FREE Study Skills Videos/DVD Offer

Dear Customer,

Thank you for your purchase from Mometrix! We consider it an honor and a privilege that you have purchased our product and we want to ensure your satisfaction.

As part of our ongoing effort to meet the needs of test takers, we have developed a set of Study Skills Videos that we would like to give you for <u>FREE</u>. These videos cover our *best practices* for getting ready for your exam, from how to use our study materials to how to best prepare for the day of the test.

All that we ask is that you email us with feedback that would describe your experience so far with our product. Good, bad, or indifferent, we want to know what you think!

To get your FREE Study Skills Videos, you can use the **QR code** below, or send us an **email** at <u>studyvideos@mometrix.com</u> with *FREE VIDEOS* in the subject line and the following information in the body of the email:

- The name of the product you purchased.
- Your product rating on a scale of 1-5, with 5 being the highest rating.
- Your feedback. It can be long, short, or anything in between. We just want to know your impressions and experience so far with our product. (Good feedback might include how our study material met your needs and ways we might be able to make it even better. You could highlight features that you found helpful or features that you think we should add.)

If you have any questions or concerns, please don't hesitate to contact me directly.

Thanks again!

Sincerely,

Jay Willis
Vice President
<u>jay.willis@mometrix.com</u>
1-800-673-8175

FTCE

PreKindergarten/Primary PK-3 Prep Book

Florida Teacher Certification Exam Secrets Study Guide

Full-Length Practice Test

Step-by-Step
Video Tutorials

3rd Edition

Copyright © 2023 by Mometrix Media LLC

All rights reserved. This product, or parts thereof, may not be reproduced, stored in a retrieval system, or transmitted in any form or by any means—electronic, mechanical, photocopy, recording, scanning, or other—except for brief quotations in critical reviews or articles, without the prior written permission of the publisher.

Written and edited by Matthew Bowling

Printed in the United States of America

This paper meets the requirements of ANSI/NISO Z39.48-1992 (Permanence of Paper).

Mometrix offers volume discount pricing to institutions. For more information or a price quote, please contact our sales department at sales@mometrix.com or 888-248-1219.

Mometrix Media LLC is not affiliated with or endorsed by any official testing organization. All organizational and test names are trademarks of their respective owners.

Paperback
ISBN 13: 978-1-5167-1832-0
ISBN 10: 1-5167-1832-1

DEAR FUTURE EXAM SUCCESS STORY

First of all, **THANK YOU** for purchasing Mometrix study materials!

Second, congratulations! You are one of the few determined test-takers who are committed to doing whatever it takes to excel on your exam. **You have come to the right place.** We developed these study materials with one goal in mind: to deliver you the information you need in a format that's concise and easy to use.

In addition to optimizing your guide for the content of the test, we've outlined our recommended steps for breaking down the preparation process into small, attainable goals so you can make sure you stay on track.

We've also analyzed the entire test-taking process, identifying the most common pitfalls and showing how you can overcome them and be ready for any curveball the test throws you.

Standardized testing is one of the biggest obstacles on your road to success, which only increases the importance of doing well in the high-pressure, high-stakes environment of test day. Your results on this test could have a significant impact on your future, and this guide provides the information and practical advice to help you achieve your full potential on test day.

Your success is our success

We would love to hear from you! If you would like to share the story of your exam success or if you have any questions or comments in regard to our products, please contact us at **800-673-8175** or **support@mometrix.com**.

Thanks again for your business and we wish you continued success!

Sincerely,
The Mometrix Test Preparation Team

> **Need more help? Check out our flashcards at:**
> **http://MometrixFlashcards.com/FTCE**

TABLE OF CONTENTS

Introduction

Thank you for purchasing this resource! You have made the choice to prepare yourself for a test that could have a huge impact on your future, and this guide is designed to help you be fully ready for test day. Obviously, it's important to have a solid understanding of the test material, but you also need to be prepared for the unique environment and stressors of the test, so that you can perform to the best of your abilities.

For this purpose, the first section that appears in this guide is the **Secret Keys**. We've devoted countless hours to meticulously researching what works and what doesn't, and we've boiled down our findings to the five most impactful steps you can take to improve your performance on the test. We start at the beginning with study planning and move through the preparation process, all the way to the testing strategies that will help you get the most out of what you know when you're finally sitting in front of the test.

We recommend that you start preparing for your test as far in advance as possible. However, if you've bought this guide as a last-minute study resource and only have a few days before your test, we recommend that you skip over the first two Secret Keys since they address a long-term study plan.

If you struggle with **test anxiety**, we strongly encourage you to check out our recommendations for how you can overcome it. Test anxiety is a formidable foe, but it can be beaten, and we want to make sure you have the tools you need to defeat it.

1

Copyright © Mometrix Media. You have been licensed one copy of this document for personal use only. Any other reproduction or redistribution is strictly prohibited. All rights reserved.
This content is provided for test preparation purposes only and does not imply an endorsement by Mometrix of any particular political, scientific, or religious point of view.

Secret Key #1 – Plan Big, Study Small

There's a lot riding on your performance. If you want to ace this test, you're going to need to keep your skills sharp and the material fresh in your mind. You need a plan that lets you review everything you need to know while still fitting in your schedule. We'll break this strategy down into three categories.

Information Organization

Start with the information you already have: the official test outline. From this, you can make a complete list of all the concepts you need to cover before the test. Organize these concepts into groups that can be studied together, and create a list of any related vocabulary you need to learn so you can brush up on any difficult terms. You'll want to keep this vocabulary list handy once you actually start studying since you may need to add to it along the way.

Time Management

Once you have your set of study concepts, decide how to spread them out over the time you have left before the test. Break your study plan into small, clear goals so you have a manageable task for each day and know exactly what you're doing. Then just focus on one small step at a time. When you manage your time this way, you don't need to spend hours at a time studying. Studying a small block of content for a short period each day helps you retain information better and avoid stressing over how much you have left to do. You can relax knowing that you have a plan to cover everything in time. In order for this strategy to be effective though, you have to start studying early and stick to your schedule. Avoid the exhaustion and futility that comes from last-minute cramming!

Study Environment

The environment you study in has a big impact on your learning. Studying in a coffee shop, while probably more enjoyable, is not likely to be as fruitful as studying in a quiet room. It's important to keep distractions to a minimum. You're only planning to study for a short block of time, so make the most of it. Don't pause to check your phone or get up to find a snack. It's also important to **avoid multitasking**. Research has consistently shown that multitasking will make your studying dramatically less effective. Your study area should also be comfortable and well-lit so you don't have the distraction of straining your eyes or sitting on an uncomfortable chair.

 The time of day you study is also important. You want to be rested and alert. Don't wait until just before bedtime. Study when you'll be most likely to comprehend and remember. Even better, if you know what time of day your test will be, set that time aside for study. That way your brain will be used to working on that subject at that specific time and you'll have a better chance of recalling information.

Finally, it can be helpful to team up with others who are studying for the same test. Your actual studying should be done in as isolated an environment as possible, but the work of organizing the information and setting up the study plan can be divided up. In between study sessions, you can discuss with your teammates the concepts that you're all studying and quiz each other on the details. Just be sure that your teammates are as serious about the test as you are. If you find that your study time is being replaced with social time, you might need to find a new team.

Copyright © Mometrix Media. You have been licensed one copy of this document for personal use only. Any other reproduction or redistribution is strictly prohibited. All rights reserved.
This content is provided for test preparation purposes only and does not imply an endorsement by Mometrix of any particular political, scientific, or religious point of view.

Secret Key #2 – Make Your Studying Count

You're devoting a lot of time and effort to preparing for this test, so you want to be absolutely certain it will pay off. This means doing more than just reading the content and hoping you can remember it on test day. It's important to make every minute of study count. There are two main areas you can focus on to make your studying count.

Retention

It doesn't matter how much time you study if you can't remember the material. You need to make sure you are retaining the concepts. To check your retention of the information you're learning, try recalling it at later times with minimal prompting. Try carrying around flashcards and glance at one or two from time to time or ask a friend who's also studying for the test to quiz you.

To enhance your retention, look for ways to put the information into practice so that you can apply it rather than simply recalling it. If you're using the information in practical ways, it will be much easier to remember. Similarly, it helps to solidify a concept in your mind if you're not only reading it to yourself but also explaining it to someone else. Ask a friend to let you teach them about a concept you're a little shaky on (or speak aloud to an imaginary audience if necessary). As you try to summarize, define, give examples, and answer your friend's questions, you'll understand the concepts better and they will stay with you longer. Finally, step back for a big picture view and ask yourself how each piece of information fits with the whole subject. When you link the different concepts together and see them working together as a whole, it's easier to remember the individual components.

Finally, practice showing your work on any multi-step problems, even if you're just studying. Writing out each step you take to solve a problem will help solidify the process in your mind, and you'll be more likely to remember it during the test.

Modality

Modality simply refers to the means or method by which you study. Choosing a study modality that fits your own individual learning style is crucial. No two people learn best in exactly the same way, so it's important to know your strengths and use them to your advantage.

For example, if you learn best by visualization, focus on visualizing a concept in your mind and draw an image or a diagram. Try color-coding your notes, illustrating them, or creating symbols that will trigger your mind to recall a learned concept. If you learn best by hearing or discussing information, find a study partner who learns the same way or read aloud to yourself. Think about how to put the information in your own words. Imagine that you are giving a lecture on the topic and record yourself so you can listen to it later.

For any learning style, flashcards can be helpful. Organize the information so you can take advantage of spare moments to review. Underline key words or phrases. Use different colors for different categories. Mnemonic devices (such as creating a short list in which every item starts with the same letter) can also help with retention. Find what works best for you and use it to store the information in your mind most effectively and easily.

3

Copyright © Mometrix Media. You have been licensed one copy of this document for personal use only. Any other reproduction or redistribution is strictly prohibited. All rights reserved.
This content is provided for test preparation purposes only and does not imply an endorsement by Mometrix of any particular political, scientific, or religious point of view.

Secret Key #3 – Practice the Right Way

Your success on test day depends not only on how many hours you put into preparing, but also on whether you prepared the right way. It's good to check along the way to see if your studying is paying off. One of the most effective ways to do this is by taking practice tests to evaluate your progress. Practice tests are useful because they show exactly where you need to improve. Every time you take a practice test, pay special attention to these three groups of questions:

- The questions you got wrong
- The questions you had to guess on, even if you guessed right
- The questions you found difficult or slow to work through

This will show you exactly what your weak areas are, and where you need to devote more study time. Ask yourself why each of these questions gave you trouble. Was it because you didn't understand the material? Was it because you didn't remember the vocabulary? Do you need more repetitions on this type of question to build speed and confidence? Dig into those questions and figure out how you can strengthen your weak areas as you go back to review the material.

 Additionally, many practice tests have a section explaining the answer choices. It can be tempting to read the explanation and think that you now have a good understanding of the concept. However, an explanation likely only covers part of the question's broader context. Even if the explanation makes perfect sense, **go back and investigate** every concept related to the question until you're positive you have a thorough understanding.

As you go along, keep in mind that the practice test is just that: practice. Memorizing these questions and answers will not be very helpful on the actual test because it is unlikely to have any of the same exact questions. If you only know the right answers to the sample questions, you won't be prepared for the real thing. **Study the concepts** until you understand them fully, and then you'll be able to answer any question that shows up on the test.

It's important to wait on the practice tests until you're ready. If you take a test on your first day of study, you may be overwhelmed by the amount of material covered and how much you need to learn. Work up to it gradually.

On test day, you'll need to be prepared for answering questions, managing your time, and using the test-taking strategies you've learned. It's a lot to balance, like a mental marathon that will have a big impact on your future. Like training for a marathon, you'll need to start slowly and work your way up. When test day arrives, you'll be ready.

Start with the strategies you've read in the first two Secret Keys—plan your course and study in the way that works best for you. If you have time, consider using multiple study resources to get different approaches to the same concepts. It can be helpful to see difficult concepts from more than one angle. Then find a good source for practice tests. Many times, the test website will suggest potential study resources or provide sample tests.

Copyright © Mometrix Media. You have been licensed one copy of this document for personal use only. Any other reproduction or redistribution is strictly prohibited. All rights reserved. This content is provided for test preparation purposes only and does not imply an endorsement by Mometrix of any particular political, scientific, or religious point of view.

Practice Test Strategy

If you're able to find at least three practice tests, we recommend this strategy:

UNTIMED AND OPEN-BOOK PRACTICE

Take the first test with no time constraints and with your notes and study guide handy. Take your time and focus on applying the strategies you've learned.

TIMED AND OPEN-BOOK PRACTICE

Take the second practice test open-book as well, but set a timer and practice pacing yourself to finish in time.

TIMED AND CLOSED-BOOK PRACTICE

Take any other practice tests as if it were test day. Set a timer and put away your study materials. Sit at a table or desk in a quiet room, imagine yourself at the testing center, and answer questions as quickly and accurately as possible.

Keep repeating timed and closed-book tests on a regular basis until you run out of practice tests or it's time for the actual test. Your mind will be ready for the schedule and stress of test day, and you'll be able to focus on recalling the material you've learned.

Copyright © Mometrix Media. You have been licensed one copy of this document for personal use only. Any other reproduction or redistribution is strictly prohibited. All rights reserved.
This content is provided for test preparation purposes only and does not imply an endorsement by Mometrix of any particular political, scientific, or religious point of view.

Secret Key #4 – Pace Yourself

Once you're fully prepared for the material on the test, your biggest challenge on test day will be managing your time. Just knowing that the clock is ticking can make you panic even if you have plenty of time left. Work on pacing yourself so you can build confidence against the time constraints of the exam. Pacing is a difficult skill to master, especially in a high-pressure environment, so **practice is vital**.

Set time expectations for your pace based on how much time is available. For example, if a section has 60 questions and the time limit is 30 minutes, you know you have to average 30 seconds or less per question in order to answer them all. Although 30 seconds is the hard limit, set 25 seconds per question as your goal, so you reserve extra time to spend on harder questions. When you budget extra time for the harder questions, you no longer have any reason to stress when those questions take longer to answer.

Don't let this time expectation distract you from working through the test at a calm, steady pace, but keep it in mind so you don't spend too much time on any one question. Recognize that taking extra time on one question you don't understand may keep you from answering two that you do understand later in the test. If your time limit for a question is up and you're still not sure of the answer, mark it and move on, and come back to it later if the time and the test format allow. If the testing format doesn't allow you to return to earlier questions, just make an educated guess; then put it out of your mind and move on.

On the easier questions, be careful not to rush. It may seem wise to hurry through them so you have more time for the challenging ones, but it's not worth missing one if you know the concept and just didn't take the time to read the question fully. Work efficiently but make sure you understand the question and have looked at all of the answer choices, since more than one may seem right at first.

Even if you're paying attention to the time, you may find yourself a little behind at some point. You should speed up to get back on track, but do so wisely. Don't panic; just take a few seconds less on each question until you're caught up. Don't guess without thinking, but do look through the answer choices and eliminate any you know are wrong. If you can get down to two choices, it is often worthwhile to guess from those. Once you've chosen an answer, move on and don't dwell on any that you skipped or had to hurry through. If a question was taking too long, chances are it was one of the harder ones, so you weren't as likely to get it right anyway.

On the other hand, if you find yourself getting ahead of schedule, it may be beneficial to slow down a little. The more quickly you work, the more likely you are to make a careless mistake that will affect your score. You've budgeted time for each question, so don't be afraid to spend that time. Practice an efficient but careful pace to get the most out of the time you have.

6

Copyright © Mometrix Media. You have been licensed one copy of this document for personal use only. Any other reproduction or redistribution is strictly prohibited. All rights reserved. This content is provided for test preparation purposes only and does not imply an endorsement by Mometrix of any particular political, scientific, or religious point of view.

Secret Key #5 – Have a Plan for Guessing

When you're taking the test, you may find yourself stuck on a question. Some of the answer choices seem better than others, but you don't see the one answer choice that is obviously correct. What do you do?

The scenario described above is very common, yet most test takers have not effectively prepared for it. Developing and practicing a plan for guessing may be one of the single most effective uses of your time as you get ready for the exam.

In developing your plan for guessing, there are three questions to address:

- When should you start the guessing process?
- How should you narrow down the choices?
- Which answer should you choose?

When to Start the Guessing Process

Unless your plan for guessing is to select C every time (which, despite its merits, is not what we recommend), you need to leave yourself enough time to apply your answer elimination strategies. Since you have a limited amount of time for each question, that means that if you're going to give yourself the best shot at guessing correctly, you have to decide quickly whether or not you will guess.

Of course, the best-case scenario is that you don't have to guess at all, so first, see if you can answer the question based on your knowledge of the subject and basic reasoning skills. Focus on the key words in the question and try to jog your memory of related topics. Give yourself a chance to bring the knowledge to mind, but once you realize that you don't have (or you can't access) the knowledge you need to answer the question, it's time to start the guessing process.

It's almost always better to start the guessing process too early than too late. It only takes a few seconds to remember something and answer the question from knowledge. Carefully eliminating wrong answer choices takes longer. Plus, going through the process of eliminating answer choices can actually help jog your memory.

Summary: Start the guessing process as soon as you decide that you can't answer the question based on your knowledge.

7

Copyright © Mometrix Media. You have been licensed one copy of this document for personal use only. Any other reproduction or redistribution is strictly prohibited. All rights reserved.
This content is provided for test preparation purposes only and does not imply an endorsement by Mometrix of any particular political, scientific, or religious point of view.

How to Narrow Down the Choices

The next chapter in this book (**Test-Taking Strategies**) includes a wide range of strategies for how to approach questions and how to look for answer choices to eliminate. You will definitely want to read those carefully, practice them, and figure out which ones work best for you. Here though, we're going to address a mindset rather than a particular strategy.

Your odds of guessing an answer correctly depend on how many options you are choosing from.

Number of options left	5	4	3	2	1
Odds of guessing correctly	20%	25%	33%	50%	100%

You can see from this chart just how valuable it is to be able to eliminate incorrect answers and make an educated guess, but there are two things that many test takers do that cause them to miss out on the benefits of guessing:

- Accidentally eliminating the correct answer
- Selecting an answer based on an impression

We'll look at the first one here, and the second one in the next section.

To avoid accidentally eliminating the correct answer, we recommend a thought exercise called **the $5 challenge**. In this challenge, you only eliminate an answer choice from contention if you are willing to bet $5 on it being wrong. Why $5? Five dollars is a small but not insignificant amount of money. It's an amount you could afford to lose but wouldn't want to throw away. And while losing

$5 once might not hurt too much, doing it twenty times will set you back $100. In the same way, each small decision you make—eliminating a choice here, guessing on a question there—won't by itself impact your score very much, but when you put them all together, they can make a big difference. By holding each answer choice elimination decision to a higher standard, you can reduce the risk of accidentally eliminating the correct answer.

The $5 challenge can also be applied in a positive sense: If you are willing to bet $5 that an answer choice *is* correct, go ahead and mark it as correct.

Summary: Only eliminate an answer choice if you are willing to bet $5 that it is wrong.

Copyright © Mometrix Media. You have been licensed one copy of this document for personal use only. Any other reproduction or redistribution is strictly prohibited. All rights reserved. This content is provided for test preparation purposes only and does not imply an endorsement by Mometrix of any particular political, scientific, or religious point of view.

Which Answer to Choose

You're taking the test. You've run into a hard question and decided you'll have to guess. You've eliminated all the answer choices you're willing to bet $5 on. Now you have to pick an answer. Why do we even need to talk about this? Why can't you just pick whichever one you feel like when the time comes?

The answer to these questions is that if you don't come into the test with a plan, you'll rely on your impression to select an answer choice, and if you do that, you risk falling into a trap. The test writers know that everyone who takes their test will be guessing on some of the questions, so they intentionally write wrong answer choices to seem plausible. You still have to pick an answer though, and if the wrong answer choices are designed to look right, how can you ever be sure that you're not falling for their trap? The best solution we've found to this dilemma is to take the decision out of your hands entirely. Here is the process we recommend:

Once you've eliminated any choices that you are confident (willing to bet $5) are wrong, select the first remaining choice as your answer.

Whether you choose to select the first remaining choice, the second, or the last, the important thing is that you use some preselected standard. Using this approach guarantees that you will not be enticed into selecting an answer choice that looks right, because you are not basing your decision on how the answer choices look.

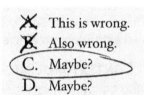

This is not meant to make you question your knowledge. Instead, it is to help you recognize the difference between your knowledge and your impressions. There's a huge difference between thinking an answer is right because of what you know, and thinking an answer is right because it looks or sounds like it should be right.

Summary: To ensure that your selection is appropriately random, make a predetermined selection from among all answer choices you have not eliminated.

9

Copyright © Mometrix Media. You have been licensed one copy of this document for personal use only. Any other reproduction or redistribution is strictly prohibited. All rights reserved.
This content is provided for test preparation purposes only and does not imply an endorsement by Mometrix of any particular political, scientific, or religious point of view.

Test-Taking Strategies

This section contains a list of test-taking strategies that you may find helpful as you work through the test. By taking what you know and applying logical thought, you can maximize your chances of answering any question correctly!

It is very important to realize that every question is different and every person is different: no single strategy will work on every question, and no single strategy will work for every person. That's why we've included all of them here, so you can try them out and determine which ones work best for different types of questions and which ones work best for you.

Question Strategies

⊘ READ CAREFULLY

Read the question and the answer choices carefully. Don't miss the question because you misread the terms. You have plenty of time to read each question thoroughly and make sure you understand what is being asked. Yet a happy medium must be attained, so don't waste too much time. You must read carefully and efficiently.

⊘ CONTEXTUAL CLUES

Look for contextual clues. If the question includes a word you are not familiar with, look at the immediate context for some indication of what the word might mean. Contextual clues can often give you all the information you need to decipher the meaning of an unfamiliar word. Even if you can't determine the meaning, you may be able to narrow down the possibilities enough to make a solid guess at the answer to the question.

⊘ PREFIXES

If you're having trouble with a word in the question or answer choices, try dissecting it. Take advantage of every clue that the word might include. Prefixes can be a huge help. Usually, they allow you to determine a basic meaning. *Pre-* means before, *post-* means after, *pro-* is positive, *de-* is negative. From prefixes, you can get an idea of the general meaning of the word and try to put it into context.

⊘ HEDGE WORDS

Watch out for critical hedge words, such as *likely, may, can, sometimes, often, almost, mostly, usually, generally, rarely,* and *sometimes.* Question writers insert these hedge phrases to cover every possibility. Often an answer choice will be wrong simply because it leaves no room for exception. Be on guard for answer choices that have definitive words such as *exactly* and *always.*

⊘ SWITCHBACK WORDS

Stay alert for *switchbacks.* These are the words and phrases frequently used to alert you to shifts in thought. The most common switchback words are *but, although,* and *however.* Others include *nevertheless, on the other hand, even though, while, in spite of, despite,* and *regardless of.* Switchback words are important to catch because they can change the direction of the question or an answer choice.

Copyright © Mometrix Media. You have been licensed one copy of this document for personal use only. Any other reproduction or redistribution is strictly prohibited. All rights reserved. This content is provided for test preparation purposes only and does not imply an endorsement by Mometrix of any particular political, scientific, or religious point of view.

⊘ FACE VALUE

When in doubt, use common sense. Accept the situation in the problem at face value. Don't read too much into it. These problems will not require you to make wild assumptions. If you have to go beyond creativity and warp time or space in order to have an answer choice fit the question, then you should move on and consider the other answer choices. These are normal problems rooted in reality. The applicable relationship or explanation may not be readily apparent, but it is there for you to figure out. Use your common sense to interpret anything that isn't clear.

Answer Choice Strategies

⊘ ANSWER SELECTION

The most thorough way to pick an answer choice is to identify and eliminate wrong answers until only one is left, then confirm it is the correct answer. Sometimes an answer choice may immediately seem right, but be careful. The test writers will usually put more than one reasonable answer choice on each question, so take a second to read all of them and make sure that the other choices are not equally obvious. As long as you have time left, it is better to read every answer choice than to pick the first one that looks right without checking the others.

⊘ ANSWER CHOICE FAMILIES

An answer choice family consists of two (in rare cases, three) answer choices that are very similar in construction and cannot all be true at the same time. If you see two answer choices that are direct opposites or parallels, one of them is usually the correct answer. For instance, if one answer choice says that quantity x increases and another either says that quantity x decreases (opposite) or says that quantity y increases (parallel), then those answer choices would fall into the same family. An answer choice that doesn't match the construction of the answer choice family is more likely to be incorrect. Most questions will not have answer choice families, but when they do appear, you should be prepared to recognize them.

⊘ ELIMINATE ANSWERS

Eliminate answer choices as soon as you realize they are wrong, but make sure you consider all possibilities. If you are eliminating answer choices and realize that the last one you are left with is also wrong, don't panic. Start over and consider each choice again. There may be something you missed the first time that you will realize on the second pass.

⊘ AVOID FACT TRAPS

Don't be distracted by an answer choice that is factually true but doesn't answer the question. You are looking for the choice that answers the question. Stay focused on what the question is asking for so you don't accidentally pick an answer that is true but incorrect. Always go back to the question and make sure the answer choice you've selected actually answers the question and is not merely a true statement.

⊘ EXTREME STATEMENTS

In general, you should avoid answers that put forth extreme actions as standard practice or proclaim controversial ideas as established fact. An answer choice that states the "process should be used in certain situations, if…" is much more likely to be correct than one that states the "process should be discontinued completely." The first is a calm rational statement and doesn't even make a definitive, uncompromising stance, using a hedge word *if* to provide wiggle room, whereas the second choice is far more extreme.

Copyright © Mometrix Media. You have been licensed one copy of this document for personal use only. Any other reproduction or redistribution is strictly prohibited. All rights reserved. This content is provided for test preparation purposes only and does not imply an endorsement by Mometrix of any particular political, scientific, or religious point of view.

⊘ Benchmark

As you read through the answer choices and you come across one that seems to answer the question well, mentally select that answer choice. This is not your final answer, but it's the one that will help you evaluate the other answer choices. The one that you selected is your benchmark or standard for judging each of the other answer choices. Every other answer choice must be compared to your benchmark. That choice is correct until proven otherwise by another answer choice beating it. If you find a better answer, then that one becomes your new benchmark. Once you've decided that no other choice answers the question as well as your benchmark, you have your final answer.

⊘ Predict the Answer

Before you even start looking at the answer choices, it is often best to try to predict the answer. When you come up with the answer on your own, it is easier to avoid distractions and traps because you will know exactly what to look for. The right answer choice is unlikely to be word-for-word what you came up with, but it should be a close match. Even if you are confident that you have the right answer, you should still take the time to read each option before moving on.

General Strategies

⊘ Tough Questions

If you are stumped on a problem or it appears too hard or too difficult, don't waste time. Move on! Remember though, if you can quickly check for obviously incorrect answer choices, your chances of guessing correctly are greatly improved. Before you completely give up, at least try to knock out a couple of possible answers. Eliminate what you can and then guess at the remaining answer choices before moving on.

⊘ Check Your Work

Since you will probably not know every term listed and the answer to every question, it is important that you get credit for the ones that you do know. Don't miss any questions through careless mistakes. If at all possible, try to take a second to look back over your answer selection and make sure you've selected the correct answer choice and haven't made a costly careless mistake (such as marking an answer choice that you didn't mean to mark). This quick double check should more than pay for itself in caught mistakes for the time it costs.

⊘ Pace Yourself

It's easy to be overwhelmed when you're looking at a page full of questions; your mind is confused and full of random thoughts, and the clock is ticking down faster than you would like. Calm down and maintain the pace that you have set for yourself. Especially as you get down to the last few minutes of the test, don't let the small numbers on the clock make you panic. As long as you are on track by monitoring your pace, you are guaranteed to have time for each question.

⊘ Don't Rush

It is very easy to make errors when you are in a hurry. Maintaining a fast pace in answering questions is pointless if it makes you miss questions that you would have gotten right otherwise. Test writers like to include distracting information and wrong answers that seem right. Taking a little extra time to avoid careless mistakes can make all the difference in your test score. Find a pace that allows you to be confident in the answers that you select.

12

Copyright © Mometrix Media. You have been licensed one copy of this document for personal use only. Any other reproduction or redistribution is strictly prohibited. All rights reserved.
This content is provided for test preparation purposes only and does not imply an endorsement by Mometrix of any particular political, scientific, or religious point of view.

⊘ Keep Moving

Panicking will not help you pass the test, so do your best to stay calm and keep moving. Taking deep breaths and going through the answer elimination steps you practiced can help to break through a stress barrier and keep your pace.

Final Notes

The combination of a solid foundation of content knowledge and the confidence that comes from practicing your plan for applying that knowledge is the key to maximizing your performance on test day. As your foundation of content knowledge is built up and strengthened, you'll find that the strategies included in this chapter become more and more effective in helping you quickly sift through the distractions and traps of the test to isolate the correct answer.

Now that you're preparing to move forward into the test content chapters of this book, be sure to keep your goal in mind. As you read, think about how you will be able to apply this information on the test. If you've already seen sample questions for the test and you have an idea of the question format and style, try to come up with questions of your own that you can answer based on what you're reading. This will give you valuable practice applying your knowledge in the same ways you can expect to on test day.

Good luck and good studying!

Copyright © Mometrix Media. You have been licensed one copy of this document for personal use only. Any other reproduction or redistribution is strictly prohibited. All rights reserved.
This content is provided for test preparation purposes only and does not imply an endorsement by Mometrix of any particular political, scientific, or religious point of view.

Copyright © Mometrix Media. You have been licensed one copy of this document for personal use only. Any other reproduction or redistribution is strictly prohibited. All rights reserved.
This content is provided for test preparation purposes only and does not imply an endorsement by Mometrix of any particular political, scientific, or religious point of view.

Child Growth, Development, and Relationships with Families and the Community

Transform passive reading into active learning! After immersing yourself in this chapter, put your comprehension to the test by taking a quiz. The insights you gained will stay with you longer this way. Scan the QR code to go directly to the chapter quiz interface for this study guide. If you're using a computer, simply visit the bonus page at **mometrix.com/bonus948/ftceprekinprim** and click the Chapter Quizzes link.

Overview of Human Developmental Theories

ISSUES OF HUMAN DEVELOPMENT

Historically, there have been a number of arguments that theories of human development seek to address. These ideas generally lie on a spectrum, but are often essential concepts involved in developmental theories. For instance, the nature vs. nurture debate is a key concept involved in behaviorist camps of development, insisting that a substantial portion of a child's development may be attributed to his or her social environment.

- **Universality vs. context specificity**: Universality implies that all individuals will develop in the same way, no matter what culture they live in. Context specificity implies that development will be influenced by the culture in which the individual lives.
- **Assumptions about human nature** (3 doctrines: original sin, innate purity, and tabula rasa):
  - Original sin says that children are inherently bad and must be taught to be good.
  - Innate purity says that children are inherently good.
  - Tabula rasa says that children are born as "blank slates," without good or bad tendencies, and can be taught right vs. wrong.
- **Behavioral consistency**: Children either behave in the same manner no matter what the situation or setting, or they change their behavior depending on the setting and who is interacting with them.
- **Nature vs. nurture**: Nature is the genetic influences on development. Nurture is the environment and social influences on development.
- **Continuity vs. discontinuity**: Continuity states that development progresses at a steady rate and the effects of change are cumulative. Discontinuity states that development progresses in a stair-step fashion and the effects of early development have no bearing on later development.
- **Passivity vs. activity**: Passivity refers to development being influenced by outside forces. Activity refers to development influenced by the child himself and how he responds to external forces.
- **Critical vs. sensitive period**: The critical period is that window of time when the child will be able to acquire new skills and behaviors. The sensitive period refers to a flexible time period when a child will be receptive to learning new skills, even if it is later than the norm.

15

Copyright © Mometrix Media. You have been licensed one copy of this document for personal use only. Any other reproduction or redistribution is strictly prohibited. All rights reserved.
This content is provided for test preparation purposes only and does not imply an endorsement by Mometrix of any particular political, scientific, or religious point of view.

THEORETICAL SCHOOLS OF THOUGHT ON HUMAN DEVELOPMENT

- **Behaviorist Theory** – This philosophy discusses development in terms of conditioning. As children interact with their environments, they learn what behaviors result in rewards or punishments and develop patterns of behaviors as a result. This school of thought lies heavily within the nurture side of the nature/nurture debate, arguing that children's personalities and behaviors are a product of their environments.
- **Constructivist Theory** – This philosophy describes the process of learning as one in which individuals build or construct their understanding from their prior knowledge and experiences in an environment. In constructivist thought, individuals can synthesize their old information to generate new ideas. This school of thought is similar to behaviorism in that the social environment plays a large role in learning. Constructivism, however, places greater emphasis on the individual's active role in the learning process, such as the ability to generate ideas about something an individual has not experienced directly.
- **Ecological Systems Theory** – This philosophy focuses on the social environments in and throughout a person's life. Ecological systems theorists attempt to account for all of the complexities of various aspects of a person's life, starting with close relationships, such as family and friends, and zooming out into broader social contexts, including interactions with school, communities, and media. Alongside these various social levels, ecological systems discuss the roles of ethnicity, geography, and socioeconomic status in development across a person's lifespan.
- **Maturationist Theory** – This philosophy largely focuses on the natural disposition of a child to learn. Maturationists lean heavily into the nature side of the nature/nurture argument and say that humans are predisposed to learning and development. As a result, maturationists propose that early development should only be passively supported.
- **Psychoanalytic Theory** – Psychoanalytic theorists generally argue that beneath the conscious interaction with the world, individuals have underlying, subconscious thoughts that affect their active emotions and behaviors. These subconscious thoughts are built from previous experiences, including developmental milestones and also past traumas. These subconscious thoughts, along with the conscious, interplay with one another to form a person's desires, personality, attitudes, and habits.

FREUD'S PSYCHOSEXUAL DEVELOPMENTAL THEORY

Sigmund Freud was a neurologist who founded the psychoanalytic school of thought. He described the distinction between the conscious and unconscious mind and the effects of the unconscious mind on personality and behavior. He also developed a concept of stages of development, in which an individual encounters various conflicts or crises, called psychosexual stages of development. The way in which an individual handles these crises were thought to shape the individual's personality over the course of life. This general formula heavily influenced other psychoanalytic theories.

ERIKSON'S PSYCHOSOCIAL DEVELOPMENTAL THEORY

Eric Erikson's psychosocial development theory was an expansion and revision of Freud's psychosexual stages. Erikson describes eight stages in which an individual is presented with a crisis, such as an infant learning to trust or mistrust his or her parents to provide. The choice to trust or mistrust is not binary, but is on a spectrum. According to the theory, the individual's resolution of the crisis largely carries through the rest of his or her life. Handling each of the eight conflicts well theoretically leads to a healthy development of personality. The conflicts are spaced out throughout life, beginning at infancy and ending at death.

Copyright © Mometrix Media. You have been licensed one copy of this document for personal use only. Any other reproduction or redistribution is strictly prohibited. All rights reserved. This content is provided for test preparation purposes only and does not imply an endorsement by Mometrix of any particular political, scientific, or religious point of view.

KOHLBERG'S STAGES OF MORAL DEVELOPMENT

Kohlberg's stages of moral development are heavily influenced by Erikson's stages. He describes three larger levels of moral development with substages. In the first level, the **preconventional level**, morality is fully externally controlled by authorities and is motivated by avoidance of punishment and pursuit of rewards. In the second level, the **conventional level**, the focus shifts to laws and social factors and the pursuit of being seen by others as good or nice. In the third and final level, the **postconventional** or **principled level**, the individual looks beyond laws and social obligations to more complex situational considerations. A person in this stage might consider that a law may not always be the best for individuals or society and a particular situation may warrant breaking the rule for the true good.

GEORGE HERBERT MEAD'S PLAY AND GAME STAGE DEVELOPMENT THEORY

George Herbert Mead was a sociologist and psychologist who described learning by stepping into **social roles**. According to his theory, children first interact with the world by imitating and playing by themselves, in which a child can experiment with concepts. Mead describes this development in terms of three stages characterized by increasing complexity of play. A child in the **preparatory stage** can **play** pretend and learn cooking concepts by pretending to cook. As a child develops socially, they learn to step in and out of increasingly abstract and complex **roles** and include more interaction. This is known as the **play stage**, including early interactive roles. For instance, children may play "cops and robbers," which are more symbolically significant roles as they are not natural roles for children to play in society. As social understanding develops, children enter the **game stage**, in which the child can understand their own role and the roles of others in a game. In this stage, children can participate in more complex activities with highly structured rules. An example of a complex game is baseball, in which each individual playing has a unique and complex role to play. These stages are thought to contribute to an individual's ability to understand complex social roles in adulthood.

IVAN PAVLOV

Ivan Pavlov was a predecessor to the behaviorist school and is credited with being the first to observe the process of classical conditioning, also known as Pavlovian conditioning. Pavlov observed that dogs would begin salivating at the sound of a bell because they were conditioned to expect food when they heard a bell ring. According to classical conditioning, by introducing a neutral stimulus (such as a bell) to a naturally significant stimulus (such as the sight of food), the neutral stimulus will begin to create a conditioned response on its own.

JOHN B. WATSON

Watson is credited as the founder of behaviorism and worked to expand the knowledge base of conditioning. He is famous for his experiments, including highly unethical experiments such as the "Little Albert" experiment in which he used classical conditioning to cause an infant to fear animals that he was unfamiliar with. Watson proposed that psychology should focus only on observable behaviors.

B.F. SKINNER

Skinner expanded on Watson's work in behaviorism. His primary contributions to behaviorism included studying the effect of **reinforcement** and **punishment** on particular behaviors. He noted that stimuli can be both additive or subtractive may be used to either increase or decrease behavior frequency and strengths.

Copyright © Mometrix Media. You have been licensed one copy of this document for personal use only. Any other reproduction or redistribution is strictly prohibited. All rights reserved. This content is provided for test preparation purposes only and does not imply an endorsement by Mometrix of any particular political, scientific, or religious point of view.

Lev Vygotsky

Vygotsky's sociocultural theory describes development as a social process, in which individuals mediate knowledge through social interactions and can learn by interacting with and watching others. Vygotsky's ideas have been widely adopted in the field of education, most notably his theory of the "**zone of proximal development**." This theory describes three levels of an individual's ability to do tasks, including completely incapable of performing a task, capable with assistance, and independently capable. As an individual's experience grows, they should progress from less capable and independent to more capable and independent.

> **Review Video: Instructional Scaffolding**
> Visit mometrix.com/academy and enter code: 989759

Bandura's Social Learning Theory

Albert Bandura's social learning theory argues against some of the behaviorist thoughts that a person has to experience stimulus and response to learn behaviors, and instead posits that an individual can learn from other peoples' social interactions. Bandura would say that most learning takes place from observing and predicting social behavior, and not through direct experience. This becomes a more efficient system for learning because people are able to learn information more synthetically.

Bowlby's Attachment Theory

Bowlby's attachment theory describes the impact that early connections have on lifelong development. Working from an evolutionary framework, Bowlby described how infants are predisposed to be attached to their caregivers as this increases chance of survival. According to Bowlby's theory, infants are predisposed to stay close to known caregivers and use them as a frame of reference to help with learning what is socially acceptable and what is safe.

Piaget's Cognitive Development Theory

Piaget's theory of cognitive development describes how as individuals develop, their cognitive processes are able to become more complex and abstract. In the early stages, an infant may be able to recognize an item, such as a glass of water, on sight only. As that individual grows, they are able to think, compare, and eventually develop abstract thoughts about that concept. According to Piaget, this development takes place in all individuals in predictable stages.

Maslow's Hierarchy of Needs

Maslow defined human motivation in terms of needs and wants. His **hierarchy of needs** is classically portrayed as a pyramid sitting on its base divided into horizontal layers. He theorized that, as humans fulfill the needs of one layer, their motivation turns to the layer above. The layers consist of (from bottom to top):

- **Physiological**: The need for air, fluid, food, shelter, warmth, and sleep.
- **Safety**: A safe place to live, a steady job, a society with rules and laws, protection from harm, and insurance or savings for the future.
- **Love/Belonging**: A network consisting of a significant other, family, friends, co-workers, religion, and community.
- **Esteem or self-respect**: The knowledge that you are a person who is successful and worthy of esteem, attention, status, and admiration.

Copyright © Mometrix Media. You have been licensed one copy of this document for personal use only. Any other reproduction or redistribution is strictly prohibited. All rights reserved. This content is provided for test preparation purposes only and does not imply an endorsement by Mometrix of any particular political, scientific, or religious point of view.

- **Self-actualization**: The acceptance of your life, choices, and situation in life and the empathetic acceptance of others, as well as the feeling of independence and the joy of being able to express yourself freely and competently.

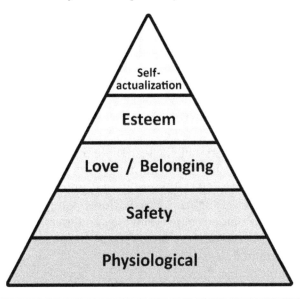

Review Video: Maslow's Hierarchy of Needs
Visit mometrix.com/academy and enter code: 461825

Cognitive Development

PIAGET'S THEORY OF COGNITIVE DEVELOPMENT

Jean Piaget's theory of cognitive development consists of four stages that a child moves through throughout life. The four stages are the **sensorimotor stage** (birth-2 years), **preoperational stage** (2-7 years), **concrete operational stage** (7-11 years), and **formal operational stage** (12 years and beyond). Piaget believed that the way children think changes as they pass through these stages. In the **sensorimotor stage**, infants exist in the present moment and investigate their world for the first time through their five senses, reflexes, and actions. Key skills infants acquire during this stage include object permanence and self-recognition. In the **preoperational stage**, children learn to express ideas symbolically, including through language and pretend play. Markers of this stage include engaging in animism, egocentrism, and the inability to understand conservation (the knowledge that the quantity of something does not change when its appearance does). In the **concrete operational stage**, children develop logical thought and begin understanding conservation. The **formal operational stage** brings the ability to think abstractly and hypothetically. Piaget believed that children learn through experimenting and building upon knowledge from experiences. He asserted that educators should be highly qualified and trained to create experiences that support development in each of these stages.

Copyright © Mometrix Media. You have been licensed one copy of this document for personal use only. Any other reproduction or redistribution is strictly prohibited. All rights reserved. This content is provided for test preparation purposes only and does not imply an endorsement by Mometrix of any particular political, scientific, or religious point of view.

SKILLS TYPICALLY ACQUIRED AT EACH STAGE OF COGNITIVE DEVELOPMENT

- **Sensorimotor:** As children in the sensorimotor stage gain an increasing awareness of their bodies and the world around them, a wide range of skills are acquired as they mature from infancy to toddlerhood. Early skills at this stage include sucking, tasting, smiling, basic vocalizations, and **gross motor skills** such as kicking and grasping. These skills increase in complexity over time and come to include abilities such as throwing and dropping objects, crawling, walking, and using simple words or phrases to communicate. As children near the end of this stage, they are typically able to exhibit such skills as stacking, basic problem solving, planning methods to achieve a task, and attempting to engage in daily routines such as dressing themselves or brushing their hair.
- **Preoperational:** This stage is marked by significant leaps in **cognition** and **gross motor skills**. Children in the preoperational stage are able to use increasingly complex language to communicate, and develop such skills as jumping, running, and climbing as they gain increasing control over their bodies. Preoperational children begin learning the basic categorization of alike objects, such as animals, flowers, or foods. This stage is also characterized by the development of pretend play and includes such skills as creating imaginary friends, role playing, and using toys or objects to symbolize something else, such as using a box as a pretend house.
- **Concrete Operational:** In this stage, children begin developing **logical reasoning** skills that allow them to perform increasingly complex tasks. Concrete operational children are able to distinguish subcategories, including types of animals, foods, or flowers, and can organize items in ascending or descending order based upon such characteristics as height, weight, or size. Children at this stage develop the understanding that altering the appearance of an object or substance does not change the amount of it. A classic example of this is the understanding that liquid transferred from one container to another retains its volume. This concept is known as **conservation**.
- **Formal Operational:** The formal operational stage is characterized by the development of **abstract** and **hypothetical** cognitive skills. Children at this stage are able to solve increasingly complex math equations, hypothesize and strategically devise a plan for engaging in science experiments, and develop creative solutions to problems. They are also able to theorize potential outcomes to hypothetical situations, as well as consider the nuances of differing values, beliefs, morals, and ethics.

SUBSTAGES OF THE SENSORIMOTOR STAGE

Piaget's sensorimotor stage is divided into six substages. In each, infants develop new skills for representing and interacting with their world. In the first substage, infants interact **reflexively** and involuntarily to stimuli in the form of muscle jerking when startled, sucking, and gripping. Subsequent stages are circular, or repetitive, in nature, and are based on interactions with the self and, increasingly, the environment. **Primary circular reactions**, or intentionally repeated actions, comprise the second substage. Infants notice their actions and sounds and purposefully repeat them, but these actions do not extend past the infant's body. Interaction with the environment begins in the third substage as infants engage in **secondary circular reactions**. Here, infants learn that they can interact with and manipulate objects within their environment to create an effect, such as a sound from pressing a button. They then repeat the action and experience joy in this ability. In the fourth substage, secondary circular reactions become coordinated as infants begin planning movements and actions to create an effect. **Tertiary circular reactions** allow for exploration in the fifth substage, as infants start experimenting with cause and effect. In the sixth substage, infants begin engaging in **representational thought** and recall information from memory.

Copyright © Mometrix Media. You have been licensed one copy of this document for personal use only. Any other reproduction or redistribution is strictly prohibited. All rights reserved. This content is provided for test preparation purposes only and does not imply an endorsement by Mometrix of any particular political, scientific, or religious point of view.

EXAMPLES OF PRIMARY, SECONDARY, AND TERTIARY CIRCULAR REACTIONS

The following are some common examples of primary, secondary, and tertiary circular reactions:

- **Primary:** Primary circular reactions are comprised of repeated **bodily** actions that the infant finds enjoyable. Such actions include thumb sucking, placing hands or feet in the mouth, kicking, and making basic vocalizations.
- **Secondary:** Secondary circular reactions refer to repeated enjoyable interactions between the infant and objects within their **environment** in order to elicit a specific response. Such actions include grasping objects, rattling toys, hitting buttons to hear specific sounds, banging two objects together, or reaching out to touch various items.
- **Tertiary:** Tertiary circular reactions are comprised of intentional and planned actions using objects within the environment to **achieve a particular outcome**. Examples include stacking blocks and knocking them down, taking toys out of a bin and putting them back, or engaging in a repeated behavior to gauge a caretaker's reaction each time.

DEFINING CHARACTERISTICS OF THE PREOPERATIONAL STAGE OF DEVELOPMENT

The preoperational stage of development refers to the stage before a child can exercise operational thought and is associated with several defining characteristics including **pretend play**, **animism**, and **egocentrism**. As children learn to think and express themselves symbolically, they engage in pretend play as a means of organizing, understanding, and representing the world around them as they experience it. During this stage, children do not understand the difference between inanimate and animate objects, and thus demonstrate animism, or the attribution of lifelike qualities to inanimate objects. Egocentrism refers to the child's inability to understand the distinction between themselves and others, and consequentially, the inability to understand the thoughts, perspectives, and feelings of others. During the preoperational stage, the brain is not developed enough to understand **conservation**, which is the understanding that the quantity of something does not change just because its appearance changes. Thus, children in this stage exhibit **centration**, or the focusing on only one aspect of something at a time at. Additionally, children struggle with **classification** during this stage, as they are not cognitively developed enough to understand that an object can be classified in multiple ways.

MILESTONES ACHIEVED DURING THE CONCRETE OPERATIONAL STAGE OF DEVELOPMENT

The concrete operational stage marks the beginning of a child's ability to think logically about the concrete world. In this stage, children develop many of the skills they lacked in the preoperational phase. For example, egocentrism fades as children in this stage begin to develop empathy and understand others' perspectives. Additionally, they develop an understanding of conservation, or the idea that the quantity of something does not change with its appearance. Children in this stage begin to learn to classify objects in more than one way and can categorize them based on a variety of characteristics. This allows them to practice **seriation**, or the arranging of objects based on quantitative measures.

DEVELOPMENT OF COGNITIVE ABILITIES IN THE FORMAL OPERATIONAL STAGE

In the formal operational stage, children can think beyond the concrete world and in terms of abstract thoughts and hypothetical situations. They develop the ability to consider various outcomes of events and can think more creatively about solutions to problems than in previous stages. This advanced cognitive ability contributes to the development of personal identity. In considering abstract and hypothetical ideas, children begin to formulate opinions and develop personal stances on intangible concepts, thus establishing individual character. The formal operational stage continues to develop through adulthood as individuals gain knowledge and experience.

Copyright © Mometrix Media. You have been licensed one copy of this document for personal use only. Any other reproduction or redistribution is strictly prohibited. All rights reserved.
This content is provided for test preparation purposes only and does not imply an endorsement by Mometrix of any particular political, scientific, or religious point of view.

LEV VYGOTSKY'S THEORY OF COGNITIVE DEVELOPMENT

Lev Vygotsky's theory on cognitive development is heavily rooted in a **sociocultural** perspective. He argued that the most important factors for a child's cognitive development reside in the cultural context in which the child grows up and social interactions that they have with adults, mentors, and more advanced peers. He believed that children learn best from the people around them, as their social interactions, even basic ones such as smiling, waving, or facial expressions, foster the beginning of more complex cognitive development. He is well-known for his concept of the **Zone of Proximal Development (ZPD)**, which is the idea that as children mature, there are tasks they can perform when they receive help from a more advanced individual. He believed that children could move through the ZPD and complete increasingly complicated tasks when receiving assistance from more cognitively advanced mentors. According to Vygotsky, children develop the most when passing through the ZPD. Vygotsky's contributions are heavily embedded in modern education, and often take the form of teacher-led instruction and scaffolding to assist learners as they move through the ZPD.

Zone of Proximal Development

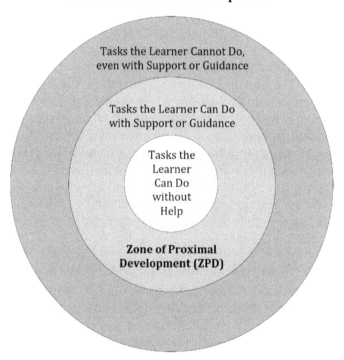

Review Video: <u>Zone of Proximal Development (ZPD)</u>
Visit mometrix.com/academy and enter code: 555594

Social and Emotional Development

ERIK ERIKSON'S EIGHT STAGES OF PSYCHOSOCIAL DEVELOPMENT

Erik Erikson defined eight predetermined stages of psychosocial development from birth to late adulthood in which an individual encounters a crisis that must be resolved to successfully transition to the next stage. The first is **trust vs. mistrust** (0-18 months), where the infant learns that the world around them is safe and they can trust caregivers to tend to their basic needs. The next stage is **autonomy vs. shame** (18 months-3 years), where children learn to control their actions and establish independence. In the **initiative vs. guilt stage** (3-5 years), children acquire a

22

Copyright © Mometrix Media. You have been licensed one copy of this document for personal use only. Any other reproduction or redistribution is strictly prohibited. All rights reserved. This content is provided for test preparation purposes only and does not imply an endorsement by Mometrix of any particular political, scientific, or religious point of view.

sense of purpose and initiative through social interactions. Next, children enter the **industry vs. inferiority stage** (6-11 years), where they develop mastery and pride in completing a task. The next stage is **identity vs. role confusion** (12-18 years), in which children explore and develop characteristics that will comprise their identity and determine their role in society. The sixth stage is **intimacy vs. isolation** (19-40 years), where one forms relationships by sharing the identity developed in the previous stage with others. **Generativity vs. stagnation** (40-65 years) occurs in middle adulthood and focuses on contributing to society's next generation through finding one's life purpose. The last stage is **ego integrity vs. despair** (65 to death), in which one reflects on the productivity and success of their life.

EXPECTED BEHAVIORS AT EACH STAGE OF PSYCHOSOCIAL DEVELOPMENT

Stage	Examples of expected behaviors
Trust vs. mistrust	In this stage, the infant's primary goal is ensuring the fulfillment of their **basic needs**. Infants will cry or make other vocalizations to indicate to caregivers when they want something, such as to be fed or picked up. Separation anxiety from parents is also typical during this stage.
Autonomy vs. shame	Children in this stage begin attempting to perform daily tasks **independently**, such as making food, dressing themselves, bathing, or combing their hair. As children in this stage begin to realize they have a separate identity, they often begin attempting to assert themselves to parents and caregivers.
Initiative vs. guilt	Children at this stage often begin actively engaging and playing with other children. In play settings, these children will often assume **leadership roles** among a group of peers, create new games or activities, and devise their own rules for them. The initiative vs. guilt stage is also characterized by the development of feelings of sadness or guilt when making a mistake or hurting another's feelings.
Industry vs. inferiority	In this stage, children begin attempting to master concepts or skills with the intention of seeking **approval** and **acceptance** from others, particularly those older than themselves, in order to secure a feeling of competency. Children in this stage often become more involved in striving to succeed academically, extracurricular activities, and competitive sports.
Identity vs. role confusion	This stage is characterized by experimentation and uncertainty as young adolescents strive to establish an **independent identity**. Typical behaviors include interacting with new peer groups, trying new styles of dress, engaging in new activities, and considering new beliefs, values, and morals. As young adolescents in this stage are impressionable, they may potentially engage in risky or rebellious behavior as a result of peer pressure.
Intimacy vs. isolation	Individuals in this stage have typically established their identities and are ready to seek **long-term relationships**. This stage marks the development of a social network comprised of close friends and long-term romantic partners.
Generativity vs. stagnation	During this stage, individuals begin engaging in **productive** activities to benefit others and elicit personal fulfillment. Such activities include advancing in a career, parenting, or participating in community service projects.

Copyright © Mometrix Media. You have been licensed one copy of this document for personal use only. Any other reproduction or redistribution is strictly prohibited. All rights reserved. This content is provided for test preparation purposes only and does not imply an endorsement by Mometrix of any particular political, scientific, or religious point of view.

Stage	Examples of expected behaviors
Integrity vs. despair	This stage occurs at the end of one's life and is characterized by **reflection** upon lifetime accomplishments and positive contributions to society. Doing so allows the individual to assess whether their life purpose was fulfilled and begin accepting death.

INCORPORATING LIFE SKILLS INTO CURRICULUM

In addition to academic achievement, the ultimate goal of education is to develop the whole child and provide a successful transition to independence and adulthood. Incorporating such valuable life skills as decision-making, goal setting, organization, self-direction, and workplace communication in early childhood through grade 12 curriculum is vital in ensuring students become productive contributors to society. Furthermore, the implementation of these life skills in early childhood is integral in allowing children to successfully progress in independence and maturity. The acquisition of such skills instills in students the self-motivation and ability to set goals, make decisions on how to effectively organize and manage time to complete them, and overcome obstacles. Additionally, teaching students to apply these skills promotes effective communication when working with others toward a goal. Through incorporating life skills into curriculum, teachers instill a growth mindset and foster self-empowered, confident lifelong learners with the necessary tools to navigate real-life situations and achieve success as they transition to adulthood. In the classroom, activities that promote leadership skills, cooperative learning, goal setting, self-monitoring, and social interaction foster an increasing sense of independence as children develop.

EFFECT OF EXTERNAL ENVIRONMENTAL FACTORS ON SOCIAL AND EMOTIONAL DEVELOPMENT

Social and emotional development is heavily influenced by a child's home environment. Children learn social and emotional skills such as self-regulation, self-awareness, coping, and relationship building through modeling from parents and caregivers. A positive and supportive home environment is integral for proper social and emotional development. External factors, including lack of affection and attention, parental divorce, and homelessness, pose profound negative impacts on this development. In terms of social development, such external factors could lead to attachment or abandonment issues, as well as distrust. Furthermore, children exposed to negative environmental factors could struggle forging relationships, cooperating, and following societal rules. Emotionally, negative impacts on development cause aggression, poor self-regulation, insecurity, anxiety, isolation, and depression. Since developmental domains are interconnected, the impacts that external factors have on social and emotional development ultimately damage cognitive and physical development. Underdeveloped social skills impair cognitive development because the inability to properly interact with peers impedes the ability to learn from them. Additionally, inadequate emotional skills can inhibit concentration and understanding in school, thus inhibiting cognitive development. Physically, struggling to interact with others leads to impaired development of gross and fine motor skills as well as large muscle development that would be achieved through play.

Physical Development

PHYSICAL CHANGES OCCURRING IN EARLY CHILDHOOD THROUGH ADOLESCENCE

As children pass through stages of development from early childhood through middle childhood and adolescence, they experience significant physical changes. Children in early childhood experience rapid growth in height and weight as they transition away from physical characteristics of infancy. In this stage, children begin to gain independence as they develop and improve upon

Copyright © Mometrix Media. You have been licensed one copy of this document for personal use only. Any other reproduction or redistribution is strictly prohibited. All rights reserved. This content is provided for test preparation purposes only and does not imply an endorsement by Mometrix of any particular political, scientific, or religious point of view.

gross and fine motor skills. By early childhood, children develop the ability to walk, run, hop, and as they mature through this stage, learn to throw, catch, and climb. They learn to hold and manipulate small objects such as zippers and buttons, and can grasp writing utensils to create shapes, letters, and drawings with increasing accuracy. Physical growth varies for individual children in middle childhood as some children begin experiencing prepubescent bodily changes. Children in middle childhood experience further improvements and refinements of gross and fine motor skills and coordination. Significant physical and appearance changes occur in adolescence as children enter puberty. These changes often occur quickly, resulting in a period of awkwardness and lack of coordination as adolescents adjust to this rapid development.

IMPACT OF EXTERNAL FACTORS ON PHYSICAL DEVELOPMENT

As children pass through physical development stages from early childhood to adolescence, it is important that environmental factors are supportive of proper growth and health. Physical development can be hindered by external factors, such as poor nutrition, lack of sleep, prenatal exposure to drugs, and abuse, as these can cause significant and long-lasting negative consequences. Exposure to such factors can lead to stunted physical growth, impaired brain development and function, poor bone and muscle development, and obesity. Furthermore, the negative impacts from such external factors ultimately impedes cognitive, social, and emotional development. Impaired brain development and function negatively affect cognitive development by impacting the ability to concentrate and grasp new concepts. In terms of emotional development, physical impairments due to external factors can cause a child to become depressed, withdrawn, aggressive, have low self-esteem, and unable to self-regulate. Improper physical growth and health impacts social development in that physical limitations could hinder a child's ability to properly interact with and play with others. Impacted brain development and function can limit a child's ability to understand social cues and norms.

Language Development

STAGES OF LANGUAGE DEVELOPMENT

The first stage of language development and acquisition, the **pre-linguistic stage**, occurs during an infant's first year of life. It is characterized by the development of gestures, making eye contact, and sounds like cooing and crying. The **holophrase** or **one-word sentence stage** develops in infants between 10 and 13 months of age. In this stage, young children use one-word sentences to communicate meaning in language. The **two-word sentence stage** typically develops by the time a child is 18 months old. Each two-word sentence usually contains a noun or a verb and a modifier, such as "big balloon" or "green grass." Children in this stage use their two-word sentences to communicate wants and needs. **Multiple-word sentences** form by the time a child is two to two and a half years old. In this stage, children begin forming sentences with subjects and predicates, such as "tree is tall" or "rope is long." Grammatical errors are present, but children in this stage begin demonstrating how to use words in appropriate context. Children ages two and a half to three years typically begin using more **complex grammatical structures**. They begin to include grammatical structures that were not present before, such as conjunctions and prepositions. By the age of five or six, children reach a stage of **adult-like language development**. They begin to use words in appropriate context and can move words around in sentences while maintaining appropriate sentence structure. Language development and acquisition has a wide range of what is considered normal development. Some children do not attempt to speak for up to two years and then may experience an explosion of language development at a later time. In these cases, children often emerge from their silent stage with equivalent language development to babies who were

Copyright © Mometrix Media. You have been licensed one copy of this document for personal use only. Any other reproduction or redistribution is strictly prohibited. All rights reserved.
This content is provided for test preparation purposes only and does not imply an endorsement by Mometrix of any particular political, scientific, or religious point of view.

more expressive early on. A child who does not speak after two years, however, may be exhibiting signs of a developmental delay.

ORAL LANGUAGE DEVELOPMENT

Oral language development begins well before students enter educational environments. It is learned first without formal instruction, with **environmental factors** being a heavy influence. Children tend to develop their own linguistic rules as a result of genetic disposition, their environments, and how their individual thinking processes develop. Oral language refers to both speaking and listening. Components of oral language development include phonology, syntax, semantics, morphology, and pragmatics. **Phonology** refers to the production and recognition of sounds. **Morphology** refers to how words are formed from smaller pieces, called morphemes. **Semantics** refers to meaning of words and phrases and has overlap with morphology and syntax, as morphemes and word order can both change the meaning of words. Semantic studies generally focus on learning and understanding vocabulary. **Syntax** refers to how words and morphemes are combined to make up meaningful phrases. In English, word order is the primary way that many components of grammar are communicated. Finally, **pragmatics** refers to the practical application of language based on various social situations. For instance, a college student is likely to use different vocabulary, complexity, and formality of language when speaking with a professor than when speaking with his or her peer group. Each of these five components of language are applied in oral language. Awareness and application of these components develops over time as students gain experience and education in language use. **Oral language development** can be nurtured by caregivers and teachers well before children enter educational environments. Caregivers and teachers can promote oral language development by providing environments full of language development opportunities. Additionally, teaching children how conversation works, encouraging interaction among children, and demonstrating good listening and speaking skills are good strategies for nurturing oral language development.

> **Review Video: Components of Oral Language Development**
> Visit mometrix.com/academy and enter code: 480589

HELPING STUDENTS DEVELOP ORAL LANGUAGE ABILITIES

Children pick up oral language skills in their home environments and build upon these skills as they grow. Early language development is influenced by a combination of genetic disposition, environment, and individual thinking processes. Children with **oral language acquisition difficulties** often experience difficulties in their **literacy skills**, so activities that promote good oral language skills also improve literacy skills. **Strategies** that help students develop oral language abilities include developing appropriate speaking and listening skills; providing instruction that emphasizes vocabulary development; providing students with opportunities to communicate wants, needs, ideas, and information; creating language learning environments; and promoting auditory memory. Developing appropriate speaking and listening skills includes teaching turn-taking, awareness of social norms, and basic rules for speaking and listening. Emphasizing **vocabulary development** is a strategy that familiarizes early learners with word meanings. Providing students with opportunities to **communicate** is beneficial for developing early social skills. Teachers can create **language learning environments** by promoting literacy in their classrooms with word walls, reading circles, or other strategies that introduce language skills to

26

Copyright © Mometrix Media. You have been licensed one copy of this document for personal use only. Any other reproduction or redistribution is strictly prohibited. All rights reserved. This content is provided for test preparation purposes only and does not imply an endorsement by Mometrix of any particular political, scientific, or religious point of view.

students. Promoting **auditory memory** means teaching students to listen to, process, and recall information.

Review Video: <u>Types of Vocabulary Learning (Broad and Specific)</u>
Visit mometrix.com/academy and enter code: 258753

HELPING STUDENTS MONITOR ERRORS IN ORAL LANGUAGE

Oral language is the primary way people communicate and express their knowledge, ideas, and feelings. As oral language generally develops, their **speaking and listening skills** become more refined. This refinement of a person's language is called fluency, which can be broken down into the subdisciplines of language, reading, writing, speaking, and listening. **Speaking fluency** usually describes the components of rate, accuracy, and prosody. **Rate** describes how fast a person can speak and **prosody** describes the inflection and expressions that a person puts into their speech. **Accuracy** describes how often a person makes an error in language production. In early stages of language development, individuals generally do not have enough language knowledge to be able to monitor their own speech production for errors and require input from others to notice and correct their mistakes. As an individual becomes more proficient, they will be able to monitor their own language usage and make corrections to help improve their own fluency. In the classroom, the teacher needs to be an active component of language monitoring to help facilitate growth. Teachers can monitor **oral language errors** with progress-monitoring strategies. Teachers can also help students monitor their own **oral language development** as they progress through the reading curriculum. Students can monitor their oral language by listening to spoken words in their school and home environments, learning and practicing self-correction skills, and participating in reading comprehension and writing activities. Students can also monitor oral language errors by learning oral language rules for phonics, semantics, syntax, and pragmatics. These rules typically generalize to developing appropriate oral language skills.

EXPRESSIVE AND RECEPTIVE LANGUAGE

Expressive language refers to the aspects of language that an individual produces, generally referring to writing and speaking. **Receptive language** refers to the aspects of language that an individual encounters or receives, and generally refers to reading and listening. Both expressive and receptive language are needed for communication from one person to another.

	Expressive	Receptive
Written	Writing	Reading
Oral	Speaking	Listening

Copyright © Mometrix Media. You have been licensed one copy of this document for personal use only. Any other reproduction or redistribution is strictly prohibited. All rights reserved. This content is provided for test preparation purposes only and does not imply an endorsement by Mometrix of any particular political, scientific, or religious point of view.

EXPRESSIVE LANGUAGE SKILLS

Expressive language skills include the ability to use vocabulary, sentences, gestures, and writing. People with good **expressive language skills** can label objects in their environments, put words in sentences, use appropriate grammar, demonstrate comprehension verbally by retelling stories, and more. This type of language is important because it allows people to express feelings, wants and needs, thoughts and ideas, and individual points of view. Strong expressive language skills include pragmatic knowledge, such as using gestures and facial expressions or using appropriate vocabulary for the listener or reader and soft skills, such as checks for comprehension, use of analogies, and grouping of ideas to help with clarity. Well-expressed language should be relatively easy for someone else to comprehend.

RECEPTIVE LANGUAGE SKILLS

Receptive language refers to a person's ability to perceive and understand language. Good receptive language skills involve gathering information from the environment and processing it into meaning. People with good **receptive language skills** perceive gestures, sounds and words, and written information well. Receptive language is important for developing appropriate communication skills. Instruction that targets receptive language skills can include tasks that require sustained attention and focus, recognizing emotions and gestures, and listening and reading comprehension. Games that challenge the players to communicate carefully, such as charades or catchphrase, can be a great way to target receptive language skills. As one student tries to accurately express an idea with words or gestures, the rest of the class must exercise their receptive language skills. Lastly, focusing on **social skills and play skills instruction** encourages opportunities for children to interact with their peers or adults. This fosters receptive language skills and targets deficits in these skills.

STAGES OF LITERACY DEVELOPMENT

The development of literacy in young children is separated into five stages. Names and ranges of these stages sometimes vary slightly, but the stage milestones are similar. Stage 1 is the **Emergent Reader stage**. In this stage, children ages 6 months to 6 years demonstrate skills like pretend reading, recognizing letters of the alphabet, retelling stories, and printing their names. Stage 2 is the **Novice/Early Reader stage** (ages 6–7 years). Children begin to understand the relationships between letters and sounds and written and spoken words, and they read texts containing high-frequency words. Children in this stage should develop orthographic conventions and semantic knowledge. In Stage 3, the **Decoding Reader stage**, children ages 7–9 develop decoding skills in order to read simple stories. They also demonstrate increased fluency. Stage 4 (ages 8–15 years) is called the **Fluent, Comprehending/Transitional Reader stage**. In this stage, fourth to eighth graders read to learn new ideas and information. In Stage 5, the **Expert/Fluent Reader stage**, children ages 16 years and older read more complex information. They also read expository and narrative texts with multiple viewpoints.

> **Review Video: Stages of Reading Development**
> Visit mometrix.com/academy and enter code: 121184

RELATIONSHIP BETWEEN LANGUAGE DEVELOPMENT AND EARLY LITERACY SKILLS

Language development and early literacy skills are interconnected. **Language concepts** begin and develop shortly after birth with infant/parent interactions, cooing, and then babbling. These are the earliest attempts at language acquisition for infants. Young children begin interacting with written and spoken words before they enter their grade school years. Before they enter formal classrooms, children begin to make **connections** between speaking and listening and reading and writing. Children with strong speaking and listening skills demonstrate strong literacy skills in early grade school. The development of **phonological awareness** is connected to early literacy skills. Children

Copyright © Mometrix Media. You have been licensed one copy of this document for personal use only. Any other reproduction or redistribution is strictly prohibited. All rights reserved. This content is provided for test preparation purposes only and does not imply an endorsement by Mometrix of any particular political, scientific, or religious point of view.

with good phonological awareness recognize that words are made up of different speech sounds. For example, children with appropriate phonological awareness can break words (e.g., "bat" into separate speech sounds, "b-a-t"). Examples of phonological awareness include rhyming (when the ending parts of words have the same or similar sounds) and alliteration (when words all have the same beginning sound). Success with phonological awareness (oral language) activities depends on adequate development of speech and language skills.

PROMOTING LITERACY DURING THE EARLY STAGES OF LITERACY DEVELOPMENT

Teachers and parents can implement strategies at different stages of literacy development in order to build **good reading skills** in children with and without disabilities. During the **Emergent Reader stage**, teachers and parents can introduce children to the conventions of reading with picture books. They can model turning the pages, reading from left to right, and other reading conventions. Book reading at this stage helps children begin to identify letters, letter sounds, and simple words. Repetitive reading of familiar texts also helps children begin to make predictions about what they are reading. During the **Novice/Early Reader** and **Decoding Reader stages**, parents and teachers can help children form the building blocks of decoding and fluency skills by reading for meaning and emphasizing letter-sound relationships, visual cues, and language patterns. In these stages, increasing familiarity with sight words is essential. In the **Fluent, Comprehending/Transitional Reader stage**, children should be encouraged to read book series, as the shared characters, settings, and plots help develop their comprehension skills. At this stage, a good reading rate (fluency) is an indicator of comprehension skills. **Expert/Fluent readers** can independently read multiple texts and comprehend their meanings. Teachers and parents can begin exposing children to a variety of fiction and non-fiction texts before this stage in order to promote good fluency skills.

Review Video: Phonics (Encoding and Decoding)
Visit mometrix.com/academy and enter code: 821361

Review Video: Fluency
Visit mometrix.com/academy and enter code: 531179

Family Involvement and Collaboration

EFFECTIVELY WORKING AND COMMUNICATING WITH FAMILIES

Utilizing multiple means of communication when working with students' families ensures information is **accessible** to and **inclusive** of all involved family members. As students' home lives are dynamic, conveying information through several avenues allows families in various situations to participate in their child's education. This is invaluable in establishing and maintaining the positive relationships necessary between students' families and schools for effective teaching and learning. General classroom information, including concepts being taught, important dates, assignments, or suggestions for activities to do at home that reinforce learning in the classroom, can be communicated both digitally and in written form. Newsletters, calendars, or handouts can be both printed and included on a class website to ensure accessibility for all families. Updates regarding individual students can be communicated electronically, through writing, or in person. Email, digital communication apps, and the telephone allow for frequent communication to address students' progress, express concerns, or offer praise. Teachers and families can also communicate through handwritten notes, progress reports, or students' daily agendas. In-person communication, such as during a scheduled conference, is beneficial for discussing individual students' progress and goals related to the education program in depth, as well as ways to support their success in learning.

Copyright © Mometrix Media. You have been licensed one copy of this document for personal use only. Any other reproduction or redistribution is strictly prohibited. All rights reserved. This content is provided for test preparation purposes only and does not imply an endorsement by Mometrix of any particular political, scientific, or religious point of view.

BUILDING POSITIVE RELATIONSHIPS THAT ENHANCE OVERALL LEARNING

Students are more supported and learn more effectively when the relationships between their teachers and families are founded on **mutual respect**, **understanding**, and **cooperation**. Establishing this positive rapport requires the teacher to work and communicate frequently with students' families. Doing so creates an inviting learning atmosphere in which family members feel welcomed and included as **equal contributors** to the educational program. This sentiment empowers and encourages family members to take an active role in their children's education, thus strengthening students' support system and enhancing the overall learning experience. In addition, family members that feel a strong connection to their children's school are more likely to model positive attitudes toward education and reinforce learning at home. When teachers and family members communicate frequently, they develop a mutual sense of trust for one another. This allows for **productive collaboration** and the exchange of valuable insight regarding how to best support students' learning needs both within and outside of the classroom.

APPROPRIATE COLLABORATION AND COMMUNICATION WITH FAMILIES

To effectively collaborate and communicate with students' families, the teacher must carefully consider appropriate methods for doing so. Communication and collaboration must always be **positive**, **respectful,** and **inclusive** to all families to ensure they feel welcomed as equal participants in their children's education. As such, the teacher must be mindful and responsive to the fact that students come from a variety of backgrounds, family dynamics and living situations. This includes demonstrating **cultural competency** when interacting with families from different backgrounds, providing multiple and varied opportunities for family involvement, and communicating through a variety of means. Doing so ensures that families of varying situations have access to pertinent information and feel equally included in the educational program. The teacher must also be mindful of the nature and purpose of communication in order to ensure that sensitive details about individual students are shared only with appropriate family members. General classroom information, such as important dates, events, or assignments, may be shared publicly among the classroom community, whereas such matters as individual student progress or behavior records must be reserved for private communication with the appropriate family members.

INVOLVEMENT OF FAMILIES, PARENTS, GUARDIANS, AND LEGAL CAREGIVERS
STRATEGIES TO ENCOURAGE ENGAGEMENT

As students' family dynamics are diverse, it is important that the teacher implement a variety of methods to engage parents, guardians, and legal caregivers into the educational program. Doing so creates an inviting atmosphere in which family members of all situations feel encouraged to participate in their children's education. Efforts to engage families must always be **positive, inclusive**, and **accommodating** to a variety of needs, schedules, and situations. This includes ensuring that all opportunities for involvement are culturally sensitive, meaningful, and accepting of all families. Utilizing a variety of **communication methods**, such as weekly newsletters, calendars, phone calls, and electronic communication, ensures that opportunities to engage in the educational program are accessible to all families. Providing **multiple** and **varied** opportunities for involvement, such as family nights, field trips, award ceremonies, or inviting families to participate in classroom activities, further encourages family engagement in the educational program. This enables families in various situations to become involved in their children's education in the way that best suits their needs and abilities.

Copyright © Mometrix Media. You have been licensed one copy of this document for personal use only. Any other reproduction or redistribution is strictly prohibited. All rights reserved. This content is provided for test preparation purposes only and does not imply an endorsement by Mometrix of any particular political, scientific, or religious point of view.

FORMS OF ACTIVE INVOLVEMENT

Active involvement in the educational program can take a variety of forms both within and outside of the classroom to accommodate differences in families' schedules, dynamics, and abilities. Providing multiple avenues for involvement engages families of various situations to actively participate in their children's education. Within the classroom, family members can **volunteer** their time to assist as teacher's aides, tutors, or chaperones. In addition, if a family member is skilled in an area related to instruction, the teacher can ask them to come in to speak or teach a lesson. Inviting family members to **visit the classroom** or participate in special class activities allows them to actively engage in the learning process and gain insight into the educational program. Outside of daily classroom activities, family members can be encouraged to participate by attending **family nights, school social events, fundraisers**, or **parent-teacher association meetings**. Active involvement in the educational program can also occur at home. By frequently communicating with teachers, assisting with projects or homework, and emphasizing the importance of learning at home, family members can be informed and actively involved in their children's education.

IMPORTANCE IN CHILDREN'S EDUCATION

As students spend a great deal of time between school and home, the degree to which their family is involved in the educational program significantly influences the quality of the learning experience. When teachers take measures to engage families in their children's education, they establish a welcoming tone that facilitates relationships founded on mutual respect, understanding, and acceptance. These positive relationships are necessary for encouraging and empowering families to actively participate in the learning process. Such involvement contributes to establishing a **positive learning community** in which teachers and families can collaborate productively to enhance students' learning. When students' families are actively involved in their education, it strengthens the **support system** in both influential areas of their lives, thus establishing a sense of security that allows them to confidently engage in learning. Families that participate in the educational program are more likely to emphasize its value at home by extending and reinforcing learning outside of the classroom. This is highly beneficial in promoting positive attitudes toward learning, academic achievement, and social and emotional development.

INFLUENCE ON STUDENT LEARNING AND DEVELOPMENT

The degree of family involvement in the educational program significantly influences the quality of students' learning and development. Learning is more effective when parents, guardians, or legal caregivers are actively engaged in their child's education, as this promotes positive relationships between students' school and home lives that strengthen their **support system** and encourage the extension of learning beyond the classroom. Families that participate in the educational program are likely to emphasize and model its importance at home, thus influencing students to adopt the same positive attitudes toward learning. This facilitates **academic achievement, decreased absences** from school, and **positive learning habits**. In addition, when families are actively involved in the educational process, they are more effectively able to support students with resources at home that reinforce concepts learned in the classroom to strengthen connections and understanding. Students develop healthy **social and emotional skills** as well when their families are actively involved in the educational program. This facilitates positive self-esteem and interpersonal skills that contribute to academic success and fewer behavioral issues in the classroom.

BENEFITS FOR PARENTS, FAMILIES, GUARDIANS, AND LEGAL CAREGIVERS

Families, parents, guardians, and legal caregivers that are actively involved in the educational program gain greater **insight**, **understanding**, and **resources** that enable them to support their children's learning more effectively both within and outside of the classroom. Active engagement in

31

Copyright © Mometrix Media. You have been licensed one copy of this document for personal use only. Any other reproduction or redistribution is strictly prohibited. All rights reserved. This content is provided for test preparation purposes only and does not imply an endorsement by Mometrix of any particular political, scientific, or religious point of view.

the educational program fosters a positive rapport founded on mutual respect and support among family members, teachers, and school. This provides family members with a sense of **confidence** in the merits of the educational program while contributing to the sense that they are **equal participants** in the learning process. These family members are more informed regarding what is being taught in the classroom, as well as beneficial resources to reinforce learning at home. This leaves family members feeling more **empowered** and willing to reinforce their students' learning. In addition, participating in the learning process provides family members with a greater understanding of the characteristics and capabilities of their children's developmental level, thus equipping them with the knowledge to effectively support learning and growth.

BENEFITS FOR EFFECTIVE TEACHING

The involvement of families, parents, guardians, and legal caregivers in the educational program is highly beneficial for effective teaching. Family members that actively participate in the learning process are likely to develop a greater sense of **understanding** and **appreciation** of the teacher's role within it. Such involvement also facilitates positive and frequent communication with families that fosters relationships founded on mutual respect and increases the teacher's **morale**, and therefore effectiveness, in the classroom. Active engagement from family members also allows the teacher to gain a better understanding of how to support individual students' needs. Family members provide valuable insight regarding students' cultures, values, beliefs, educational goals, and learning needs to allow for more effective teaching. In addition, family members that are involved in their children's education are more likely to reinforce and extend learning at home, thus allowing for more effective teaching in the classroom.

POSITIVE RAPPORT

A positive rapport between teachers and families enhances the quality of the learning experience. Establishing these positive relationships requires that teachers frequently take measures to engage families in the educational program in ways that are **meaningful**, **relevant**, and **responsive** to varying situations, backgrounds, and needs. In doing so, teachers communicate the sentiment that all families are welcomed, valued, and considered equal participants in the learning process. This serves to create an open, inviting learning atmosphere in which family involvement is encouraged, thus fostering the **participation** and **communication** necessary for developing a mutual positive rapport. Working to build positive relationships strengthens the connection between schools and families that facilitates productive **collaboration** to best support and enhance students' learning.

INTERACTING WITH FAMILIES OF VARIOUS BACKGROUNDS
DIVERSITIES THAT MAY BE ENCOUNTERED

Appropriate interaction when working and communicating with students' families requires the teacher to recognize the wide range of diversities in characteristics, backgrounds, and needs that they will inevitably encounter. With **culturally diverse** families, the teacher will likely experience variances in language, values, traditions, and customs, including differences in beliefs regarding best practices for raising and educating children. **Socioeconomic** differences may influence the degree to which families have the ability and access to resources to support their children in learning. In some instances, socioeconomic differences may also impact the level of education that family members have attained and potentially the value they place on the importance of education. The teacher must also be mindful of the diversities that exist among **family dynamics**. Some families may have a single caregiver, whereas others may have many. Students may be only children, have several siblings, or come from a blended family. Differences in dynamics also include varying work schedules, lifestyle demands, and living situations that the teacher must consider when working and communicating with families. By acknowledging the diverse characteristics,

Copyright © Mometrix Media. You have been licensed one copy of this document for personal use only. Any other reproduction or redistribution is strictly prohibited. All rights reserved. This content is provided for test preparation purposes only and does not imply an endorsement by Mometrix of any particular political, scientific, or religious point of view.

backgrounds, and needs of students' families, the teacher can take measures to ensure appropriate and inclusive interactions that enhance the learning experience.

APPROPRIATE AND PRODUCTIVE INTERACTIONS

Recognizing the diverse nature of students' cultures, backgrounds, and experiences provides teachers with insight regarding how to interact with their families appropriately and productively. By self-educating to become **culturally competent** and building relationships with students, teachers develop an understanding of the unique characteristics, values, beliefs, and needs of each family. This enables teachers to tailor their communication with individual families in a way that is respectful, **culturally sensitive**, and responsive to their concerns and needs. Doing so ensures that all families feel welcomed and supported in the school environment, thus establishing positive relationships that encourage families to actively engage in the educational program and collaborate productively with teachers to enhance students' learning.

POSSIBLE OBSTACLES

As teachers work and interact with families of diverse backgrounds and experiences, they likely will encounter obstacles that must be addressed to facilitate effective communication. **Cultural differences** in values, beliefs, language, and nonverbal communication may cause misinterpretations between teachers and families that make it difficult to understand one another. It is, therefore, important that the teacher educate themselves regarding students' backgrounds to learn how to communicate in a culturally sensitive manner. When language barriers are present, learning common words and phrases in the language or utilizing an interpreter is beneficial in facilitating communication. Family members may have experienced **negative interactions** with teachers in the past that affect their willingness to engage in communication. Taking measures to establish an inviting, accepting atmosphere that promotes open communication is beneficial in encouraging these families to become involved. **Lifestyle differences**, including varying work schedules, living situations, and family dynamics, may make it difficult to establish effective communication. In addition, **accessibility issues**, including lack of access to transportation, technology devices, or the internet, may hinder family members' abilities to maintain frequent communication. To address these issues, teachers must utilize several communication methods that accommodate families' varying needs and situations.

CONSIDERATIONS TO ENSURE BENEFICIAL INTERACTIONS

The ultimate goal when working and communicating with families is to benefit students' learning and development. When teachers and families develop a positive rapport between one another, it fosters productive collaboration to support the students' educational and developmental goals. Doing so requires that teachers ensure all interactions with students' families are appropriate, respectful, and considerate. This includes demonstrating awareness of varying **backgrounds, characteristics**, and **needs** of each family and interacting in a way that is responsive and accepting of differences. Teachers must practice **cultural competency** when communicating with families, including recognizing differences in perspectives, values, beliefs, and nonverbal communication. Teachers must also consider families' unique situations, including differing **work schedules, living arrangements**, and **family dynamics** to ensure that all interactions are considerate of their time, accommodating to their needs, and supportive of their role in the educational program. When interacting with families, it is important that teachers practice active listening and respond appropriately, meaningfully, and constructively. This communicates to families that their opinions, goals, and concerns related to the educational program are respected, thus encouraging them to actively participate in supporting their children's progress and development.

Copyright © Mometrix Media. You have been licensed one copy of this document for personal use only. Any other reproduction or redistribution is strictly prohibited. All rights reserved.
This content is provided for test preparation purposes only and does not imply an endorsement by Mometrix of any particular political, scientific, or religious point of view.

REGULAR COMMUNICATION WITH FAMILIES

STUDENTS' PROGRESS AND IMPORTANT CLASSROOM INFORMATION

Frequent communication regarding individual student progress and important classroom information is essential to actively engaging family members as equal contributors to the educational program. Doing so creates an inviting atmosphere focused on open and productive dialogue to enhance students' learning and development. Regular communication with families through a variety of methods establishes a strong connection between students' school and home lives that supports their achievement. When families are consistently updated and informed regarding their children's progress in the educational program, they can more effectively collaborate with the teacher to **proactively** address concerns and **implement necessary supports** for successful learning. Frequently communicating important classroom information, including curriculum, assignments, events, and opportunities for involvement, ensures that families are always informed regarding their children's educational program and ways in which they can actively participate. This equips family members with the knowledge and resources necessary to effectively support and reinforce learning both in the classroom and at home.

> **Review Video: Collaborating with Families**
> Visit mometrix.com/academy and enter code: 679996

POSITIVE RAPPORT THAT ENHANCES TEACHING AND LEARNING

Regularly interacting and working with students' families facilitates the **continuous** and **open** line of communication necessary to establishing and sustaining a positive rapport. Building such positive relationships is integral to quality teaching and learning, as frequent communication allows families and teachers to develop a sense of mutual respect, trust, and understanding over time. By frequently communicating with families, teachers create a welcoming, inclusive learning environment in which family members feel encouraged and empowered to contribute as **equal participants** in their child's educational program. This facilitates productive collaboration between teachers and families that supports and enhances students' learning. Developing a positive rapport with family members is also valuable in providing teachers with insight regarding strategies to best support and accommodate students' learning styles, needs, and individual differences. When teachers and families have a positive relationship with one another, students feel more supported in their learning both within and outside of the classroom, thus promoting positive attitudes toward learning and academic achievement.

LISTENING AND RESPONDING TO FAMILIES' CONCERNS

Actively **listening** and **responding** to students' families when interacting with them is an important part of building positive relationships that enhance teaching and learning. By listening attentively to families' concerns, ideas, and information regarding their child and the educational program, teachers gain a greater awareness of their unique backgrounds, characteristics, and experiences. With this understanding in mind, teachers can ensure that they respond to family members in a **sensitive**, **accepting**, and **empathetic** manner to promote the development of a mutual positive rapport. Doing so conveys the sentiment that family members are valued and respected as equal participants in the educational program, thus encouraging them to engage in positive communication to support their children's learning. Families can provide valuable insight regarding their children's learning styles, needs, and behaviors. When teachers listen and respond constructively to this information, they foster positive relationships with families by validating and including them in the learning process. In addition, listening and responding appropriately to students' families indicates acknowledgement and appreciation for their participation in the

Copyright © Mometrix Media. You have been licensed one copy of this document for personal use only. Any other reproduction or redistribution is strictly prohibited. All rights reserved. This content is provided for test preparation purposes only and does not imply an endorsement by Mometrix of any particular political, scientific, or religious point of view.

educational program that contributes to building positive relationships and encourages continued communication.

CONFERENCES

BUILDING POSITIVE RELATIONSHIPS BETWEEN SCHOOLS AND FAMILIES

Frequently conducting conferences with parents, guardians, and legal caregivers facilitates the consistent **in-person communication** necessary for building positive relationships founded on mutual understanding and respect. The conference setting provides a space in which teachers, school staff, and families can discuss the educational program and the student's individual progress, as well as address concerns and collaborate in developing goals. By conducting conferences regularly, teachers, school staff, and families can maintain a continuous, **open dialogue** that provides insight regarding one another's perspectives, intentions, and roles in the educational program. This allows for increased understanding and appreciation for one another that contributes to building positive relationships. Families that attend conferences regularly feel more included in the educational program as equal contributors to their children's learning, thus encouraging them to establish positive strong connections with the school.

SUPPORT OF STUDENTS' SUCCESS IN LEARNING

Effective conferences between teachers and families are focused on open communication, productive collaboration, and strengthening the connection between students' home and school lives. When families and teachers work together in conferences to benefit the student, it strengthens their **support system** in both influential areas of their lives. This is beneficial in enhancing students' **academic achievement**, promoting **healthy development**, and encouraging **positive attitudes toward learning**. Conducting conferences frequently ensures that family members are consistently **informed** and **involved** as equal participants in their child's progress and the educational program. This equips families with the information, understanding, and resources to more effectively support their child's learning both within and outside of the classroom. In addition, effective conferences provide teachers with insight from families regarding students' learning needs, behaviors, and individual situations. With this knowledge in mind, teachers can work with families to develop a plan and implement strategies that best support students' learning and development.

GUIDELINES FOR EFFECTIVENESS

Family conferences are a valuable opportunity to discuss students' individual progress, collaborate to develop educational goals, and address concerns. To ensure conferences are productive, teachers must take measures to make families feel welcomed, respected, and included in the process. Conferences must be scheduled at a **convenient time** for all attending family members in order to accommodate varying needs and situations. It is also important that conferences take place in a comfortable, **inviting atmosphere**, as this establishes a positive tone and facilitates discussion. Teachers must arrive **on time** and **prepared** with specific information to discuss regarding the student, including positive remarks that highlight their strengths. This demonstrates that teachers know the student well and want them to succeed, thus making family members feel comfortable in discussing their child. Asking **open-ended questions**, encouraging families to talk, and practicing active listening is important in facilitating productive discussion, as well as ensuring families feel heard and respected in their concerns. **Direct criticism** of the student must always be avoided; rather, teachers should focus on discussing ways that student can apply their strengths to improve in other areas.

Copyright © Mometrix Media. You have been licensed one copy of this document for personal use only. Any other reproduction or redistribution is strictly prohibited. All rights reserved. This content is provided for test preparation purposes only and does not imply an endorsement by Mometrix of any particular political, scientific, or religious point of view.

FAMILY SUPPORT RESOURCES THAT ENHANCE FAMILY INVOLVEMENT

Families that are supported through school, community, and interagency resources are equipped to effectively support their child's learning and development. Often, families may be hesitant to become actively involved in their children's education because they lack the skills and understanding of how to do so. These support systems are beneficial in providing family members with the **tools, knowledge**, and **resources** that prepare them to effectively participate in the educational program and extend learning outside of the classroom. Such resources are valuable in educating families on the characteristics, needs, and abilities of their children's developmental level, as well as strategies for developing and engaging in age-appropriate activities that support learning at home. This instills a sense of confidence within families regarding their ability to successfully support their children's learning that empowers and encourages them to become actively involved.

When families are supported through **school**, **community**, and **interagency** resources, they are able to more effectively become involved in the educational program. Numerous resources dedicated to educating families on ways they can support their children's learning are available to accommodate varying situations, needs, and abilities. Within the school, **teachers**, **guidance counselors**, and other **staff members** can provide valuable information regarding students' developmental characteristics, needs, and abilities, as well as ways families can become involved to enhance learning within and outside of the classroom. **Support groups** hosted by the school enable families to share experiences and discuss ways to become involved in the learning process. Community support resources are often tailored to address the specific needs of families within the community. These resources offer **family education services** such as classes, meetings, or programs designed to provide families with the training, strategies, and knowledge necessary to become actively involved in their children's education. Several **national family support agencies** are also available to educate families on ways to become involved in their children's learning. Such agencies often have multiple locations, as well as an array of digitally printed information, discussion forums, and training opportunities to enhance family involvement in learning.

Chapter Quiz

Ready to see how well you retained what you just read? Scan the QR code to go directly to the chapter quiz interface for this study guide. If you're using a computer, simply visit the bonus page at **mometrix.com/bonus948/ftceprekinprim** and click the Chapter Quizzes link.

Copyright © Mometrix Media. You have been licensed one copy of this document for personal use only. Any other reproduction or redistribution is strictly prohibited. All rights reserved. This content is provided for test preparation purposes only and does not imply an endorsement by Mometrix of any particular political, scientific, or religious point of view.

Professionalism and Foundations of Early Childhood Education

Transform passive reading into active learning! After immersing yourself in this chapter, put your comprehension to the test by taking a quiz. The insights you gained will stay with you longer this way. Scan the QR code to go directly to the chapter quiz interface for this study guide. If you're using a computer, simply visit the bonus page at **mometrix.com/bonus948/ftceprekinprim** and click the Chapter Quizzes link.

Early Childhood Legal Responsibilities

LEGAL RESPONSIBILITIES OF EARLY CHILDHOOD PROFESSIONALS

Historically, special education was introduced with the purpose of separating special-needs children from their normally developing peers. However, since 1991, the IDEA legislation has established the necessity of inclusion in normal care and educational environments, including early childhood (EC) settings, for children with disabilities. EC professionals know excluding any child is illegal. Another example of legal responsibilities is the "mandated reporter" status of caregivers, teachers, and other adults working with children and families. They are legally required to report suspected child abuse and neglect; the law penalizes them for not reporting. For example, say an EC teacher sees injuries to a child. The child knows the mother has a new boyfriend, displays a fearful attitude, and responds evasively to teacher questions. Later, the child tells the teacher that he or she has been hurt by the boyfriend. The teacher pities the mother, realizing she needs the boyfriend financially and emotionally, and reporting suspected abuse could make the mother lose her children or their home. Regardless, the teacher must report suspicions by law, which was enacted to stop violence against children.

REGULATIONS REGARDING THE CONFIDENTIALITY OF RECORDS

In early childhood settings, records kept about children and their families must be treated with strict confidentiality. Early childhood centers/programs/preschools/agencies should limit access to student records to children's immediate family members, only those employees authorized, and agencies having legal authority to access records. Confidentiality of records and restricted access to them in all centers/programs/preschools/agencies that receive federal funding are mandated by the **Family Educational Rights and Privacy Act (FERPA)**. Moreover, with the ongoing trend toward educational inclusion, many EC settings serve children with disabilities, whose student records are additionally subject to regulations under the federal **Individuals with Disabilities Education Act (IDEA)** and also to the special education laws of their respective US states. An exception to the laws regarding records confidentiality is mandated reporting by EC personnel of suspected child abuse and neglect. Laws applying to child abuse and neglect supersede FERPA regulations. Legally, EC employees are required to report the suspected abuse and neglect of children, and they are immune from liability for releasing child records information relevant to their reporting.

QUALITY CARE AND ECONOMIC CONSIDERATIONS

To furnish and sustain quality care in early childhood settings is always challenging to care providers. It is even more so during difficult economic times. Many early childhood centers must

37

Copyright © Mometrix Media. You have been licensed one copy of this document for personal use only. Any other reproduction or redistribution is strictly prohibited. All rights reserved. This content is provided for test preparation purposes only and does not imply an endorsement by Mometrix of any particular political, scientific, or religious point of view.

face whether to downsize the services they offer or to go out of business. When administrators choose to remain in operation, they encounter equally difficult decisions regarding how to reduce services, but not at the expense of quality. A legal issue related to such economic considerations is that EC personnel are often placed at legal risk when service quality is compromised. While EC employers, employees, young children's parents, and educational researchers are all interested in and pursue a definition of quality care, no single operational definition has been attained. However, early childhood professionals with ample work experience in EC centers have contributed various definitions. The consensus of their contributions includes the following common elements: a nurturing environment; employees trained in EC development and methods; age-appropriate curricula; sufficient space, equipment, and materials; safety and good maintenance of physical environments; and good parent-teacher communication.

MEDICAL CARE AND TREATMENT EMPHASIZED IN LEGAL REGULATIONS

The child care licensing regulations of each US state government mostly govern children's medical care and treatment in early childhood settings. Overall, state regulations emphasize four areas of medical care and treatment:

- Health requirements for all employees, such as having no communicable diseases, passing a TB test, having no health conditions preventing active child care, and maintaining accurate employee and child health records
- Administration by staff of medication to children being served in EC settings
- Management by EC staff of emergencies due to illness, injury, and accidents
- Treatment of nonemergency minor illnesses, injuries, and accidents occurring to children in EC settings

To protect children's health and safety, EC programs/schools/centers must maintain written policies and procedures for emergency and nonemergency care. To protect personnel from litigation, they must adhere scrupulously to written policies and procedures. Litigation for damages or injury is likely when not following procedures. Not reporting suspected or observed child abuse/neglect and not completing accident reports also invite lawsuits.

ADMINISTRATION OF MEDICATION GUIDELINES

The administration of medication to children in early childhood settings has been subject to much controversy due to obvious issues of dangers and liability. EC centers and programs must write their policies and procedures to include their state government's licensing requirements for medical care and treatment, which they must follow closely. Experts recommend that parent and doctor permission be required for administering any prescription and nonprescription medications to children. EC settings should keep on file written parental consent for each medication and review these records regularly for changes. They should also post separate charts, easily accessible to staff, with each child's name, medication, dosage, administration time, and teacher initials. These provide documentation of teachers following parent directions and can prevent mistakes. Staff should label all medications with the drug name, child's name, doctor's name and contact information, and administration instructions. EC centers seasonally and frequently contain many children simultaneously recovering from a variety of illnesses; labeling prevents giving children the wrong medication. Empty drug containers should be returned to parents.

TRANSPORTATION FROM EARLY CHILDHOOD LOCATIONS AND EMERGENCY MEDICAL TREATMENT

For a child's non-life-threatening medical emergencies, early childhood personnel should request transportation by the child's parents. However, if parents cannot transport the child, or in a more

Copyright © Mometrix Media. You have been licensed one copy of this document for personal use only. Any other reproduction or redistribution is strictly prohibited. All rights reserved.
This content is provided for test preparation purposes only and does not imply an endorsement by Mometrix of any particular political, scientific, or religious point of view.

severe emergency, EC administrators should call an ambulance. In life-threatening emergencies that preclude waiting for an ambulance, EC administrators must designate the vehicle and responsible employee for transporting the child to the hospital; this information should be posted in the facility's emergency procedures. Administrators should keep the number of staff involved in emergency medical treatment to a minimum. Those employees they designate for involvement should be willing to take on the responsibility and should have current first aid training. The administrators can include a clause in these employees' job descriptions providing for their transporting children in the event of an emergency. The EC facility may also pay for additional or separate liability insurance coverage of the employees they designate as responsible for providing necessary emergency medical treatment.

CHILD CUSTODY ISSUES INVOLVING EARLY CHILDHOOD FACILITIES

EC facilities are affected by two types of issues involving child custody:

- Parents are pursuing legal and/or physical custody of the child, but they are not living together.
- State authorities have removed a child from the parents' legal and physical custody.

Parents frequently demand the right to visit with and/or take the child home on occasion. Two types of custody are legal custody, defined as an individual's or agency's right to make decisions on a child's behalf regarding the child's place of residence, medical treatment, and education; and physical custody, defined as an individual's or agency's right and responsibility to provide a child with immediate care, and a household or care facility for the present and immediate future. Physical custody does not include all of the rights of full legal custody. It is serious for a child to be in the middle of a custody battle between divorcing parents or between parents and foster parents; therefore, early childhood facilities need the most concise, clear-cut guidelines possible.

EMERGENCY MEDICAL TREATMENT AND FIRST AID RECOMMENDATIONS

EC programs and preschools must write specific, detailed procedures regarding emergency treatment and keep these on file. Children's parents as well as early childhood administrators and staff need to be informed regarding what will occur in the event of a child's serious illness or injury. EC settings must also keep written, signed parental consent forms on file, as well as parent contact information, parental physician and hospital preferences, and health insurance information. EC staff should have current, regularly updated first aid training. First aid equipment should be stored in locations accessible to personnel, who should be frequently reminded of these locations. Lists of each staff member's first aid responsibilities and training should be posted, also accessibly. Licensing regulations require early childhood facilities to notify parents of emergencies; not doing so is subject to legal action. In non-life-threatening emergencies, staff should ask parents to furnish transportation and medical treatment. For grave emergencies, parental consent forms should be filed and updated semiannually, including physician and hospital names, ambulance service, and other transportation procedures.

NON-EMERGENCY MEDICAL ILLNESSES

EC programs must keep procedures for, and reports on, nonemergency medical treatment of children on file just as they do for emergency procedures and reporting. Staff must contact and notify a sick child's parents, who decide if the child should leave the center/preschool. If so, parents should transport their child. Parental consent forms should authorize a doctor or nurse to provide routine medical treatment. early childhood centers/preschools should have sick children wait to be picked up in a location that is separate from other children and activities but closely supervised by staff. For children with allergies, diabetes, and other chronic medical conditions, early childhood

39

Copyright © Mometrix Media. You have been licensed one copy of this document for personal use only. Any other reproduction or redistribution is strictly prohibited. All rights reserved. This content is provided for test preparation purposes only and does not imply an endorsement by Mometrix of any particular political, scientific, or religious point of view.

centers/preschools should not only keep this information on file in records but also post it accessibly at all times for staff reference. Instructions for any special treatment should be included. For any health impairments a child has that could potentially involve emergency treatment, directions for staff should be visibly posted, including specific employees designated to administer treatment. This protects children from harm and caregivers and educators from legal liability.

CUSTODY STATUS

It is recommended that during a child's enrollment, early childhood programs procure a signed, dated document clarifying the child's custody status, including names, contact information, and relationships of all individuals authorized to pick up the child. Copies of any separation agreement or court decree should also be filed. Any time EC staff do not recognize an individual coming to pick up a child, they should ask the person to produce photo identification, which they should closely inspect. EC program administrators cannot make decisions regarding who has legal or physical custody of a child they serve. When a parent or other adult enrolls a child in an early childhood program, that adult is asked to list other persons to be contacted in the event of an emergency. EC administrators are advised to present all parents/guardians with a statement that the early childhood center will only release their child to someone the enrolling parent/adult listed on the emergency form as authorized to pick up the child.

PICKING UP CHILDREN

NON-CUSTODIAL OR NON-AUTHORIZED ADULTS ATTEMPTING TO PICK UP CHILDREN

EC centers should always have up-to-date documentation on file of a child's custodial arrangements, signed and dated by the enrolling adult. If an adult not authorized to pick up the child attempts to do so, an early childhood administrator should inform that adult of the center's policies and procedures regarding custody. They may even show the unauthorized adult their copy of the custodial court order if needed. If the unauthorized adult then departs, the administrator must notify the enrolling adult of the incident; file a written report of it; meet with the custodial adult to clarify custody arrangements anew; document this meeting, including its date and signatures; and file the document in the child's record. If the unauthorized adult refuses to leave and makes a scene or threatens/displays violence, the EC administrator should call the police if needed. The EC center's having a procedure in place for protecting children against emotionally upsetting scenes and/or violent adult behavior is crucial to the children's safety and well-being.

LEGAL RESPONSIBILITIES WHEN CHILDREN ARE NOT PICKED UP TIMELY

If a child is not picked up on time from an early childhood center at the end of its defined day, the EC center has the legal responsibility for the child's welfare as long as the child is on the premises. In the event that a child is left at the EC center for a long time and the parent/authorized adult has not notified the center why and/or when the child will be picked up, EC personnel are advised that keeping the child at the center is less likely to incur legal liability than for the child to stay at an EC staff member's home, for example. If the child has to be removed, it is important for EC staff to inform the police of this and where they are taking the child. If parents are chronically tardy picking up children, EC staff should review the child's information and/or inquire further of parents to ascertain reasons and possible solutions because they are legally responsible for reporting suspected child neglect.

ATTRIBUTES INDICATING EARLY CHILDHOOD EDUCATORS' PROFESSIONALISM AND PROFESSIONAL RESPONSIBILITY

While care and instruction of young children are delivered through a variety of program types, early childhood educators share common general goals. They appreciate early childhood as a unique period in life. They work to educate holistically, considering the mind, feelings, and body of

40

Copyright © Mometrix Media. You have been licensed one copy of this document for personal use only. Any other reproduction or redistribution is strictly prohibited. All rights reserved. This content is provided for test preparation purposes only and does not imply an endorsement by Mometrix of any particular political, scientific, or religious point of view.

the whole child. The educational goals they develop are designed to support each child's fulfilling his or her individual potential within relationship contexts. EC professionals realize children are inseparable from their social milieus of family, society, and culture; they work to relate to and understand children in these contexts while also appreciating and supporting family ties. They apply their knowledge of child development, teaching according to how children learn and what they need, and apply research in the field to differentiate common assumptions and myths from valid scientific findings. They have appropriate behavioral expectations for children at each developmental stage. EC professionals realize the significance of confidentiality; they never gossip or tell families personal information about other families. Lifelong learners, they set their own professional goals, pursuing ongoing professional development.

INTERACTIONS WITH ADULTS IN THE LEARNING ENVIRONMENT

Regarding teachers' roles, much of the focus is on observing children and their behaviors, helping children manage peer interactions, and giving children opportunities for developing peer-group social skills. Too often, a similar emphasis is not accorded to teachers' reflecting on their interactions and behaviors with other adults, learning to collaborate with other adults, and developing skills for conflict resolution and managing disagreements with other adults. Some experts say teachers should work diligently and deliberately to make adult interactions integral parts of daily classroom activity. For group early childhood education settings to attain their goals, adults must make and implement plans collaboratively. However, mandatory staff meetings are commonly occupied with curricular and administrative requirements; beyond these, little or no attention or time is applied to nurturing adult-adult relationships. Adults interact during in-service trainings and professional development experiences but rarely outside of daily classroom settings. Nevertheless, these experiences can be used as foundations for better adult-adult communication within early childhood education contexts. Conscious efforts to develop adult-adult relationships benefiting children's growth, development, and learning are necessary.

POSITIVE INTERACTIONS AMONG ADULTS WITHIN THE EARLY CHILDHOOD EDUCATION SETTING

Adults engage in positive interactions with each other within early childhood education programs when they make time to share their anecdotal records and observations of their young students and collaboratively plan instruction based on their collective contributions. When adults share information and communicate with one another about the children and their families with whom they work, they interact positively together. When EC educators engage in problem-solving activities and dialogues, these help them identify which learning goals and experiences they can make more effective for the children and how they can do this. Adults within early childhood education settings should engage in reciprocal exchanging of ideas about the EC learning environment and about how to share responsibilities for performing instructional tasks, rearranging classrooms as needed, setting up class projects, taking care of class pets and plants, and other such daily duties.

ADULT-ADULT INTERACTIONS

Early childhood education research contains little work addressing adults' cooperation and collaborative expertise with each other and the influences of these on children. However, the HighScope curriculum model, The Creative Curriculum, and similar curriculum models and approaches do address adult-adult interactions by stressing how important teamwork is in planning lessons and sharing responsibilities and information. In addition, some educational experts have written about power struggles and other interactional dynamics in adult-adult relationships that can impede employee performance in a variety of settings. Professional development and training programs rarely include adult conflict-resolution techniques, instruction

41

Copyright © Mometrix Media. You have been licensed one copy of this document for personal use only. Any other reproduction or redistribution is strictly prohibited. All rights reserved. This content is provided for test preparation purposes only and does not imply an endorsement by Mometrix of any particular political, scientific, or religious point of view.

in working collaboratively, or adult learning principles. Hence, educators must consider how their adult-adult interactions can support children's development of competence, capability, and confidence. Sharing instructional goals, planning learning experiences that support goals, and sharing responsibilities as a team for implementing projects establishes climates of safety and trust for children.

APPLYING QUALITY TIME TO EARLY CHILDHOOD EDUCATORS' INTERACTIONS WITH ADULTS

Educators have noted that attitudes and things we commonly say to children, such as, "Your actions speak louder than your words," would equally benefit us in addressing our own behaviors as adults. Applying the same principles we teach children to interactions among adults in the learning community can positively influence those interactions, which in turn affects adult-child/teacher-student interactions and overall classroom atmospheres. Without such atmospheres conducive to trust and honesty in adult relationships, educators can fall prey to misunderstandings and internalizing negative attitudes, which influence not only coworker interactions but moreover classroom climates. One solution is for adults in early childhood education to establish occasions affording "quality adult time." Psychotherapist and psychological theorist Virginia Satir, pioneer of family therapy, found interpersonal dynamics influenced by positive adult-adult communication. Trust-building, mutual colleague support, and sharing experiences/feelings—related or unrelated to classrooms—promote adult relationships that benefit teacher-learner relationships and thus enhance young children's development and learning.

Early Childhood Programs and Approaches

MONTESSORI METHOD
SECTIONS OF THE MONTESSORI METHOD OF EARLY CHILDHOOD INSTRUCTION

- **The Practical Life Area**: These Montessori classes helps children develop care for self, others, and the environment. Children learn many daily skills, including buttoning, pouring liquids, preparing meals, and cleaning up after meals and activities.
- **The Sensorial Area**: This area gives young children experience with learning through all five senses. They participate in activities like ordering colors from lightest to darkest, sorting objects from roughest to smoothest texture, and sorting items from biggest to smallest/longest to shortest. They learn to match similar tastes, textures, and sounds.
- **The Language Arts Area**: This area encourages young children to express themselves in words, and they learn to identify letters, match them with corresponding phonemes (speech sounds), and manually trace their shapes as preparation for learning reading, spelling, grammar, and writing. In the
- **Mathematics and Geometry Area**: Children learn to recognize numbers, count, add, subtract, multiply, divide, and use the decimal system via hands-on learning with concrete materials. In the
- **Cultural Subjects Area**: Children learn science, art, music, movement, time, history, geography, and zoology.

ASPECTS OF THE PHILOSOPHY OF THE MONTESSORI METHOD AS A CURRICULUM APPROACH

Maria Montessori's method emphasizes children's engagement in self-directed activities, with teachers using clinical observations to act as children's guides. In introducing and teaching concepts, the Montessori Method also employs self-correcting ("autodidactic") equipment. This method focuses on the significance and interrelatedness of all life forms and the need for every individual to find his or her place in the world and to find meaningful work. Children in Montessori schools learn complex math skills and gain knowledge about diverse cultures and languages.

Copyright © Mometrix Media. You have been licensed one copy of this document for personal use only. Any other reproduction or redistribution is strictly prohibited. All rights reserved.
This content is provided for test preparation purposes only and does not imply an endorsement by Mometrix of any particular political, scientific, or religious point of view.

Montessori philosophy puts emphasis on adapting learning environments to individual children's developmental levels. The Montessori Method also believes in teaching both practical skills and abstract concepts through the medium of physical activities. Montessori teachers observe and identify children's movements into sensitive periods when they are best prepared to receive individual lessons in subjects of interest to them that they can grasp readily. Children's senses of autonomy and self-esteem are encouraged in Montessori programs. Montessori instructors also strive to engage parents in their children's education.

GENERAL PRACTICES IN THE MONTESSORI METHOD

What Montessori calls "work" refers to developmentally appropriate learning materials. These are set out so each student can see the choices available. Children can select items from each of Montessori's five sections: Practical Life, Sensorial, Language Arts, Mathematics and Geometry, and Cultural Subjects. When a child is done with a work, he or she replaces it for another child to use and selects another work. Teachers work one-on-one with children and in groups; however, the majority of interactions are among children, as Montessori stresses self-directed activity. Not only teachers but also older children help younger ones in learning new skills, so Montessori classes usually incorporate 2- or 3-year age ranges. Depending on students' ages and the individual school, Montessori school days are generally half-days, 9 a.m.–noon or 12:30 p.m. Most Montessori schools also offer afternoon and/or early evening options. Children wanting to "do it myself" benefit from Montessori, as do special-needs children. Individualized attention, independence, and hands-on learning are emphasized. Montessori schools prefer culturally diverse students and teach about diverse cultures.

BANK STREET CURRICULUM APPROACH TO EARLY CHILDHOOD EDUCATION

Lucy Sprague Mitchell founded the **Bank Street** curriculum, applying theoretical concepts from Jean Piaget, Erik Erikson, John Dewey, and others. Bank Street is called a developmental-interaction approach. It emphasizes children's rich, direct interactions with a wide variety of ideas, materials, and people in their environments. The Bank Street method gives young children opportunities for physical, cognitive, emotional, and social development through engagement in various types of child care programs. Typically, multiple subjects are included and taught to groups. Children can learn through a variety of methods and at different developmental levels. By interacting directly with their geographical, social, and political environments, children are prepared for lifelong learning through this curriculum. Using blocks, solving puzzles, going on field trips, and doing practical lab work are among the numerous learning experiences Bank Street offers. Its philosophy is that school can simultaneously be stimulating, satisfying, and sensible. School is a significant part of children's lives, where they inquire about and experiment with the environment and share ideas with other children as they mature.

CLASSROOM CHARACTERISTICS FOR 5- TO 6-YEAR-OLDS

The Bank Street approach to teaching recommends that children 5–6 years old should have classrooms that are efficient, organized, conducive to working, and designed to afford them sensory and motor learning experiences. Classrooms should include rich varieties of appealing colors, which tend to energize children's imaginations and activity and encourage them to interact with the surroundings and participate in the environment. "Interest corners" in classrooms are advocated by the Bank Street approach. These are places where children can display their artworks, use language, and depict social life experiences. This approach also recommends having multipurpose tables in the classroom that children can use for writing, drawing, and other classroom activities. The Bank Street approach also points out the importance of libraries in schools, not just for supporting classroom content but for providing materials for children's extracurricular reading.

Copyright © Mometrix Media. You have been licensed one copy of this document for personal use only. Any other reproduction or redistribution is strictly prohibited. All rights reserved. This content is provided for test preparation purposes only and does not imply an endorsement by Mometrix of any particular political, scientific, or religious point of view.

REQUIREMENTS AND ROLES OF CLASSROOMS AND TEACHERS

The Bank Street approach requires educators to create well-designed classrooms: this curriculum approach finds children are enabled to develop discipline by growing up in such controlled environments. Teachers are considered to be extremely significant figures in their young students' lives. The Bank Street approach requires that teachers always treat children with respect, to enable children to develop strong senses of self-respect. Teachers' having faith in their students and believing in their ability to succeed are found to have great impacts on young children's performance and their motivation to excel in school and in life. The Bank Street Curriculum emphasizes the importance of providing transitions from one type of activity to another. It also stresses changing the learning subjects at regular time intervals. This facilitates children's gaining a sense of direction and taking responsibility for what they do. Bank Street views these practices as helping children develop internal self-control, affording them discipline for dealing with the external world.

FROEBEL'S EDUCATIONAL THEORY REGARDING LEARNING AND TEACHING

Friedrich Froebel (1782–1852) originated the concept and practice of kindergarten (German for "child's garden"). He found that observation, discovery, play, and free, self-directed activity facilitated children's learning. He observed that drawing/art activities develop higher-level cognitive skills and that virtues are taught through children's games. He also found nature, songs, fables, stories, poems, and crafts to be effective learning media. He attributed reading and writing development to children's self-expression needs. Froebel recommended activities to develop children's motor skills and stimulate their imaginations. He believed in equal rather than authoritarian teacher-student relationships, and advocated family involvement/collaboration. He pointed out the critical nature of sensory experiences, and the value of life experiences for self-expression. He believed teachers should support students' discovery learning rather than prescribing what to learn. Like Piaget, Dewey, and Montessori, Froebel embraced constructivist learning, i.e. children construct meaning and reality through their interactions with the environment. He stressed the role of parents, particularly mothers, in children's educational processes.

FROEBEL'S FAMOUS ACHIEVEMENT

Froebel's theory of education had widespread influences, including using play-based instruction with young children. Froebel's educational theory emphasized the unity of humanity, nature, and God. Froebel believed the success of the individual dictates the success of the race, and that school's role is to direct students' will. He believed nature is the heart of all learning. He felt unity, individuality, and diversity were important values achieved through education. Froebel said education's goals include developing self-control and spirituality. He recommended curricula include math, language, design, art, health, hygiene, and physical education. He noted school's role in social development. According to Froebel, schools should impart meaning to life experiences; show students relationships among external, previously unrelated knowledge; and associate facts with principles. Froebel felt human potential is defined through individual accomplishments. He believed humans generally are productive and creative, attaining completeness and harmony via maturation.

SIEGFRIED ENGELMANN'S CONTRIBUTIONS TO EARLY CHILDHOOD EDUCATION

Siegfried Engelmann (b. 1931) cofounded the **Bereiter-Engelmann Program** with **Carl Bereiter** with funding from the US Office of Education. This project demonstrated the ability of intensive instruction to enhance cognitive skills in disadvantaged preschool-aged children, establishing the **Bereiter-Engelmann Preschool Program**. Bereiter and Engelmann also conducted experiments reexamining Piaget's theory of cognitive development, specifically concerning the ability to

44

Copyright © Mometrix Media. You have been licensed one copy of this document for personal use only. Any other reproduction or redistribution is strictly prohibited. All rights reserved.
This content is provided for test preparation purposes only and does not imply an endorsement by Mometrix of any particular political, scientific, or religious point of view.

conserve liquid volume. They showed it could be taught, contrary to Piaget's contention that this ability depended solely on a child's cognitive-developmental stage. Engelmann researched curriculum and instruction, including preschoolers with Down syndrome and children from impoverished backgrounds, establishing the philosophy and methodology of Direct Instruction. He designed numerous reading, math, spelling, language, and writing instruction programs, as well as achievement tests, videos, and games. Engelmann worked with Project Head Start and Project Follow Through. The former included his and Wesley Becker's comparison of their Engelmann-Becker model of early childhood instruction with other models in teaching disadvantaged children. The latter is often considered the biggest controlled study ever comparing teaching models and methods.

ENGELMANN'S METHODS AND FEATURES OF HIS CURRICULUM

In the 1960s, Engelmann noted a lack of research into how young children learn. Wanting to find out what kinds of teaching affected retention and what the extent was of individual differences among young learners, Engelmann conducted research, as Piaget had done, using his own children and those of colleagues and neighbors. With a previous advertising background, Engelmann formed focus groups of preschool children to test-market teaching methods. Main features of the curricula Engelmann developed included emphasizing phonics and computation early in young children's instruction; using a precise logical sequence to teach new skills; teaching new skills in small, separate, "child-sized" pieces; correcting learners' errors immediately; adhering strictly to designated teaching schedules; constantly reviewing to integrate new learning with previously attained knowledge; and scrupulous measurement techniques for assessing skills mastery. To demonstrate the results of his methods for teaching math, Engelmann sent movies he made of these to educational institutions. They showed that with his methods, toddlers could master upper-elementary-grade-level computations and even simple linear equations.

DIRECT INSTRUCTION METHOD OF TEACHING CHILDREN

Direct Instruction (DI) is a behavioral method of teaching. Therefore, learner errors receive immediate corrective feedback, and correct responses receive immediate, obvious positive reinforcement. DI has a fast pace—10–14 learner responses per minute overall—affording more attention and less boredom, reciprocal teacher-student feedback, immediate indications of learner problems to teachers, and natural reinforcement of teacher activities. DI thus promotes more mutual student and teacher learning than traditional "one-way" methods. Children are instructed in small groups according to ability levels. Their attention is teacher-focused. Teacher presentations follow scripts designed to give instruction the proper sequence, including prewritten prompts and questions developed through field-testing with real students. These optimized prepared lessons allow teachers to attend to extra instructional and motivational aspects of learning. Cued by teachers, who control the pace and give all learners with varying response rates chances for practice, children respond actively in groups and individually. Small groups are typically seated in semicircles close to teachers, who use visual aids like blackboards and overhead projectors.

PROJECT FOLLOW THROUGH

In 1967, President Lyndon B. Johnson declared his War on Poverty. This initiative included **Project Follow Through**, funded by the US Office of Education and Office of Economic Opportunity. Research had previously found that Project Head Start, which offered early educational interventions to disadvantaged preschoolers, had definite positive impacts, but these were often short-lived. Project Follow Through was intended to discover how to maintain Head Start's benefits. Siegfried Engelmann and Wesley Becker, who had developed the Engelmann-Becker instructional model, invited others to propose various other teaching models in communities selected to participate in Project Follow Through. The researchers asked parents in each

Copyright © Mometrix Media. You have been licensed one copy of this document for personal use only. Any other reproduction or redistribution is strictly prohibited. All rights reserved.
This content is provided for test preparation purposes only and does not imply an endorsement by Mometrix of any particular political, scientific, or religious point of view.

community to choose from among the models provided. The proponents of each model were given funds to train teachers and furnish curriculum. Models found to enhance disadvantaged children's school achievement were to be promoted nationally. Engelmann's Direct Instruction model showed positive results surpassing all other models. However, the US Office of Education did not adopt this or other models found best.

APPROACHES TO REMEDIAL OR COMPENSATORY EDUCATION

A huge comparative study of curriculum and instruction methods, Project Follow Through incorporated three main approaches: Affective, Basic Skills, and Cognitive. Affective approaches used in Project Follow Through included the Bank Street, Responsive Education, and Open Education models. These teaching models aim to enhance school achievement by emphasizing experiences that raise children's self-esteem, which is believed to facilitate their acquisition of basic skills and higher-order problem-solving skills. Basic Skills approaches included the Southwest Labs, Behavior Analysis, and Direct Instruction models. These models find that mastering basic skills facilitates higher-order cognitive and problem-solving skills, and higher self-esteem. Cognitive approaches included the Parent Education, TEEM, and Cognitively Oriented Curriculum models. These models focus on teaching higher-order problem-solving and thinking skills as the optimal avenue to enhancing school achievement and to improving lower-order basic skills and self-esteem. Affective and Cognitive models have become popular in most schools of education. Basic Skills approaches are less popular but are congruent with other, very effective methods of specialized instruction.

CONTRIBUTIONS OF CONSTANCE KAMII TO EARLY CHILDHOOD EDUCATION

Professor of early childhood education **Constance Kamii**, of Japanese ancestry, was born in Geneva, Switzerland. She attended elementary school in both Switzerland and Japan, completing secondary school and higher education degrees in the United States. She studied extensively with Jean Piaget, also of Geneva. She worked with the **Perry Preschool Project** in the 1960s, fueling her subsequent interest in theoretically grounded instruction. Kamii believes in basing early childhood educational goals and objectives upon scientific theory of children's cognitive, social, and moral development, and moreover that Piaget's theory of cognitive development is the sole explanation for child development from birth to adolescence. She has done much curriculum research in the US and published a number of books on how to apply Piaget's theory practically in early childhood classrooms. Kamii agrees with Piaget that education's overall, long-term goal is developing children's intellectual, social, and moral autonomy. Kamii has said, "A classroom cannot foster the development of autonomy in the intellectual realm while suppressing it in the social and moral realms."

THEORETICAL ORIENTATION, PHILOSOPHY, AND APPROACH OF THE KAMII-DEVRIES APPROACH

Constance Kamii and Rheta DeVries formulated the **Kamii-DeVries Constructivist Perspective** model of preschool education. It is closely based upon Piaget's theory of child cognitive development and on the constructivist theory to which Piaget and others subscribed, which dictates that children construct their own realities through their interactions with the environment. Piaget's particular constructivism included the principle that through their interacting with the world within a logical-mathematical structure, children's intelligence, knowledge, personalities, and morality develop. The Kamii-DeVries approach finds that children learn via performing mental actions, which Piaget called operations, through the vehicle of physical activities. This model favors using teachers experienced in traditional preschool education, who employ a child-centered approach and establish active learning settings, are in touch with children's thoughts, respond to children from children's perspectives, and facilitate children's extension of their ideas. The Kamii-

Copyright © Mometrix Media. You have been licensed one copy of this document for personal use only. Any other reproduction or redistribution is strictly prohibited. All rights reserved.
This content is provided for test preparation purposes only and does not imply an endorsement by Mometrix of any particular political, scientific, or religious point of view.

DeVries model has recently been applied to learning assessments using technology (2003) and to using constructivism in teaching physics to preschoolers (2011).

HighScope Curriculum

David Weikart and colleagues developed the **HighScope Curriculum** in the 1960s and 1970s, testing it in the Perry Preschool and Head Start Projects, among others. The HighScope philosophy is based on Piaget's constructivist principles that active learning is optimal for young children; that they need to become involved actively with materials, ideas, people, and events; and that children and teachers learn together in the instructional environment. Weikart and colleagues' early research focused on economically disadvantaged children, but the HighScope approach has since been extended to all young children and all kinds of preschool settings. This model recommends dividing classrooms into well-furnished, separate "interest areas" and regular daily class routines, affording children time to plan, implement, and reflect upon what they learn and to participate in large and small group activities. Teachers establish socially supportive atmospheres; plan group learning activities; organize settings and set daily routines; encourage purposeful child activities, problem-solving, and verbal reflection; and interpret child behaviors according to HighScope's key child development experiences.

HighScope Curriculum's Key Experiences for Preschoolers

The HighScope Curriculum model identified a total of **58 "key experiences"** it found critical for preschool child development and learning. These key experiences are subdivided into ten main categories:

- **Creative representation**, which includes recognizing symbolic use, imitating, and playing roles
- **Language and literacy**, which include speaking, describing, scribbling, and narrating/dictating stories
- **Initiative and social relations**, including solving problems, making decisions and choices, and building relationships
- **Movement**, including activities like running, bending, stretching, and dancing
- **Music**, which includes singing, listening to music, and playing musical instruments
- **Classification**, which includes sorting objects, matching objects or pictures, and describing object shapes
- **Seriation**, or arranging things in prescribed orders (e.g., by size or number)
- **Numbers**, which for preschoolers focuses on counting
- **Space**, which involves activities like filling and emptying containers
- **Time**, including concepts of starting, sequencing, and stopping actions.

Technology Use, School Day Durations and Settings, and Targets for Its Application

The HighScope Curriculum frequently incorporates computers as regular program components, including developmentally appropriate software, for children to access when they choose. School days may be full-day or part-day, determined by each individual program. Flexible hours accommodate individual family needs and situations. HighScope programs work in both child care and preschool settings. HighScope was originally designed to enhance educational outcomes for young children considered at-risk due to socioeconomically disadvantaged, urban backgrounds and was compatible with Project Head Start. This model of early childhood curriculum and instruction advocates individualizing teaching to each child's developmental level and pace of learning. As such, the HighScope approach is found to be effective for children who have learning disabilities and also for children with developmental delays. It works well with all children needing individual attention. HighScope is less amenable to highly structured settings that use more adult-directed instruction.

47

Copyright © Mometrix Media. You have been licensed one copy of this document for personal use only. Any other reproduction or redistribution is strictly prohibited. All rights reserved. This content is provided for test preparation purposes only and does not imply an endorsement by Mometrix of any particular political, scientific, or religious point of view.

HEAD START PROGRAM

Head Start was begun in 1964, extended by the Head Start Act of 1981, and revised in its 2007 reauthorization. It is a program of the US Department of Health and Human Services designed to give low-income families and their young children comprehensive services of health, nutrition, education, and parental involvement. While Head Start was initially intended to "catch up" low-income children over the summer to reach kindergarten readiness, it soon became obvious that a six-week preschool program was inadequate to compensate for having lived in poverty for one's first five years. Hence, the Head Start Program was expanded and modified over the years with the aim of remediating the effects of system-wide poverty upon child educational outcomes. Currently, Head Start gives local public, private, nonprofit, and for-profit agencies grants for delivering comprehensive child development services to promote disadvantaged children's school readiness by improving their cognitive and social development. It particularly emphasizes developing early reading and math abilities preschoolers will need for school success.

GENESIS AND RATIONALE OF THE HEAD START PROGRAM

After research had accumulated considerable evidence of how important children's earliest years are to their ensuing growth and development, the US Department of Health and Human Services Administration for Children and Families' Office of Head Start established the Early Head Start Program in 1995. Early Head Start works to improve prenatal health, improve infant and toddler development, and enhance healthy family functioning. It serves children from 0–3 years. Like the original program, Early Head Start stresses parental engagement in children's growth, development, and learning.

PLAY-BASED CURRICULUM

To plan a curriculum based on children's natural play with building blocks (Hoisington, 2008), a teacher can first arrange the environment to stimulate further such play. Then he or she can furnish materials for children to make plans/blueprints for and records and models of buildings they construct. The teacher can make time during the day for children to reflect upon and discuss their individual and group-building efforts. Teachers can also utilize teaching strategies that encourage children to reflect on and consider in more depth the scientific principles related to their results. A teacher can provide building materials of varied sizes, shapes, textures, and weights, and can provide props to add realism, triggering more complex structures and creative, dramatic, emotional, and social development. Teachers can take photos of children's structures as documents for discussions, stimulating language and vocabulary development. Supplying additional materials to support and stick together blocks extends play-based learning. Active teacher participation by offering observations and asking open-ended questions promotes children's standards-based learning of scientific, mathematical, and linguistic concepts, processes, and patterns.

SUPPORTING AND INTEGRATING STANDARDS-BASED LEARNING IN SCIENTIFIC, MATHEMATICAL, AND LINGUISTIC DOMAINS

When children play at building with blocks, for example, they investigate material properties such as various block shapes, sizes, and weights and the stability of carpet vs. hard floor as bases. They explore cause-and-effect relationships, make conclusions regarding the results of their trial-and-error experiments, draw generalizations about observed patterns, and form theories about what does and does not work to build high towers. Ultimately, they construct their knowledge of how reality functions. Teachers support this by introducing relevant learning standards in the play context meaningful to children. For example, math standards, including spatial awareness, geometry, number, operations, patterns, and measurement, can be supported through planning play. By encouraging and guiding children's discussion and documentation of their play constructions, and supplying nonfictional and fictional books about building, a teacher also

48

Copyright © Mometrix Media. You have been licensed one copy of this document for personal use only. Any other reproduction or redistribution is strictly prohibited. All rights reserved.
This content is provided for test preparation purposes only and does not imply an endorsement by Mometrix of any particular political, scientific, or religious point of view.

integrates learning goals and objectives for language and literacy development. Teachers can plan activities specifically to extend learning in these domains, like counting blocks, comparison/contrast, matching, sorting, sequencing, phonological awareness, alphabetic awareness, print awareness, book appreciation, listening, comprehension, speech, and communication.

USING THEMATIC TEACHING UNITS

To develop a thematic teaching unit, a teacher designs a collection of related activities around certain themes or topics that crosses several curriculum areas or domains. **Thematic units** create learning environments for young children that promote all children's active engagement, as well as their process learning. By studying topics children find relevant to their own lives, thematic units build upon children's preexisting knowledge and current interests and also help them relate information to their own life experiences. Varied curriculum content can be more easily integrated through thematic units in ways that young children can understand and apply meaningfully. Children's diverse individual learning styles are also accommodated through thematic units. Such units involve children physically in learning; teach them factual information in greater depth; teach them learning process-related skills, such as "learning how to learn"; holistically integrate learning; encourage cohesion in groups; meet children's individual needs; and provide motivation to both children and their teachers.

PROJECT APPROACH

The **Project Approach** (Katz and Chard, 1989) entails having young children choose a topic interesting to them, studying this topic, researching it, and solving problems and questions as they emerge. This gives children greater practice with creative thinking and problem-solving skills, which supports greater success in all academic and social areas. For example, if a class of preschoolers shows interest in the field of medicine, their teacher can plan a field trip to a local hospital to introduce a project studying medicine in depth. During the trip, the teacher can record children's considerations and questions, and then use these as guidelines to plan and conduct relevant activities that will further stimulate the children's curiosity and imagination. Throughout this or any other in-depth project, the teacher can integrate specific skills for reading, writing, math, science, social studies, and creative thinking. This affords dual benefits: enabling both children's skills advancement and their gaining knowledge they recognize is required and applies in their own lives. Children become life-long learners with this recognition.

INTEGRATED CURRICULUM AND EARLY CHILDHOOD EDUCATION

An **integrated curriculum** organizes early childhood education to transcend the boundaries between the various domains and subject content areas. It unites different curriculum elements through meaningful connections to allow study of wider areas of knowledge. It treats learning holistically and mirrors the interactive nature of reality. The principle that learning consists of series of interconnections is the foundation for teaching through use of an integrated curriculum. Benefits of integrated curricula include an organized planning mechanism, greater flexibility, and the ability to teach many skills and concepts effectively, include more varied content, and enable children to learn most naturally. By identifying themes children find most interesting, teachers can construct webs of assorted themes, which can provide the majority of their curriculum. Research has proven the effectiveness of integrated teaching units for both children and their teachers. Teachers can also integrate new content into existing teaching units they have identified as effective. Integrated units enable teachers to ensure children are learning pertinent knowledge and applying it to real-life situations.

49

Copyright © Mometrix Media. You have been licensed one copy of this document for personal use only. Any other reproduction or redistribution is strictly prohibited. All rights reserved. This content is provided for test preparation purposes only and does not imply an endorsement by Mometrix of any particular political, scientific, or religious point of view.

SKILLS, TOPICS, STRATEGIES, AND BENEFITS RELATED TO CREATING THEMATICALLY-BASED TEACHING UNITS

EC teachers can incorporate many skills into units organized by theme. This includes state governments' educational standards/benchmarks for various skills. Teachers can base units on topics of interest to young children, such as building construction, space travel, movie-making, dinosaurs, vacations, nursery rhymes, fairy tales, pets, wildlife, camping, the ocean, and studies of particular authors and book themes. Beginning with a topic that motivates the children is best; related activities and skills will naturally follow. In planning units, teachers should establish connections among content areas like literacy, physical activity, dramatic play, art, music, math, science, and social studies. Making these connections permits children's learning through their strongest/favored modalities and supports learning through meaningful experiences, which is how they learn best. Theme-based approaches effectively address individual differences and modality-related strengths, as represented in Gardner's theory of multiple intelligences. Thematic approaches facilitate creating motivational learning centers and hands-on learning activities and are also compatible with creating portfolio assessments and performance-based assessments. Teachers can encompass skill and conceptual benchmarks for specific age/developmental levels within engaging themes.

Equity in Education

EQUALITY VS. EQUITY

Equality refers to providing everyone with the same resources when working toward a goal, regardless of the unique needs or situation of the individual. **Equity** means considering an individual's needs and circumstances to provide the proper supports that allow them a fair opportunity to achieve a common goal. In the classroom, creating an equitable environment requires the consideration of students' individual learning styles, needs, and personal situations, and using this knowledge to instill necessary supports to help each student achieve the same objectives relative to their peers. Equity in the classroom is especially important for closing the achievement gap, particularly in low socioeconomic areas, because many of these students come from disadvantaged situations and need additional help to gain a fair opportunity for academic success.

> **Review Video: Equality vs Equity**
> Visit mometrix.com/academy and enter code: 685648

SUPPORTS UTILIZED TO PROVIDE AN EQUITABLE LEARNING ENVIRONMENT

The nature of academic, physical, and behavioral supports depends largely on the needs of the individual student. However, some common supports are effective in addressing an array of needs to facilitate an equitable learning environment. Students with **learning disabilities** may benefit from such academic supports as preferential seating near the front of the room and minimized distractions to enhance focus. Modified test questions or alternate assignments, graphic organizers, scaffolded texts, extra copies of class notes, and individualized instruction as necessary are also valuable in enhancing focus, preventing overwhelm, and ensuring learning activities are aligned with students' capabilities. Students with **physical disabilities** may require wheelchair access, a sign language interpreter or scribe, braille text, enlarged fonts, or the use of technology devices to aid in reading and writing. Common **behavioral supports** in the classroom include opportunities for frequent breaks or movement as needed, a daily check-in with a caseworker or other dedicated staff member, or a behavior chart to allow students to self-monitor.

Copyright © Mometrix Media. You have been licensed one copy of this document for personal use only. Any other reproduction or redistribution is strictly prohibited. All rights reserved.
This content is provided for test preparation purposes only and does not imply an endorsement by Mometrix of any particular political, scientific, or religious point of view.

ESTABLISHING HIGH ACADEMIC EXPECTATIONS

In any classroom, establishing high academic standards is imperative for motivating and empowering students to succeed. By communicating high expectations clearly and frequently, the teacher demonstrates belief that each student can overcome obstacles and excel academically, thus inspiring student engagement, curiosity for learning, and an overall positive and productive learning environment. To create an environment of high academic standards, the teachers' expectations must be apparent in instruction. The teacher must provide lessons and activities that are rigorous but not so challenging that students are unable to complete them without assistance, as this would disempower and disengage students from learning. The teacher must set achievable learning goals based on knowledge of student abilities and encourage self-reflection. Additionally, the teacher must utilize knowledge of students' individual needs to instill necessary supports to help students in achieving tasks and create an equitable environment for learning. This will ultimately empower students to overcome obstacles and motivate them for academic success.

Roles and Responsibilities within the Local Education System

DEPARTMENT CHAIRPERSONS

Department chairpersons are appointed to act as **leaders** within their subject area. These individuals are responsible for a variety of instructional and administrative duties to ensure the **efficacy** of their academic department in supporting the goals and mission of the school. This includes contributing to curriculum development, communicating instructional expectations from administration to their colleagues, and ensuring that daily instruction within the department aligns with campus and district academic standards. Department chairpersons also serve as **resources** for their team, including collaborating with them to design instructional activities and assessments, offering support, and facilitating positive communication with administration. When working with administration, department chairpersons discuss the progress of their department in meeting academic goals, collaborate to develop strategies for assisting faculty in supporting student learning, and ensure their colleagues have the support, materials, and resources necessary for effective instruction. In addition, department chairpersons are often responsible for coordinating department activities and programs that promote student achievement and contribute to creating a positive school community.

SCHOOL PRINCIPAL

The primary role of the **principal** is establishing and maintaining a **school culture** that supports students, teachers, staff, and families in the educational program. This role comprises a multifaceted array of responsibilities that extend to nearly every aspect of the school. The principal is responsible for supervising the **daily operations** of the school to ensure a safe, orderly environment in which teachers, staff, and students are working in alignment with the school's mission. To achieve this, the principal must communicate expectations for a positive, productive school community, ensure academic and behavioral policies are followed by staff and students, and assign staff members specific duties to facilitate an organized, efficient learning environment. In addition, it is important that the principal support staff, students, and families by engaging in frequent, open communication, addressing concerns, and providing resources necessary to promote growth and achievement. The principal is also responsible for ensuring that the school's educational program is effective in supporting teachers, staff, and students in the achievement of academic standards. This includes overseeing curriculum, monitoring instructional practices, measuring their school's performance in relation to district academic standards, as well as communicating the progress and needs of the school to the board of education.

Copyright © Mometrix Media. You have been licensed one copy of this document for personal use only. Any other reproduction or redistribution is strictly prohibited. All rights reserved. This content is provided for test preparation purposes only and does not imply an endorsement by Mometrix of any particular political, scientific, or religious point of view.

BOARD OF TRUSTEES

Each school within a district is overseen by a **board of trustees** responsible for making decisions to ensure that the educational program supports students' learning needs for academic achievement. The board of trustees is comprised of a group of **elected individuals** that are typically members of the community in which they serve. As such, they have an understanding of the educational needs of the students within the community and can apply this knowledge to make effective decisions regarding the learning program. Members within a board of trustees are responsible for creating an educational program in alignment with students' needs, as well as setting goals and developing strategies that support students in achieving them. This includes determining a **budget plan, allocating resources**, and making **administrative decisions** that benefit the school. In addition, board members are responsible for analyzing assessment data to make informed decisions regarding strategies to best support individual schools within the district and ensuring that measures are being implemented to effectively meet students' learning needs.

CURRICULUM COORDINATORS

Curriculum coordinators are responsible for the **development** and **implementation** of curriculum that is aligned with campus and district academic goals. These individuals work closely with teachers and administrators to analyze student progress in relation to the educational program, primarily through **assessment scores**, to determine the overall effectiveness of the curriculum in supporting students' achievement. Analyzing student progress enables curriculum coordinators to identify strengths and areas for improvement within the curriculum to make adjustments that best meet students' learning needs as they work to achieve learning targets. Ensuring that curriculum aligns with academic standards and students' learning needs facilitates more effective teaching and learning. Doing so provides teachers with a clear understanding of how to adequately prepare students for success, thus allowing them to design focused instruction and implement necessary supports to promote the achievement of campus and district academic standards.

SCHOOL TECHNOLOGY COORDINATORS

Incorporating technology into the classroom is highly valuable in diversifying instructional strategies to promote student learning and engagement. School **technology coordinators** facilitate this integration to enhance teaching and learning, as they are responsible for the **organization, maintenance**, and **allocation** of available technology resources within the school building. This includes ensuring that all technology is functional, updated, properly stored, and accessible to teachers. These individuals are also responsible for **staying current** on developing digital resources that could be implemented to improve the learning experience, as well as communicating with the board of education regarding **acquiring** technology resources for their school. Doing so ensures that teachers have the materials necessary to best support students' learning. In addition, technology coordinators **educate** teachers and staff on the uses of technology resources, as well as strategies to implement them in the classroom for more effective instruction.

SPECIAL EDUCATION PROFESSIONALS

Special education professionals work with students of various disabilities, their teachers, and families to provide an equitable, inclusive environment that supports learning and development. These individuals are responsible for creating an educational plan that is tailored to support the unique needs of disabled students and ensuring that this plan is followed in all areas of the school. Special educators develop **individualized education programs** (IEPs) according to students' areas of need, develop academic and behavioral goals, as well as provide supports and modifications to accommodate students in achieving them. Special education professionals work with teachers to

Copyright © Mometrix Media. You have been licensed one copy of this document for personal use only. Any other reproduction or redistribution is strictly prohibited. All rights reserved. This content is provided for test preparation purposes only and does not imply an endorsement by Mometrix of any particular political, scientific, or religious point of view.

educate them on the proper implementation of individualized accommodations to ensure all students have the support necessary to successfully engage in learning. This includes collaborating with teachers to adapt and modify curriculum, instructional activities, and assessments to meet the individual needs of students with disabilities. In addition, special educators may work alongside classroom teachers in a team-teaching setting or provide individualized instruction as necessary. Students' academic and behavioral progress is monitored over time, and special educators communicate this information to families in order to collaborate in developing future goals and strategies to support achievement.

ROLES AND RESPONSIBILITIES OF PROFESSIONALS WITHIN THE EDUCATION PROGRAM

The roles and responsibilities of various professionals within the educational program are described as follows:

- **Principal**—The principal is responsible for ensuring that the daily operations of the school function in a safe, orderly manner that aligns with the goals of the educational program. This includes delegating tasks to staff, enforcing academic and behavioral policies, ensuring instructional practices support student achievement, and communicating with students, staff, and families to establish a positive learning environment.
- **Vice Principal**—The vice principal's role is to assist the principal in supervising the daily operations of the school to create a safe, orderly, and productive learning environment. They are responsible for working with teachers, staff, students, and families to support them in the educational program. This includes enforcing academic and behavioral policies, addressing concerns, facilitating communication, and ensuring instructional practices support student achievement of campus and district academic goals.
- **Board of Trustees**—The board of trustees is responsible for developing an educational program that reflects the learning needs of students within the community. This includes developing educational goals, strategies to support students in achieving them, and ensuring that schools within the district are in alignment with the educational program. The board of trustees is also responsible for such administrative decisions as developing a budget plan and allocating resources to schools within the district according to students' needs.
- **Curriculum Coordinator**—Curriculum coordinators are responsible for developing a curriculum that aligns with campus and district academic goals, and ensuring it is implemented properly to support student achievement. This includes working with teachers and administrators to measure student progress within the curriculum and adjusting instructional strategies as necessary to support student success.
- **Assessment Coordinator**—Assessment coordinators schedule, disperse, and collect standardized assessments and testing materials within the school building. They are responsible for educating teachers on proper assessment protocols to ensure that all practices align with district policies, collaborating with them to develop strategies that support student achievement, and ensuring all students are provided with necessary accommodations according to individual need.
- **Technology Coordinator**—Technology coordinators facilitate the integration of digital resources into the curriculum. They are responsible for acquiring, organizing, maintaining, and allocating technology within the school. These individuals also work with teachers and staff to educate them on ways to utilize technology resources to enhance instruction.

Copyright © Mometrix Media. You have been licensed one copy of this document for personal use only. Any other reproduction or redistribution is strictly prohibited. All rights reserved. This content is provided for test preparation purposes only and does not imply an endorsement by Mometrix of any particular political, scientific, or religious point of view.

- **Department Chair**—Department chairpersons act as leaders among the teachers within their content area. Their responsibilities include contributing to curriculum development, facilitating communication between administration and their colleagues, and ensuring instructional practices align with the educational program. They also collaborate with members of their team to develop instructional practices that best support student achievement of campus and district academic goals.
- **Teacher Assistant**—The teacher assistant's role is to support the classroom teacher in both instructional and non-instructional duties. This includes assisting with the preparation, organization, and cleanup of lesson materials, working with small groups of students, managing student behavior, and ensuring the classroom functions in a safe, orderly manner.
- **Paraprofessional**—Paraprofessionals are licensed within the field of education and are responsible for assisting the teacher with daily classroom operations. This includes working with individual or small groups of students to provide instructional support, assisting with the preparation of lesson plans and materials, managing student behavior, and completing administrative duties.
- **Speech-Language Pathologist**—Speech-Language pathologists are special education professionals that work with students that have varying degrees of language and communication difficulties. They are responsible for evaluating and diagnosing disabilities related to speech and language, as well as developing individualized treatment programs. Speech-language pathologists then work with these students to remedy language and communication disabilities, as well as collaborate with teachers, staff, and families regarding ways to support their progress.
- **ESL Specialist**—ESL (English as a second language) specialists work with students for whom English is not their native language. They are responsible for evaluating students' levels of English language proficiency across the domains of reading, writing, speaking, and listening, determining necessary linguistic supports, and working with teachers to develop strategies that support English language acquisition. ESL specialists also work with individual or small groups of students to monitor progress and develop English language proficiency skills.
- **Guidance Counselor**—The role of guidance counselors is to support students' social, emotional, academic, and behavioral needs. This includes providing counseling services, mediation, and for upper grade level students, advice regarding course selection and career choices. These individuals communicate with teachers, staff, and families to develop and implement plans to support students' personal growth and academic achievement.
- **School Nurse**—The school nurse is responsible for providing a range of healthcare to students and staff in the school building. This includes evaluating the physical, mental, and emotional health of students and staff, as well as delivering general first-aid treatments. School nurses are also responsible for organizing and dispersing prescribed medications to students in accordance with their healthcare plan and educating teachers and staff regarding best practices for ensuring students' health and safety. School nurses may work with special education professionals to assess students' needs in the development of an individualized education program.
- **Building Service Worker**—Building service workers are responsible for the general maintenance of the school building and outside campus. This includes ensuring that all areas, equipment, and furniture are clean, functional, and safe for student and staff use. These individuals are also responsible for transporting heavy equipment and furniture throughout the school building.

54

Copyright © Mometrix Media. You have been licensed one copy of this document for personal use only. Any other reproduction or redistribution is strictly prohibited. All rights reserved. This content is provided for test preparation purposes only and does not imply an endorsement by Mometrix of any particular political, scientific, or religious point of view.

- **Secretary**—The school secretary is responsible for assisting the principal, vice principal, and other office personnel in daily administrative duties. This individual assumes a variety of responsibilities to ensure the efficient function of daily operations within the school. Their responsibilities include communicating with students, families, and other office visitors, directing phone calls to the appropriate location, handling financial matters, and coordinating the school calendar.
- **Library/Media Specialist**—Library and media specialists coordinate the organization, maintenance, and allocation of all library and media resources within the school building. They are responsible for educating students regarding the proper use of library and media resources to locate information, including how to navigate the internet safely and appropriately for educational purposes. Library and media specialists also direct students toward reading material aligned with their literacy skills and provide teachers with learning materials to incorporate into instruction.
- **Instructional Leadership Team (ILT)**—An instructional leadership team is comprised of individuals responsible for educating teachers regarding current and relevant instructional philosophies and practices to enhance student learning. These individuals collaborate with teachers to educate them regarding how to implement instructional strategies, activities, and assessments to effectively meet students' learning needs and support their achievement of campus and district academic goals.
- **School Resource Officer**—The role of the school resource officer is to maintain a safe, orderly environment for teachers, staff, and students. They are responsible for ensuring the physical security of the school, handling legal infractions within the school, and addressing conflicts among students. The school resource officer also works with administration and staff to develop emergency drill procedures.
- **Pupil Personnel Worker (PPW)**—Pupil personnel workers are responsible for addressing issues that hinder the academic achievement of at-risk students. These individuals communicate with teachers, administration, staff, and families to ensure these students are supported both within and outside of the school building. This includes addressing issues related to behavior, crisis intervention, attendance, and home lives. Pupil personnel workers direct families toward school and community support resources and collaborate with teachers to implement supports that facilitate success in learning.

Professional Development

AVAILABLE RESOURCES AND SUPPORT SYSTEMS

Effective educators continuously seek professional development opportunities to refine their teaching practice. There are multiple resources and support systems that teachers can utilize to develop their professional knowledge and skills. Within the school building, mentors are available to offer ideas, advice, and support in developing teaching practices and strategies to implement in the classroom for effective teaching and learning. The school's **instructional leadership team** (ILT) is also a valuable resource for educating teachers regarding current instructional practices to enhance student engagement and learning. Teachers can continue their professional education by enrolling in university courses or participating in state-initiated programs to stay informed on relevant pedagogical theories and practices. Service centers are also available that offer workshops, training, and conferences on a variety of topics related to education to support teachers' professional development. In addition, numerous digital support resources are available that allow teachers to enroll in courses, participate in informational webinars, and collaborate with other educators in professional learning communities to build and enhance their teaching practice.

Copyright © Mometrix Media. You have been licensed one copy of this document for personal use only. Any other reproduction or redistribution is strictly prohibited. All rights reserved.
This content is provided for test preparation purposes only and does not imply an endorsement by Mometrix of any particular political, scientific, or religious point of view.

EXAMPLE OPPORTUNITIES THAT CAN ENHANCE TEACHING PRACTICE

Professional development opportunities are available to address a variety of needs for refining one's practice and developing pedagogical knowledge. Professional development trainings can serve to educate teachers on how to utilize and incorporate current technologies into the classroom, as well as teach strategies for implementing relevant and engaging instructional techniques, materials, and resources into the classroom. These opportunities can also be beneficial in teaching educators how to demonstrate cultural competency and skills for productive collaboration with colleagues to enhance student learning. Teachers can also seek professional development opportunities to learn best practices for addressing a variety of student needs, such as intellectual, physical, social, or emotional disabilities, or linguistic needs of ELLs. Actively seeking and participating in professional development trainings helps to ensure teachers stay current on pedagogical theories that can serve as a framework for their instructional practice.

EFFECTIVELY UTILIZING RESOURCES AND SUPPORT SYSTEMS

The field of education is multifaceted and continuously evolving. As such, it is important that teachers of all experience levels engage in the vast array of **available resources** and **support systems** to develop and refine their professional skills. Doing so enhances students' learning, as teachers that actively seek professional development are more current on pedagogical theories and practices, as well as instructional strategies, resources, and technologies to incorporate in the classroom. This allows teachers to design and implement more effective instruction, as it provides them with an increased range of knowledge and tools to enhance student engagement and understanding. In addition, as students' individual needs are diverse, participating in resources and support systems allows teachers to educate themselves on how to properly accommodate them to enhance the learning experience. Utilizing resources and support systems also enables teachers to learn from and collaborate with other educators in professional learning communities to continuously develop new skills, ideas, and instructional methods that enhance student learning.

TEACHER APPRAISALS
CHARACTERISTICS, GOALS, AND PROCEDURES

Teacher appraisals are a method of evaluation intended to provide the teacher with continuous feedback regarding their **performance** and areas in which they can improve their professional skills to enhance student learning. Feedback is provided periodically throughout the school year and derives from classroom **observations** typically conducted by the principal or grade-level administrator. Observations can either be **formally** scheduled and last the duration of a lesson, or can be in the form of shorter, informal **walk-through** evaluations. In both instances, the observer watches and collects information as the teacher delivers instruction, directs learning activities, and interacts with students. The teacher's performance is then measured against **criteria** across several domains pertaining to planning, preparing, and delivering instruction. This score is used to provide the teacher with detailed feedback in post-observation meetings regarding their strengths and specific areas in which they can improve their practice to more effectively meet students' learning needs. Feedback is used to support the teacher in developing specific **professional goals** and strategies for improving their teaching skills.

BENEFITS OF APPRAISAL RESULTS IN IMPROVING PROFESSIONAL SKILLS

The results of teacher appraisals are beneficial in providing educators with **specific feedback** regarding areas in which they can improve their professional skills. Effective teachers understand the value of continuously **refining their practice** to enhance student learning, and therefore, actively seek opportunities to do so. However, it may prove difficult for teachers to objectively assess their own efficacy in the classroom. Appraisal results communicate feedback from the

Copyright © Mometrix Media. You have been licensed one copy of this document for personal use only. Any other reproduction or redistribution is strictly prohibited. All rights reserved.
This content is provided for test preparation purposes only and does not imply an endorsement by Mometrix of any particular political, scientific, or religious point of view.

outside perspective of the observer for a comprehensive evaluation of their performance, thus providing teachers with clarity regarding their strengths and areas for growth. This allows educators to effectively develop **professional goals** to improve their skills in targeted areas and **strategies** to achieve these goals successfully.

WORKING WITH SUPERVISORS, MENTORS, AND COLLEAGUES
ENHANCING PROFESSIONAL KNOWLEDGE AND SKILLS

When teachers collaborate with supervisors, mentors, and other colleagues, it facilitates a productive **professional learning community** that supports the continuous development of knowledge and skills related to education. Doing so provides teachers with the opportunity to work with educational professionals of varying backgrounds, experiences, and expertise. This exposes teachers to a wide range of **perspectives**, **approaches**, and **philosophies** that they can learn from to build and enhance their practice. In such a setting, teachers can interact with other professionals within the school community to share ideas, support one another, and collaborate productively in developing strategies to improve their efficacy in the classroom. Additionally, actively engaging with supervisors, mentors, and colleagues facilitates the open communication necessary for productive collaboration in effectively addressing issues to enhance the school community.

ADDRESSING ISSUES AND BUILDING PROFESSIONAL SKILLS

Productive collaboration with supervisors, mentors, and colleagues is essential to addressing issues related to the educational program and continuously developing professional practices. There are multiple opportunities for such collaboration within the school community that accommodate varying purposes. By participating in **professional learning communities**, members of the educational program can collaborate and support one another in addressing concerns and building professional skills. In subject-area **department** or **team meetings**, educators can work together to share ideas, strategies, and resources related to their content area for more effective instruction. Working with supervisors and mentors in **post-observation conferences** provides teachers with valuable feedback regarding their strengths and areas for improvement. Such collaboration is beneficial in creating specific goals and strategies for professional growth. Additionally, engaging in collaborative **professional development opportunities**, including workshops, conferences, programs, and courses, is beneficial in allowing educators to build upon one another's experiences, backgrounds, and expertise to enhance professional practices.

PROFESSIONAL DEVELOPMENT RESOURCES

The various professional development resources available to teachers and staff are discussed below:

- **Mentors/Support Systems**: Mentors and other dedicated support resources within the school system are intended to provide teachers with guidance to enhance their professional knowledge, skills, and expertise. These individuals are typically highly experienced and work with teachers to develop effective instructional strategies, classroom management techniques, and learning materials to improve their teaching skills.
- **Conferences**: Education conferences are multifaceted events in which teachers can learn about current developments in their field to improve their professional knowledge, pedagogical skills, and technical expertise. Conference events are comprised of numerous professional development opportunities, including presentations on current pedagogical theories and practices, collaborative workshops, and training sessions regarding the implementation of new instructional strategies and technology resources. At these events, teachers can also network with one another to connect and share resources, ideas, and strategies that enhance their teaching practice.

Copyright © Mometrix Media. You have been licensed one copy of this document for personal use only. Any other reproduction or redistribution is strictly prohibited. All rights reserved. This content is provided for test preparation purposes only and does not imply an endorsement by Mometrix of any particular political, scientific, or religious point of view.

- **Professional Associations**: Education associations provide teachers with access to numerous professional development opportunities for improving knowledge, pedagogical skills, and technical expertise. These associations can be related to general education or content specific, and offer information regarding education conferences, workshops, training opportunities, and courses to enhance teaching practices. Professional education associations also allow teachers the opportunity to network with one another to build professional knowledge by sharing ideas, resources, and strategies to implement in the classroom.

- **Online Resources**: Numerous online resources, including websites, blogs, webinar trainings, and discussion forums are available to support teachers in enhancing their professional knowledge, skills, and technical expertise on a variety of topics. Teachers can utilize these resources to learn current pedagogical theories and practices, instructional and classroom management strategies, as well as relevant technology resources to implement in the classroom for enhanced student learning. Online resources are also valuable for collaborating with other teachers in building professional knowledge and sharing ideas, learning materials, and resources that improve instructional practices.

- **Workshops**: Workshop training sessions provide teachers the opportunity to build professional knowledge, skills, and expertise by educating them on current instructional strategies, classroom management techniques, and digital resources in a hands-on setting. Workshops are typically dedicated to a specific pedagogical topic and allow teachers to collaborate with one another in learning how to implement it in their classroom.

- **Journals**: Education journals publish newly researched information regarding pedagogical theories and practices teachers can utilize to enhance their professional knowledge. These journals include scholarly articles and case studies regarding topics such as instructional strategies and practices, classroom management techniques, and the implementation of digital resources. Education journals allow teachers to stay current on pedagogical developments in order to continuously improve their teaching skills.

- **Coursework**: Engaging in coursework is beneficial in continuing formal professional education to enhance knowledge, pedagogical skills, and technical expertise. Doing so allows teachers to learn from other experienced educators regarding current educational theories, practices, instructional strategies, and technology resources. By participating in formal coursework, teachers can continuously build upon their teaching skills and stay current regarding developments in their field.

REFLECTION AND SELF-ASSESSMENT
IMPROVING TEACHING PERFORMANCE AND ACHIEVING PROFESSIONAL GOALS

Just as students are encouraged to reflect upon their academic performance, it is important that teachers **reflect** on and **self-assess** their own efficacy in the classroom. Doing so is integral for improving professional knowledge and skills to enhance student learning. Effective teachers continuously self-evaluate their performance to ensure they are providing engaging, relevant instruction that effectively meets students' learning needs for success. Frequently reflecting upon and assessing the effectiveness of their lesson plans, instructional strategies, assessments, and approaches to classroom management is beneficial in providing teachers with insight regarding their **professional strengths** as well as specific **areas for growth**. With this insight, teachers can identify the knowledge, skills, and strategies they need to improve upon to deliver more effective instruction. This ultimately allows teachers to set relevant professional goals to enhance their teaching practice and determine the steps they need to take in achieving them.

Copyright © Mometrix Media. You have been licensed one copy of this document for personal use only. Any other reproduction or redistribution is strictly prohibited. All rights reserved. This content is provided for test preparation purposes only and does not imply an endorsement by Mometrix of any particular political, scientific, or religious point of view.

METHODS

Continuous reflection and self-assessment through a variety of methods is beneficial in providing teachers with insight into the effectiveness of their teaching practice. **Reflecting on lessons** after they are finished allows teachers to self-assess their instruction by identifying specific elements that were successful, as well as components that can be improved in the future to enhance student learning. By eliciting **student feedback**, teachers can evaluate whether their instructional strategies, lesson activities, and assessments promote student engagement and understanding. Working with **mentors** and **colleagues** to discuss the effectiveness of lessons, instructional approaches, and classroom management techniques is also valuable in facilitating self-evaluation of teaching practices to seek areas for improvement. In addition, teachers are typically provided the opportunity to **respond to post-observation feedback** prior to attending an appraisal conference. This provides teachers with the opportunity to reflect on their overall performance and prepare to collaborate with the observer in developing professional goals.

Team Teaching and Professional Collaboration

TEAM TEACHING

Team teaching refers to the collaboration of two or more teachers, paraprofessionals, instructional aides, or special education workers in planning and delivering instruction and assessments. There are **several structures** to this approach to accommodate varying teaching styles and student needs. One teacher may provide direct instruction while another engages in lesson activities or monitors student progress. Similarly, one teacher may instruct while another observes and collects information to improve future planning. Students may be grouped with teachers according to their needs to provide differentiation, or teachers may participate simultaneously and equally in all aspects of the learning process. The intention of this approach is to create a **student-centered environment** focused on enhancing and deepening the learning experience. Team teaching is beneficial in allowing increased **individualized instruction** that more effectively meets students' learning needs. Additionally, when multiple teachers are present, students have access to varying **ideas** and **perspectives** that strengthen their understanding. Team teaching also benefits teachers, as it enables them to utilize one another's strengths for improved instruction. There are, however, limitations to this approach. Differences in **classroom management** styles, **teaching practices**, and **personalities**, when not addressed properly through respectful communication and flexibility, hinder the effectiveness of team teaching.

VERTICAL TEAMING

Communication and collaboration among teachers of varying grade levels is integral to effective instruction that supports students' learning and development. Through **vertical teaming**, content specific teachers **across grade levels** have the opportunity to work together in discussing and planning curriculum, instruction, assessments, and strategies that prepare students for achievement. Teachers of lower grade levels are often unsure of what students in upper grade levels are learning. As a result, these teachers may be uncertain of the skills and abilities their students need to be adequately prepared for success as they transition through grade levels. Likewise, teachers of upper grade levels are often unsure of what students have learned in previous grades, thus hindering their ability to adequately plan instruction and implement necessary learning supports. Vertical teaming facilitates the communication necessary for teachers across grade levels to collaborate in **establishing expectations for preparedness** at each grade level and developing a common curriculum path. This enhances teaching and learning, in that teachers are more effectively able to plan instruction that is aligned with learning targets and prepare students with the necessary knowledge, tools, and supports for continued academic success.

Copyright © Mometrix Media. You have been licensed one copy of this document for personal use only. Any other reproduction or redistribution is strictly prohibited. All rights reserved. This content is provided for test preparation purposes only and does not imply an endorsement by Mometrix of any particular political, scientific, or religious point of view.

HORIZONTAL TEAMING

Horizontal teaming refers to the collaboration of **same-grade level** teachers and staff that work with a common group of students. These teams may comprise teachers within a **single subject area** or **across disciplines** and may also include special education workers, grade-level administrators, paraprofessionals, and guidance counselors. Horizontal teaming is beneficial in facilitating the **coordinated planning** of curriculum, instruction, and assessments, as well as discussion regarding students' progress in the educational program. In addition, this method of teaming provides teachers and staff the opportunity to work together in developing educational goals, addressing areas of need, and implementing strategies to support students' success in learning. Horizontal teaming is also beneficial in encouraging teachers and staff to cooperate with one another in alignment with the goals and mission of the school to create a positive learning community focused on promoting student achievement.

BENEFITS OF MENTORS IN ENHANCING PROFESSIONAL KNOWLEDGE AND SKILLS

Mentors within the school community are typically experienced teachers that are available to offer support, guidance, and expertise to new teachers. As these individuals typically have a great deal of experience as educators, they are highly valuable resources in increasing professional knowledge and improving teaching skills. Mentors can provide **strategies, tools**, and **advice** for planning and delivering instruction, classroom management, and meeting students' learning needs to promote achievement. This includes suggesting ideas and resources for lesson activities and assessments, as well as techniques for differentiating instruction, enhancing student engagement, and promoting positive behavior. In addition, mentors can offer insight on how to effectively **navigate the school community**, including how to interact appropriately with colleagues and superiors, complete administrative duties, and communicate effectively with students' families. Regularly working with mentors in the school building ensures that new teachers are supported in developing the knowledge and skills necessary to become effective educators.

INTERACTION WITH PROFESSIONALS IN THE SCHOOL COMMUNITY

In order for an educational community to function effectively, professionals in the building must work together cohesively on a daily basis to support the school's mission and student learning. The nature of these interactions significantly determines the climate and culture of the school environment. Appropriate, professional interactions are important in facilitating the productive collaboration necessary to create a positive school community that promotes student success in learning. All interactions must therefore be **respectful**, **constructive**, and **sensitive** to the varying backgrounds, cultures, and beliefs among professionals in the school community. This includes using **appropriate language**, practicing **active listening**, and ensuring that discussions regarding colleagues, superiors, students, and other individuals in the building remain positive. When interacting in a team setting, it is important to maintain open dialogue and support one another's contributions to the educational program. All professionals in the school building must understand one another's roles and appreciate how these roles function together to support the educational program. Doing so ensures that collaboration is productive, purposeful, and aligned with enhancing students' learning experience.

SUPPORTIVE AND COOPERATIVE RELATIONSHIPS WITH PROFESSIONAL COLLEAGUES
SUPPORTS LEARNING AND ACHIEVEMENT OF CAMPUS AND DISTRICT GOALS

Effective collaboration among school staff and faculty members is reliant on establishing and maintaining supportive, cooperative professional relationships. Doing so facilitates a sense of **mutual respect** and **open communication** that allows colleagues to work together constructively in developing educational goals, plans to support students in achieving them, and strategies to

Copyright © Mometrix Media. You have been licensed one copy of this document for personal use only. Any other reproduction or redistribution is strictly prohibited. All rights reserved. This content is provided for test preparation purposes only and does not imply an endorsement by Mometrix of any particular political, scientific, or religious point of view.

address areas of need within the educational program. Mutual support and cooperation are also beneficial in fostering the **coordinated planning** of curriculum, learning activities, assessments, and accommodations to meet students' individual needs for academic achievement. Such professional relationships allow for more effective teaching and learning, as students are supported by a school community that works together cohesively to promote learning and the achievement of campus and district academic goals.

STRATEGIES FOR ESTABLISHING AND MAINTAINING RELATIONSHIPS

Building and maintaining professional relationships founded on mutual support and cooperation is integral in creating a positive, productive school community focused on student achievement. **Frequent communication** with colleagues in a variety of settings is an important factor in establishing and sustaining such professional relationships. Maintaining continuous and open communication allows professional colleagues in the school building to develop the respect for and understanding of one another necessary to establish a strong rapport. By participating together in **school activities**, **events**, and **programs**, teachers and staff members can build connections while contributing to enhancing the school community and climate. **Community building** strategies, such as participating in activities or games that require teamwork, are also valuable opportunities for developing supportive and cooperative professional relationships among colleagues. In addition, **collaborating** with one another in regard to curriculum, lesson planning, and promoting student achievement, contributes significantly to developing positive professional relationships. There are multiple avenues for such collaboration, including participating in professional learning communities (PLC's), department meetings, vertical or horizontal teaming, or engaging in team teaching. Doing so provides teachers and staff the opportunity to communicate and develop mutual goals that support the educational program and student learning.

Disability Education Laws

INDIVIDUALS WITH DISABILITIES EDUCATION ACT

The Individuals with Disabilities Education Act (**IDEA**) includes six major principles that focus on students' rights and the responsibilities public schools have for educating children with **disabilities**. One of the main principles of the IDEA law is to provide a **free and appropriate public education (FAPE)** suited to the individual needs of a child with a disability. This requires schools to provide special education and related services to students identified as having disabilities. Another purpose of IDEA is to require schools to provide an appropriate **evaluation** of a child with a suspected disability and an **Individualized Education Program (IEP)** for a child with a disability who qualifies under IDEA. Students with IEPs are guaranteed **least restrictive environment (LRE)**, or a guarantee that they are educated in the general education classroom as much as possible. IDEA also ensures **parent participation**, providing a role for parents as equal participants and decision makers. Lastly, **procedural safeguards** also serve to protect parents' rights to advocate for their children with disabilities.

PEOPLE PROTECTED BY PARTS B AND C OF IDEA LAW

Early intervention services are provided to children with special needs from birth to age three under **IDEA Part C**. Children from birth to age 3 who are identified as having disabilities and qualify under IDEA receive **Individualized Family Service Plans (IFSPs)**.

Special education and related services are provided to children with disabilities from ages 3 to 21 under **IDEA Part B**. Children ages 3 to 21 who are identified as having disabilities and qualify under IDEA receive educational documents, called **Individualized Education Programs (IEPs)**.

Copyright © Mometrix Media. You have been licensed one copy of this document for personal use only. Any other reproduction or redistribution is strictly prohibited. All rights reserved. This content is provided for test preparation purposes only and does not imply an endorsement by Mometrix of any particular political, scientific, or religious point of view.

Individualized Education Programs vs. Individualized Family Service Plans

IFSPs and IEPs are both educational documents provided under IDEA to service the rights of children with disabilities and their families. The major differences between IEPs and IFSPs, aside from the ages they service, is that **IFSPs** cover **broader services** for children with disabilities and their families. IFSP services are often provided in the children's homes. **IEPs** focus on special education and related services within the children's **school settings**.

Purpose of IEPs and Function of the PLOPs

An IEP is a written statement for a child with a disability. Its primary purposes are to establish **measurable annual goals** and to list the **services** needed to help the child with a disability meet the annual goals.

The IDEA law mandates that a statement of the child's academic achievement and functional performance be included within the IEP. This statement is called **Present Levels of Performance (PLOPs)**. It provides a snapshot of the student's current performance in school. Present Levels of Performance should also report how a student's disability is affecting, or not affecting, progress in school.

The IDEA law mandates that an **Annual Goals section** be provided within the IEP. Annual goals outline what a student is expected to learn within a 12-month period. These goals are influenced by the student's PLOPs and are developed using objective, measurable data based on the student's previous academic performance.

> **Review Video: 504 Plans and IEPs**
> Visit mometrix.com/academy and enter code: 881103

Child Find Law

Child Find is part of the Individuals with Disabilities Education Act (IDEA) and states that schools are legally required to find children who have **disabilities** and need **special education** or other services. According to the **Child Find law**, all school districts must have processes for identifying students who need special education and related services. Children with disabilities from birth to age 21, children who are homeschooled, and children in private schools are all covered by the Child Find law. Infants and toddlers can be identified and provided with services so that parents have the right tools in place to meet their children's needs before they enter grade school. The Child Find law does not mean that public schools need to agree to evaluate students when evaluations are requested. Schools may still refuse evaluation if school professionals do not suspect the children of having disabilities.

Steps to Implementing IEPs

The five most important steps in the **Individualized Education Program (IEP)** process are the identification via "Child Find" or the referral for special education services, evaluation, determination of eligibility, the first IEP meeting at which the IEP is written, and the ongoing provision of services during which progress is measured and reported. The referral can be initiated by a teacher, a special team in the school district, the student's parent, or another professional. The evaluation provides a snapshot of a student's background history, strengths, weaknesses, and academic, behavioral, or social needs. An IEP team of professionals as well as the student's parents/guardians use the evaluation and any other reports regarding a student's progress to determine if the student is eligible for special education services. Once a student has been found eligible for special education, the first IEP meeting is held during which an IEP is written by a special education teacher or other specialist familiar with the student. The IEP meeting, either

Copyright © Mometrix Media. You have been licensed one copy of this document for personal use only. Any other reproduction or redistribution is strictly prohibited. All rights reserved. This content is provided for test preparation purposes only and does not imply an endorsement by Mometrix of any particular political, scientific, or religious point of view.

initial or annual, is held before the new IEP is implemented. Once the IEP meeting has occurred, services will be provided as detailed in the written IEP, during which the student's progress will continually be measured and reported. The IEP team includes the student, parents/guardians, special education teacher, general education teacher, school psychologist, school administrator, appropriate related service professionals, and any other professionals or members that can comment on the student's strengths.

MANIFESTATION DETERMINATION

Manifestation determination is a process defined by the Individuals with Disabilities Education Act (IDEA). The **manifestation determination process** is put into effect when a student receiving special education needs to be removed from the educational setting due to a suspension, expulsion or alternative placement. Manifestation determination is the process that determines if the **disciplinary action** resulted from a **manifestation of the student's disability**. This is important because if the action was a manifestation of the disability, the outcome of the disciplinary action may change. During the initial part of this process, relevant data is collected about the student and the circumstances of the offending behavior. The student's Individualized Education Program team determines whether or not the student's behavior was related to the disability. If they determine that the behavior was not related to the disability, the disciplinary action is carried out. If the behavior is determined to be related to the disability, the student is placed back into the original educational setting.

PROVISION OF TITLE III OF THE AMERICANS WITH DISABILITIES ACT

Title III of ADA prohibits the discrimination of people with disabilities in **public accommodations**. Title III seeks to level the playing field of access for people with disabilities participating in public activities. Businesses open to the public, such as schools, restaurants, movie theaters, day care facilities, recreation facilities, doctor's offices, and restaurants, are required to comply with **ADA standards**. Additionally, commercial facilities, such as privately-owned businesses, factories, warehouses, and office buildings, are required to provide access per ADA standards. Title III of ADA outlines the general requirements of the **reasonable modifications** that businesses must provide. Title III also provides detailed, specific requirements for reasonable modifications within businesses and requires new construction and building alterations to abide by ADA regulations. Title III also outlines rules regarding **enforcement of ADA regulations**, such as the consequences for a person or persons participating in discrimination of a person with a disability. Title III provides for **certification of state laws or local building codes**. This means that a state's Assistant Attorney General may issue certification to a place of public accommodation or commercial facility that meets or exceeds the minimum requirements of Title III.

LARRY P. V. RILES

The *Larry P. v. Riles* (1977) court case examined possible **cultural discrimination** of African-American students. The court case questioned whether an intelligence quotient (IQ) test was an accurate measurement of a student's true intelligence. The case argued that there was a disproportionate number of African-American students identified as needing special education services (EMR program services). The court plaintiff Larry P. argued that IQ tests were **biased** against African-American students, which resulted in their placements in limiting educational settings. The defendant Riles argued that the prevalence of African-American students in the EMR classes was due to genetics and social and environmental factors. The court ultimately ruled that the IQ tests were discriminatory and resulted in the disproportionate placement of African-American students in the EMR setting. It was determined that these particular assessments were **culturally biased**, and the students' performances would be more accurately measured using adaptive behavior assessments, diagnostic tests, observations, and other assessments.

Copyright © Mometrix Media. You have been licensed one copy of this document for personal use only. Any other reproduction or redistribution is strictly prohibited. All rights reserved. This content is provided for test preparation purposes only and does not imply an endorsement by Mometrix of any particular political, scientific, or religious point of view.

DIANA V. STATE BOARD OF EDUCATION

Diana v. State Board of Education (1970) is a court case that examined the case of a student who was placed in special education after results of the Stanford Binet Intelligence test indicated she had a mild case of "mental retardation." This class-action lawsuit was developed on behalf of nine **Mexican-American children**, arguing that IQ scores were not an adequate measurement to determine special education placement in the EMR setting. The case argued that Mexican-American children might be at a disadvantage because the IQ tests were written and administered in English. This might possibly constitute **discrimination**. The plaintiffs in the case argued that IQ scores were not a valid measurement because the children might have been unable to comprehend the test written in English. In the conclusive results of this case, the court ordered children to be tested in their primary language, if it was not English. As a result of this case, IQ tests were no longer used as the sole assessments for determining **special education placement**. There was also increased focus on **cultural and linguistic diversity** in students.

WINKELMAN V. PARMA CITY BOARD OF EDUCATION

This court case began as an argument against a **free and appropriate public education** as required by the Individuals with Disabilities Education Act (IDEA). The parents of Jacob Winkelman believed their son was not provided with a FAPE in his special education setting in Parma City Schools. The disagreement became about whether or not children can be **represented by their parents** per IDEA law in federal court. The U.S Court of Appeals for the Sixth Circuit argued that IDEA protected the rights of the children and not the parents. In the end, the District Court ruled that parents could represent their children within disputes over a free and appropriate public education as constituted by IDEA. Ultimately, this settled the question of whether or not **parents have rights under IDEA**, in addition to their children. The court case determined that parents play a significant role in the education of their children on Individualized Education Programs (IEPs) and are IEP team members. Therefore, parents are entitled to litigate *pro se* for their children.

HONIG V. DOE

Honig v. Doe (1998) was a Supreme Court case examining the violation of the **Education for All Handicapped Children Act** (EAHCA, an earlier version of the Individuals with Disabilities Education Act) against the California School Board. The offense occurred when a child was suspended for a violent behavior outburst that was related to his disability. The court case centered on two plaintiffs. Both were diagnosed with an Emotional Disturbance and qualified for special education under EAHCA. Following the violent incident, the school suspended the students and recommended them for expulsion. The plaintiff's case argued that the suspension/expulsion went against the **stay-put provision of EAHCA**, which states that children with disabilities must remain in their current educational placements during review proceedings unless otherwise agreed upon by both parents and educational representatives. The defendant argued that the violence of the situation marked an exception to the law. The court determined that schools are able to justify the placement removal of a student when maintaining a **safe learning environment** outweighs a student's right to a free and appropriate public education.

PENNSYLVANIA ASSOCIATION FOR RETARDED CHILDREN V. COMMONWEALTH OF PENNSYLVANIA

The Commonwealth of Pennsylvania was accused by the Pennsylvania Association for Retarded Children (PARC 1971), now known as the Arc of Pennsylvania, of denying a **free and appropriate public education** to students with disabilities. The Commonwealth of Pennsylvania was accused of refusing to educate students who had not met the "mental age of 5." The groups argued before the District Court of the Eastern District of Pennsylvania. This case was significant because PARC was

Copyright © Mometrix Media. You have been licensed one copy of this document for personal use only. Any other reproduction or redistribution is strictly prohibited. All rights reserved. This content is provided for test preparation purposes only and does not imply an endorsement by Mometrix of any particular political, scientific, or religious point of view.

one of the first institutions in the country to challenge the **placement of students with special needs**. The plaintiffs argued that all children should and would benefit from some sort of educational instruction and training. Ultimately, this was the beginning of instituting the state requirement of a free and appropriate public education (**FAPE**) for all children in public education from ages 6–21. The Commonwealth of Pennsylvania was tasked with providing a FAPE and sufficient education and training for all eligible children receiving special education. They could no longer deny students based on their mental ages. This triggered other state institutions to make similar decisions and led to the creation of similar federal policies in the **Education for All Handicapped Children Act** (1974).

1990 AMENDMENTS TO THE IDEA

The **Individuals with Disabilities Education Act (IDEA)** replaced the Education for All Handicapped Children Act in 1990. IDEA amendments changed the **age range** for children to receive special education services to ages 3–21. IDEA also changed the language of the law, changing the focus onto the **individuals with disabilities** rather than the **handicapped children**. Therefore, the focus shifted from the conditions or disabilities to the individual children and their needs. IDEA amendments also **categorized** different disabilities. IDEA 1997 increased the emphasis on the individualized education plans for students with disabilities and increased parents' roles in the educational decision-making processes for their children with disabilities. Part B of the 1997 amendment provided services to children ages 3–5, mandating that their learning needs be outlined in **Individualized Education Programs** or **Individualized Family Service Plans**. Part C of IDEA provided **financial assistance** to the families of infants and toddlers with disabilities. Part C states that educational agencies must provide **early intervention services** that focus on children's developmental and medical needs, as well as the needs of their families. Part C also gives states the option to provide services to children who are at risk for developmental disabilities.

EFFECT OF THE INDIVIDUALS WITH DISABILITIES EDUCATION IMPROVEMENT ACT OF 2004 ON IDEA

In 2004, the Individuals with Disabilities Education Act implemented the **Individuals with Disabilities Education Improvement Act**. IDEA was reauthorized to better meet the needs of children in special education programs and children with special needs. As a result of these changes:

- Special educators are required to achieve **Highly Qualified Teacher status** and be **certified in special education**.
- Individualized Education Programs must contain measurable **annual goals** and descriptions of how progress toward the goals will be **measured and reported**.
- Schools or agencies must provide science or research-based **interventions** as part of the evaluation process to determine if children have specific learning disabilities. This may be done in addition to assessments that measure achievement or intelligence.

The changes made to require science or research-based interventions resulted in many districts implementing **Response to Intervention procedures**. These procedures meet the IDEA 2004 requirement of providing interventions in addition to achievement reports or intelligence tests on the Individualized Education Programs for children with disabilities.

DEVELOPMENT OF EDUCATIONAL LAWS LIKE GOALS 2000 AND NO CHILD LEFT BEHIND

President Bill Clinton signed the **National Educational Goals Act**, also known as Goals 2000, into effect in the 1990s to trigger standardized educational reform. The act focused on **outcomes-based education** and was intended to be completed by the year 2000. The goals of this act included

Copyright © Mometrix Media. You have been licensed one copy of this document for personal use only. Any other reproduction or redistribution is strictly prohibited. All rights reserved.
This content is provided for test preparation purposes only and does not imply an endorsement by Mometrix of any particular political, scientific, or religious point of view.

ensuring that children are ready to learn by the time they start school, increasing high school graduation rates, demonstration of competency by students in grades 4, 8, and 12 in core content areas, and positioning the United States as first in the world in mathematics and science achievement. Goals 2000 was withdrawn when President George W. Bush implemented the **No Child Left Behind Act (NCLB)** in 2001. NCLB also supported standards-based reform, and it mandated that states develop more **skills-based assessments**. The act emphasized state testing, annual academic progress, report cards, and increased teacher qualification standards. It also outlined changes in state funding. NCLB required schools to meet **Adequate Yearly Progress (AYP)**. AYP was measured by results of achievement tests taken by students in each school district, and consequences were implemented for school districts that missed AYP during consecutive years.

EVERY STUDENT SUCCEEDS ACT OF 2015

NCLB was replaced in 2015 by the Every Student Succeeds Act (**ESSA**). ESSA built upon the foundations of NCLB and emphasized **equal opportunity** for students. ESSA currently serves as the main K–12 educational law in the United States. ESSA affects students in public education, including students with disabilities. The purpose of ESSA is to provide a **quality education** for all students. It also aims to address the achievement of **disadvantaged students**, including students living in poverty, minority groups, students receiving special education services, and students with limited English language skills. ESSA determined that states may decide educational plans as long as they follow the government's framework. ESSA also allows states to develop their own educational standards and mandates that the curriculum focus on preparing students for post-secondary educations or careers. The act requires students to be tested annually in math and reading during grades 3–8 and once in high school. Students must also be tested in science once in elementary school, middle school, and high school. **School accountability** was also mandated by ESSA. The act requires states to have plans in place for any schools that are underperforming.

ESL RIGHTS FOR STUDENTS AND PARENTS

As public schools experience an influx of English as a Second Language (ESL) students, knowledge of their **rights** becomes increasingly important. The **Every Student Succeeds Act (ESSA)** of 2015 addresses funding discrepancies for ESL students and families. ESSA allocates funds to schools and districts where low-income families comprise 40% or more of the enrollment. This is intended to assist with ESL students who are underperforming or at risk for underperforming. ESSA also provides funding for ESL students to become English proficient and find academic success. However, in order for schools and districts to receive this funding, they must avoid discrimination, track ESL student progress, assess ESL student English proficiency, and notify parents of their children's ESL status. Avoiding discrimination includes preventing the over-identification of ESL students for special education services. The referral and evaluation process must be carried out with caution to ensure that students' perceived disabilities are actual deficits and not related to their English language learning abilities.

REHABILITATION ACT OF 1973

The Rehabilitation Act of 1973 was the law that preceded IDEA 1975. The Rehab Act serves to protect the rights of people with disabilities in several ways.

- It protects people with disabilities against discrimination relating to **employment**.
- It provides students with disabilities equal access to the **general education curriculum** (Section 504).

Copyright © Mometrix Media. You have been licensed one copy of this document for personal use only. Any other reproduction or redistribution is strictly prohibited. All rights reserved. This content is provided for test preparation purposes only and does not imply an endorsement by Mometrix of any particular political, scientific, or religious point of view.

AMERICANS WITH DISABILITIES ACT OF 1990 (ADA)

The Americans with Disabilities Act (1990) also protects the rights of people with disabilities.

- The ADA provides **equal employment** for people with disabilities. This means employers must provide reasonable accommodations for people with disabilities in their job and work environments.
- It provides **access** for people with disabilities to both public and private places open to the public (i.e. access ramps and automatic doors).
- It provides **telecommunications access** to people with disabilities. This ensures people with hearing and speech disabilities can communicate over the telephone and Internet.

ELEMENTARY AND SECONDARY EDUCATION ACT (ESEA)

The Elementary and Secondary Education Act (ESEA) also protects the rights of people with disabilities.

- Passed by President Johnson in 1965, ESEA was part of the president's "War on Poverty." The law sought to allow **equal access to a quality education**.
- ESEA extended more funding to secondary and primary schools and emphasized high **standards and accountability**.
- This law was authorized as **No Child Left Behind** (2001) under President Bush, then reauthorized as the **Every Student Succeeds Act** (ESSA) under President Obama.

SECTION 504

A Section 504 Plan comes from the civil rights law, Section 504 of the Rehabilitation Act of 1973, and protects the rights of individuals with disabilities. A 504 Plan is a formal plan or blueprint for how the school will provide services to a student with a disability. This essentially removes barriers for individuals with disabilities by ensuring that **appropriate services** are provided to meet their special needs. A 504 Plan includes:

- **Accommodations**: A 504 Plan includes accommodations a student with a disability may need to be successful in a regular education classroom. For example, a student with ADHD may need to sit near the front of the room to limit distractions.
- **Related Services**: A 504 Plan includes related services, such as speech therapy or occupational therapy, a student may need to be successful in the general education classroom.
- **Modifications**: Although it is rare for a 504 Plan to include modifications, sometimes they are included. Modifications change what the student is expected to do, such as being given fewer homework assignments.

504 PLANS VS. INDIVIDUALIZED EDUCATION PROGRAMS

- A 504 Plan and an Individualized Education Program are similar in that they serve as a blueprint for a student with a disability. However, a 504 Plan serves as a blueprint for how the student will have **access to school**, whereas the IEP serves as a blueprint for a student's **special education experience**.
- A 504 Plan helps level the playing field for a student with a disability by providing services and changes to the **learning environment**. An IEP provides individualized special education and related services to meet the **unique needs of a student with a disability**. Both IEPs and 504 Plans are provided at no cost to parents.

Copyright © Mometrix Media. You have been licensed one copy of this document for personal use only. Any other reproduction or redistribution is strictly prohibited. All rights reserved.
This content is provided for test preparation purposes only and does not imply an endorsement by Mometrix of any particular political, scientific, or religious point of view.

- The 504 Plan was established under the **Rehabilitation Act of 1973** as a civil rights law. The Individualized Education Program was established under the **Individuals with Disabilities Education Act** (1975 and amended in 2004).
- Unlike an IEP, a 504 Plan does **not** have to be a planned, written document. An IEP is a **planned, written document** that includes unique annual learning goals and describes related services for the student with a disability.

INFORMED PARENTAL CONSENT

The Individuals with Disabilities Education Act (IDEA) requires that parents be **informed** before a student is evaluated for special education services. IDEA mandates that a school district receive **parental consent** to initiate an evaluation of a student for special education services. Consent means the school district has fully informed the parent of their intentions or potential reasons for evaluation of the student. Legally, the request must be written in the parent's native language. This consent does not mean the parent gives consent for a student's placement in special education. In order for a student to be initially placed in special education or receive special education services, parental consent must be given for this issue separately. At any time, parents can withdraw consent for special education placement or special education services. Schools are able to file **due process** if they disagree with the parental withdrawal of consent. Parents also have a right to consent to parts of a student's Individualized Education Program (IEP), but not necessarily all of the IEP. Once parental consent is granted for all parts of the IEP, it can be implemented.

TIERS OF THE RESPONSE TO INTERVENTION MODEL

- **Tier 1: High Quality Classroom Instruction, Screening, and Group Interventions**: In Tier 1, all students are screened using universal screening and/or the results of statewide assessments. Students identified as at risk receive supplemental instruction. Students who make adequate progress are returned to their regular instruction. Students who do not make adequate progress move to Tier 2.
- **Tier 2: Targeted Interventions**: These interventions are designed to improve the progress of the students who did not make adequate progress in Tier 1. Targeted instruction is usually in the areas of reading and math and does not last longer than one grading period.
- **Tier 3: Intensive Interventions and Comprehensive Evaluation**: Students who are not successful in Tier 2 move on to Tier 3. They receive intensive interventions that target their specific deficits. Students who do not meet progress goals during intensive interventions are referred to receive comprehensive evaluations and are considered to be eligible for special education under IDEA.

STAKEHOLDERS IN SPECIAL EDUCATION

Stakeholders that play roles in educating students with disabilities include the students, parents, general educators, administrators, and community members. Students should receive an educational **curriculum** based on strict standards, such as the Common Core Content Standards. This ensures that they receive good educational foundations from which to grow and expand upon during their school careers. Parents, legal guardians, and sometimes agencies act in the best interests of their children. If they do not think the Individualized Education Programs suit the needs of their children, they can request **due process hearings** in court. FAPE and LRE ensure that students are educated alongside peers in general education classrooms by general educators. General educators collaborate with special educators to create **successful inclusion classrooms**. When inclusion is done successfully, the students with disabilities meet their IEP goals.

Copyright © Mometrix Media. You have been licensed one copy of this document for personal use only. Any other reproduction or redistribution is strictly prohibited. All rights reserved. This content is provided for test preparation purposes only and does not imply an endorsement by Mometrix of any particular political, scientific, or religious point of view.

INFORMATION TO BE EVALUATED DURING MULTI-FACTORED EVALUATIONS OR EVALUATION TEAM REPORTS

Multi-Factored Evaluations are processes required by the Individuals with Disabilities Education Act to determine if a student is eligible for special education. When a student is suspected of having a disability, the parent or school district can initiate the evaluation process. **Student information** that is evaluated in a Multi-Factored Evaluation includes background information, health information, vision testing, hearing testing, social and emotional development, general intelligence, past and current academic performance, communication needs, gross and fine motor abilities, results of aptitude or achievement tests, academic skills, and current progress toward Individualized Education Program (IEP) goals. Progress reporting on IEP goals is only appropriate during an annual MFE when a student has already qualified for special education services. The purpose of an MFE is to provide **comprehensive information** about a student for professionals working with the student. An MFE also helps determine what academic or behavioral **goals** or related services might be appropriate for a student with disabilities.

FREE AND APPROPRIATE PUBLIC EDUCATION COMPONENTS

The Individuals with Disabilities Education Act (IDEA) defines free and appropriate public education (FAPE) as an educational right for children with disabilities in the United States. FAPE stands for:

- **Free**: All students found eligible for special education services must receive free services, expensed to the public instead of the parents.
- **Appropriate**: Students are eligible for educations that are appropriate for their specific needs, as stated in their Individualized Education Programs (IEPs).
- **Public**: Students with disabilities have the right to be educated in public schools.
- **Education**: An education must be provided to any school-aged child with a disability. Education and services are defined in a student's IEP.

Ideally, FAPE components are put in place in order to guarantee the best education possible that also suits the individual needs of a student with a disability. FAPE should take place in the least restrictive environment, or the environment with the fewest barriers to learning for the individual student with a disability.

MULTI-FACTORED EVALUATION OR EVALUATION TEAM REPORT

A Multi-Factored Evaluation (**MFE**), sometimes referred to as an Evaluation Team Report (**ETR**), serves as a snapshot of a child's abilities, strengths, and weaknesses. An MFE is conducted to determine a student's eligibility for special education. Once a student with a disability qualifies for special education, an MFE is conducted at least every three years after the initial MFE date. MFEs are conducted for students ages 3 to 21 who are on IEPs. The purpose of the MFE is to influence a student's **Individualized Education Program**. An MFE reports on a student's **current abilities** and how the disability may affect **educational performance**. MFEs can also determine if a student qualifies for related services, such as occupational therapy or speech-language therapy. An MFE can be requested by a parent or school district when a child is suspected of having a disability. The school district typically has 30 days or less to respond to a parental request to evaluate a student, giving consent or refusal for an evaluation. While initial MFEs are conducted as a means to determine special education qualification, annual MFEs are conducted to address any changes in the needs or services of a student already receiving special education services.

Copyright © Mometrix Media. You have been licensed one copy of this document for personal use only. Any other reproduction or redistribution is strictly prohibited. All rights reserved. This content is provided for test preparation purposes only and does not imply an endorsement by Mometrix of any particular political, scientific, or religious point of view.

LEAST RESTRICTIVE ENVIRONMENTS TO DELIVER SPECIAL EDUCATION SERVICES

Special education services are delivered to students that qualify with a **disability** defined by the Individuals with Disabilities Education Act (IDEA). IDEA law also requires that students who qualify for special education must receive special education services in **least restrictive environments** that provide the fewest barriers to their learning. A student's most appropriate instructional setting is written out in the **Individualized Education Program (IEP)**. Some special education instructional settings include:

- no instructional setting
- mainstream setting
- resource room
- self-contained classroom
- homebound instruction

With **no instructional setting**, students participate in the general education curriculum but may receive related services, such as speech-language therapy or occupational therapy. In the **mainstream setting**, students are instructed in the general education classroom for most or part of the day and provided with special education supports, accommodations, modifications, and related services. A **resource room** is an environment where students receive remedial instruction when they cannot participate in the general curriculum for one or more subject areas. A **self-contained classroom** is a setting for students who need special education and related services for more than 50% of the day. **Homebound instruction** is for students who are homebound or hospital bound for more than four consecutive weeks.

DUE PROCESS RIGHTS AVAILABLE TO PARENTS AND LEGAL GUARDIANS

When parents or legal guardians and school districts cannot agree on components of a student with a disability's Individualized Education Program (IEP), parents and legal guardians have a right to **due process**. Due process is a legal right under the Individuals with Disabilities Education Act (IDEA) that usually involves the school district violating a legal rule. Examples of these violations include a school district not running an IEP meeting, failing to conduct a tri-annual evaluation, or failing to implement a student's IEP. Disputes often involve a student's instructional placement, appropriate accommodations or modifications, related services, or changes to IEPs. School districts' due process policies vary depending on the district. IDEA, however, mandates that a **due process legal form** be completed by the parent or legal guardian in order to move forward. This form must be completed within two years of a dispute. **Mediation**, or the process of coming to an agreement before filing due process, can be a solution to the dispute. IEP meetings, even when it is not time for an annual review, are also appropriate options for resolving a dispute before filing due process.

PURPOSE OF MEDIATION IN LIEU OF A PARENT OR LEGAL GUARDIAN FILING FOR DUE PROCESS

Mediation is a process used to address a dispute prior to a parent or legal guardian filing for due process. The purpose of mediation is to **resolve a dispute** between the parent or legal guardian of a student with a disability and the school district. Disputes occur when the parent or legal guardian does not agree with an IEP component, such as what related services are provided or the way a student's IEP is being implemented. Mediation is not a parent or legal guardian's legal right, but school districts often support mediation to offset a **due process filing**. Mediation involves the attempt to resolve a dispute and includes a meeting between the parent or legal guardian, school district member, and a neutral third party, such as a mediator provided by the state. States have lists of **mediators** available for these situations. Agreements that come out of the mediation process are put into writing and, if appropriate, put into a student's IEP. Disagreements can

Copyright © Mometrix Media. You have been licensed one copy of this document for personal use only. Any other reproduction or redistribution is strictly prohibited. All rights reserved. This content is provided for test preparation purposes only and does not imply an endorsement by Mometrix of any particular political, scientific, or religious point of view.

continue to be mediated, or the decision may be made to file due process. Prior to mediation, parents or legal guardians and school districts have the option of holding IEP meetings (outside of annual meetings) to resolve disputes.

MAINTAINING CONFIDENTIALITY AND PRIVACY OF STUDENT RECORDS

Similar to the Health Insurance Portability and Accountability Act of 1966 (HIPAA), **FERPA** is a law that protects privacy. However, FERPA is specific to the privacy of students. The FERPA law applies to any school or agency that receives funds from the US Department of Education. This ensures that schools or agencies cannot share any confidential information about a student without a parent or student's written consent. **Student educational records** can be defined as records, files, documents, or other materials which contain a student's personal information. **Individualized Education Programs (IEPs)** and **Evaluation Team Reports (ETRs)** are examples of private documents under the FERPA law. The responsibility of a school covered by FERPA is to maintain confidentiality and privacy. The members of an IEP team, such as special educators, related service professionals, general educators, or other professionals, cannot share any identifying, private information about a student. Information addressing the needs of individual students found on an IEP, Evaluation Team Report, or other identifying document must remain confidential unless express written consent is given by the parent or legal guardian.

PRE-REFERRAL/REFERRAL PROCESS FOR IDENTIFYING AND PLACING A STUDENT WITH A DISABILITY

The purpose of a pre-referral process for a child with a suspected disability is to attempt **reasonable modifications and accommodations** before the child is referred for special education services. Schools often have **pre-referral teams** whose purpose is to identify the strengths and needs of a child, put reasonable strategies into action, and evaluate the results of this pre-referral intervention. If the results do not show any change, another intervention can be attempted, or the student can be referred for a special education evaluation.

If a child is suspected of having a disability and did not succeed with pre-referral interventions, the school or parent can request an **evaluation**. During the evaluation process, the school compiles information to see if the student needs special education or related services. This information is used to determine if the student's disability is affecting school performance and if the student qualifies for special education. The evaluation lists and examines the student's strengths, weaknesses, and development and determines what supports the student needs in order to learn. An evaluation must be completed before special education services can be provided.

ROLE OF A SCHOOL PSYCHOLOGIST IN SPECIAL EDUCATION

School psychologists are certified members of school teams that **support the needs of students and teachers**. They help students with overall academic, social, behavioral, and emotional success. School psychologists are trained in data collection and analysis, assessments, progress monitoring, risk factors, consultation and collaboration, and special education services. In special education, school psychologists may work directly with students and collaborate with teachers, administrators, parents, and other professionals working with particular students. They may also be involved in counseling students' parents, the Response to Intervention process, and performing initial evaluations of students who are referred for special education services. School psychologists also work to improve academic achievement, promote positive behavior and health by implementing school-wide programs, support learning needs of diverse learners, maintain safe school environments, and strengthen and maintain good school-parent relationships.

Copyright © Mometrix Media. You have been licensed one copy of this document for personal use only. Any other reproduction or redistribution is strictly prohibited. All rights reserved. This content is provided for test preparation purposes only and does not imply an endorsement by Mometrix of any particular political, scientific, or religious point of view.

OVERREPRESENTATION OF STUDENTS FROM DIVERSE BACKGROUNDS

Disproportionate representation occurs when there is not an equal representation of students from different **cultural and linguistic backgrounds** identified for special education services. Students from different cultural and linguistic groups should be identified for special education services in similar proportions. This ensures that no one group is **overrepresented** and **overidentified as having special needs** due to their cultural or linguistic differences. Disproportionality can occur based on a child's sex, language proficiency, receipt of free and reduced lunch, or race and ethnicity. Historically, most disproportionality has been a civil rights issue and due to a child's cultural or linguistic background. Recently, the focus has been on the disproportional number of students who spend time in special education classrooms instead of being educated alongside regularly educated peers.

The referral process, **Response to Intervention (RTI)**, provides safeguards against disproportionality. The RTI process requires instruction and intervention catered to the unique, specific needs of the individual student. The purpose of RTI is not the identification of a disability or entitlement to services. Instead, it focuses on data used to make educational decisions about individuals, classrooms, schools, or districts. Models like RTI address disproportionate representation, but they are not perfect.

Chapter Quiz

Ready to see how well you retained what you just read? Scan the QR code to go directly to the chapter quiz interface for this study guide. If you're using a computer, simply visit the bonus page at **mometrix.com/bonus948/ftceprekinprim** and click the Chapter Quizzes link.

Copyright © Mometrix Media. You have been licensed one copy of this document for personal use only. Any other reproduction or redistribution is strictly prohibited. All rights reserved. This content is provided for test preparation purposes only and does not imply an endorsement by Mometrix of any particular political, scientific, or religious point of view.

Developmentally Appropriate Practices and Curricula

Transform passive reading into active learning! After immersing yourself in this chapter, put your comprehension to the test by taking a quiz. The insights you gained will stay with you longer this way. Scan the QR code to go directly to the chapter quiz interface for this study guide. If you're using a computer, simply visit the bonus page at **mometrix.com/bonus948/ftceprekinprim** and click the Chapter Quizzes link.

Health Needs in Early Childhood

EFFECT OF MATURATIONAL FACTORS ON THE DEVELOPMENT AND LEARNING

Many physiological factors affect the development of babies and young children. These dictate which kinds of learning activities are appropriate or ineffective for certain ages. For example, providing a newborn with visual stimuli from several feet away is wasted, as newborns cannot yet focus on distant objects. Adults cannot expect infants younger than about 5 months to sit up unsupported, as they have not yet developed the strength for it. Adults cannot expect toddlers who have not yet attained stable walking gaits to hop or balance upon one foot successfully. It is not coincidental that first grade begins at around 6 years: younger children cannot physically sit still for long periods and have not developed long enough attention spans to prevent distraction. This is also why kindergarten classes feature varieties of shorter-term activities and more physical movement. Younger children also have not yet developed the self-regulation to keep from shouting out on impulse, getting up and running around, etc.—behaviors disruptive to formal schooling but developmentally normal.

NUTRITIONAL FACTORS IN DIET AFFECTING EARLY CHILDHOOD DEVELOPMENT

Babies are typically nourished via the mother's milk or infant formula, and then with baby food; however, young children mostly eat the same foods as adults by the age of 2 years. Though they eat smaller quantities, young children have similar nutritional needs to those of adults. Calcium can be more important in early childhood to support the rapid bone growth occurring during this period; young children should receive 2–3 servings of dairy products and/or other calcium-rich foods. For all ages, whole-grain foods are nutritionally superior for their fiber and nutrients than refined flours, which have had these removed. Refined flours provide "empty calories," causing wider blood-sugar fluctuations and insulin resistance—type 2 diabetes risks—than whole grains, which stabilize blood sugar and offer more naturally occurring vitamins and minerals. Darkly and brightly colored produce are most nutritious. Adults should cut foods into small, bite-sized pieces to prevent choking in young children, who have not yet perfected their biting, chewing, and swallowing skills.

CONSIDERATIONS FOR EARLY CHILDHOOD NUTRITION

Raw or lightly steamed vegetables are best because excess heat destroys nutrients and frying adds fat calories. Fresh, in-season and flash-frozen fruits are more nutritious and less processed than canned. Adults should monitor young children's diets to limit highly processed produce, which can have excessive sugar, salt, or preservatives. Good protein sources include legumes, nuts, lean poultry, and fish. Serving nut butters instead of whole nuts is safer, but spread thinly on whole-grain breads, crackers, or vegetable pieces, because young children can choke on large globs of nut

73

Copyright © Mometrix Media. You have been licensed one copy of this document for personal use only. Any other reproduction or redistribution is strictly prohibited. All rights reserved. This content is provided for test preparation purposes only and does not imply an endorsement by Mometrix of any particular political, scientific, or religious point of view.

butter as well. Omega-3 fatty acids from salmon, mackerel, herring, flaxseeds, and walnuts control inflammation, prevent heart arrhythmias, and lower blood pressure. Monounsaturated fats from avocados, olives, peanuts, and their oils, as well as canola oil, prevent heart disease, lower bad cholesterol, and raise good cholesterol. Polyunsaturated fats from nuts and seeds and from corn, soy, sesame, sunflower, and safflower oils lower cholesterol. These fats/oils should be served in moderation, and saturated fats should be avoided.

CONSIDERATIONS FOR FEEDING YOUNG CHILDREN

Saturated fats from meats and full-fat dairy should be limited; they can cause health problems like high cholesterol, cardiovascular disease, obesity, and diabetes. Trans fats are produced chemically by hydrogenating normally liquid unsaturated fats and converting them to solid, saturated fats as in margarine and shortening used in many baked goods. These are considered even unhealthier than regular saturated fats and should be avoided. (The words *partially hydrogenated* in the ingredients signal trans fats.) Infants derive enough water from their mother's milk or from formula, but young children should be given plenty of water and/or milk in "sippy cups" to stay hydrated. The common practice of giving young children fruit juice should be avoided. Even without added sugars, fruit juices crowd out room in small stomachs for food nutrients and cause dental cavities and weaken permanent teeth before they erupt. Children can also gain weight, as juice calories do not replace food calories the way actual fruit does with its fiber and solids. Young children should eat two-thirds of adult-sized portions.

CHARACTERISTICS OF YOUNG CHILDREN'S NUTRITIONAL NEEDS

Young children have smaller stomachs than adults and cannot eat as much at one time as teens or adults. However, it is common practice for today's restaurants to provide oversized portions. The historical tradition of encouraging young children to "clean their plates" is ill-advised, considering these excessive portions and the abundance of food in America today. Adults can help young children by teaching them instead to respond to their own bodies' signals and eat only until they are satisfied. Adults can also place smaller portions of food on young children's plates and request to-go containers at restaurants to take leftovers home. Because young children cannot eat a lot at once, they must maintain their blood sugar and energy throughout the day by snacking between meals. However, "snack foods" need not be high in sugar, salt, and unhealthy fats. Cut pieces of fresh fruits and vegetables, whole-grain crackers and low-fat cheeses, and portable yogurt tubes make good snacks for young children.

DEVELOPMENT OF NUTRITIOUS EATING HABITS AND ATTITUDES

Early childhood is an age range often associated with "finicky" eaters. Adults can experiment by substituting different foods that are similar sources of protein or other nutrients to foods young children dislike. Preparing meals to look like happy faces or animals or to have appealing designs can entice young children to eat varied foods. Engaging children age-appropriately in selecting and preparing meals with supervision can also motivate them to consume foods when they have participated in their preparation. Adults should model healthy eating habits for young children, who imitate admired adults' behaviors. Early childhood is when children form basic food-related attitudes and habits and so is an important time for influencing these. Children are exposed to unhealthy foods in advertising, at school, in restaurants, and with friends, so adult modeling and guidance regarding healthy choices are important to counteract these influences. However, adults should also impart the message early that no foods are "bad" or forbidden, allowing some occasional indulgences in small amounts to prevent the development of eating disorders.

Copyright © Mometrix Media. You have been licensed one copy of this document for personal use only. Any other reproduction or redistribution is strictly prohibited. All rights reserved. This content is provided for test preparation purposes only and does not imply an endorsement by Mometrix of any particular political, scientific, or religious point of view.

RELATIONSHIP OF SLEEP QUALITY TO BLOOD SUGAR CONTROL IN CHILDREN WITH TYPE 1 DIABETES

Researchers find blood sugar stability problematic for many children with type 1 (juvenile) diabetes, despite all efforts by parents and children to follow diabetic health care rules, because of sleep differences. Diabetic children spend more time in lighter than deeper stages of sleep compared to nondiabetic children. This results in higher levels of blood sugar and poorer school performance. Lighter sleep and resulting daytime sleepiness tend to increase blood sugar levels. Sleep apnea is a sleep disorder that causes a person's breathing to be interrupted often during sleeping. These breathing interruptions result in poorer sleep quality, fatigue, and daytime sleepiness. Sleep apnea has previously been associated with type 2 diabetes—historically adult-onset, though now children are developing it, too. It is now known that apnea is also associated with type 1 diabetes in children: roughly one-third of diabetic children studied have sleep apnea, regardless of their weight (being overweight can contribute to apnea). Sleep apnea is additionally associated with much higher blood sugars in diabetic children.

GENERAL SLEEP NEEDS AND BEHAVIORS OF YOUNG CHILDREN

Sleep allows the body to become repaired and recharged for the day and is vital for young children's growth and development. Children aged 2–5 years generally need 10–12 hours of sleep daily. Children 5–7 years old typically need 9–11 hours of sleep. Their sleep schedules should be fairly regular. While occasionally staying up later or missing naps for special events is not serious, overall inconsistent/disorganized schedules cause lost sleep and lethargic and/or cranky children. Some young children sleep fewer hours at night but need long daytime naps, while others need longer, uninterrupted nighttime sleep but seldom nap. Young children are busy exploring and discovering new things; they have a lot of energy and are often excited even when tired. Because they have not developed much self-regulation, they need adult guidance to calm down enough to go to sleep and will often resist bedtimes. Adults should plan bedtime routines. These can vary, but their most important aspect is consistency. Children then expect routines' familiar steps, and anticipating these steps comfort them.

COMPONENTS AND CHARACTERISTICS OF GOOD BEDTIME ROUTINES

Bedtime routines serve as transitions from young children's exciting, adventurous daytime activities to the tranquility needed for healthful rest. Adults should begin routines by establishing and enforcing a rule that daytime activities like rough-and-tumble physical play or TV-watching stop at a specific time. While preschoolers may be less interested in video games than older children, establishing limits early will help parents enforce stopping these activities at bedtime when they are older, too. Bath time is one good way to begin bedtime routines. Toys and games make baths fun, and bath washes with lavender and other soothing ingredients are now available to relax young children. Also, since young children eat smaller meals, healthy bedtime snacks are important. Too much or too little food will disrupt sleep, and too much liquid can cause bedwetting. Adults should plan nighttime snacks appropriately for the individual child. Bedtime reading promotes interest in books and learning and adult-child/family bonding, and calms children. Singing lullabies, hugging, and cuddling also support bonding, relax children, and make them feel safe and secure.

HELPING YOUNG CHILDREN TRANSITION FROM CRIBS TO REGULAR BEDS

One of young children's significant transitions from infancy is moving from a crib to a "big bed." Some become very motivated to escape cribs. For example, some bright, adventurous toddlers and even babies have untied padded crib bumpers, stacked them, and climbed out of the crib. For such children, injury is a greater danger from a crib than a bed. Others, whose cognitive and verbal skills

Copyright © Mometrix Media. You have been licensed one copy of this document for personal use only. Any other reproduction or redistribution is strictly prohibited. All rights reserved. This content is provided for test preparation purposes only and does not imply an endorsement by Mometrix of any particular political, scientific, or religious point of view.

are more developed than motor skills, may stand or jump up and down, repeatedly calling, "Hey, I'm up!" until a parent comes. These children should be moved to regular beds, with guardrails and/or body pillows to prevent rolling and falling-out accidents. If a child is moved to a bed to free the crib for a new baby, this should be done weeks ahead of the infant's arrival if possible, to separate these two significant life events. Most young children are excited about "grown-up" beds. Some, if hesitant, can sleep in the crib and nap in the bed for a gradual transition until ready for the bed full-time.

CONSIDERATIONS IN CHILDREN'S BEDROOMS AND FAMILY BEDS

The majority of early childhood experts think young children should not have adults in their rooms every night while they fall asleep. They believe this can interfere with young children's capacity for "self-soothing" and falling asleep on their own, making them dependent on an adult presence to fall asleep. Parents/caregivers are advised to help children relax until sleepy, and then leave, saying "Good night" and "I love you." Young children frequently feel more comfortable going to bed with a favorite blanket or stuffed animal and/or a night light. Regardless, fears and nightmares are still fairly common in early childhood. "Family beds" (i.e., children sleeping in the same bed or adjacent beds with parents) are subject to controversy. However, this is traditional in many developing countries and was historically so in America. Whatever the individual family choice, it should be consistent, as young children will be frustrated by inconsistent practices and less likely to develop good sleeping habits.

HYGIENE IN EARLY CHILDHOOD

IMPORTANCE OF HAND-WASHING

A major change during early childhood is that hygiene transforms from something adults do for children to something children learn to do themselves. Toddlers are typically learning toilet-training, getting many germs on their hands. Preschoolers today are also often exposed to germs in daycare or school settings. Adults must explain to young children using concrete, easily understood terms how germs spread, how hand-washing removes germs, and when and how to wash their hands. Adults also need to remind children frequently to wash their hands until it becomes a habit. Hand-washing should be required before eating, after toileting, after being outdoors, after sneezing/coughing, and after playing with pets. Because young children have short attention spans and can be impatient, they are unlikely to wash long or thoroughly enough. Adults can encourage this by teaching children to sing "Happy Birthday" or other 15- to 20-second songs/verses while washing, both assuring optimal hand-washing duration and making the process more fun.

BATHING

While infants are bathed by adults, by the time they are toddlers or preschoolers, they generally have learned to sit in a bathtub and wash themselves. However, regardless of their ability to bathe, young children should never be left unsupervised by adults in the bath. Young children can drown very quickly, even in an inch of water; an adult should always be in the bathroom. Also, adults should not let young children run bathwater: they are likely to make it too cold or hot. Adults can prevent scalding accidents by turning down the water heater temperature. The adult should adjust water temperature and test it on his or her own inner arm (an area with more sensitive skin). Parents/caregivers should choose baby shampoos, soaps, and washes that do not irritate young eyes or skin, and keep adult bath products out of children's reach and sight. Very active children may need to bathe daily; others suffering dry, itchy skin should bathe every other day and/or have parents/caregivers apply mild moisturizing lotion.

Copyright © Mometrix Media. You have been licensed one copy of this document for personal use only. Any other reproduction or redistribution is strictly prohibited. All rights reserved. This content is provided for test preparation purposes only and does not imply an endorsement by Mometrix of any particular political, scientific, or religious point of view.

PROMOTING AND TEACHING DENTAL HYGIENE

Even while young children still have their deciduous teeth ("baby" teeth), dental hygiene practices can affect their permanent adult teeth before they erupt. For example, excessive sugar can weaken adult teeth before they even appear above the gumline. Adults should not only teach young children how important it is to brush their teeth twice and floss once daily at a minimum, they should also model these behaviors. Children are far more likely to imitate parents' dental hygiene practices than do what parents only tell them but do not do themselves. Integrating tooth brushing into morning and bedtime routines promotes the habit. Adults can help motivate resistant children with entertaining toothbrushes that play music, spin, light up, and/or have cartoon illustrations. Young children have not developed the fine motor skills sufficient for flossing independently and will need adult supervision until they are older. Individual flossers are easier for them to use with help than traditional string dental floss.

EXERCISE BENEFITS FOR YOUNG CHILDREN

Young children need daily physical exercise to strengthen their bones, lungs, hearts, and other muscles. Throwing, catching, running, jumping, kicking, and swinging actions develop young children's gross motor skills. Children sleep better with regular physical activity and are at less risk for obesity. Playing actively with other children also develops social skills, including empathy, sharing, cooperation, and communication. Family playtimes strengthen bonding and let parents model positive exercise habits. Outdoor play is fun for youngsters; running and laughing lift children's moods. Pride at physical attainments moreover boosts children's self-images and self-esteem. At least 60 minutes of physical activity most days is recommended for children. This includes jungle gyms, slides, swings, and other playground equipment; family walks, bike-riding, playing backyard catch, baseball, football, or basketball; adult-supervised races or obstacle courses; and age-appropriate community sports activities/leagues. Adults should plan and supervise activities to prevent injuries. They should also provide repeated sunscreen applications for outdoor activities to prevent sunburn and long-term skin damage.

EXPOSURE TO TV/OTHER MEDIA AND OPTIMAL ENVIRONMENTAL CONDITIONS FOR LEISURE ACTIVITIES

Preschool-aged children are not yet cognitively able to distinguish between reality and fantasy. Therefore, overly violent or intense content in TV or other media can frighten them. Additionally, exposure to video violence has been proven to increase aggressive behaviors in young children. Moreover, using TV as a babysitter for long times excludes more cognitively stimulating and interactive pursuits. Parents/caregivers can provide young children with paints, crayons, and modeling clay. They can play board games and simple card games, do puzzles, sing songs, and read stories with young children. Pretend/make-believe play develops during early childhood, so adults can encourage their playing "house," "dress-up," or "auto shop." Park/playground trips afford outdoor play and physical activity/exercise. Visiting local museums, zoos, or planetariums combine education and entertainment with outings. In multiple-child families, it is important for each child to get some one-on-one time with parents regularly, even in unstructured activities like going to the hardware store with Daddy or keeping Mommy company while she washes dishes.

DISADVANTAGES/ADVANTAGES AND RISK/PROTECTIVE FACTORS IN ECONOMICALLY DEPRIVED AND CULTURALLY DIVERSE ENVIRONMENTS

Historically, research on the effects of poverty has been focused on the disadvantages coming from a lack of necessary resources and the presence of risk factors. Due to the lack of resources, children in economically deprived communities commonly have fewer stimulating toys, less diverse verbal interaction, and commonly inadequate nutrition. Other risk factors often include unhealthy family

Copyright © Mometrix Media. You have been licensed one copy of this document for personal use only. Any other reproduction or redistribution is strictly prohibited. All rights reserved.
This content is provided for test preparation purposes only and does not imply an endorsement by Mometrix of any particular political, scientific, or religious point of view.

environments, medical illness without treatment, and insufficient social-services, such as education, policing, and medical care. However, more recent research also identifies poverty's advantages, including opportunities for young children to play with peers and older children with little adult intervention, promoting empathy, cooperation, self-control, self-reliance, and sense of belonging; experience with multiple teaching styles, especially modeling, observation, and imitation; and language acquisition within a culturally-specific context through rich cultural traditions of stories, songs, games, and toys. These findings illuminate the resiliency or stress resistance of some children. Recent research also identifies protective factors against risk factors. These protections contribute to child resiliency, including the child's personality traits; having stable, supportive, cohesive family units; and having external support systems promoting positive values and coping skills.

INFLUENCE OF CULTURES AND CULTURAL VALUES ON EARLY CHILDHOOD DEVELOPMENT

The culture in a society influences and determines one's individual values, as do both historical and current social and political occurrences. One's values then influence the ways in which children are valued and raised. American educators can understand the "American" perspective on early childhood better through understanding cultural diversity. Americans tend to fixate on their own culture's beliefs of truth as the only existing reality, but depending on personal histories and values and current conditions, there can actually be multiple right ways of doing things. For example, Western cultures value children's early attainment of independence and individuality, but Eastern cultures value interdependence and group harmony more than individualism. In affluent societies, letting children explore the environment early and freely is valued, but in poor and/or developing societies, parents protect children, keeping them close and even carrying them while working, and thus do not value early freedom and exploration.

EFFECT OF AGE, ETHNICITY, AND INCOME ON HEALTH AND SCHOOL OUTCOMES

Research traces many variations in well-being and health to early childhood. These differences come from inequities in service access and treatment, congenital health problems, and early exposure to greater familial and community risk factors. Child groups at risk that are overrepresented in the American population include young children, low-income children, and minority children. These risk factors also carry a high correlation with one another as minority groups tend to be overrepresented below the **federal poverty level (FPL)** and low-income families statistically carry the highest birth rate. Childhood poverty has long-lasting effects on students' developmental, socioeconomic, and academic success. Furthermore, the earlier a student is in poverty, the more likely they are to encounter the adverse effects of poverty, as they may miss certain milestones or lack the support needed to keep up with their peers.

ENVIRONMENT, SOCIAL AND EMOTIONAL SUPPORT, SELF-IMAGE, AND SUCCESS

Researchers have recently found that a child's sense of self is significant in predicting success in life. Even when a child's family environment involves multiple stressors, having a good relationship with one parent mitigates a child's psychosocial risks. As a child grows older, a close, supportive, lasting relationship with an adult outside the family can confer similar protection. Such relationships promote self-esteem in a child. Children with positive self-esteem are more able to develop feelings of control, mastery, and self-efficacy to achieve tasks, and they are more able to manage stressful life experiences. Such children demonstrate more initiative in forming relationships and accomplishing tasks. They reciprocally derive more positive experiences from their environments. Children with positive self-concepts pursue, develop, and sustain experiences and relationships that support success. Their positive self-images are further enhanced by these successes, generating additional supportive relationships and experiences. While we often hear

Copyright © Mometrix Media. You have been licensed one copy of this document for personal use only. Any other reproduction or redistribution is strictly prohibited. All rights reserved. This content is provided for test preparation purposes only and does not imply an endorsement by Mometrix of any particular political, scientific, or religious point of view.

about negative cycles of poverty, abuse, or failure, positive cycles of success can be equally as self-perpetuating.

INDIVIDUALISTIC VERSUS COLLECTIVISTIC CULTURES

Anthropologists have classified various world cultures along a continuum of how individualistic or interdependent their structures and values are. Investigating these differences is found to afford much insight and application for early childhood education. The predominant culture in America is considered very individualistic. Children are encouraged to assert themselves and make their own choices to realize their highest potentials, with the ultimate goal of individual self-fulfillment. Collectivistic/sociocentric cultures, however, place the highest importance on group well-being; if collective harmony is disrupted by individual assertiveness, such self-assertion is devalued. Some educators characterize this contrast as the difference between standing out (individualist) and fitting in (collectivist). Researchers note that when asked to finish "I am..." statements, members of interdependent cultures tend to supply a family role, religion, or organization (e.g., "a father/a Buddhist"), whereas members of individualistic cultures cite personal qualities (e.g., "intelligent/hardworking"). Research finds American culture most individualistic, Latin American and Asian cultures most interdependent, and European cultures in the middle.

HEALTH STATISTICS RELATED TO RACE AND ETHNICITY

Children are at higher risk for inadequate development when they are born prematurely or with low birth weights. Recent research found racial and ethnic disparities in these birth conditions. For example, average rates of low birth weights between 2018 and 2020 were almost double for African Americans as for whites (14 percent versus 6.9 percent). Latinos had similar but slightly higher risk than whites for low birth weight (7.5 percent versus 6.9 percent). Native American/Alaska Natives had slightly higher risk than whites (8.1 percent versus 6.9 percent), as did Asian/Pacific Islanders (8.6 percent versus 6.9 percent). The CDC reported that in 2017 and 2018, the prevalence of obesity among different racial groups varied greatly. Non-Hispanic Asians reported the lowest average 17.4 percent of obesity, whereas non-Hispanic White demonstrated a 42.2 percent obesity rate, followed by 44.8 percent for Hispanic and 49.6 percent for Non-Hispanic Black adults. These two statistics demonstrate a sample of correlated health risks present among varied socioeconomic groups.

Learning Environments in Early Childhood

GUIDELINES FOR INDOOR AND OUTDOOR SPACE USE

Indoor and outdoor early childhood learning environments should be safe, clean, and attractive. They should include at least 35 square feet indoors and 75 square feet outdoors of usable play space per child. Staff must have access to prepare spaces before children's arrival. Gyms or other larger indoor spaces can substitute if outdoor spaces are smaller. The youngest children should be given separate outdoor times/places. Outdoor scheduling should ensure enough room and prevent altercations/competition among different age groups. Teachers can assess if enough space exists by observing children's interactions and engagement in activities. Children's products and other visuals should be displayed at child's-eye level. Spaces should be arranged to allow individual, small-group, and large-group activity. Space organization should create clear pathways enabling children to move easily among activities without overly disturbing others, and should promote positive social interactions and behaviors; activities in each area should not distract children in other areas.

Copyright © Mometrix Media. You have been licensed one copy of this document for personal use only. Any other reproduction or redistribution is strictly prohibited. All rights reserved. This content is provided for test preparation purposes only and does not imply an endorsement by Mometrix of any particular political, scientific, or religious point of view.

ARRANGEMENT OF LEARNING ENVIRONMENTS
ARRANGING INDOOR LEARNING ENVIRONMENTS ACCORDING TO CURRICULAR ACTIVITIES

EC experts indicate that rooms should be organized to enable various activities, but not necessarily to limit activities to certain areas. For example, mathematical and scientific preschool activities may occur in multiple parts of a classroom, though the room should still be laid out to facilitate their occurrence. Sufficient space for infants to crawl and toddlers to toddle is necessary, as are both hard and carpeted floors. Bolted-down/heavy, sturdy furniture is needed for infants and toddlers to use for pulling up, balancing, and cruising. Art and cooking activities should be positioned near sinks/water sources for cleanup. Designating separate areas for activities like block-building, book-reading, musical activities, and dramatic play facilitates engaging in each of these. To allow ongoing project work and other age-appropriate activities, school-aged children should have separate areas. Materials should be appropriate for each age group and varied. Books, recordings, art supplies, and equipment and materials for sensory stimulation, manipulation, construction, active play, and dramatic play, all arranged for easy, independent child access and rotated for variety, are needed.

ARRANGING LEARNING ENVIRONMENTS TO CHILDREN'S PERSONAL, PRIVACY, AND SENSORY NEEDS

In any early childhood learning environment, the indoor space should include easily identifiable places where children and adults can store their personal belongings. Since early childhood involves children in groups for long time periods, they should be given indoor and outdoor areas allowing solitude and privacy while still easily permitting adult supervision. Playhouses and tunnels can be used outdoors, while small interior rooms and partitions can be used indoors. Environments should include softness in various forms like grass outdoors; carpet, pillows, and soft chairs indoors; adult laps to sit in and be cuddled; and soft play materials like clay, Play-Doh, finger paints, water, and sand. While noise is predictable, even desirable in early childhood environments, undue noise causing fatigue and stress should be controlled by noise-absorbing elements like rugs, carpets, drapes, acoustic ceilings, and other building materials. Outdoor play areas supplied by a school or community should be separated from roadways and other hazards by fencing and/or natural barriers. Awnings can substitute for shade, and inclines/ramps for hills, when these are not naturally available. Surfaces and equipment should be varied.

Learning Across the Curriculum

USING INTEGRATED CURRICULA

Integrating subject/domain content across the curriculum has been used for years at every educational level, from higher education to early childhood education. However, recent demands for accountability, as exemplified and escalated by No Child Left Behind, can distract educators from holistic and overall learning toward preoccupation with developing isolated skills and using test scores to measure achievement. But rather than discarding teaching methods proven effective, early childhood educators need to integrate newer, mandate-related practices into existing plans and methods. Teaching integrated curricula in early childhood classrooms has proven effective for both children and teachers. Integrating learning domains and subject content, in turn, integrates the child's developing skills with the whole child. When teachers use topics children find interesting and exciting, in-depth projects focusing on particular themes, and good children's literature, they give children motivation to learn the important concepts and skills they need for school and life success. Children should bring home from preschool not only further developed skills but also knowledge useful and meaningful in life.

Copyright © Mometrix Media. You have been licensed one copy of this document for personal use only. Any other reproduction or redistribution is strictly prohibited. All rights reserved. This content is provided for test preparation purposes only and does not imply an endorsement by Mometrix of any particular political, scientific, or religious point of view.

USING MANIPULATIVES FOR PRESCHOOL MATH LEARNING

Young children learn primarily through visually inspecting, touching, holding, and manipulating concrete objects. While they are less likely to understand abstract concepts presented abstractly, such concepts are likelier accessible to preschoolers through the medium of real things they can see, feel, and manipulate. **Manipulatives** are proven as effective learning devices; some early math curricula (e.g., Horizons) even require them. They are also particularly useful for children with tactile or visual learning styles. Many math manipulatives are available for sale, such as linking cubes; 3-dimensional geometric shapes and "geoboards"; large magnetized numbers for whiteboards; weights, scales, and balances for measurements; math blocks; math games; number boards and color tiles; flashcards; play money and toy cash registers, and activities; objects for sorting and patterning; or tangrams for recognizing shapes, reproducing and designing patterns, and spatial problem-solving. Teachers can create homemade math manipulatives using bottle caps/lids; seashells, pebbles/stones; buttons; keys; variously sized, shaped, and colored balls; coffee stirrers; or cardboard tubes from paper products.

HELPING YOUNG CHILDREN USE INQUIRY AND DISCOVERY IN SCIENCE

Early childhood teachers are advised to "teach what they know," meaning use materials with which they are familiar. For example, teachers who like plants can have young children plant beans, water them, and watch them grow, moreover incorporating this activity with the story "Jack and the Beanstalk." Teachers can bring in plants, leaves, and flowers for children to observe and measure their sizes, shapes, or textures. Experts recommend teachers utilize their everyday environments to procure learning materials, such as pine needles and cones, loose feathers and leaves found outdoors, animal fur from pets or groomers, and/or snakeskins or turtle shells from local pet stores. Experts advise teachers to use their observational skills during inquiry and discovery activities: if children apply nonstandard and/or unusual uses of some materials, teachers should observe what could be a new discovery, wherein students teach adults new learning, too. Teachers should let children play with and explore new materials to understand their purposes, uses, and care before using them in structured activities.

PROCESS SKILLS DEVELOPED BY PRESCHOOL SCIENCE PROGRAMS

Experts find three process skills that good early childhood science programs help develop are **observation**, **classification**, and **communication**. Young children are inherently curious about the world and hence enjoy many activities involving inquiry and discovery. Teachers can uncover science in many existing preschool activities. For example, since young children relate to activities focusing on themselves, teachers can have them construct skeletons of dry pasta, using their pictures as heads. Cooking activities involve science, as do art activities. Teachers can have children explore various substances' solubility in water and which colors are produced by mixing which other colors. They can have them compare and contrast different objects. They can create inexpensive science centers using animal puppets; models; thematically-related games, puzzles, books, and writing materials; mirrors, prisms, and magnifiers; scales; magnets; and various observable, measurable objects. Teachers should regularly vary materials to sustain children's interest.

PRESCHOOL ACTIVITIES FOR DEVELOPING PHYSICAL COORDINATION, FINE MOTOR SKILLS, AND LARGE MUSCLE SKILLS

Preschoolers are more likely to fall because their lower bodies are not yet developed equally to their upper bodies, giving them higher centers of gravity. Therefore, seeing how long they can balance on one foot and hopping exercises help improve balance and coordination. Hopping races let preschoolers participate in groups and observe peer outcomes, which can also enhance self-

81

Copyright © Mometrix Media. You have been licensed one copy of this document for personal use only. Any other reproduction or redistribution is strictly prohibited. All rights reserved. This content is provided for test preparation purposes only and does not imply an endorsement by Mometrix of any particular political, scientific, or religious point of view.

confidence and supporting others. "Freeze dancing" (like musical chairs without the chair-sitting), without eliminations, provides physical activity and improves coordination. Using writing implements, tying shoes, and playing with small items develop fine motor skills. With preschoolers, it is more effective and developmentally appropriate to incorporate fine motor activities into playtime than to separate quiet activity from play. For example, on nature walks, teachers can have children collect pebbles and twigs and throw them into a stream, developing coordination and various muscles. Running, skipping, and playing tag develop large muscle skills. Kicking, throwing, and catching balls give good unstructured exercise without game rules preschoolers cannot understand. Preschoolers' short attention spans preclude long activity durations.

BENEFITS OF AESTHETIC EXPERIENCES

To help children learn color names and develop sensory discrimination and classification abilities, some art museums offer preschool lessons, which teachers can also use as models. For example, a teacher can read a children's story or sing a song about color, then present artwork for children to examine, and then a separate display with different shapes of different colors used by the artist, asking children to name these and any other colors they know, and identify any other colors the artist used not represented in the second display. The teacher then demonstrates how mixing produces other colors. After this demonstration with children's discussion, the teacher gives each child a piece of heavy-duty paper and a brush. The teacher pours about an inch-sized puddle of each of the three primary colors—red, blue, and yellow—in the middle of each child's paper. The teacher then tells the children to use their brushes to explore mixing colors and see the variety of other colors they can create.

BENEFITS OF THE LINE IN VISUAL ARTS

Activities focusing on lines in art help young children expand their symbol recognition, develop their comparison-making ability, and facilitate shape recognition. Teachers can begin by singing a song or reading a children's story about lines. Then they can present one painting, drawing, or other artwork and help children point at various kinds of lines that the artist used. The teacher can draw various line types on a separate piece of paper (e.g. wavy, pointy, spiral) and ask children to find similar lines in the artwork. Then the teacher can ask children to try drawing these different lines themselves. Teachers should also inform children of various tools for drawing lines, such as crayons, pencils, markers, chalk, and paint, and let them experiment with these. An early childhood teacher can also supply butcher paper or other roll paper for each child to lie down on in whatever creative body positions they can make. The teacher outlines their body shapes with a marker. Then the teacher has the children explore drawing different kinds of lines, using various kinds of drawing tools, to enhance and personalize their individual body outlines.

AESTHETIC EXPERIENCES INVOLVING SHAPE

Giving young children learning activities that focus on shapes used in art helps them develop their abilities to form concepts and identify discrepancies. Manipulating basic geometric shapes also stimulates their creative thinking skills and imaginations, as well as developing early geometric math skills. For example, an early childhood teacher can first read aloud a children's book about shapes, of which many are available. After reading it through, the teacher can go back through the story, asking children to point to and name shapes they recognize. Then the teacher can show children an artwork. Using line drawings and/or solid geometric shapes, they discuss what shapes the artist used. The teacher can help children arrange solid shapes to form different images (people, flowers, houses). The teacher can then give children paper pulp trays, heavy paper, and/or board; assorted wooden, cardboard, and/or plastic shapes; and instructions to think and arrange shapes they can make with them, and then give them glue to affix the shapes to their trays, paper, and/or board. They can paint their creations after the glue dries.

Copyright © Mometrix Media. You have been licensed one copy of this document for personal use only. Any other reproduction or redistribution is strictly prohibited. All rights reserved. This content is provided for test preparation purposes only and does not imply an endorsement by Mometrix of any particular political, scientific, or religious point of view.

Exploring Texture in Art

Preschoolers learn much through looking at and touching concrete materials. Activities involving visual and tactile examination and manipulation plus verbal discussion enhance young children's representational/symbolic thinking abilities. Such activities also enable children to explore various ways of representing different textures visually. Teachers can provide "feely bags or boxes"—bags or boxes with variously textured items inside, such as sandpaper, fleece, clay, wool, or tree bark—for children to feel and describe textures before seeing them, and identify objects based on feel. A teacher can then show children a selected artwork, and they can discuss together which textures are included(e.g., smooth, rough, jagged, bumpy, sharp, prickly, soft, or slippery). The teacher can then demonstrate using plaster, thickened paste, or clay how to create various textures using assorted tools (e.g., tongue depressors, plastic tableware, chopsticks, small toys, or child-safe pottery tools) and have children experiment with discovering and producing as many different textures as they can. After children's products dry, they can paint them the next day.

Providing Affective Learning Experiences

Providing affective experiences supports young children's emotional development, including understanding and expressing their emotions. These enable development of emotional self-regulation/self-control. Emotional development is also prerequisite to and supportive of social interactions and development. Affective activities also help teachers understand how children feel, which activities they find most fascinating, and/or why they are not participating. "Feelings and Faces" activities are useful. For example, a teacher can have each child draw four different "feeling" faces on paper plates (e.g., happy, sad, angry, confused, excited) and discuss each. A teacher can offer various scenarios, like learning a new song, painting a picture, getting a new pet, or feeling sick, and ask children how they feel about each. Then the teacher can give them new paper plates, having them draw faces showing feelings they often have. Gluing Popsicle sticks to the plates turns them into "masks." The teacher can prompt the children on later days to hold up their masks to illustrate how they feel on a given day and about specific activities/experiences.

Most Important Social Skills

Experts find it crucial for young children's later success in school and life to have experiences that develop understanding of their own and others' emotions, constructive management of their strong feelings, and skills in forming and maintaining relationships. Young children use earlier developed motor skills like pushing/shoving, biting, hitting, or kicking, to get what they want rather than later developing verbal skills. Since physical aggression is antisocial, social development includes learning more acceptable, verbal emotional expressions. "Punch and Judy"–type puppet-shows depicting aggression's failures entertain preschoolers; discussing puppet behavior develops social skills. Teachers have children say which puppets they liked or disliked and considered good or bad, what happened, what might happen next, and how puppets could act differently. Teachers can reinforce children's discussion of meeting needs using words, not violence. Many read-aloud stories explain why people behave certain ways in social contexts; discussion/question-and-answer groups promote empathy, understanding, and listening skills. Assigning collaborative projects, like scrapbooking in small groups, helps young children learn cooperation, turn-taking, listening, and verbally expressing what they want.

Providing Affective Experiences and Promoting Emotional Development, Physical Activity, and Creativity

Early childhood teachers can help children understand their feelings and others' feelings, express their emotions, engage in physical exercise, use creative thinking, and have fun by using emotional movement activities. For example, the teacher can begin with prompting the children to

Copyright © Mometrix Media. You have been licensed one copy of this document for personal use only. Any other reproduction or redistribution is strictly prohibited. All rights reserved.
This content is provided for test preparation purposes only and does not imply an endorsement by Mometrix of any particular political, scientific, or religious point of view.

demonstrate various types of body movements and postures, like crawling, walking, tiptoeing, skipping, hopping, crouching, slouching, limping, or dancing. Then the teacher can ask the children which feelings they associate with each type of movement and body position. The teacher can play some music for children to move to, and give them instructions such as "Move like you are happy... like you are sad... like you are scared... like you are surprised... like you are angry..." Teachers can also use "freeze"/"statue" dances or games, wherein children move to music and must freeze in position like statues when the music stops; for affective practice, teachers instruct children to depict a certain emotion each time they freeze in place.

Developmentally Appropriate Practices

DEVELOPMENTALLY APPROPRIATE PRACTICE

Developmentally Appropriate Practice **(DAP)** is an approach to teaching grounded in theories of child development. It is derived from the belief that children are naturally curious to learn, and when provided a stimulating environment, are encouraged to take initiative in their own learning. This approach allows for a great deal of choice in learning experiences. The teacher's role is to facilitate active learning by creating developmentally appropriate activities based on the awareness of similarities between children in various developmental stages and the knowledge that each child develops at their own rate. With this knowledge, the teacher can then adjust the curriculum, activities, and assessments to fit the needs of individual students based on an awareness of age, cultural, social, and individual expectations.

CREATING INSTRUCTION TAILORED TO COGNITIVE DEVELOPMENT

A developmentally responsive teacher understands that the needs of students change as they mature through the stages of cognitive development. Furthermore, an effective teacher uses this knowledge to plan instruction that coincides with each developmental level. The early childhood teacher understands the needs and abilities of preoperational children, and designs instruction that focuses on interacting with the world around them through hands-on activities and pretend play. Such activities foster exploration of the environment, roles, and connections. Developmentally responsive elementary school teachers are aware of the logical thinking patterns that occur during the concrete operational stage. Thus, they create instruction that allows children to interact with tangible materials to help them draw logical conclusions about their environment and understand abstract ideas. As children reach adolescence, a developmentally responsive teacher understands the increased ability to think abstractly, hypothetically, and reflectively in the formal operational stage. They use this knowledge to create instruction that encourages discussion, debate, creative problem solving, and opportunities to develop opinions, beliefs, and values.

COGNITIVE DEVELOPMENT

IMPORTANCE IN DESIGN OF APPROPRIATE LEARNING EXPERIENCES THAT FACILITATE GROWTH

The teacher must understand their students' cognitive developmental ability relative to their grade level in order to create effective, engaging learning experiences that facilitate growth. This understanding allows teachers to develop age-appropriate instruction, activities, and assessment that challenges students based on their skills and abilities but is attainable based on their cognitive developmental level. In knowing how students in a given grade level think and learn, the teacher can develop instruction that effectively facilitates learning and growth, such as creating opportunities for purposeful play with young children, opportunities for middle-school aged students to engage in logical problem solving, or activities that promote the development of abstract thinking and reasoning with adolescents. In addition, understanding students' cognitive

Copyright © Mometrix Media. You have been licensed one copy of this document for personal use only. Any other reproduction or redistribution is strictly prohibited. All rights reserved.
This content is provided for test preparation purposes only and does not imply an endorsement by Mometrix of any particular political, scientific, or religious point of view.

abilities of each developmental level allow the teacher to better understand the nuances that exist within them, as students ultimately develop at their own pace and have individual learning needs.

IMPACT ON TEACHING AND LEARNING

Students' thinking and learning develops as they mature, as their thought processes and worldview changes. Consequently, teaching and learning must adapt to accommodate these changes and facilitate growth. In the early years of cognitive development, children learn through interacting with the surrounding environment using their physical senses and engage in independent play. To facilitate this, young children need learning experiences that stimulate their development through exploration. As children reach early elementary school, they begin to think symbolically and play with others. Purposeful play and interaction with learning materials becomes an important part of learning at this stage. Teachers should act as facilitators and provide multiple opportunities for children to engage in purposeful, self-directed play with interactive materials as they learn to categorize the world around them. By later childhood, children think concretely and logically, and thus, need hands-on learning experiences that provide opportunities for classification, experimentation, and problem-solving skills to facilitate their level of cognition and promote development. As children reach adolescence, they are increasingly able to think abstractly and consider hypothetical situations beyond what is concretely present. To enhance learning, teachers must provide opportunities for exploring different perspectives, values, and synthesizing information to engage in creative problem solving.

APPROPRIATE INSTRUCTIONAL ACTIVITIES

The following are some examples of appropriate instructional activities for early childhood, middle-level, and high school students:

- **Early childhood:** Activities that allow for exploration, play, and movement while teaching young children to function and cooperate in a group setting are most valuable in early childhood classrooms. **Movement activities** such as dancing, jumping rope, using outdoor play equipment, as well as structured and unstructured play, are beneficial in developing gross motor skills and teaching young children to properly interact with others. **Whole-group** activities such as circle time, class songs, and read-aloud sessions are also valuable in teaching young children appropriate communication skills within a group. **Thematic learning stations**, such as a science center, dramatic play area, library corner, block area, art center, and technology center, allow young children to explore their own interests on a variety of topics while developing creative and imaginative skills. **Sensory play** stations that include such items as a sand box or water table, are beneficial in further developing motor skills and allowing young children to explore and experiment with a variety of textures. Young children also require opportunities for quiet activities, such as naptime, self-selected reading, or meditation throughout the day in order to process information, reflect, and rest after active movement.

Copyright © Mometrix Media. You have been licensed one copy of this document for personal use only. Any other reproduction or redistribution is strictly prohibited. All rights reserved.
This content is provided for test preparation purposes only and does not imply an endorsement by Mometrix of any particular political, scientific, or religious point of view.

- **Middle-level**: Students at this age are best supported by the implementation of **hands-on** learning activities that develop **logical reasoning** and **collaboration** skills. Collaborative activities such as science experiments, mathematical word problems, the use of manipulatives, and projects that allow opportunities for building, creating, disassembling, and exploring, are beneficial in facilitating such a learning experience. Social and emotional learning activities are also important in developing middle school students' skills in these domains. Incorporating such activities as class meetings, community building activities, and self-reflection activities, are valuable methods for teaching social and emotional skills. In addition, cooperative learning opportunities should be implemented frequently across subject areas to further develop students' ability to work productively with others. Examples include literacy circles, creating teams for class review games, or group presentations.
- **High School:** Instructional activities for high school students should be designed to foster the development of **abstract** and **hypothetical** thinking abilities while preparing them to become productive members of society as they enter adulthood. Activities such as debates, class discussions, and mock trials are beneficial in providing high school students the opportunity to employ abstract reasoning, consider solutions to hypothetical situations, and develop empathy for opposing viewpoints. Assignments that require students to engage in the research process are valuable opportunities for developing higher-order thinking skills, as they encourage students to analyze, compare, and interpret information, as well as seek evidence to support their claims. In addition, incorporating activities that benefit the community, such as fundraisers or food and clothing drives, are beneficial in teaching high school students the importance of positively contributing to society.

EFFECTIVE AND DEVELOPMENTALLY APPROPRIATE LEARNING EXPERIENCES AND ASSESSMENTS

Effective developmentally appropriate instruction requires careful consideration when planning to ensure that students' individual needs across domains are supported to facilitate growth and a positive learning experience. The teacher must consider the developmental stage of their students based upon their age group, as well as students' individual differences. With this knowledge in mind, teachers must ensure that they provide an inclusive learning environment that fosters growth and development by creating challenging, yet attainable activities based on students' needs. Likewise, teachers must evaluate whether learning experiences and assessments are age, developmentally, and culturally appropriate while ensuring that they are tailored to students' unique learning differences. Learning experiences must provide opportunities for hands-on, cooperative, and self-directed learning, exploration, and participation to allow students to interact with their environment and build experiences. Additionally, lessons and activities should be flexible in nature to allow for inquiry and build upon students' prior experiences. Effective developmentally appropriate assessments are aimed at monitoring student progress and allow for flexibility based on students' learning differences. They should be intended to provide feedback to the teacher on how to better adapt instruction to meet students' individual needs and foster developmental growth.

FACILITATING DEVELOPMENT OF LIFE SKILLS AND ATTITUDES IN MIDDLE SCHOOL-AGE CHILDREN

Middle school-age children are at a pivotal development point in which they experience rapid and profound change. In this transition, they often demonstrate characteristics of younger and older children and are therefore at a critical stage for developing the beliefs, attitudes, and habits that will be the foundation for their future. Teachers must understand the implications of these changes and design instruction that addresses students' learning needs and facilitates the development of such

Copyright © Mometrix Media. You have been licensed one copy of this document for personal use only. Any other reproduction or redistribution is strictly prohibited. All rights reserved. This content is provided for test preparation purposes only and does not imply an endorsement by Mometrix of any particular political, scientific, or religious point of view.

important life skills as working and getting along with others, appreciating diversity, and committing to continued schooling. Cooperative learning and team building strategies instill the importance of working together positively to problem solve, building on one another's strengths, and valuing other's perspectives. These strategies also teach students to appreciate diversity through encouraging them to work with peers with different backgrounds and experiences. Additionally, teachers can teach students to embrace diversity through creating a culturally responsive classroom environment that models acceptance and incorporates elements of students' differences into instruction to demonstrate the value of diverse perspectives. Teachers promote positive attitudes toward academics that encourage a commitment to continued schooling by teaching organization, time management, and goal-setting skills that instill a growth mindset and provide a foundation for success.

IMPACT OF STUDENT CHARACTERISTICS ON TEACHING AND LEARNING
YOUNG CHILDREN

The developmental level of young children is characterized by defining attributes that impact teaching and learning, and for which several considerations must be made to design and implement effective instruction. As the attention span of young children is limited, the teacher must think about how to effectively act as a facilitator for learning more often than directly instructing students. **Direct instruction** must be delivered in small, manageable chunks to accommodate students' attention spans and ensure they retain and understand new concepts. Thus, the teacher must evaluate which elements of the curriculum require structured learning, while allowing for flexibility within instruction to accommodate student inquiry. Young children also need frequent **movement**, **physical activity**, and **social interaction**, as they learn and build experiences concretely through moving, playing, interacting with, and exploring their environment. To create a learning environment that accommodates these characteristics, the teacher must consider the physical arrangement of the classroom, and whether it adequately allows for movement. Additionally, teachers must incorporate **structured** and **unstructured activities** that foster and promote exploration, inquiry, play, cooperative learning, and hands-on interactions with the learning environment. With these considerations in mind, the teacher enhances students' learning experience by tailoring instruction to their developmental characteristics.

MIDDLE SCHOOL-AGED CHILDREN

As middle school-age children transition from childhood to adolescence, they experience vast changes across all developmental domains. Consequently, they exhibit characteristics that affect teaching and learning that require careful consideration when adapting instruction to their unique learning needs. While these students require increasing independence as they mature, they still need a structured, predictable environment to ease the transition into high school. The teacher must create a balance between fostering independence and growth while providing a schedule and routine. Opportunities for self-directed learning and student choice, as well as strategies for self-assessment and reflection foster autonomy and self-responsibility over learning while the teacher facilitates and monitors progress. Strategies to teach effective organizational and time management skills further promote independence and prepare students for success upon entering high school. As middle school-age students develop, the importance of peers becomes increasingly prevalent as they begin to search for their identity and shape their own values and beliefs. Teachers must ensure to provide opportunities for cooperative and small group learning to facilitate students' social development while considering the importance of promoting positive peer relationships at this impressionable developmental level.

Copyright © Mometrix Media. You have been licensed one copy of this document for personal use only. Any other reproduction or redistribution is strictly prohibited. All rights reserved.
This content is provided for test preparation purposes only and does not imply an endorsement by Mometrix of any particular political, scientific, or religious point of view.

ADOLESCENT CHILDREN

The developmental changes that occur in adolescence result in distinct characteristics as students in this age group transition into young adulthood. During this stage, students are discovering their identities, values, and beliefs and begin to explore long-term career and life choices. As they navigate their development and shape the person they will become, social relationships come to be increasingly important. Teachers must consider the impact of these characteristics when developing instruction to effectively address the unique needs of this age group and establish foundational attitudes, habits, and skills necessary for success in life. Effective instruction encourages adolescents to consider different perspectives, morals, and values to broaden their worldview and foster the development of their own beliefs. Lessons and activities should allow for exploration of personal interests, skills, and abilities as students shape their personalities and begin to consider long-term life goals. Moreover, the teacher should incorporate strategies that assist adolescents in goal setting to successfully foster a growth mindset and provide a foundation for success. Additionally, as socialization is highly influential at this stage, teachers must consider the importance of incorporating cooperative learning strategies and opportunities for socialization within instruction to encourage healthy peer relationships and foster positive identity development.

INTERCONNECTION OF DEVELOPMENTAL DOMAINS

Developmental domains are deeply interconnected. If one area of a child's development is negatively impacted, it is likely to pose negative consequences on other developmental areas. Proper physical development is key to developing cognitively, socially, and emotionally in that physical development allows children to acquire the necessary gross and fine motor skills to explore and experiment with the world around them, as well as interact with others. Physical development includes development of the brain, and factors such as poor nutrition, sleep, or prenatal exposure to drugs potentially hinder brain development. Consequentially, this may result in cognitive delays, and ultimately lead to social or emotional developmental delays through negatively impacting the child's ability to interact with others, build relationships, emotionally regulate, or communicate effectively.

FACTORS TO CONSIDER WHEN SELECTING MATERIALS FOR LEARNING AND PLAY

To plan meaningful, integrated, and active learning and play experiences, the teacher must have a deep understanding of both the developmental stage of the students and an understanding of students' individual needs. With this knowledge in mind, there are several factors that the teacher must consider when choosing materials that support active learning and play experiences, and ultimately, the development of the whole child. Materials should be adaptable in use to facilitate development in multiple areas. Versatility is also important in fostering imagination and creativity. The teacher must consider how the chosen materials will support understanding of concepts covered in instruction, as well as how they will support conceptual, perceptual, and language development. Furthermore, the teacher must ensure that materials are age-appropriate, stimulating, and encourage active participation both independently and cooperatively.

CHARACTERISTICS OF A DEVELOPMENTALLY RESPONSIVE CLASSROOM

A developmentally responsive classroom is one in which the teacher understands the cognitive, physical, social, and emotional developmental stages of students while recognizing nuances and individual developmental differences within these stages. The teacher understands that developmental domains are interconnected, and effectively responds to unique developmental differences by designing a learner-centered curriculum and classroom environment that caters to each students' abilities, needs, and developmental levels to develop the whole child. The

Copyright © Mometrix Media. You have been licensed one copy of this document for personal use only. Any other reproduction or redistribution is strictly prohibited. All rights reserved. This content is provided for test preparation purposes only and does not imply an endorsement by Mometrix of any particular political, scientific, or religious point of view.

developmentally responsive classroom is engaging, supportive, and provides challenging learning opportunities based on individual learner abilities. There are several factors the teacher must consider in the developmentally responsive classroom when planning an appropriate, engaging, and challenging learning experience. The teacher must have a deep understanding of which teaching strategies will most effectively appeal to students of varying developmental levels and be prepared to teach content in multiple ways. Furthermore, the teacher must consider how to plan and organize activities, lessons, breaks, and the overall classroom environment. This would include considering how to arrange the classroom, which activity areas to include, spacing, and classroom equipment. The developmentally responsive classroom should promote positivity and productivity through creating a supportive yet challenging learning atmosphere that welcomes and respects differences, thus encouraging students' curiosity and excitement for learning.

Role of Play in Learning and Development

CHARACTERISTICS OF THE DEVELOPMENTAL PLAY STAGES

As children develop, so do their styles of play. Developmental play stages are divided into five primary phases: **solitary play** (Birth-2 years), **onlooker play** (2 years), **parallel play** (2-3 years), **associative play** (3-4 years) and **cooperative play** (4 years and beyond). During the **solitary play** stage, children play alone and are uninterested in playing with others, or what other children around them are doing. When they reach the **onlooker play** stage, children will watch other children play, but will not actively engage in playing with others. In **parallel play**, children do not play with one another, but will often play next to each other and will use similar materials. They may be curious about what other children are doing, and may copy them, but will not directly play with them. Children begin to intentionally play with others in the **associative play** stage, but the play is unorganized and still largely individual in its goals. In **cooperative play**, children begin to intentionally play and share materials in organized groups, and often have a common purpose or goal when playing.

Parallel Play

Cooperative Play

PURPOSES AND BENEFITS OF PLAY IN EARLY CHILDHOOD EDUCATION

Purposeful play is an integral part of learning and development in the early childhood classroom. Its purpose is to aid and allow children to incorporate all aspects of development and thus provides cognitive, social, emotional, and physical benefits. Purposeful play deepens children's understanding of new concepts through allowing them to explore and experiment in the world around them using imagination and creativity. Integrating purposeful play into the early childhood classroom is further beneficial in that it allows children to construct and build on knowledge through experiences and helps develop divergent and convergent thinking. The socialization

Copyright © Mometrix Media. You have been licensed one copy of this document for personal use only. Any other reproduction or redistribution is strictly prohibited. All rights reserved.
This content is provided for test preparation purposes only and does not imply an endorsement by Mometrix of any particular political, scientific, or religious point of view.

children get from play strengthens their language skills through speaking to one another, using new vocabulary, and listening to others. Purposeful play strengthens physical-motor development in that it calls for children to move their bodies in games, running, jumping, etc. Play is necessary for building important emotional and social skills that are necessary for being a successful member of society later in life.

Instructional Planning

DESIGNING AND SEQUENCING LESSON PLANS AND UNITS TO ALIGN WITH INSTRUCTIONAL GOALS

The effective sequencing of units and lesson plans is key to developing coherent, comprehensible instruction that aligns with instructional goals and fosters success in learning. The teacher must first determine the instructional goals that students will be expected to achieve based on state academic standards as a framework, as well as students' individual needs, knowledge, and abilities. The teacher must then logically arrange specific units of instruction aimed toward achieving the determined instructional goals. Each unit should build upon knowledge from the prior unit. Within each unit, the teacher must determine what students must achieve as they work toward instructional goals and determine objectives that facilitate success based on individual need and ability. Once objectives are defined, teachers must design lesson plans in a logical sequence that will facilitate students in reaching these objectives and increasingly build upon knowledge as students work toward achieving the learning goal. When planning lessons, teachers must decide which activities, procedures, and materials are necessary for successfully completing lesson objectives while ensuring that individual learning needs are met. The teacher must also decide what will be assessed at the end of each lesson and unit to determine student success in achieving instructional goals.

CREATING DEVELOPMENTALLY APPROPRIATE LEARNING EXPERIENCES AND ASSESSMENTS

Multiple factors must be considered when designing developmentally appropriate learning experiences and assessments that effectively facilitate student growth and achievement. Teachers must consider the general cognitive, physical, social, and emotional developmental levels of students, as well as individual differences in background, skill, knowledge, and learning needs. With this understanding, teachers must then evaluate whether learning experiences are simultaneously appropriate to students' developmental levels and individual needs. This includes ensuring that learning activities and teaching strategies are varied in approach, tailored to students' interests and incorporate student choice in learning. Learning experiences must build upon students' background knowledge and experiences and provide challenging, yet attainable learning opportunities based on individual skills and abilities. Additionally, the teacher must consider whether learning experiences promote student participation and engagement as well as cooperative learning to ensure development across domains. Just as with learning experiences, the developmental appropriateness of assessments must also be evaluated. The teacher must consider whether assessments allow for choice in how students demonstrate their learning so as to address individual learning needs. Furthermore, it is important that teachers consider the purpose of each assessment regarding the feedback they are seeking and how it can help determine further instruction.

ROLE OF LEARNING THEORY IN INSTRUCTIONAL PROCESS AND STUDENT LEARNING

Multiple learning theories exist to explain how people acquire knowledge, abilities, and skills. Each theory proposes its own approach for best practices in teaching and learning, and therefore, each is most effective and applicable based on the context of learning and individual student needs. Thus, learning theory has a significant role as the framework for the instructional process and facilitating

Copyright © Mometrix Media. You have been licensed one copy of this document for personal use only. Any other reproduction or redistribution is strictly prohibited. All rights reserved. This content is provided for test preparation purposes only and does not imply an endorsement by Mometrix of any particular political, scientific, or religious point of view.

student learning. The teacher must understand the principles of various learning philosophies as well as their students' unique learning needs to effectively design and implement instruction from the perspective of the most applicable theory. Learning theories serve as a context from which, upon identifying desired learning outcomes, teachers can make informed decisions about designing instruction, activities, and assessments that are most effective based on their students' learning styles, skills, and abilities. In developing an understanding of students' learning needs, teachers can determine which learning theory is appropriate in order to design the most effective instruction possible. This facilitates student learning in that it allows for the implementation of student-centered methodologies tailored to students' learning needs and preferences and enhances instruction through allowing the teacher to implement methods from the theory most relevant to students' needs.

The following are examples of some common learning theories that can be used as a framework in the instructional process:

- **Constructivism (Jean Piaget):** This theory proposes that students learn by interacting with the learning environment and connecting new information to their background knowledge to build understanding. This active process allows students to personalize their learning and construct their own perceptions of the world through the lens of their previous experiences.
- **Humanism (Abraham Maslow, Carl Rogers):** This theory proposes that learning should take a person-centered approach, with a focus on the individual's innate capacity for personal growth and self-actualization. It operates axiomatically from the principle that all humans have a natural desire to learn; therefore, a failure to learn is due to the learning situation or environment, rather than a person's inability to learn. Teachers should act as facilitators and strive to create a safe, accepting learning environment, celebrate students' differences, and praise academic and personal achievement.
- **Connectivism (George Siemens, Stephen Downes):** This theory proposes that learning occurs by making a series of connections across pieces of information, ideas, concepts, and perspectives. Connectivism is rooted in the notion that learning occurs externally, and technology resources facilitate connections, as learners have access to several outlets for acquiring and processing new information.
- **Experiential Learning (David Kolb):** This theory proposes that students learn and retain information best through physical exploration and interaction with the learning environment. In the classroom, teachers can facilitate this student-led approach by providing students with varying relevant experiences and opportunities for hands-on learning, such as projects or learning centers.
- **Multiple Intelligences (Howard Gardner):** Gardner's theory proposes there are several versions of intelligence, and as such, the process of learning differs among individuals. Some learners may have a stronger intelligence in one domain, but perhaps have difficulty in another, and therefore, learn best when instruction is presented through the lens of their dominant intelligence. Intelligences are categorized as logical-mathematical, verbal-linguistic, visual-spatial, bodily-kinesthetic, interpersonal, intrapersonal, musical, and naturalistic.

CONNECTING NEW INFORMATION AND IDEAS TO PRIOR KNOWLEDGE

When students connect new information to prior knowledge, learning becomes relevant and engaging. Effective instruction encourages students to connect learning to background knowledge and experiences, which increases retainment, deepens understanding, and enhances the effectiveness of the overall learning experience. Fostering personal connections to learning is

Copyright © Mometrix Media. You have been licensed one copy of this document for personal use only. Any other reproduction or redistribution is strictly prohibited. All rights reserved. This content is provided for test preparation purposes only and does not imply an endorsement by Mometrix of any particular political, scientific, or religious point of view.

achieved through incorporating an array of strategies and technologies into instruction. Activities including KWL charts, anticipatory guides, graphic organizers, and brainstorming encourage students to consider what they know before learning new concepts, thus allowing them to build upon their prior knowledge and ability to make connections that strengthen learning. Cooperative learning strategies promote sharing and building prior knowledge with other students, thus increasing students' connections to new information. Numerous technologies exist to enhance the learning experience by fostering connections between prior knowledge and new information. Teachers can incorporate a wide range of apps and games across subject areas that build upon prior knowledge by providing activities with increasing levels of difficulty. Online polls, surveys, and word association websites allow students to demonstrate prior understanding of a topic to begin making connections. Self-reflection and closure opportunities at the end of instruction further strengthen learning by encouraging students to connect new material to prior knowledge and experiences.

MAKING LEARNING MEANINGFUL AND RELEVANT

Effective instruction occurs when learning is meaningful and relevant. When the purpose of learning is clear, students are engaged, motivated, and retain new information. Instruction must be student-centered, foster personal connections, and be applicable to real-life situations to create meaningful and relevant instruction. Teachers achieve this through an array of methods and technologies that are tailored to students' learning needs. Through forging positive relationships with students, teachers learn their unique interests, preferences, and experiences. Activities such as interest inventories, surveys, and community building develop a positive rapport between teachers and students. This allows teachers to make learning meaningful by creating learner-centered instruction that facilitates personal connections and builds upon prior knowledge. Field trips and community outreach programs are effective in enhancing relevancy through demonstrating the real-world applications of instruction. Additionally, technologies including virtual field trips and tours, videos, and documentaries, assist in increasing students' understanding the purpose of learning by illustrating the real-world applications of instruction. Self-assessments make learning meaningful and relevant through encouraging student ownership and responsibility over learning as students seek areas for improvement. Moreover, closure activities serve to demonstrate overall purpose for learning through encouraging students to connect learning to the lesson's objective and their prior knowledge.

INTRADISCIPLINARY AND INTERDISCIPLINARY INSTRUCTION

Intradisciplinary and interdisciplinary instruction are both valuable strategies for teaching and learning. In **intradisciplinary** instruction, several elements of a single broad subject area are incorporated into the lesson. For example, in a science lesson, the teacher could incorporate elements of chemistry, biology, and physics into instruction. This method of instruction is beneficial in deepening students' understanding of the nuances of a particular subject area through demonstrating the various components that comprise the overarching discipline. **Interdisciplinary** instruction refers to the simultaneous integration of ideas, knowledge, and skills from several subject areas when approaching an idea, problem, or theme, and applying principles of one subject area to another. For example, in an interdisciplinary unit on food, the teacher could incorporate elements of math by teaching students to measure ingredients, language arts by teaching them to read or write a recipe, science through examining chemical reactions of the cooking process, and social studies through having students explore the impact of food agriculture on economy and society. Interdisciplinary instruction is beneficial in deepening students' understanding across subject areas and developing real-world critical thinking skills by encouraging them to make connections between disciplines and teaching them to consider an idea or problem from multiple perspectives.

Copyright © Mometrix Media. You have been licensed one copy of this document for personal use only. Any other reproduction or redistribution is strictly prohibited. All rights reserved. This content is provided for test preparation purposes only and does not imply an endorsement by Mometrix of any particular political, scientific, or religious point of view.

EXAMPLES OF INTRADISCIPLINARY INSTRUCTION

- **Language Arts:** A single language arts lesson can incorporate components of reading, writing, grammar, and listening skills. For example, a lesson on a particular poem can include a close reading of the poet's use of grammar, symbolism, imagery, and other literary techniques, as well as an audio recording of the poet reading aloud. At the end of the unit, students can be assigned to use what they learned to compose their own original poems.
- **Social Studies:** Social studies units can incorporate elements of history, anthropology, archaeology, sociology, psychology, or any other field that involves the study of humans, civilizations, cultures, and historical events. For example, a unit on the Aztec people may include an examination of their religious beliefs, customs, architecture, and agricultural practices.
- **Science:** Intradisciplinary units in science can include several branches within the field, such as chemistry, biology, physics, earth science, botany, or geology. For example, a unit on volcanoes may incorporate lessons on plate tectonics, the Earth's layers, chemicals released during a volcanic eruption, islands formed from cooled volcanic rock, as well as plants that grow best near volcanoes.
- **Mathematics:** An intradisciplinary math lesson may simultaneously include several branches within the field, such as arithmetic, algebra, or geometry. For example, in a geometry lesson on the Pythagorean theorem, students must utilize algebraic equations and arithmetic to determine the length of the sides of a right triangle.

EXAMPLES OF INTERDISCIPLINARY INSTRUCTION

- **Language Arts:** A unit based in language arts may also incorporate several other disciplines, such as social studies, art, or music. For example, a unit on William Shakespeare's *Romeo and Juliet* may include a reading of the play and an analysis of the use of literary techniques within it, as well as a study of William Shakespeare's life and the society in which he lived to incorporate social studies. Students can also act out the play to incorporate the arts and participate in a rhythmic study on iambic pentameter to incorporate music.
- **Social Studies:** Units based in social studies can include lessons focused on multiple disciplines, including language arts, music, science, and math. For example, an interdisciplinary unit on Ancient Egypt may include a historical study of the culture, religion, architecture, and practices of the Ancient Egyptians while integrating other subject areas, such as a study of hieroglyphics to incorporate language arts and creating Egyptian masks to incorporate art. Students can also study the scientific advancements of the Ancient Egyptians, as well as incorporate math to study how the ancient pyramids were constructed.
- **Science:** Scientific units can also incorporate elements of art, math, social studies, and language arts in order to become interdisciplinary. For example, a unit on Punnett squares focuses on biology and genetics but can also include several other subject areas. Math can be incorporated by integrating lessons on probability, students can be assigned to research their genetics, create a family tree, and write a report on their findings to incorporate language arts and social studies. Art can also be incorporated by having students create portraits of the potential outcomes from Punnett squares.
- **Mathematics:** Interdisciplinary units in mathematics can also include lessons focused on such disciplines as art, social studies, science, and music. For example, a geometry unit on measuring triangles may also incorporate songs to memorize equations, lessons on the pyramids of Ancient Egypt to incorporate social studies, as well as an art project in which students use only triangles to create an original piece.

Copyright © Mometrix Media. You have been licensed one copy of this document for personal use only. Any other reproduction or redistribution is strictly prohibited. All rights reserved.
This content is provided for test preparation purposes only and does not imply an endorsement by Mometrix of any particular political, scientific, or religious point of view.

INCORPORATING COOPERATIVE LEARNING ALLOWING CONSIDERATION FROM MULTIPLE VIEWPOINTS

In any classroom, teachers will encounter a wide range of diversities among students' backgrounds, cultures, interests, skills, and abilities. Thus, providing students with several opportunities for cooperative learning gives them access to others' perspectives and is highly valuable in teaching students to consider ideas from multiple viewpoints. As each student has different experiences and background knowledge, collaborative learning allows them to share their views on ideas with others. Additionally, in working together, students have the opportunity to work with others from different backgrounds that they may have otherwise never encountered and gain exposure to approaching ideas from multiple viewpoints. Cooperative learning opportunities allow students to understand and appreciate others' perspectives and teaches them that there are multiple approaches to problem solving and ideas.

LEARNING EXPERIENCES THAT DEVELOP REAL-WORLD LIFE SKILLS

The ultimate goal of education is to develop the whole child and ensure that students develop into productive, contributing members of society once they leave the classroom. Therefore, it is imperative to provide learning experiences that will develop life skills that are applicable and beneficial in the real world. In an increasingly fast-paced global society, students must be prepared to enter the professional and societal world as confident, independent, responsible, and adaptive individuals. They must have the leadership skills necessary to compete in the professional arena. Students must be able to work cooperatively with others, respect and value multiple perspectives, and be effective problem solvers and critical thinkers in order to be successful outside of the classroom. Teachers must also aim to help students develop the skills necessary to become lifelong learners to ensure continuous growth and development as they enter society. Therefore, learning experiences that promote the development of real-world life skills in addition to academic skills are necessary in adequately preparing students for success.

CROSS-CURRICULAR INSTRUCTION FOR EXPLORING CONTENT FROM VARIED PERSPECTIVES

Cross-curricular instruction allows teachers to demonstrate that elements from one subject area can be applied to ideas or problem solving in another. Thus, this instructional strategy is highly valuable in developing students' abilities to explore content from varied perspectives. As this method incorporates several disciplines in approaching a topic, it deepens students' understanding that there are several perspectives that one can take when solving a problem, and that elements of one subject area are relevant in another. In addition, cross-curricular instruction prepares students for the real world through developing critical thinking skills and allowing them to make connections between disciplines, thus allowing them to understand how to successfully approach ideas from varied perspectives.

BENEFITS OF MULTICULTURAL LEARNING EXPERIENCES

Multicultural learning experiences demonstrate to students the array of diversities that exist both inside and outside of the classroom. Just as each culture has its own values, norms, and traditions, each has its own perspectives and approaches to ideas and problem solving. Incorporating multicultural experiences in the classroom exposes students to cultures and groups that they may have otherwise never encountered and teaches them to respect and value perspectives outside of their own. As students learn other cultures' beliefs, customs, and attitudes, they develop the understanding that each culture solves problems and considers ideas from multiple viewpoints and that each approach is valuable. As students learn other perspectives, they can apply this knowledge, and ultimately build problem solving and critical thinking skills that will be beneficial in developing successful lifelong learning habits.

Copyright © Mometrix Media. You have been licensed one copy of this document for personal use only. Any other reproduction or redistribution is strictly prohibited. All rights reserved.
This content is provided for test preparation purposes only and does not imply an endorsement by Mometrix of any particular political, scientific, or religious point of view.

Incorporating Multiple Disciplines into a Thematic Unit

In **cross-curricular**, or **interdisciplinary** instruction, multiple disciplines are incorporated into a thematic unit in order to deepen students' understanding through fostering connections and demonstrating multiple perspectives and methods of problem solving. Effective interdisciplinary instruction requires careful planning to ensure that all activities are relevant to the overall lesson theme and effectively support students in achieving desired learning outcomes. The teacher must first select a thematic unit based on state academic standards and then determine desired learning outcomes. Then, the teacher must design lessons and activities for students to reach learning goals and objectives. When integrating multiple disciplines into a thematic unit, the teacher must seek out materials, resources, and activities from various subject areas that are applicable to the main topic and reinforce lesson objectives. The teacher can then integrate these elements into lesson planning to create multifaceted instruction. Additionally, the teacher can create activities that approach the overarching lesson theme from the perspective of different subject areas. The activities and materials should be coordinated and relate to one another in order to deepen students' understanding of the overall concept.

Effectively Allocating Time When Creating Lessons and Units

Effective time management is vital for successful teaching and learning. To ensure that all academic standards are covered within a school year, teachers must consider how to best allocate specific amounts of time for units and lessons that allow for review, enrichment, and reteaching. A unit plan for the school year is an effective strategy in allowing the teacher to visualize and plan the amount of content that must be covered. A unit plan can also be utilized on a smaller scale, as a framework for designing and allotting time for instructional goals, objectives, and lessons within each unit. By setting learning goals and daily objectives within individual units, the teacher can determine the amount of time available for completing each unit, thus ensuring more effective lesson planning by allowing the teacher to develop a daily schedule with dedicated time for teaching and learning. When planning lessons, the teacher must consider how much instructional time is necessary to cover each topic and the time students will need to complete lesson activities. Additionally, teachers must ensure that they allow time at the end of each lesson for reteaching if students have misconceptions, as extra time can be utilized for enrichment if reteaching is unnecessary.

Opportunities for Reflection

Opportunities for reflection within lesson plans are beneficial in enhancing learning experiences through strengthening student understanding and influencing further instruction. When students are given the opportunity to reflect, they are able to connect their learning back to the original objective and better understand the overall purpose for learning, thus fostering engagement. Reflection deepens students' understanding by allowing them to connect new concepts to their own personal experiences, which ultimately helps in comprehension and retainment through making learning relevant. Reflecting on performance empowers students to become self-motivated lifelong learners by allowing them to analyze what they understood and did well, as well as encouraging them to identify areas for improvement. Teachers can utilize students' reflections to influence and drive further instruction. Students' reflections also allow teachers to identify areas in which students excelled, areas for improvement, and can aid them in tailoring future lesson plans to adapt to students' needs and interests.

Opportunities for Self-Assessment

Self-assessments within lessons are a valuable formative assessment strategy that enriches student learning and provides insight to the teacher. Providing students with the opportunity to monitor their progress and assess their learning supports them in developing a wide range of skills that are beneficial both inside and outside of the classroom. Self-assessments empower students in their

Copyright © Mometrix Media. You have been licensed one copy of this document for personal use only. Any other reproduction or redistribution is strictly prohibited. All rights reserved.
This content is provided for test preparation purposes only and does not imply an endorsement by Mometrix of any particular political, scientific, or religious point of view.

learning by creating a sense of ownership and responsibility over their own learning, thus fostering self-motivation and engagement. They also serve to foster a sense of independence and objectivity within students to effectively review their own work and identify areas of improvement, which is a vital skill needed to becoming a lifelong learner. When students evaluate their own performance, the teacher is able to effectively assess student understanding, thus allowing them to identify areas of weakness or misconception for reteaching.

OPPORTUNITIES FOR CLOSURE ACTIVITIES

Closure activities at the end of each lesson or topic are beneficial for both students and teachers. These short activities allow teachers to formatively assess student understanding of content covered within a lesson and identify areas of misconception for reteaching. Additionally, closure activities are valuable in measuring whether the intended lesson objective was achieved before moving to the next topic. For students, closures at the end of a lesson provide structure and organization to learning, as well as emphasize the purpose for instruction by allowing them to connect what they learned back to the original objective. Moreover, in having students restate what they have learned in a closure activity, learning is strengthened by giving students the opportunity to internalize new information. In demonstrating their understanding, they can better make personal connections between their own learning, background knowledge, and experiences.

Schedules, Routines, and Activities for Young Children

IDEAL SCHEDULE FOR YOUNG CHILDREN

An ideal schedule for young children reflects their developmental characteristics and capabilities to maximize their learning. A **predictable** routine is necessary for young children to feel secure in their learning environment, and therefore, each day should follow a similar schedule while allowing room for **flexibility** if an activity takes longer than expected. Each day should begin with a clear routine, such as unpacking, a "warm-up" activity, and a class meeting to allow students to share thoughts, ask questions, and allow the teacher to discuss what will occur that day. This establishes a positive tone for the day while focusing the attention on learning. Similarly, the end of the day should have a specific routine, such as cleaning up materials and packing up for dismissal. Young children learn best by physically interacting with and exploring their environment. As such, each day should include large blocks of time for **active movement** throughout the day in the form of play, projects, and learning centers. Periods of **rest** must follow such activities, as this enables young children to process and internalize what they learned. **Direct instruction** should occur before active movement periods and last approximately 15-20 minutes to sustain engagement and attention on learning.

Example Daily Schedule for the Early Childhood Education Classroom	
8:00-8:30	Welcome, unpack, morning work
8:30-8:45	Circle time, review class calendar
8:45-9:30	Literacy/Language Arts
9:30-10:15	Learning Stations
10:15-11:00	Math
11:00-11:30	Music/Dance/Movement
11:30-12:15	Lunch
12:15-1:00	Recess/Unstructured play
1:00-1:20	Rest/Quiet time
1:20-2:00	Science

Copyright © Mometrix Media. You have been licensed one copy of this document for personal use only. Any other reproduction or redistribution is strictly prohibited. All rights reserved. This content is provided for test preparation purposes only and does not imply an endorsement by Mometrix of any particular political, scientific, or religious point of view.

| 2:00-2:45 | Creative Arts |
| 2:45-3:15 | Daily reflection, pack up, dismissal |

Some examples of restful and active movement activities for young children are discussed below:

- **Restful:** Incorporating restful activities into the early childhood classroom are beneficial in helping young children process and retain new concepts and providing them the opportunity to unwind after active movement activities. Examples of such activities include nap time, class meditation, self-reflection activities, independent art projects, or self-selected reading time. Teachers can also read aloud to students or play an audiobook during these periods.
- **Active:** Providing young children with multiple opportunities for active movement throughout the day is beneficial in promoting the development of gross motor skills, connections to learning, and the ability to function in a group setting. Active movement opportunities should include whole-class, small group, and independent activities. Examples include class dances, songs, or games, nature walks, or total participation activities such as gallery walks or four corners. Physical education activities, such as jump rope, tag, sports, or using playground equipment are also beneficial. Young children should also be provided with ample time for both structured and unstructured play throughout the day.

BALANCING RESTFUL AND ACTIVE MOVEMENT ACTIVITIES

A schedule that balances **rest** and **active movement** is necessary for positive cognitive, physical, emotional, and social development in young children. Connecting learning to active movement strengthens students' understanding of new concepts, as it allows them to physically explore and interact with their environment, experiment with new ideas, and gain new experiences for healthy **cognitive development**. In addition, incorporating active movement encourages the use of **gross motor skills** and provides students with the space to physically express themselves in an appropriate setting, thus promoting physical and emotional development. Active movement also encourages the development of positive **interpersonal skills** as young children interact and explore with one another. Restful periods are equally as important to young children's development. Incorporating rest after a period of active movement further strengthens young children's connection to learning by providing them the opportunity to reflect, process, and internalize new information.

PROVIDING LARGE BLOCKS OF TIME FOR PLAY, PROJECTS, AND LEARNING CENTERS

Providing young children with ample time for play, projects, and learning centers throughout the school day is integral to fostering their development across domains. Young children learn most effectively through active movement as they physically interact with their environment, and incorporating large blocks of time for such activities allows them to do so. Significant time dedicated to active play, projects, and learning centers on a variety of topics allows young children to explore and experiment with the world around them, test new ideas, draw conclusions, and acquire new knowledge. This supports healthy **physical** and **cognitive development**, as it provides young children the opportunity to engage in learning across subject areas while connecting it to active movement for strengthened understanding. In addition, allowing large blocks of time for these activities is necessary for **social** and **emotional development**, as it provides young children the space to interact with one another and develop important skills such as cooperation, sharing, conflict resolution, and emotional self-regulation. Dedicating large blocks of time to play, projects, and learning centers establishes a student-led, hands-on learning environment that is reflective of the developmental characteristics and needs of young children.

Copyright © Mometrix Media. You have been licensed one copy of this document for personal use only. Any other reproduction or redistribution is strictly prohibited. All rights reserved.
This content is provided for test preparation purposes only and does not imply an endorsement by Mometrix of any particular political, scientific, or religious point of view.

DEVELOPMENTAL CHARACTERISTICS OF YOUNG CHILDREN IN RELATION TO INTERACTIONS WITH OTHERS

Designing group activities that align with young children's ability to collaborate while supporting social development requires a realistic understanding of their capacity to do so. This entails understanding the **developmental characteristics** of young children at varying stages, including how the nature of their interactions with others evolves. Young children learn by exploring and interacting with their environment, so they need ample opportunities for play and active movement to do so. However, the teacher must recognize that the way young children play and collaborate develops over time. Young children typically exhibit little interest in actively playing with others until approximately age four. Until then, they progress through stages of solitary play, observing their peers, playing independently alongside others, and eventually, loosely interacting, perhaps with the same toys, while still primarily engaging in independent play. During these stages, it is important that the teacher foster **collaboration** by providing multiple opportunities for play as well as learning materials that encourage **cooperation** and **sharing**. The teacher must, however, maintain the understanding that these children have yet to develop the capacity to intentionally work with others. Once this ability is developed, the teacher can integrate coordinated group activities that encourage collaboration toward a common goal.

CONSIDERATIONS WHEN DESIGNING GROUP ACTIVITIES FOR YOUNG CHILDREN

For young children, thoughtfully designed group activities are integral in promoting development across domains. These opportunities facilitate social and emotional development by encouraging collaboration and positive communication, as well as physical and cognitive growth as children play, explore, and interact with others in the learning environment. It is therefore important that the teacher carefully consider the particulars of group activities when planning to ensure maximized learning and development. The teacher must consider the **developmental characteristics** of their students' age group, including their capacity to collaborate with others. This enables the teacher to plan group activities that align with students' abilities while promoting collaboration and development. All **learning materials** must be carefully selected to encourage collaboration, sharing, and the development of positive social skills at a developmentally appropriate level. The teacher must also consider **desired learning outcomes** and the nature of the learning taking place to determine whether group activities should be structured or unstructured. Unstructured play is valuable in allowing students to develop their social and emotional skills in a natural setting, whereas structured, teacher-led group activities allow for more focused learning. Desired outcomes also determine the size of groups for the activity to best promote collaboration and learning.

GROUP ACTIVITIES THAT REFLECT AND DEVELOP YOUNG CHILDREN'S ABILITY TO COLLABORATE

Young children benefit from a variety of **whole-class** and **small-group** activities designed to reflect and develop their collaborative skills. When the teacher incorporates group activities to encourage cooperation, sharing, and positive interactions, young children gain important social and emotional skills necessary for development across domains. Whole-group activities such as **circle time** provide young children with the opportunity to interact with others, express ideas, and ask questions in a developmentally appropriate setting. This activity develops important collaborative skills, such as taking turns, active listening, and respectful communication. Other **whole-group activities**, such as reading aloud, group songs, dances, games, or class nature walks, are effective in teaching young children how to productively contribute to and function in a group setting. **Small-group activities** can be incorporated throughout all aspects of structured and unstructured learning to develop young children's collaborative skills. Learning centers, such as a science area,

Copyright © Mometrix Media. You have been licensed one copy of this document for personal use only. Any other reproduction or redistribution is strictly prohibited. All rights reserved. This content is provided for test preparation purposes only and does not imply an endorsement by Mometrix of any particular political, scientific, or religious point of view.

pretend play area, or building block center, provide materials that encourage collaboration while allowing students to interact with others according to their abilities in a student-led setting. Problem-solving activities, such as puzzles, games, age-appropriate science experiments, or scavenger hunts, are effective in teaching young children how to work together toward a common goal.

ORGANIZING AND MANAGING GROUP ACTIVITIES TO PROMOTE COLLABORATIVE SKILLS AND INDIVIDUAL ACCOUNTABILITY

Well-planned group activities are beneficial in developing students' collaborative skills and sense of individual accountability. Such group activities are well-organized, effectively managed, and intentionally structured with a **clear goal** or problem that must be solved while allowing room for creativity to enhance the collaborative process. When designing these activities, the teacher must incorporate enough **significant components** to ensure all students within the group can productively contribute. If the assignment is too simple, students can easily complete it on their own, whereas a multifaceted activity instills a sense of interdependence within the group that fosters the development of collaborative skills. To promote individual accountability, **meaningful roles** and responsibilities should be assigned to each group member because when students feel others are relying on their contributions to complete a task, they develop a sense of ownership that motivates active participation. To further develop collaborative skills and individual accountability, students should be graded both as a **whole-group** and **individually**. This encourages group cooperation while ensuring that students' individual contributions are recognized. Including **self-assessments** at the end of group activities is beneficial in allowing students to reflect on the quality of their contributions to the group and ways they could improve their collaborative skills.

Thoughtful consideration of how to best organize and manage collaborative activities helps establish an environment that supports students in learning to work together productively and assume responsible roles within a group. When planning group activities, the teacher must consider the **desired learning outcomes** and the **nature of the task** to determine whether there are enough significant components that would benefit from collaboration. **Group size** must also be considered to most effectively foster collaboration and individual accountability when assuming responsible roles. Groups with too few students may be inadequate for addressing all the components of a complex task, whereas grouping too many students together limits productive collaboration and makes it difficult for each member to assume a significant, responsible role. The teacher must be selective regarding which students are grouped together to best facilitate productive collaboration. This includes determining which students will work well together, as well as grouping students that may need support with others that can provide scaffolding. It is also important to consider how **responsibilities** will be divided to ensure each member is given a significant role that allows them to contribute productively to the group, as well how their contributions will be monitored and **assessed**.

The Learning Environment

ESTABLISHING A POSITIVE, PRODUCTIVE CLASSROOM ENVIRONMENT
UNIQUE CHARACTERISTICS AND NEEDS OF STUDENTS AT VARYING DEVELOPMENTAL LEVELS

Students at each developmental level possess unique characteristics and needs that must be met in the classroom to ensure productivity and a positive classroom environment. For successful learning, the teacher must recognize the nuances of varying developmental levels to properly understand their students' abilities and design instruction accordingly. When the teacher is attuned to the distinct characteristics and needs of their students, they can align **curriculum**, **instructional**

Copyright © Mometrix Media. You have been licensed one copy of this document for personal use only. Any other reproduction or redistribution is strictly prohibited. All rights reserved. This content is provided for test preparation purposes only and does not imply an endorsement by Mometrix of any particular political, scientific, or religious point of view.

strategies, activities, and assessments in a way that is accessible and comprehensible to all students. This understanding enables the teacher to deliver instruction at a **pace** appropriate to students' developmental stage while ensuring they are challenged across domains based upon their ability for continuous whole-child development. In addition, knowledge of the general characteristics and needs of developmental stages enables the teacher to effectively identify and accommodate individual variances that occur within these stages for **student-centered** learning. When instruction is tailored to address the needs of varying developmental stages and individual differences, students feel supported in their learning. This ultimately fosters increased self-esteem, student engagement, and positive attitudes toward learning that contribute to an overall productive and successful classroom environment.

ADDRESSING DEVELOPMENTAL CHARACTERISTICS AND NEEDS OF YOUNGER STUDENTS

A positive and productive classroom environment for younger children requires the teacher to understand the intricacies of this developmental stage and implement strategies accordingly to promote success in learning. Younger students learn by **exploring** and **interacting** with the world around them and must be provided with multiple opportunities to do so. **Play** is integral to young students' development across domains. Therefore, both planned and free play should be incorporated throughout instruction. Play enables students to explore their environment and make connections that strengthen their learning while promoting the development of problem-solving and higher-order thinking skills. In addition, allowing frequent opportunities for play facilitates the acquisition of important social and emotional skills, such as cooperation, conflict resolution, and sharing. Likewise, incorporating frequent **movement** throughout lessons allows young students to explore their physical space and actively engage in learning for deeper understanding. Additionally, **cooperative learning** strategies encourage the development of necessary social and emotional skills and are important in teaching young children how to effectively work with others to solve a problem. When the teacher implements strategies appropriate to younger students' developmental levels, it enhances motivation, active engagement, and promotes positive attitudes toward learning for a productive classroom environment.

COLLABORATIVE OPPORTUNITIES IN ADDRESSING DEVELOPMENTAL CHARACTERISTICS AND NEEDS OF MIDDLE-LEVEL STUDENTS

Middle-level students experience significant developmental changes as they approach adolescence and therefore, have unique characteristics and needs that must be met to ensure a positive and productive learning environment. **Collaborative opportunities** are beneficial in supporting the development of cognitive, social, and emotional skills of middle-level students and should be implemented frequently. This strategy enables these students to work productively with others and promotes the development of positive **interpersonal** and **communication** skills. This is especially important in middle-level education, as students at this developmental stage begin forming their identities, attitudes toward learning, and influential peer relationships. Middle-level students build **self-confidence** through collaborative learning, as it enables them to develop positive leadership skills. Additionally, collaborative opportunities expose students to the varying backgrounds and perspectives of their classmates, thus fostering appreciation for individual differences and contributing to a positive classroom climate. Collaborative learning is also beneficial for **cognitive development**, as it allows students to build upon one another's background knowledge for enhanced learning and encourages critical and higher-order thinking while working together to solve a problem. Providing middle-level students with collaborative opportunities increases overall engagement for a positive and productive classroom environment, as well as develops necessary skills for successful transition into adolescence.

Copyright © Mometrix Media. You have been licensed one copy of this document for personal use only. Any other reproduction or redistribution is strictly prohibited. All rights reserved. This content is provided for test preparation purposes only and does not imply an endorsement by Mometrix of any particular political, scientific, or religious point of view.

PROMOTING RESPECT FOR THE COMMUNITY AND PEOPLE IN IT AMONG OLDER STUDENTS

As older students prepare for adulthood, it is important that they develop a respect for their community and the people in it. Implementing strategies to facilitate this is vital in equipping older students with **real-world skills** necessary to become productive contributors to society. By self-educating and modeling respect for the community and its people, the teacher can influence students to adopt the same sentiment. Establishing a positive community within the classroom through such activities as class meetings, discussions, and cultural activities promotes respect for others that extends to real-world situations. Strategies that demonstrate connection to the community strengthen students' overall respect and responsibility for it. This can be achieved by incorporating **authentic materials**, including news stories, art, music, and relevant speakers, to develop students' understanding and insight regarding the characteristics and needs of the community. Encouraging students to bring items from home to share fosters appreciation for their community by exposing them to the backgrounds and perspectives within it. **Community service** projects such as fundraisers, food drives, and service field trips further promote students' respect for their community while demonstrating the real-world applications of their learning. This ultimately makes learning meaningful and contributes to a positive, productive learning environment.

POSITIVE CLASSROOM CLIMATE

Classroom climate refers to the overall atmosphere that the teacher establishes and is powerful in determining the nature of the learning experience. Students are most successful in their learning when the climate is positive, encouraging, and focused on creating a collaborative, supportive community. A positive classroom climate is **welcoming**, **inclusive**, and **respectful** of all individuals. Instruction is delivered in an engaging, comprehensible way in a structured, orderly, and safe environment. The atmosphere is **visually appealing** and stimulating, yet not overwhelming, and is physically arranged in a way that maximizes learning. **Collaboration** and **supportive interactions** are encouraged throughout the learning process to enhance engagement and develop positive social and emotional skills. Such an environment builds students' self-esteem and confidence by ensuring they feel safe and empowered to participate and work with others in the learning process. In addition, it encourages positive attitudes toward learning that are necessary for active student engagement and productivity. When the classroom climate is positive, students are more self-motivated, thus strengthening their learning and promoting academic achievement.

COLLABORATION AND SUPPORTIVE INTERACTIONS

Collaboration and **supportive interactions** are key components of a positive classroom climate and should be integrated throughout instruction to promote active engagement and success in learning for all students. To achieve this, the teacher must establish a classroom community focused on respect, inclusiveness, and open dialogue. This ensures students feel safe and empowered to express themselves and interact constructively. By teaching and **modeling** active listening skills, the teacher can demonstrate and influence respectful communication in the classroom. **Team-building activities**, including class meetings, games, and discussions, are valuable strategies for creating a community that encourages productive collaboration and supportive interactions. In addition, establishing **clear expectations** for positive communication and involving students in their creation instills a sense of personal responsibility to adhere to them when working with others. Once expectations are understood, students must be provided with multiple and varied **collaborative learning** opportunities to continuously practice developing positive interpersonal skills. As students participate in learning, the teacher must be sure to consistently praise cooperation and positive interactions to reinforce the standards of communication. When the teacher promotes collaboration and supportive interactions, they create

Copyright © Mometrix Media. You have been licensed one copy of this document for personal use only. Any other reproduction or redistribution is strictly prohibited. All rights reserved.
This content is provided for test preparation purposes only and does not imply an endorsement by Mometrix of any particular political, scientific, or religious point of view.

a positive classroom climate that increases students' productivity and self-motivation to actively participate in learning for maximized achievement.

RESPECT FOR DIVERSITY AND INDIVIDUAL DIFFERENCES

An emphasis on respect for **diversity** and **individual differences** in the classroom is necessary to establish a positive, productive learning atmosphere. Teaching and modeling this sentiment to students instills the notion that everyone has unique and valuable experiences, perspectives, and characteristics to contribute to the classroom community. Emphasizing respect for all individuals ensures students feel validated and secure in their own identities while teaching them to appreciate diversities among their classmates. Such an environment promotes collaboration and supportive interactions, as it is built on a foundation of welcoming, inclusiveness, and acceptance that empowers students to confidently interact with peers as they engage in learning. When students feel respected, it increases their self-esteem and positive self-concept. Students that feel confident in the classroom are more likely to develop positive attitudes toward learning. This ultimately fosters a positive classroom climate in which students are motivated to actively engage in instruction and achieve academic success.

IMPACT OF INTERACTIONS ON CLASSROOM CLIMATE
TEACHER-STUDENT INTERACTIONS

Interactions between teachers and their students play a significant role in determining overall classroom climate and the quality of the learning experience. The way in which the teacher interacts with students influences their **social**, **emotional**, and **cognitive development**, as well as sets the tone for how students interact with each other. This ultimately shapes students' **self-esteem** and contributes to their level of engagement, attitude toward learning, and academic achievement. Therefore, it is important that the teacher ensure all interactions with students on a whole-class and individual level are positive, unbiased, encouraging, and respectful of each individual. Working to build relationships with students demonstrates a genuine interest in their lives that contributes to a positive, productive classroom climate in which students feel welcomed, accepted, and empowered to actively engage in learning. Positive interactions between the teacher and students support a healthy sense of self-esteem as well as positive social and emotional skills that contribute to cognitive development. Students with greater self-esteem are more likely to develop positive attitudes toward learning that foster increased self-motivation to actively participate in learning, thus contributing to enhanced academic achievement.

STUDENTS' INTERACTIONS WITH ONE ANOTHER

The classroom climate is dependent on the nature of **students' interactions** with one another. These interactions largely determine the quality of student learning as well as development across domains. Positive communication facilitates the development of healthy **social** and emotional skills that serve to enhance cognitive development. Students with strong social and **emotional skills** are often more motivated to actively participate in learning and are more productive in collaborative situations, as they can build upon one another's knowledge. Therefore, the teacher must implement a variety of strategies to ensure interactions among students are positive, respectful, and supportive to establish a classroom climate focused on productive learning. **Community building** exercises establish a climate built on positive and supportive communication while demonstrating the benefits of productive cooperation in achieving a goal. Teaching and **modeling** positive communication skills sets the tone and expectations for how students will interact with one another. Students should be given **frequent opportunities** to interact both during and outside of instructional time to promote the development of necessary interpersonal skills for healthy social development. In addition, **strategic student groupings** during collaborative work and consistent

Copyright © Mometrix Media. You have been licensed one copy of this document for personal use only. Any other reproduction or redistribution is strictly prohibited. All rights reserved.
This content is provided for test preparation purposes only and does not imply an endorsement by Mometrix of any particular political, scientific, or religious point of view.

monitoring help ensure maximized productivity and that the standards for communication are reinforced.

COMMUNICATING AN ENTHUSIASM FOR LEARNING

ESTABLISHING ENVIRONMENTS PROMOTING POSITIVE ATTITUDES TOWARD LEARNING

The nature of the classroom environment is reliant on the **efforts**, **behaviors**, and **attitudes** of the teacher. The teacher is responsible for setting the tone of the classroom, which determines the overall climate and has significant impacts on the quality and effectiveness of the learning experience. The classroom environment influences students' engagement, positive communication, and attitudes toward learning, which contribute to their overall academic achievement. Successful teaching and learning require the teacher to intentionally take measures to establish a welcoming, accepting, and encouraging classroom environment that promotes excitement and positive attitudes toward learning. Teachers must model genuine respect for their students and enthusiasm for learning, as well as present instruction in a way that is engaging, comprehensible, and responsive to students' needs and interests. The physical classroom must be arranged in such a way that is visually appealing, safe, and facilitative of productive learning. It is also important that the teacher establish and consistently reinforce structured routines, procedures, and behavioral expectations to contribute to an overall positive climate and ensure students feel secure and willing to participate in learning. When the classroom environment is exciting, positive, and engaging, it encourages positive attitudes toward learning that increase motivation to succeed.

INFLUENCE ON STUDENTS' MOTIVATION, PRODUCTIVITY, AND ACADEMIC ACHIEVEMENT

Modeling is perhaps one of the most powerful strategies in influencing students' attitudes, behaviors, and actions in the classroom. As students spend a great deal of time with their teachers, the level of enthusiasm for learning demonstrated by the teacher inevitably influences their own excitement in the classroom. Therefore, the teacher must conscientiously model enthusiasm for teaching and learning to positively influence students' internal motivation for productivity, learning, and achievement. Students are highly perceptive, and as such, if the teacher appears unmotivated in their practice or disinterested in the content, students will likely adopt the same sentiment and become disengaged or apathetic toward learning. The enthusiasm modeled by the teacher must be **authentic** to elicit the same genuine interest in learning from students. When the teacher demonstrates sincere excitement about the content they are teaching, it prompts curiosity for learning among students that enhances their motivation and attitudes toward learning. In addition, modeling enthusiasm for teaching and learning enhances the relationship between the teacher and students, thus contributing to a positive classroom climate that makes students excited to learn. When students have a positive attitude toward learning, they are more motivated to productively engage in learning and achieve academic success.

METHODS AND IMPACT ON CLASSROOM CLIMATE AND STUDENT ENGAGEMENT

Communicating sincere enthusiasm for teaching and learning is essential to establishing a positive, productive classroom climate focused on student engagement and achievement. Students' interest and excitement for learning are directly reflective of the sentiments exhibited by the teacher. As such, it is important that the teacher intentionally and consistently communicate excitement for their practice and content. To achieve this, the teacher must ensure that their **behaviors**, **actions**, **language**, **tone of voice**, and **interactions** with students are positive in nature. By working to build positive **interpersonal relationships** with students and demonstrating genuine interest in their lives, experiences, interests, and needs, the teacher can effectively communicate enthusiasm for their practice that motivates students to engage in learning. This is further reflected in the physical **classroom arrangement**. A classroom that is visually appealing, stimulating, and reflective of

Copyright © Mometrix Media. You have been licensed one copy of this document for personal use only. Any other reproduction or redistribution is strictly prohibited. All rights reserved. This content is provided for test preparation purposes only and does not imply an endorsement by Mometrix of any particular political, scientific, or religious point of view.

students' interests and achievements illustrates the teacher's enthusiasm and promotes a positive classroom climate in which students are excited and motivated to engage in learning.

CONVEYING HIGH EXPECTATIONS FOR ALL STUDENTS

SIGNIFICANCE IN PROMOTING PRODUCTIVITY, ACTIVE ENGAGEMENT, AND SUCCESS IN LEARNING

Communicating **high academic** and **behavioral expectations** is necessary for establishing a classroom climate focused on productivity, active engagement, and achievement. Students are heavily influenced by the teacher's expectations for them, and therefore, when high learning standards are set, students will more likely strive to achieve them. High expectations increase the **relevancy** of learning by focusing instruction and providing a clear purpose that motivates students to participate. In addition, by conveying high expectations, the teacher demonstrates a **belief in their students' abilities** to overcome personal challenges and achieve success. This notion promotes a **growth mindset** among students, which is the belief that intelligence is not inherent, but rather, can be attained and consistently improved upon. This enhances students' self-esteem and confidence, which promotes positive attitudes toward learning that foster active engagement, productivity, and success. Communicating high expectations while providing necessary supports motivates students to challenge themselves academically and gives them a sense of self-responsibility over their learning that encourages them to work to their highest potential. This ultimately creates a positive classroom climate in which students feel supported and empowered to productively engage in learning and achieve success.

STRATEGIES AND IMPACT ON CLASSROOM CLIMATE AND STUDENT ACHIEVEMENT

Communicating **high academic** and **behavioral expectations** is most effective when done so through a variety of means. This ensures that students are aware of the teacher's expectations of them and consistently reinforces high standards to establish a positive classroom climate focused on student motivation, productivity, and achievement. Expectations must always be **clear** and **visible** in the classroom, and the teacher must frequently remind students by restating them throughout instruction. Establishing learning goals and objectives that are challenging, yet attainable based on students' abilities effectively communicates high expectations and the teacher's belief that students can achieve them. This is further iterated when students encounter challenges and rather than lowering expectations, the teacher maintains the same high standards while providing necessary supports for achievement. The teacher can also communicate high expectations by ensuring they provide students with timely, clear, and constructive **feedback** on their progress and ways in which they can improve to meet them. Frequent **communication with families** is beneficial in reinforcing academic and behavioral expectations at home to ensure student awareness and maximize their effectiveness in the classroom.

LITERACY-RICH ENVIRONMENT

A **literacy-rich** classroom focuses on the development of all literacy components by immersing students in reading, writing, speaking, and listening skills across subject areas. While all students benefit from such an environment, it is especially important for **ELL students** and students with **developmental disabilities** in acquiring the literacy and language skills necessary for success. In a literacy-rich environment, the teacher provides multiple opportunities to engage in teacher-led and student-selected reading, writing, speaking, and listening activities in all areas of instruction. Students may be asked to solve word problems in math, write a report on a famous artist in art, or keep an observation log in science to encourage literacy development across content areas. Students are provided with multiple print and digital literacy materials on a variety of topics with varying levels of complexity to accommodate individual developmental levels while encouraging reading, vocabulary acquisition, and listening skills. Additionally, the teacher surrounds students with **print-rich** materials, including posters, word walls, labels, and bulletin boards on a variety of

104

Copyright © Mometrix Media. You have been licensed one copy of this document for personal use only. Any other reproduction or redistribution is strictly prohibited. All rights reserved. This content is provided for test preparation purposes only and does not imply an endorsement by Mometrix of any particular political, scientific, or religious point of view.

topics to further promote literacy development. A literacy-rich environment continuously promotes and emphasizes the importance of literacy skills in all areas of life that serve as a necessary foundation for academic and real-world success.

Review Video: Importance of Promoting Literacy in the Home
Visit mometrix.com/academy and enter code: 862347

Review Video: Characteristics of Literacy-Rich, Content-Area Classrooms
Visit mometrix.com/academy and enter code: 571455

SAFE, NURTURING, AND INCLUSIVE CLASSROOM ENVIRONMENT

A safe, nurturing, and inclusive classroom environment focuses on meeting students' emotional needs for healthy development in this domain. The overall climate in such an environment is welcoming and emphasizes **respect**, **acceptance**, and **positive communication** among the teacher and students. The classroom is brightly decorated and reflective of students' diversities, interests, and achievements to promote a sense of security and inclusivity that motivates active participation in learning. Instructional activities are also reflective of students' differences, learning styles, and interests, with necessary supports instilled to accommodate individual learning needs. This establishes an **equitable environment** that ensures all students feel respected, nurtured, and supported both academically and emotionally. Such an environment is **structured** and orderly with clear expectations, procedures, and routines to foster a sense of security as students engage in learning. Collaboration and supportive interactions among students are encouraged to create a positive, productive classroom community in which students feel confident to express themselves and participate in learning. A classroom environment that is safe, nurturing, and inclusive develops students' sense of self-concept that contributes to positive communication, relationships, and attitudes necessary for emotional development.

DEVELOPING STUDENTS' EMOTIONAL INTELLIGENCE

Emotional intelligence refers to the ability to recognize and regulate one's own emotions as well as identify and empathetically respond to the emotions of others. Developing this skill through a variety of strategies is integral to successful development across other domains. By **modeling** such skills as empathy and active listening, the teacher can influence students' abilities to identify and properly respond to their own and other's emotions. Teaching **coping strategies**, including journaling, breathing, or counting techniques, promotes students' self-regulation to manage emotions when faced with a conflict or challenge. Teaching emotional intelligence can also be integrated throughout instruction, such as prompting students to describe the feelings of a character in a book, or discuss emotions evoked from a painting. Students with strong emotional intelligence are likely to develop positive interpersonal relationships for healthy social development. This contributes to improved cognitive development in that when students collaborate productively, they build upon one another's knowledge. Emotionally intelligent students are also likely to have positive attitudes toward learning, as they have the capacity to self-regulate when faced with obstacles and properly engage in instruction for enhanced cognitive development.

MEETING AND RESPECTING STUDENTS' EMOTIONAL NEEDS, INDIVIDUAL RIGHTS, AND DIGNITY

Successful learning and whole-child development are reliant on the degree to which students' emotional needs, individual rights, and dignity are met and respected in the classroom. This establishes the tone of the overall classroom climate that determines students' sense of safety,

Copyright © Mometrix Media. You have been licensed one copy of this document for personal use only. Any other reproduction or redistribution is strictly prohibited. All rights reserved. This content is provided for test preparation purposes only and does not imply an endorsement by Mometrix of any particular political, scientific, or religious point of view.

nurturing, and inclusion when interacting with others and engaging in learning. By taking measures to prioritize students' emotional needs and create a respectful, accepting classroom community, the teacher establishes a positive learning atmosphere that promotes cognitive, social, and emotional growth for whole-child development. When students feel emotionally supported and respected in their identities, they develop a healthy sense of self-esteem that positively influences their attitude toward learning and motivation to participate. This ultimately impacts **cognitive development**, as students that actively and confidently engage in learning are more likely to be academically successful. These students are also more effectively able to develop important interpersonal communication skills necessary for healthy **social development**, as students that feel secure and accepted are more likely to be supportive of others. By meeting students' emotional needs and respecting their individual rights and dignities, the teacher effectively prepares students with the skills necessary for academic and real-world success.

Chapter Quiz

Ready to see how well you retained what you just read? Scan the QR code to go directly to the chapter quiz interface for this study guide. If you're using a computer, simply visit the bonus page at **mometrix.com/bonus948/ftceprekinprim** and click the Chapter Quizzes link.

Copyright © Mometrix Media. You have been licensed one copy of this document for personal use only. Any other reproduction or redistribution is strictly prohibited. All rights reserved. This content is provided for test preparation purposes only and does not imply an endorsement by Mometrix of any particular political, scientific, or religious point of view.

Developmentally Appropriate Intervention Strategies and Resources to Meet the Needs of All Students

Transform passive reading into active learning! After immersing yourself in this chapter, put your comprehension to the test by taking a quiz. The insights you gained will stay with you longer this way. Scan the QR code to go directly to the chapter quiz interface for this study guide. If you're using a computer, simply visit the bonus page at **mometrix.com/bonus948/ftceprekinprim** and click the Chapter Quizzes link.

Types of Disabilities and Exceptionalities and their Implications

CAUSES OF INTELLECTUAL DISABILITIES IN BABIES AND YOUNG CHILDREN
INFECTIONS

Congenital cytomegalovirus (CMV) is passed to fetuses from mothers, who may be asymptomatic. About 90% of newborns are also asymptomatic; 5–10% of these have later problems. Of the 10% born with symptoms, 90% will have later neurological abnormalities, including intellectual disabilities. **Congenital rubella**, or German measles, is also passed to fetuses from unvaccinated and exposed mothers, causing neurological damage, including blindness or other eye disorders, deafness, heart defects, and intellectual disabilities. **Congenital toxoplasmosis** is passed to fetuses by infected mothers, who can be asymptomatic, with a parasite from raw or undercooked meat that causes intellectual disabilities, vision or hearing loss, and other conditions. Encephalitis is brain inflammation caused by infection, most often viral. **Meningitis** is inflammation of the meninges, or membranes, covering the brain and is caused by viral or bacterial infection; the bacterial form is more serious. Both encephalitis and meningitis can cause intellectual disabilities. Maternal **human immunodeficiency virus** (HIV) and **acquired immunodeficiency syndrome** (AIDS) can be passed to fetuses, destroying immunity to infections, which can cause intellectual disabilities. **Maternal listeriosis**, a bacterial infection from contaminated food, animals, soil, or water, can cause meningitis and intellectual disabilities in surviving fetuses and infants.

ENVIRONMENTAL, NUTRITIONAL, AND METABOLIC INFLUENCES

Environmental deprivation syndrome results when developing children are deprived of necessary environmental elements—physical, including adequate nourishment (malnutrition); climate or temperature control (extremes of heat or cold); hygiene, like changing and bathing; and so on. It also includes lack of adequate cognitive stimulation, which can stunt a child's intellectual development, and neglect in general. Malnutrition results from starvation; vitamin, mineral, or nutrient deficiency; deficiencies in digesting or absorbing foods; and some other medical conditions. **Environmental radiation**, depending on dosage and time of exposure, can cause intellectual disabilities. **Congenital hypothyroidism** (underactive thyroid) can cause intellectual disabilities, as can hypoglycemia (low blood sugar) from inadequately controlled diabetes or occurring independently and infant **hyperbilirubinemia**. Bilirubin, a waste product of old red blood cells, is found in bile made by the liver and is normally removed by the liver; excessive bilirubin buildup in babies can cause intellectual disabilities. **Reye's syndrome**, caused by aspirin given to children with flu or chicken pox, or following these viruses or other upper respiratory

Copyright © Mometrix Media. You have been licensed one copy of this document for personal use only. Any other reproduction or redistribution is strictly prohibited. All rights reserved.
This content is provided for test preparation purposes only and does not imply an endorsement by Mometrix of any particular political, scientific, or religious point of view.

infections, or from unknown causes, produces sudden liver and brain damage and can result in intellectual disabilities.

GENETIC ABNORMALITIES AND SYNDROMES AFFECTING THE NERVOUS SYSTEM

Rett syndrome is a nervous system disorder causing developmental regression, particularly severe in expressive language and hand function. It is associated with a defective protein gene on an X chromosome. Having two X chromosomes, females with the defect on one of them can survive; with only one X chromosome, males are either miscarried, stillborn, or die early in infancy. Rett syndrome produces many symptoms, including intellectual disabilities.**Tay-Sachs disease**, an autosomal recessive disorder, is a nervous system disease caused by a defective gene on chromosome 15, resulting in a missing protein for breaking down gangliosides, chemicals in nerve tissues that build up in cells, particularly brain neurons, causing damage. Tay-Sachs is more prevalent in Ashkenazi Jews. The adult form is rare; the infantile form is commonest, with nerve damage starting in utero. Many symptoms, including intellectual disabilities, appear at 3 to 6 months, and death occurs by 4 to 5 years. Tuberous sclerosis, caused by genetic mutations, produces tumors damaging the kidneys, heart, skin, brain, and central nervous system. Symptoms include intellectual disabilities, seizures, and developmental delays.

GENETIC OR INHERITED METABOLIC DISORDERS

- **Adrenoleukodystrophy** is an X-linked genetic trait. Some female carriers have mild forms, but it affects more males more seriously. It impairs metabolism of very long-chain fatty acids, which build up in the nervous system (as well as adrenal glands and male testes). The childhood cerebral form, manifesting at ages 4 to 8, causes seizures, visual and hearing impairments, receptive aphasia, dysgraphia, dysphagia, intellectual disabilities, and other effects.
- **Galactosemia** is an inability to process galactose, a simple sugar in lactose, or milk sugar. By-product buildup damages the liver, kidneys, eyes, and brain.
- **Hunter syndrome, Hurler syndrome, and Sanfilippo syndrome** each cause the lack of different enzymes; all cause an inability to process mucopolysaccharides or glycosaminoglycans (long sugar-molecule chains). Hurler and Sanfilippo (but not Hunter) syndromes are autosomal recessive traits, meaning both parents must pass on the defect. All cause progressive intellectual disabilities.
- **Lesch Nyhan syndrome**, affecting males, is a metabolic deficiency in processing purines. It causes hemiplegia, varying degrees of intellectual disabilities, and self-injurious behaviors.
- **Phenylketonuria** (PKU), an autosomal recessive trait, causes lack of the enzyme to process dietary phenylalanine, resulting in intellectual disabilities.

PRESCRIPTION DRUGS, SUBSTANCES OF ABUSE, SOCIAL DRUGS, AND DISEASES

- **Warfarin**, a prescription anticoagulant drug to thin the blood and prevent excessive clotting, can cause microcephaly (undersized head) and intellectual disabilities in an infant when the mother has taken it during pregnancy.
- **Trimethadione**, the prescription antiseizure drug, can cause developmental delays in babies when it has been taken by pregnant mothers.
- **Maternal abuse of solvent chemicals** during pregnancy can also cause microcephaly and intellectual disabilities.
- **Maternal crack cocaine abuse** during pregnancy can cause severe and profound intellectual disabilities and many other developmental defects in fetuses, which become evident when they are newborns.

Copyright © Mometrix Media. You have been licensed one copy of this document for personal use only. Any other reproduction or redistribution is strictly prohibited. All rights reserved. This content is provided for test preparation purposes only and does not imply an endorsement by Mometrix of any particular political, scientific, or religious point of view.

- **Maternal alcohol abuse** can cause fetal alcohol syndrome, which often includes intellectual disabilities, among many other symptoms.
- **Maternal rubella** (German measles) virus can cause intellectual disabilities as well as visual and hearing impairments and heart defects.
- **Maternal herpes simplex virus** can cause microcephaly, intellectual disabilities, and microphthalmia (small or no eyes).
- **The varicella** (chicken pox) **virus** in pregnant mothers can also cause intellectual disabilities as well as muscle atrophy in babies.

CHARACTERISTICS OF INFANTS AND YOUNG CHILDREN WITH INTELLECTUAL DISABILITIES

Newborns with intellectual disabilities, especially of greater severity, may not demonstrate normal reflexes, such as rooting and sucking reflexes, necessary for nursing. They may not show other temporary infant reflexes such as the Moro, Babinski, swimming, stepping, or labyrinthine reflexes, or they may demonstrate weaker versions of some of these. In some babies, these reflexes will exist but persist past the age when they normally disappear. Babies with intellectual disabilities are likely to display developmental milestones at later-than-typical ages. The ages when they do display milestones vary according to the severity of the disability and by individual. Young children with intellectual disabilities are likely to walk, self-feed, and speak later than normally developing children. Those who learn to read and write do so at later ages. Children with mild intellectual disabilities may lack curiosity and have quiet demeanors; those with profound intellectual disabilities are likely to remain infantile in abilities and behaviors throughout life. Intellectually disabled children will score below normal on standardized IQ tests and adaptive behavior rating scales.

POTENTIAL VARIABLES CAUSING LEARNING DISABILITIES

LDs are basically neurological disorders. Though they are more specific to particular areas of learning than global disorders like intellectual disabilities, scientific research has found correlations between LDs and many of the same factors that cause intellectual disabilities, including prenatal influences like excessive alcohol or other drug consumption, diseases, and so on. Once babies are born, glandular disorders, brain injuries, exposure to secondhand smoke or other toxins, infections of the central nervous system, physical trauma, or malnutrition can cause neurological damage resulting in LDs. Hypoxia and anoxia (oxygen loss) before, during, or after birth is a cause, as are radiation and chemotherapy. These same influences often cause behavioral disorders as well as LDs. Another factor is genetic: Both LDs and behavior disorders have been observed to run in families. While research has not yet identified specific genetic factors, heritability does appear to be a component in influencing learning and behavioral disorders.

TYPES OF NEUROLOGICAL DAMAGE FOUND IN CHILDREN WITH LDS AND ADHD

Various neurological research studies have revealed that children diagnosed with LDs and ADHD have at least one of several kinds of structural damage to their brains. Scientists have found smaller numbers of cells in certain important regions of the brains of some children with learning and behavioral disorders. Some of these children are found to have brain cells of smaller than normal size. In some cases, dysplasia is discovered; that is, some brain cells migrate into the wrong area of the brain. In some children with learning and behavioral disorders, blood flow is found to be lower than normal to certain regions in the brain. Also, the brain cells of some children with learning and behavioral disabilities show lower levels of glucose metabolism; glucose (blood sugar) is the brain's main source of fuel, so inadequate utilization of glucose can affect the brain's ability to perform some functions related to cognitive processing, as in LDs, and to attention and impulse control, as in ADHD.

Copyright © Mometrix Media. You have been licensed one copy of this document for personal use only. Any other reproduction or redistribution is strictly prohibited. All rights reserved. This content is provided for test preparation purposes only and does not imply an endorsement by Mometrix of any particular political, scientific, or religious point of view.

Behavioral Variations and Characteristics of ADHD

While the chief symptoms associated with ADHD are inattentiveness, impulsive behavior, distractibility, and excessive physical activity, there is considerable variation among individual children having ADHD. For example, the degree of severity of this condition can vary widely from one child to the next. In addition, each child can vary in how much he or she exhibits each of these primary characteristics. Some children might not appear to behave very impulsively but show severe deficits in attention. Some may focus better, but only for short periods, and are very easily distracted. Some display very disruptive behavior, while others do not but may daydream excessively, not attending to programming. In general, children who have ADHD can show deficits in following rules and directions. Also, when their developmental skills are evaluated or observed, they are likely to demonstrate inconsistencies in performance over time. To identify or select specific intervention methods and strategies, professionals should use a comprehensive evaluation to obtain information about the child's specific behaviors in his or her natural environment that need remediation.

Types and Characteristics of Learning Disabilities

Dyslexia is the most common subcategory of specific learning disability that primarily affects reading but can also interfere with writing and speaking. Characteristics include reversing letters and words, for example, confusing *b* and *d* in reading and writing; reading *won* as *now*, confusing similar speech sounds like /p/ and /b/, and perceiving spaces between words in the wrong places when reading. **Dyscalculia** is difficulty doing mathematical calculations; it can also affect using money and telling time. Dysgraphia means difficulties specifically with writing, including omitting words in writing sentences or leaving sentences unfinished, difficulty putting one's thoughts into writing, and poor handwriting. **Central auditory processing disorder** causes difficulty perceiving small differences in words despite normal hearing acuity; for example, *couch* and *chair* may be perceived as *cow* and *hair*. Background noise and information overloads exacerbate the effects. Visual processing disorders affect visual perception despite normal visual acuity, causing difficulty finding information in printed text or from maps, charts, pictures, graphs, and so on; synthesizing information from various sources into one place; and remembering directions to locations.

Attachment Styles Identified in Toddlers by Mary Ainsworth

Mary Ainsworth worked with **John Bowlby**, discovering the first empirical evidence supporting his attachment theory. From her "strange situation" experiments, she identified secure, insecure and avoidant, insecure and resistant, and insecure and disorganized attachment styles. Securely attached children show normal separation anxiety when their mother leaves and happiness when she returns, avoid strangers when alone but are friendly when their mother is present, and use their mother as a safe base for environmental exploring. Insecure and resistant children show exaggerated separation anxiety, ambivalence, and resistance to their mother upon reuniting, fear strangers, cry more, and explore less than secure or avoidant babies. Insecure and avoidant children show no separation anxiety or stranger anxiety and little interest on reunions with their mother and are comforted equally by their mother or strangers. Insecure and disorganized types seem dazed and confused, respond inconsistently, and may mix resistant and ambivalent and avoidant behaviors. Secure styles are associated with sensitive, responsive caregiving and children's positive self-images and other images, resistant and ambivalent styles with inconsistent caregiving, and avoidant with unresponsive caregivers. Avoidant, resistant, and disorganized styles, associated with negative self-images and low self-esteem, are most predictive of emotional disturbances.

Copyright © Mometrix Media. You have been licensed one copy of this document for personal use only. Any other reproduction or redistribution is strictly prohibited. All rights reserved.
This content is provided for test preparation purposes only and does not imply an endorsement by Mometrix of any particular political, scientific, or religious point of view.

EMOTIONAL DISTURBANCES IN YOUNG CHILDREN CLASSIFIED AS ANXIETY DISORDERS

Anxiety disorders all share a common characteristic of overwhelming, irrational, and unrealistic fears and include:

- **Generalized anxiety disorder** (GAD) involves excessive worrying about anything or everything and free-floating anxiety.
- **Obsessive-compulsive disorder** (OCD) involves obsessive and preoccupied thoughts and compulsive or irresistible actions, including often bizarre rituals. Germ phobia, constant hand washing, repeatedly checking whether tasks are done or undone, and collecting things excessively are common.
- **Posttraumatic stress disorder** (PTSD) follows traumatic experiences/events. Children have frequent, extreme nightmares, crying, flashbacks wherein they vividly perceive or believe they are experiencing the traumatic event again, insomnia, depression, anxiety, and social withdrawal.
- **Panic Disorder** symptoms include panic attacks involving extreme fear and physical symptoms like a racing heart, cold hands and feet, pallor, hyperventilation, and feeling unable to move
- **Social phobia** includes fear and avoidance of day care, preschool, or other social settings
- **Specific phobias** are associated with specific objects, animals, or persons and are often triggered by traumatic experiences involving these

FACTORS CONTRIBUTING TO EMOTIONAL DISTURBANCES

Researchers have investigated **emotional disturbances** but have not yet established known causes for any. Some disturbances, for example, the major mental illness **schizophrenia**, seem to run in families and hence include a genetic component; childhood schizophrenia exists as a specific diagnosis. Factors contributing to emotional disturbances can be biological or environmental but more often are likely a combination of both. Dysfunctional family dynamics can often contribute to emotional disorders in children. Physical and psychological stressors on children can also contribute to the development of emotional problems. Some people have attributed emotional disturbances to diet, and scientists have also researched this but have not discovered proof of cause and effect. **Bipolar disorder** is often successfully treated with the chemical lithium, which affects sodium flow through nerve cells, so chemical imbalance may be implicated as an etiology. Pediatric bipolar disorder, which has different symptoms than adult bipolar disorder, correlates highly with histories of bipolar and other mood disorders or alcoholism in both parents.

SYMPTOMS OF PEDIATRIC BIPOLAR DISORDER

Bipolar disorder, formerly called manic-depressive disorder, has similar depressive symptoms in children as adults. However, children's mood swings often occur much faster, and children show more symptoms of anger and irritability than other adult manic symptoms. Bipolar children's most common symptoms include:

- Frequent mood swings
- Extreme irritability
- Protracted (up to several hours) tantrums or rages
- Separation anxiety
- Oppositional behavior
- Hyperactivity
- Impulsivity, and distractibility
- Restlessness and fidgetiness

Copyright © Mometrix Media. You have been licensed one copy of this document for personal use only. Any other reproduction or redistribution is strictly prohibited. All rights reserved. This content is provided for test preparation purposes only and does not imply an endorsement by Mometrix of any particular political, scientific, or religious point of view.

- Silly, giddy, or goofy behavior
- Aggression
- Racing thoughts
- Grandiose beliefs or behaviors
- Risk-taking
- Depressed moods
- Lethargy
- Low self-esteem
- Social anxiety
- Hypersensitivity to environmental or emotional triggers
- Carbohydrate (sugar or starch) cravings
- Trouble getting up in the morning

Other common symptoms include bed-wetting (especially in boys), night terrors, pressured or fast speech, obsessive or compulsive behaviors, motor and vocal tics, excessive daydreaming, poor short-term memory, poor organization, learning disabilities, morbid fascinations, hypersexuality, bossiness and manipulative behavior, lying, property destruction, paranoia, hallucinations, delusions, and suicidal ideations. Less common symptoms include migraines, bingeing, self-injurious behaviors, and animal cruelty.

CONDUCT DISORDER IN CHILDREN

Factors contributing to conduct disorders in children include genetic predispositions, neurological damage, child abuse, and other traumatic experiences. Children with conduct disorders display characteristic emotional and behavioral patterns. These include aggression: They bully or intimidate others, often start physical fights, will use dangerous objects as weapons, exhibit physical cruelty to animals or humans, and assault and steal from others. Deliberate property destruction is another characteristic—breaking things or setting fires. Young children are limited in some of these activities by their smaller size, lesser strength, and lack of access; however, they show the same types of behaviors against smaller, younger, weaker, or more vulnerable children and animals, along with oppositional and defiant behaviors against adults. Also, while truancy is impossible or unlikely in preschoolers, and running away from home is less likely, young children with conduct disorders are likely to demonstrate some forms of seriously violating rules, another symptom of this disorder.

SYMPTOMS OF CHILDHOOD-ONSET SCHIZOPHRENIA

The incidence of childhood-onset schizophrenia is rare, but it does exist. One example of differential diagnosis involves distinguishing qualitatively between true auditory hallucinations and young children's "hearing voices" otherwise: in the latter case, a child hears his or her own or a familiar adult's voice in his or her head and does not seem upset by it, while in the former, a child may hear other voices, seemingly in his or her ears, and is frightened and confused by them. Tantrums, defiance, aggression, and other acting-out, externalized behaviors are less frequent in childhood-onset schizophrenia than internalized developmental differences, for example, isolation, shyness, awkwardness, fickleness, strange facial expressions, mistrust, paranoia, anxiety, and depression. Children demonstrate nonpsychotic symptoms earlier than psychotic ones. However, it is difficult to use prepsychotic symptoms as predictors due to variance among developmental peculiarities. While psychiatrists find the course of childhood-onset schizophrenia somewhat more variable than in adults, child symptoms resemble adult symptoms. Childhood-onset schizophrenia is typically chronic and severe, responds less to medication, and has a more guarded prognosis than adolescent- or adult-onset schizophrenia.

Copyright © Mometrix Media. You have been licensed one copy of this document for personal use only. Any other reproduction or redistribution is strictly prohibited. All rights reserved.
This content is provided for test preparation purposes only and does not imply an endorsement by Mometrix of any particular political, scientific, or religious point of view.

DIAGNOSING THE EMOTIONAL DISTURBANCES IN CHILDREN CLASSIFIED AS PSYCHOTIC DISORDERS

Psychosis is a general psychiatric category referring to thought disturbances or disorders. The most common symptoms are delusions (believing things that are not true) and hallucinations (seeing, hearing, feeling, tasting, or smelling things that are not there). While early childhood psychosis is rarer than at later ages, psychiatrists confirm it does occur. Moreover, prognosis is poorer for psychosis with onset in early childhood than in adolescence or adulthood. Causes can be from known metabolic or brain disorders or unknown. Younger children are more vulnerable to environmental stressors. Also, in young children, thoughts distorted by fantasy can be from normal cognitive immaturity, due to lack of experience and a larger range of normal functioning, or pathology; where they lie on this continuum must be determined by clinicians. Believing one is a superhero who can fly can be vivid imagination or delusional; having imaginary friends can be pretend play or hallucinatory. Other developmental disorders can also cloud differential diagnosis.

VISUAL IMPAIRMENTS

DEVELOPMENTAL CHARACTERISTICS OF INFANTS AND YOUNG CHILDREN WITH VISUAL IMPAIRMENTS

Historically, it was thought that visually impaired children developed more slowly than normal; however, it is now known that ages for reaching developmental milestones are equally variable in visually impaired babies as in others and that they acquire milestones within equal age ranges. One developmental difference is in sequence: visually impaired children tend to utter their first words or subject-verb two-word sentences earlier than other children. Some visually impaired children also demonstrate higher levels of language development at younger-than-typical ages. For example, they may sing songs from memory or recall events from the past at earlier ages than other children. This is a logical development in children who must rely more on input to their hearing and other senses than to their vision when the latter is impaired. Totally blind babies reach for objects later, hence explore the environment later; hand use, eye-hand coordination, and gross and fine motor skills are delayed. Blind infants' posture control develops normally (rolling, sitting, all-fours, and standing), but mobility (raising on arms, pulling up, and walking) is delayed.

CAUSES OF VISUAL IMPAIRMENTS IN BABIES AND YOUNG CHILDREN

Syndrome-related and other malformations like cleft iris or lens dislocation causing visual impairment can have prenatal origins. Cataracts clouding the eye's lens can be congenital, traumatic, or due to maternal rubella. Eyes can be normal, but impairment in the brain's visual cortex can cause visual impairment. Infantile glaucoma, like adult glaucoma, causes intraocular fluid buildup pressure and visual impairment. Conjunctivitis and other infections cause visual impairment. Strabismus and nystagmus are ocular-muscle conditions, respectively causing eye misalignments and involuntary eye movements. Trauma damaging the eyeball(s) is another visual impairment cause. The optic nerve can suffer from atrophy (dysfunction) or hypoplasia, that is, developmental regression, usually prenatally due to neurological trauma; acuity cannot be corrected. Refractive errors like nearsightedness, farsightedness, and astigmatism are correctable. Retinoblastoma, or behind-the-eye tumors, can cause blindness and fatality; surgical or chemotherapeutic treatment is usually required before age 2. Premature infants can have retinopathy of prematurity or retrolental fibroplasia. Cryotherapeutic treatment seems to stop disease progression. Its effects range from none to severe visual impairment (approximately 25% of children) to complete blindness.

Copyright © Mometrix Media. You have been licensed one copy of this document for personal use only. Any other reproduction or redistribution is strictly prohibited. All rights reserved.
This content is provided for test preparation purposes only and does not imply an endorsement by Mometrix of any particular political, scientific, or religious point of view.

IMPACTS OF BLINDNESS UPON COGNITIVE DEVELOPMENT

Blind children have more difficulty determining and confirming characteristics of things, hence defining concepts and organizing them into more abstract levels; their problem-solving is active but harder, and they construct different realities than sighted children. Blind babies typically acquire object permanence (the understanding that unseen objects still exist) a year later than normal; they learn to reach for objects only by hearing. Understanding cause-and-effect relationships is difficult without visual evidence. Blind babies and toddlers take longer to understand an object's constancy regardless of their orientation in space, affecting their ability to orient toys and their own hands. Blind children can identify object size differences and similarities, but classifying object differences and similarities in other attributes requires longer times and more exposures to various similar objects. Blind children's development of the abilities to conserve object properties like material or substance, weight, amount and volume, length, and liquid volume is later than normal.

EFFECTS OF BLINDNESS ON EMOTIONAL AND SOCIAL DEVELOPMENT

Blind babies and children are more dependent than others on adults, affecting development. With control of their inner realities but not of their outer environments, blind children may withdraw, seeking and responding less to social interaction. They may not readily develop concepts of the external world or self-concepts as beings separate from the world and the understanding that they can be both agents and recipients of actions relative to the environment. Mother-infant smiling initiates recognition, attachment, and communication in sighted babies; blind infants smile on hearing mother's voice at 2 months. Only tactile stimuli like tickling and nuzzling evoke regular smiling in blind babies. Missing facial expressions and other visual cues, blind children have more complicated social interactions. They often do not understand the basics of playing with others and seem emotionally ambivalent or uninterested and uncommunicative. Peers may reject or avoid them; adults often overprotect them. Self-help skills like chewing, scooping, self-feeding, teeth brushing, grooming, and toilet training are delayed in blind children.

HEARING IMPAIRMENTS

PREVALENCE AND ETIOLOGIES OF HEARING IMPAIRMENTS

Half or more (50% to 60%) of infant hearing losses have genetic origins—Down and other genetically based syndromes or the existence of parental hearing loss. About 25% or more of infant hearing losses are caused by maternal infections during pregnancy, such as cytomegalovirus (CMV), postnatal complications like blood transfusions or infection with meningitis, or traumatic head injuries. Included in this 25% or more are babies having nongenetic neurological disorders or conditions that affect their hearing. Malformations of the ears, head, or face can cause hearing loss in babies. Babies spending five days or longer in neonatal intensive care units (NICUs) or having complications while in the NICU are also more likely to suffer hearing loss. Around 25% of babies are diagnosed with hearing loss whose etiology is unknown.

SIGNS OF HEARING IMPAIRMENTS

If an infant does not display a startle response to loud noises, this is a potential sign of hearing loss. This can also indicate other developmental disabilities, but because hearing loss is the most prevalent disability among newborns, hearing screening is a priority. Between birth and 3 or 4 months old, babies should turn toward the source of a sound; if they do not, it could indicate hearing loss. A child who does not utter first words like *mama* or *dada* by age 1 could have hearing impairment. When babies or young children do not turn their heads when their names are called, adults may mistake this for inattention or ignoring; however, children turning upon seeing adults, but not upon hearing their names, can indicate hearing loss. Babies and children who seem to hear certain sounds but not others may have partial hearing losses. Delayed speech-language

Copyright © Mometrix Media. You have been licensed one copy of this document for personal use only. Any other reproduction or redistribution is strictly prohibited. All rights reserved. This content is provided for test preparation purposes only and does not imply an endorsement by Mometrix of any particular political, scientific, or religious point of view.

development or unclear speech, not following directions, saying "Huh?" often, and wanting higher TV or music volumes can indicate hearing loss in children.

SPEECH AND LANGUAGE IMPAIRMENTS
FACTORS CONTRIBUTING TO SPEECH AND LANGUAGE IMPAIRMENTS

Some speech and language disorders in children have unknown causes. Others have known causes such as hearing loss: speech and language are normally acquired primarily through the auditory sense, so children with impaired hearing have delayed and impaired development of speech and language. Brain injuries, neurological disorders, viral diseases, and some medications can also cause problems with developing language or speech. Children with intellectual disabilities are more likely to have delayed language development, and their speech is also more likely to develop more slowly and to be distorted. Cerebral palsy causes neuromuscular weakness and incoordination of speech. When severe, it can cause the inability to produce recognizable speech sounds; some children without speech can still vocalize, and some cannot. A cleft palate or lip and other physical impairments affect speech. Inadequate speech-language modeling at home inhibits speech-language development. Vocal abuse in children (screaming, coughing, throat clearing, or excessive talking) can cause vocal nodules or polyps, causing voice disorders. Stuttering can be related to maturation, anxiety or stress, auditory feedback defects, or unknown causes.

CHARACTERISTICS

In speech, most phonological disorders are articulatory; that is, children fail to pronounce specific speech sounds or phonemes correctly beyond the normal developmental age for achieving accuracy. Stuttering, disfluency, and rate and rhythm disorders cause children to repeat phonemes, especially initial word sounds; to repeat words; to prolong vowels or consonants; or to block, straining so hard to produce a sound that, pressure builds, but no sound issues. Their speech rates may also increase and decrease irregularly. Children with voice disorders can have voices that sound hoarse, raspy, overly nasal, higher- or lower-pitched than normal, overly weak or strident, and whispery or harsh. Hoarseness is common with vocal nodules and polyps. Cleft palate commonly causes hypernasality. In language, one of the most common impairments is delayed language development due to environmental deprivation, intellectual disabilities, neurological damage or defects, hearing loss, visual impairment, and so on. Children with neurological damage or disorders may exhibit aphasias, language disorders characterized by receptive difficulty with understanding spoken or written language, or expressive difficulty constructing spoken or written language.

PHYSICAL AND HEALTH IMPAIRMENTS
EXAMPLES OF PHYSICAL AND HEALTH IMPAIRMENTS

In the special education field of early childhood education, "other health impairment" is a term referring to health and physical conditions that rob a child of strength, vitality, or alertness or that cause excessive alertness to environmental stimuli, all having the end result of impeding the child's ability to attend or respond to the educational environment. Health problems can be acute(short-term or temporary but serious) or chronic (long-term, persistent, or recurrent). Some examples of such health and physical impairments include cerebral palsy, spina bifida, amputations or missing limbs, muscular dystrophy, cystic fibrosis, asthma, rheumatic fever, sickle-cell anemia, nephritis or kidney disease, leukemia, Tourette syndrome, hemophilia, diabetes, heart disease, AIDS, and lead poisoning. All these conditions and others can interfere with a child's development and ability to attend and learn. In addition to seizure disorders, which often cause neurological damage, seizure-controlling medications also frequently cause drowsiness, interfering with attention and cognition. Attention deficit and attention deficit hyperactivity disorders (ADD and ADHD) limit attention span,

Copyright © Mometrix Media. You have been licensed one copy of this document for personal use only. Any other reproduction or redistribution is strictly prohibited. All rights reserved. This content is provided for test preparation purposes only and does not imply an endorsement by Mometrix of any particular political, scientific, or religious point of view.

focus, and concentration and thus are sometimes classified as health impairments requiring special education services.

CHARACTERISTICS OF BABIES AND CHILDREN WITH PHYSICAL AND HEALTH IMPAIRMENTS

The characteristics of children having various physical or health impairments can range from having no limitations to severe limitations in their activities. Children with cerebral palsy, for example, usually have deficiencies in gross and fine motor development and deficits in speech-language development. Physical and health conditions causing severe debilitation in some children not only seriously limit their daily activities but also cause multiple primary disabilities and impair their intellectual functioning. Other children with physical or health impairments function at average, above-average, or gifted intellectual and academic levels. An important consideration when working with babies and young children having physical or health impairments is handling and positioning them physically. Correctly picking up, holding, carrying, giving assistance, and physically supporting younger children and arranging play materials for them based on their impairment is not only important for preventing injury, pain, and discomfort; it also enables them to receive instruction better and to manipulate materials and perform most efficiently. Preschoolers with physical impairments also tend to have difficulty with communication skills, so educators should give particular attention to facilitating and developing these.

DEVELOPMENTAL DELAYS
FACTORS LEADING TO DEVELOPMENTAL DELAYS

Developmental delays can come from genetic or environmental causes or both. Infants and young children with intellectual disabilities are most likely to exhibit developmental delays. Their development generally proceeds similarly to that of normal children but at slower rates; milestones are manifested at later-than-typical ages. Sensory impairments such as with hearing and vision can also delay many aspects of children's development. Children with physical and health impairments are likely to exhibit delays in their motor development and performance of physical activities. Another factor is environmental: children deprived of adequate environmental stimulation commonly show delays in cognitive, speech-language, and emotional and social development. Children with autism spectrum disorders often have markedly delayed language and speech development; many are nonverbal. Autistic children also typically have impaired social development, caused by an inability or difficulty with understanding others' emotional and social nonverbal communications. When they cannot interpret these, they do not know how to respond and also cannot imitate them; however, they can often learn these skills with special instruction.

CHARACTERISTICS INDICATING DEVELOPMENTAL DELAYS

Developmental delays mean that a child does not reach developmental milestones at the expected ages. For example, if most babies normally learn to walk between 12 and 15 months of age, a 20-month-old who is not beginning to walk is considered as having a developmental delay. Delays can occur in cognitive, speech-language, social-emotional, gross motor skill, or fine motor skill development. Signs of delayed motor development include stiff or rigid limbs, floppy or limp body posture for the child's age, using one side of the body more than the other, and clumsiness unusual for the child's age. Behavioral signs of children's developmental delays include inattention or shorter-than-normal attention span for the age, avoiding or infrequent eye contact, focusing on unusual objects for long times or preferring objects over social interaction, excessive frustration when attempting tasks normally simple for children their age, unusual stubbornness; aggressive and acting-out behaviors; daily violent behaviors, rocking, excessive talking to oneself, and not soliciting love or approval from parents.

Copyright © Mometrix Media. You have been licensed one copy of this document for personal use only. Any other reproduction or redistribution is strictly prohibited. All rights reserved. This content is provided for test preparation purposes only and does not imply an endorsement by Mometrix of any particular political, scientific, or religious point of view.

Traumatic Brain Injury (TBI)
IDEA's Legal Definition of Traumatic Brain Injury

TBI is defined by the **IDEA law** (the Individuals with Disabilities Education Act) as "an acquired injury to the brain from external physical force, resulting in total or partial functional disability or psychosocial impairment, or both, that adversely affect a child's educational performance." This definition excludes injuries from birth trauma, congenital injuries, and degenerative conditions. TBI is the foremost cause of death and disability in children (and teens) in the USA. The most common causes of TBI in children include falls, motor vehicle accidents, and physical abuse. In spite of the IDEA's definition, aneurysms and strokes are three examples of internal traumas that can also cause TBI in babies and young children. External head injuries that can result in TBI include both open and closed head injuries. Shaken baby syndrome is caused by forcibly shaking an infant. This causes the brain literally to bounce against the insides of the skull, causing rebound injuries, resulting in TBI and even death.

> **Review Video: Medical Conditions in Education**
> Visit mometrix.com/academy and enter code: 531058

Characteristics

TBI can impair a child's cognitive development and processing. It can impede the language development of children, which is dependent upon cognitive development. Children who have sustained TBI often have difficulties with attention, retention, and memory; reasoning, judgment, understanding abstract concepts, and thinking abstractly; and problem-solving abilities. TBIs can also impair a child's motor functions and physical abilities. The sensory and perceptual functions of children with TBI can be abnormal. Their ability to process information is often compromised. Their speech can also be affected. In addition, TBIs can impair a child's psychosocial behaviors. Memory deficits are commonest, tend to be more long-lasting, and are often area-specific; for example, a child may recall personal experiences but not factual information. Other common characteristics of TBI include cognitive inflexibility or rigidity, damaged conceptualization and reasoning, language loss or poor verbal fluency, problems with paying attention and concentrating, inadequate problem solving, and problems with reading and writing.

Etiologies and Characteristics of Multiple Disabilities

The term **multiple disabilities** refers to any combination of more than one disabling condition. For example, a child may be both blind and deaf due to causes such as having rheumatic fever in infancy or early childhood. Anything causing neurological damage before, during, or shortly after birth can result in multiple disabilities, particularly if it is widespread rather than localized. For example, infants deprived of oxygen or suffering traumatic brain injuries in utero, during labor or delivery, or postnatally can sustain severe brain damage. So can babies having encephalitis or meningitis and those whose mothers abused drugs prenatally. Infants with this type of extensive damage can often present with multiple disabilities, including intellectual disabilities, cerebral palsy, physical paralysis, mobility impairment, visual impairment, hearing impairment, and speech-language disorders. They may have any combination of or all of these disabilities as well as others. In addition to a difficulty or inability with normal physical performance, multiple disabled children often have difficulty acquiring and retaining cognitive skills and transferring or generalizing skills among settings and situations.

Prematurity or Preterm Birth

Babies born before 37 weeks' gestation are classified as **premature** or **preterm**. Premature infants can have difficulty with breathing, as their lungs are not fully developed, and with regulating their

117

Copyright © Mometrix Media. You have been licensed one copy of this document for personal use only. Any other reproduction or redistribution is strictly prohibited. All rights reserved. This content is provided for test preparation purposes only and does not imply an endorsement by Mometrix of any particular political, scientific, or religious point of view.

body temperatures. Premature infants may be born with pneumonia, respiratory distress, extra air or bleeding in the lungs, jaundice, sepsis or infection, hypoglycemia (low blood sugar), severe intestinal inflammation, bleeding into the brain or white-matter brain damage, or anemia. They have lower-than-normal birth weights, body fat, muscle tone, and activity. Additional typical characteristics of premature infants include apnea (interrupted breathing); lanugo (a coating of body hair that full-term infants no longer have); thin, smooth, shiny, translucent skin through which veins are visible; soft, flexible ear cartilage; cryptorchidism (undescended testicles) and small, non-ridged scrotums in males; enlarged clitorises in females; and feeding difficulties caused by weak or defective sucking reflexes or incoordination of swallowing with breathing.

DISABLING CONDITIONS RESULTING FROM PREMATURE BIRTHS

Physicians find it impossible to predict the long-term results of prematurity for any individual baby based on an infant's gestational age and birth weight. However, some related immediate and long-term effects can be identified. Generally, the lower the birth weight and the more prematurely a child is born, the greater the risk is for complications. Infants born at less than 34 weeks of gestation typically cannot coordinate their sucking and swallowing and may temporarily need feeding or breathing tubes or oxygen. They also need special nursery care until able to maintain their body temperatures and weights. Long-term complications of prematurity can include bronchopulmonary dysplasia, a chronic lung condition; delayed physical growth and development; delayed cognitive development; mental or physical delays or disabilities; and blindness, vision loss, or retinopathy of prematurity (formerly called retrolental fibroplasia). While some premature infants sustain long-term disabilities, some severe, other babies born prematurely grow up to show no effects at all; any results within this range can also occur.

Diverse Student Populations

UNDERSTANDING STUDENTS' DIVERSE BACKGROUNDS AND NEEDS
SELF-EDUCATION

Educating oneself on students' diverse backgrounds and needs enhances one's overall understanding of their students and creates a culturally sensitive, accepting classroom environment tailored to students' individual needs. There are several avenues through which teachers should educate themselves in an effort to build an accepting and respectful classroom climate. Communication is key for learning about diversities; thus, it is important for teachers to foster and maintain positive communications with students' families to deepen understanding of cultures, beliefs, lifestyles, and needs that exist within their classroom. This could include learning some language of students with different cultural backgrounds, attending family nights at school, or participating in social events within their students' communities to integrate themselves into the culture. Furthermore, teachers can learn more about their students' backgrounds and needs through gaining an understanding of student differences, incorporating these diversities into the curriculum, and encouraging students to participate in learning by sharing aspects of their lives with the class.

TEACHING, LEARNING, AND CLASSROOM CLIMATE BENEFITS

A deep understanding of students' diverse backgrounds and needs provides multiple benefits for teaching, learning, and overall classroom climate. Knowledge of students' diversities allows teachers to understand the individual needs and abilities of their students, and tailor instruction accordingly to maximize student development and achievement. Additionally, it allows teachers to know which authentic materials to incorporate in lessons and instructions to best create an engaging, relevant, and respectful learning experience that fosters student interest in learning and

Copyright © Mometrix Media. You have been licensed one copy of this document for personal use only. Any other reproduction or redistribution is strictly prohibited. All rights reserved.
This content is provided for test preparation purposes only and does not imply an endorsement by Mometrix of any particular political, scientific, or religious point of view.

promotes success. Furthermore, by enhancing understanding of students' diverse backgrounds and needs, teachers consequently begin to model an attitude of inclusivity, acceptance, and respect for differences, which is then reflected by students and achieves a positive, welcoming classroom climate that promotes diversity.

IMPLICATIONS FOR TEACHING, LEARNING, AND ASSESSMENT IN DIVERSE CLASSROOMS

In any classroom, a teacher will encounter a wide range of variances among individual students that inevitably will influence teaching, learning, and assessment. Diversities in ethnicity, gender, language background, and learning exceptionality will likely exist simultaneously in a single classroom. Educators must be prepared to teach to these diversities while concurrently teaching students the value and importance of diversity. The curriculum and classroom environment must be adjusted to meet individual student needs and create an **inclusive**, **respectful**, and **equitable** environment that welcomes differences and allows for success in learning. This begins with the teacher developing an understanding of the unique diversities that exist within their students and using this knowledge to **differentiate** curriculum, materials, activities, and assessments in such a way that students of all needs, interests, backgrounds, and abilities feel encouraged and included. Furthermore, the teacher must understand how to instill appropriate supports to accommodate the diverse needs of students, as well as how to modify the classroom environment in such a way that is reflective of the diversity of the students.

CONSIDERATIONS FOR TEACHING IN DIVERSE CLASSROOMS

ETHNICALLY-DIVERSE CLASSROOMS

As society becomes increasingly diverse, teachers will certainly encounter classrooms with students of multiple ethnicities. Thus, to create an accepting and respectful classroom environment that allows for success in learning for all students, there are several factors to consider. Teachers must educate themselves on the various ethnicities within their classroom. This includes being mindful of **social norms, values, beliefs, traditions,** and **lifestyles** of different ethnic groups, and learning to communicate with students and families in a respectful, culturally sensitive manner. Additionally, the teacher must make a conscious effort to incorporate aspects of each ethnicity into the curriculum, activities, and classroom environment to create an inclusive atmosphere that teaches the acceptance, respect for, and celebration of differences. Teachers must be **culturally competent** and ensure that all materials are accurate, relevant, authentic, and portray the different ethnicities within the classroom in a respectful, unbiased manner. Furthermore, teachers must consider how their own ethnicity impacts their teaching style and interactions with students, how they may be perceived by other ethnic groups, and how to respond in a manner that fosters respect and inclusivity.

GENDER-DIVERSE CLASSROOMS

When approaching a gender-diverse classroom, teachers need to consider their perceptions, interactions with, and expectations of different genders, as well as how the classroom environment and materials portray gender differences. Teachers must work to eliminate possible stereotypical beliefs so all students feel respected, accepted, and encouraged to participate. Furthermore, teachers must consider how their behavior acts as a model for how students perceive gender roles and should act in a way that eliminates gender divisiveness. Teachers should use gender-neutral language when addressing students and ensure that all students receive equal attention. Teachers must maintain equal academic and behavioral expectations between genders and be sure to equally praise and discipline students so that neither gender feels superior or inferior to another. Regarding curriculum and classroom materials, teachers must ensure that the classroom environment encourages equal participation in, access to, and choice of all activities and procedures. Activities and materials should provide equal opportunities and foster collaboration

Copyright © Mometrix Media. You have been licensed one copy of this document for personal use only. Any other reproduction or redistribution is strictly prohibited. All rights reserved. This content is provided for test preparation purposes only and does not imply an endorsement by Mometrix of any particular political, scientific, or religious point of view.

between genders. Furthermore, teachers must ensure that curriculum materials avoid gender stereotypes, and highlight each gender equally in order to create an accepting and respectful learning environment that provides equal opportunities for students of all genders to develop their individual identities and abilities.

LINGUISTICALLY DIVERSE CLASSROOMS

In a **linguistically diverse** classroom, teachers must consider how to effectively demonstrate value for students' native languages while simultaneously supporting the development of necessary language skills to thrive in the school setting. By accepting and encouraging students to use their native languages, teachers can establish an inclusive learning environment that celebrates linguistic differences, and therefore, encourages students to want to build upon their language skills. Through this, teachers create an equitable learning environment that allows for academic success. To develop English language skills, the teacher must first consider each students' language ability and level of exposure to English prior to entering the classroom, as well as the level of language learning support each student has at home. Teachers can then implement effective instructional strategies and supports to modify curriculum in a way that addresses students' language needs. Teachers must also consider the implications of the classroom environment on language acquisition. By creating an atmosphere that encourages language acquisition through **literacy-rich resources** and **cooperative learning**, teachers promote the use of language skills and ultimately provide opportunities for success for all students.

LINGUISTIC SUPPORTS AND INSTRUCTIONAL STRATEGIES PROMOTING ENGLISH LANGUAGE PROFICIENCY

Incorporating a variety of linguistic aids and instructional strategies is beneficial in supporting ELL students of varying levels of English language proficiency. **Visual representations** to accompany instruction, such as posters, charts, pictures, slide shows, videos, tables, or anchor charts, are valuable in providing clarification and reference while promoting vocabulary acquisition. When delivering instruction, **body language** such as hand gestures, eye contact, and movement to mimic verbal directions and explanations can provide clarification to enhance understanding. These students may also require **translation devices** for clarification, an interpreter to help with understanding instructions and new concepts, alternate assignments with simplified language, or **individualized instruction** from an ESL teacher. Frequently checking for understanding and providing clarification as necessary throughout instruction are necessary to ensuring ELL students understand learning materials, instructions, and assessments. In addition, creating a print and literacy-rich environment by including word walls for new vocabulary, reading materials that vary in complexity, labels, and opportunities for speaking, reading, and writing within instruction are valuable in promoting English language acquisition.

LEARNING DISABILITIES AND OTHER EXCEPTIONALITIES

In a classroom where learning disabilities and exceptionalities are present, teachers must consider accommodations for students of various learning needs while fostering an atmosphere of respect and acceptance. Teachers must understand the individual learning needs of each student and differentiate instruction accordingly to create an equitable and inclusive learning atmosphere. For **learning disabled** students, teachers must consider accommodations that allow for inclusion in all areas of curriculum and instruction. Such considerations may include extended work time, individualized instruction, and cooperative learning activities to ensure that learning disabled students are provided the necessary supports to achieve academic success. For students with other exceptionalities, such as **gifted and talented** students, teachers need to consider ways to provide challenging and stimulating opportunities for expansion and enrichment of curriculum. Furthermore, the teacher must be aware of their own interactions with students in order to

Copyright © Mometrix Media. You have been licensed one copy of this document for personal use only. Any other reproduction or redistribution is strictly prohibited. All rights reserved. This content is provided for test preparation purposes only and does not imply an endorsement by Mometrix of any particular political, scientific, or religious point of view.

demonstrate and encourage respect and acceptance among students. By providing supports for individual student success, teachers can effectively highlight students' strengths and therefore, teach students to accept and celebrate differences in learning abilities.

Educating Students about Diversity

GOALS OF TEACHING DIVERSITY IN THE CLASSROOM

Teaching diversity in the classroom aims to establish a welcoming and inclusive classroom environment that encourages academic achievement and whole-child development. Diversity education works to develop students' understanding, acceptance, and respect for others' perspectives while instilling the concept that people are ultimately more alike than different, and that diversities should be celebrated. Teaching the importance of differences creates a positive, inclusive classroom atmosphere in which all students feel respected, safe, and valued by their teacher and peers. Such an environment promotes academic achievement among students in that it encourages participation in learning and builds the self-esteem necessary for positive growth and development. Furthermore, teaching diversity has a significant role in **whole-child development** in that it instills the ability to understand and respect multiple frames of reference, thus increasing their ability to problem solve, cooperate with others, and develop a broader global perspective. Additionally, it allows for the development of cultural competency and ultimately creates accepting and respectful contributors to society.

> **Review Video: Multiculturalism/Celebrating All Cultures**
> Visit mometrix.com/academy and enter code: 708545

RECOGNIZING AND ELIMINATING PERSONAL BIASES

Personal biases are often subtle and unconscious, yet it is essential that teachers work to recognize and eliminate them to create an accepting and respectful classroom environment. Personal biases may negatively impact teaching style, interactions with students, and ultimately, student learning and self-esteem. In eliminating personal bias, teachers ensure that they establish an inclusive classroom environment where each student is treated fairly. Furthermore, students' beliefs toward diversity are influenced by the attitudes and behaviors modeled by their teacher, and therefore, eradicating personal bias is vital in positively influencing students to accept and respect differences. To eliminate personal bias, teachers must **reflect** on their own culture's attitudes toward diversity, as well as how these attitudes influence their interactions toward other groups, and work to make positive changes. Teachers must **educate** themselves on the diversities among their students and work to deepen their understanding of different groups through **communicating** with families, **integrating** themselves into students' communities, and participating in **professional development** that focuses on **cultural competency** and the importance of teaching diversity. Through making positive changes against personal biases, teachers foster a classroom environment that promotes diversity and empowers all students to be successful.

IMPACT OF DIVERSE CULTURAL CLIMATE IN THE CLASSROOM

Creating a diverse cultural climate in the classroom results in an empowering and engaging learning environment that facilitates academic success. An atmosphere that respects and accepts differences fosters a sense of inclusivity and welcoming among teachers and students, which allows students to feel comfortable with differences, safe in their own identities, and consequently, comfortable to engage in learning. This fosters a positive attitude toward learning that promotes academic achievement. Additionally, when students accept one another's differences in a diverse

121

Copyright © Mometrix Media. You have been licensed one copy of this document for personal use only. Any other reproduction or redistribution is strictly prohibited. All rights reserved. This content is provided for test preparation purposes only and does not imply an endorsement by Mometrix of any particular political, scientific, or religious point of view.

cultural climate, they are better able to work together and adopt creative problem-solving solutions through others' perspectives, which results in success in learning. Furthermore, a successfully diverse cultural climate reflects the diversity of the students within it, which ultimately creates a more engaging and relevant academic environment that sparks motivation and curiosity toward learning. Learning environments that reflect students' diversity create a sense of unity and belonging in the classroom and positively contribute to success in learning through building students' self-esteem and self-concept to empower them in believing they can achieve academic success.

Authentic Classroom Materials

Authentic classroom materials are artifacts from various cultures, events, or periods of time. These items enhance the relevancy of instruction by promoting students' real-world connection to learning and may also be used to incorporate students' backgrounds and experiences into the classroom to increase engagement. Such materials include magazines, newspapers, advertisements, restaurant menus, and recipes. In addition, resources such as video clips, films, television shows, documentaries, news segments, and music serve as authentic media sources to incorporate into instruction. Original works or documents, including art pieces, literature, poetry, maps, or historical records, are also valuable authentic resources for providing students with a real-world learning experience.

Locating and Implementing

Authentic classroom materials and resources are integral in creating a classroom environment that fosters engaging, relevant, and positive learning experiences. Teachers must work to develop an understanding of the diversities among their students and use this knowledge to locate and implement authentic classroom materials into daily instruction. In doing so, teachers create a positive learning environment that accepts and respects differences through incorporating **relevant** and **familiar** materials that make students from all backgrounds feel valued and included in instruction. When students can see aspects of their culture reflected in authentic learning materials, they can make **personal connections** between what they are learning and their own lives, and learning becomes more valuable, engaging, and relevant, thereby promoting success in learning.

Incorporating Diversity Education into the Classroom

Incorporating diversity into the classroom maximizes student opportunities for academic success through creating a welcoming, empowering, and inclusive atmosphere. Teachers can implement multiple strategies to incorporate **diversity education** into the curriculum both as its own unit and woven into content instruction once they develop an understanding of the diversities among their own students. Through **building relationships** with students, teachers can use their knowledge of students' lives to incorporate aspects of their backgrounds into the curriculum by creating specific **cultural lessons** on food, music, language, art, and history. Additionally, **cultural comparison** studies are an effective method of teaching students the value of diversity, as well as highlighting the fact that people from different backgrounds often have more similarities than differences. Teachers can further implement diversity education by encouraging students to participate in learning through having them share elements of their culture and background with the class through activities such as show and tell or hosting family nights. Furthermore, integrating **cooperative learning** activities into instruction allow and encourage students from different backgrounds to work together and gain an understanding of the perspectives and backgrounds of others.

Copyright © Mometrix Media. You have been licensed one copy of this document for personal use only. Any other reproduction or redistribution is strictly prohibited. All rights reserved. This content is provided for test preparation purposes only and does not imply an endorsement by Mometrix of any particular political, scientific, or religious point of view.

INCORPORATING DIVERSITY IN THE CURRICULUM

Incorporating diversity into the curriculum is vital for teaching the value and importance of differences and for contributing to a respectful and accepting environment. Additionally, it is imperative that diversity education extend from the curriculum to the entire classroom environment to maximize student growth and opportunity to reach potential. When students learn in an atmosphere that celebrates diversity and identifies strengths in differences, they feel a sense of belonging and confidence that encourages them to engage in learning, thus maximizing the potential for academic success. Teachers can effectively integrate diversity into the classroom environment through making authentic cultural materials such as texts, music, and art readily accessible for students. Additionally, providing several opportunities for students to collaborate and socialize in a natural setting allows them to gain an understanding and respect for their peers' backgrounds. By encouraging students to share aspects of their own lives and backgrounds with the class through cultural activities, teachers facilitate a diverse climate that celebrates differences.

CULTURALLY RESPONSIVE TEACHING

Culturally responsive teaching is an instructional approach in which the teacher practices awareness, inclusivity, and sensitivity regarding the social and cultural diversities that are present within the classroom. With this awareness in mind, the culturally responsive teacher designs curriculum, instruction, activities, and assessments that are inclusive and reflective of students' social and cultural backgrounds and experiences. When planning instruction and learning experiences, the teacher can demonstrate awareness of social and cultural norms through consciously educating themselves on the beliefs, values, and norms of their students. This is achieved through connecting with students and building positive relationships to learn about their individual backgrounds and locate authentic learning materials that are reflective of their experiences. Through communicating with students' parents, family members, and members of the community, the teacher can practice and build awareness of the diverse social and cultural norms of their students to gain an understanding of how to design culturally responsive instruction. By educating themselves on the social and cultural norms of their students, the teacher can effectively ensure that students' diversities are reflected in all areas of instruction in a culturally sensitive manner to create an empowering learning environment that engages all students.

	Practices for Culturally Responsive Teaching
1	Create an inclusive classroom environment
2	Recognize personal biases and work to eliminate them
3	Self-educate on the community and students' social and cultural backgrounds
4	Use curriculum that reflects students' diversities using authentic materials
5	Frequently communicate with students' families
6	Build positive interpersonal relationships with students
7	Be involved in the community

Supporting Students with Varied Learning Needs

PLANNING AND ADAPTING LESSONS TO ADDRESS STUDENTS' NEEDS
VARIED BACKGROUNDS

Effectively planning lessons and adapting instruction to address students' varied backgrounds requires teachers to gain an understanding of individual students, and educate themselves on **customs, norms**, and **values** of the cultures in their classroom. This allows teachers to effectively

Copyright © Mometrix Media. You have been licensed one copy of this document for personal use only. Any other reproduction or redistribution is strictly prohibited. All rights reserved.
This content is provided for test preparation purposes only and does not imply an endorsement by Mometrix of any particular political, scientific, or religious point of view.

plan **culturally responsive** lessons with **authentic materials** to make learning valuable, interesting, relevant, and allow students to feel included. Understanding students' backgrounds means teachers recognize variances in their knowledge and experiences on different topics and can effectively plan engaging and inclusive lessons that build upon it. Teachers must assess students' knowledge on material prior to creating lessons to effectively plan instruction that adapts to the needs of students' varied backgrounds and reflects students' experiences. Teachers must plan lesson materials such as texts, art, music, and language that accurately and sensitively reflect students' diverse backgrounds. Cooperative learning strategies should be incorporated to facilitate communication among students with varying backgrounds, as it helps them build knowledge from others' experiences, as well as teaches them to respect and value differences among their peers. Teachers must plan instruction that communicates high academic expectations for all students and adapt instruction as necessary by implementing supports to create equity and address the needs of varying backgrounds.

> **Review Video: <u>Adapting and Modifying Lessons or Activities</u>**
> Visit mometrix.com/academy and enter code: 834946

DIFFERENCES IN INDIVIDUAL STUDENTS' SKILLS

Teachers must use their knowledge of differences in students' skills to plan multifaceted, adaptable lessons that highlight students' strengths while providing instructional supports where needed based on individual skill level. To effectively plan, teachers must incorporate multiple strategies and mediums for instruction, activities, and assessments to allow students of all skill levels equitable and enriching access to content material. This includes allowing multiple opportunities for **student choice** in learning and demonstration of understanding through such strategies as choice boards, learning centers, project menus, and digital resources that allow students to approach content in multiple ways. In doing so, teachers effectively plan instruction that allows students to grasp new material and demonstrate learning in a way that best suits their skill level. Additionally, teachers must plan to incorporate **scaffolds** into their lessons and plan to adapt instruction as needed through continuous **formative assessments** to provide additional support for students of lower skill levels, while adding opportunities for enrichment and acceleration for gifted students. Supports can also be effectively planned into lessons through providing several opportunities for small-group activities in which students of various skill levels can work together, provide peer tutoring, and build upon one another's knowledge.

DIFFERENCES IN STUDENTS' INDIVIDUAL INTERESTS

In order to plan engaging instruction that fosters success in learning, teachers must plan lessons and adapt instruction to address differences in students' individual interests. To accomplish this, teachers first need to work to build relationships with students and develop an understanding of their unique interests to effectively tailor instruction that taps into these interests. Through **differentiated instruction** and the incorporation of **student-choice** opportunities for learning and assessment, teachers can effectively plan **student-centered** lessons that teach content in multiple ways that appeal to varying interests. Additionally, interest centers in the classroom foster engagement in learning, are easily adaptable, and can be planned into daily instruction. By frequently conducting **formative assessments**, teachers can gauge student interest in activities and adjust as necessary. This ultimately promotes self-direction, motivation, and curiosity in learning through providing students the opportunity to build content knowledge based on their individual interests.

Copyright © Mometrix Media. You have been licensed one copy of this document for personal use only. Any other reproduction or redistribution is strictly prohibited. All rights reserved. This content is provided for test preparation purposes only and does not imply an endorsement by Mometrix of any particular political, scientific, or religious point of view.

DIFFERENCES IN STUDENTS' INDIVIDUAL LEARNING NEEDS

Differences in backgrounds, abilities, skills, and interests results in a wide spectrum of student learning needs that must be addressed when planning effective and adaptable instruction. Teachers must recognize the individual learning needs of students to plan lessons that are accommodating, equitable, and promote success in learning. Through **student-centered** and **differentiated** instruction, teachers can effectively provide multiple avenues for content instruction, learning, and assessment based on individual need. Planning for **student-choice** and **self-directed learning** allows teachers to successfully address all learning styles and needs. Additionally, teachers must incorporate scaffolds into their lessons to adapt instruction. This can be done through incorporating such supports as graphic organizers, outlines, charts, and visuals, as well as planning for small, mixed-ability group instruction based on learning needs to provide scaffolding. Teachers should plan to check frequently for understanding during instruction in order to adapt activities and adjust instruction to meet individual learning needs.

ELL STUDENTS

English language learners (ELLs) need support in both understanding content material and building their English proficiency levels. To effectively plan and adapt instruction to accommodate them and facilitate success in learning, it is important that teachers demonstrate respect for the student's native language while encouraging the acquisition of English language skills. Teachers should plan for some content instruction to be in the student's native language to begin to build knowledge. To effectively assist ELLs in building vocabulary on specific content areas, lessons should be planned around **themed units**. Additionally, planning multiple cooperative learning and peer-tutoring activities allows ELLs to practice and develop their English skills in a natural setting, as well provides support for understanding new instructional concepts. Teachers must plan to scaffold content material, texts, and writing assignments to align with students' proficiency levels through adding such supports as graphic organizers, labels, and charts. Incorporating **linguistic aids** such as verbal cues, gestures, pictures, and digital resources allow teachers to effectively adapt instruction as necessary to support understanding and develop English language skills.

STUDENTS WITH DISABILITIES

Students with disabilities may require **instructional or physical supports** in order to have an equitable learning experience that facilitates their academic success. Teachers must be cognizant of any student disabilities and work to effectively plan instruction in a subtle, sensitive, and inclusive manner. Students with learning disabilities may require the planning of supports such as preferential seating, extra time for work and assessments, graphic organizers, and shorter or chunked assignments. These students may need to be paired with others that can provide scaffolding and peer-tutoring or may require individualized instruction or small focused groups. Students with physical disabilities may require such supports as a modified classroom environment to address their physical needs, audiovisual supplements, enlarged font, or braille texts. Teachers must work to incorporate these supports into their lesson planning to ensure that all students are included and empowered to learn, while allowing for flexibility in their lesson plans to allow for necessary adaptations.

CULTURAL AND SOCIOECONOMIC DIFFERENCES

ADDRESSING DIFFERENCES IN AN INCLUSIVE AND EQUITABLE CLASSROOM ENVIRONMENT

In a **culturally responsive** classroom, the teacher recognizes and is sensitive to the importance of planning instruction that addresses cultural and socioeconomic differences among students for creating an **inclusive** and **equitable** learning environment. The teacher responds to differences in norms, values, interests, and lifestyles through designing relevant instruction that builds on

Copyright © Mometrix Media. You have been licensed one copy of this document for personal use only. Any other reproduction or redistribution is strictly prohibited. All rights reserved.
This content is provided for test preparation purposes only and does not imply an endorsement by Mometrix of any particular political, scientific, or religious point of view.

students' experiences and facilitates personal connections that foster engagement in learning. This is important in conveying to students the value of their diverse experiences and highlighting their strengths in a manner that empowers them to achieve academic success while providing support where needed. It is important that the teacher incorporate supports in instructional planning to address academic, social, behavioral, and emotional needs of students from different cultural and socioeconomic backgrounds to provide all students an equitable opportunity for success in learning while maintaining high academic expectations.

POSSIBLE IMPACTS ON ACADEMIC ACHIEVEMENT

If not properly addressed, cultural and socioeconomic differences among students pose potentially negative impacts on academic achievement. It is vital that teachers recognize and accommodate these differences to instill the proper supports for engagement and success in learning. Students from different cultural or socioeconomic backgrounds may feel excluded from curriculum and instruction, which may result in lowered self-concept, self-esteem, and ultimately, disengagement toward learning. Thus, teachers must practice **culturally responsive teaching** to create instruction in which all students feel valued and included. These students may lack the support or resources for education at home due to various cultural and social challenges, and students from low socioeconomic backgrounds may face health, behavioral, or emotional challenges that impact their development and ability to learn. It is important that the teacher recognize these challenges and subtly address them in the classroom to establish an inclusive, equitable, and empowering environment that fosters engagement in learning. Some strategies for addressing these differences include providing community classroom materials, extra time for tutoring and assistance outside of classroom hours, individualized instruction, or opportunities to use the internet at school for students who lack access at home.

SIGNIFICANCE OF VARIED STUDENT LEARNING NEEDS AND PREFERENCES
IMPLICATIONS ON INSTRUCTION

Variances in students' learning needs and preferences implies that instruction must be **differentiated**, flexible, and allow for adaptations as necessary to accommodate students' individual needs, abilities, and interests. Furthermore, it means that teachers must work to build relationships with their students to develop an understanding of their different needs and preferences. This allows teachers to design instruction that emphasizes individual strengths while challenging students academically based on their abilities and providing instructional supports where necessary to ensure student success. To accomplish this, teachers must plan and deliver instructional material in multiple ways to address differences in learning needs and preferences, as well as allow for student choice in learning, processing, and demonstrating understanding of content.

POSSIBLE VARIANCES THAT MAY BE ENCOUNTERED

Teachers will inevitably encounter an array of learning needs and preferences among their students. As students have varying **learning styles**, including but not limited to visual, auditory, or kinesthetic, their methods for acquiring, processing, and retaining information will differ, as well as their **preferred modalities** for doing so. Some students may prefer written assignments in which they work independently, while others may prefer activities that involve active movement within a group. Similarly, some students require more individualized attention, while others may function better in a small group or whole-class setting. Students will also come to the classroom with differing **academic abilities**, and therefore, will require varying levels of assistance, support, and guidance to facilitate their success in learning. In addition, students may have specific learning, physical, social, or emotional **disabilities**, and as such, will need varying degrees of supports and accommodations to support their ability to learn effectively.

Copyright © Mometrix Media. You have been licensed one copy of this document for personal use only. Any other reproduction or redistribution is strictly prohibited. All rights reserved. This content is provided for test preparation purposes only and does not imply an endorsement by Mometrix of any particular political, scientific, or religious point of view.

IMPORTANCE OF TAILORING CURRICULUM, INSTRUCTION, AND ASSESSMENTS

Through tailoring curriculum, instruction, and assessments according to student learning needs and preferences, teachers create a **student-centered** learning environment. This motivates and empowers students to take ownership of their learning and allows every student an equal opportunity to achieve academic success. By creating a flexible curriculum and presenting instruction through multiple methods, teachers ensure that the learning needs and preferences of all students are met by facilitating a dynamic and engaging learning environment in which students can learn in the way that best suits their needs. Furthermore, in adapting assessments based upon students' learning needs and preferences by allowing **student choice**, teachers maximize student understanding of content material, allowing them to demonstrate learning according to their interests and abilities.

Chapter Quiz

Ready to see how well you retained what you just read? Scan the QR code to go directly to the chapter quiz interface for this study guide. If you're using a computer, simply visit the bonus page at **mometrix.com/bonus948/ftceprekinprim** and click the Chapter Quizzes link.

Copyright © Mometrix Media. You have been licensed one copy of this document for personal use only. Any other reproduction or redistribution is strictly prohibited. All rights reserved. This content is provided for test preparation purposes only and does not imply an endorsement by Mometrix of any particular political, scientific, or religious point of view.

Diagnosis, Assessment, and Evaluation

Transform passive reading into active learning! After immersing yourself in this chapter, put your comprehension to the test by taking a quiz. The insights you gained will stay with you longer this way. Scan the QR code to go directly to the chapter quiz interface for this study guide. If you're using a computer, simply visit the bonus page at **mometrix.com/bonus948/ftceprekinprim** and click the Chapter Quizzes link.

Screening in Early Childhood

SCREENING FOR PARTICULAR DELAY CRITERION

Initial screenings are required, but if a young child has been screened for developmental disorders or delays within the past 6 months and no changes have been observed or reported, repeat screening may be waived. Hearing and vision screenings are mandatory when screening young children. Formal developmental measures are also required, which may include screening tests of motor skills development, cognitive development, social-emotional development, and self-help skills development. Formal screening tests of speech-language development are also required. Additional tests recommended during screening include informal measures. For example, checklists, rating scales, and inventories may be used to screen a child's behavior, mood, and performance of motor skills, cognitive skills, self-help skills, and social and emotional skills. On checklists, parents or caregivers check whether the child does or does not demonstrate listed behaviors, or assessors may complete them via parent or caregiver interviews or interviewing and observing the child. Rating scales ask parents, caregivers, and assessors to rate a child's behaviors, affect, mood, and so on, within a range of numbered and labeled descriptions. Inventories list demonstrated skills and needs. Behavioral observations and existing records and information are also used.

FEATURES OF DEVELOPMENTAL SCREENINGS AND EVALUATIONS

If a child's development is suspected of being delayed—for example, the child is not reaching developmental milestones during expected age ranges—a developmental screening may be administered. Screening tests are quickly performed and yield more general results. The hospital or doctor's office may give a questionnaire to the parent or caregiver to complete for a screening. Alternatively, a health or education professional may administer a screening test to the child. Screening tests are not intended to diagnose specific conditions or give details; they are meant to identify children who may have some problem. Screenings can overidentify or under-identify developmental delays in children. Hence, if the screening identifies a child as having developmental delays, the child is then referred for a developmental evaluation—a much longer, more thorough, comprehensive, in-depth assessment using multiple tests, administered by a psychologist or other highly-trained professional. Evaluation provides a profile of a child's strengths and weaknesses in all developmental domains. Determination of needs for early intervention services or treatment plans is based on evaluation results.

DEVELOPMENTAL EVALUATION DATA TYPES

The child's social history should be obtained, which is typically done by a social worker. Details of the child's developmental progress up until present day; the family's composition, socioeconomic status, and situation; and the child's and family's health and medical histories and status should be

Copyright © Mometrix Media. You have been licensed one copy of this document for personal use only. Any other reproduction or redistribution is strictly prohibited. All rights reserved. This content is provided for test preparation purposes only and does not imply an endorsement by Mometrix of any particular political, scientific, or religious point of view.

emphasized. A physician's or nurse's medical assessment is required, including a **physical examination** and, if indicated, a specialist's examination. A psychologist typically assesses intellectual and **cognitive development**; at least one such test is generally required. At least one test of adaptive behavior is also required to assess **emotional-social development**. **Self-help skills** are evaluated; this may be included within cognitive, adaptive behavior, or programming assessments. **Communication skills** are typically evaluated by a speech-language pathologist. Both receptive and expressive language must be tested comprehensively rather than simply by single-word vocabulary tests. As indicated, **speech articulation** is also tested. At least one test of **motor skills**, typically administered by a physical or occupational therapist, is required. **Programming** evaluation requires at least one criterion-referenced or curriculum-based measure, typically administered by an educator.

CHILD FIND

Child Find is an ongoing process with the aim of locating, identifying, and referring young children with disabilities and their families as early as possible for service programs. This process consists of activities designed to raise public awareness and screenings and evaluations to identify and diagnose disabilities. The federal IDEA law mandates under Part B that disabled children are guaranteed early childhood special education services and under Part C that infants and toddlers at risk for developmental delays are guaranteed early intervention programs. (Eligibility guidelines vary by US state.) The IDEA requires school districts to find, identify, and evaluate children with disabilities in their attendance areas. School districts have facilitated this Child Find process by establishing community-informed referral networks whose members refer children who may have exceptional educational needs (EENs). Network members typically include parents, doctors, birth-to-3 programs, child care programs, Head Start programs, public health agencies, social service agencies, and any other community members with whom the young children come into contact.

CURRENT COLLABORATIVE APPROACHES AND MODELS OF SCREENING

Historically, the tradition was to conduct kindergarten screenings of children entering schools around age 5. However, in recent years, school districts have developed community referral networks to assist in the processes of Child Find, screening, evaluation, and referral for early intervention and early childhood special education and related services. Current models are more informal, proactive, and collaborative. Cooperative educational interagency service efforts give parents information about normal early childhood development and available community resources and offer opportunities for developmental screenings of their young children. Specific procedures are governed by individual US state laws. Generally, district networks implementing current models send developmental review forms to parents to complete in advance, and then they attend a developmental screening at a community site. Parents discuss normal early childhood growth and development with program staff, while, in the same room, trained professionals observe their children as they play. Children's vision and hearing are also screened. Parents can discuss their children's current development with psychologists, early childhood educators, or counselors. Thereafter, they can learn about community resources.

DEFINING DEVELOPMENTAL DELAYS IN INFANTS AND TODDLERS

The IDEA Part C specifies the areas of development that states must include in **defining developmental delays**. However, individual states must identify the criteria they use to determine eligibility, including pertinent diagnostic instruments, procedures, and functional levels. States currently use quantitative and qualitative measures. Quantitative criteria for developmental delay include the difference between chronological age and performance level, expressed as a percentage of chronological age; performance at a given number of months below chronological age; or number of standard deviations (SDs) below mean of performance on a norm-referenced test.

Copyright © Mometrix Media. You have been licensed one copy of this document for personal use only. Any other reproduction or redistribution is strictly prohibited. All rights reserved. This content is provided for test preparation purposes only and does not imply an endorsement by Mometrix of any particular political, scientific, or religious point of view.

Qualitative criteria include the development considered atypical or delayed for established norms or observed behaviors considered atypical. At least one state differentially defines delay according to a child's age in months, with the rationale that a 25% delay, for example, is very different for a 1-year-old than a 3-year-old. Quantitative criteria for defining delay and determining eligibility vary widely among states. A 25% or 20% delay (2 SDs below mean in 1+ areas or 1.5 SD below mean in 2+ areas) is some common state criteria.

RISK FACTORS IN INFANTS AND TODDLERS

Scientists find that developmental outcomes for children are not reliably predicted by any one risk factor or event. **Developmental risk** increases with increased biological, medical, or environmental risk factors. However, researchers have found some variables that afford resiliency in children to offset risk factors. These can include the child's basic temperament, the child having high self-esteem, the child having a good emotional relationship with at least one parent, and the child having experiences of successful learning. These findings indicate that assessments should include criteria for multiple biological and environmental risk factors, for cumulative biological and environmental risk factors, and for protective or resilience factors, considering all of these in the context of change occurring over time. Under the IDEA, US states have the option to provide early intervention services to children considered at risk for adverse developmental outcomes as well as those already identified with them. Some states apply multiple-risk models, requiring three to five risk factors for service eligibility. Some states also determine eligibility with less DD when biological, medical, or environmental risk factors also exist.

INFORMATION SOURCES ON EARLY INTERVENTION AND PRESCHOOL SPECIAL EDUCATION SERVICES

Military families stationed both in the United States and overseas who have young special needs children can seek information and assistance from the federally funded organization Specialized Training of Military Families (STOMP). The staff of STOMP is composed of parents having special needs children themselves, who also have been trained to work with other parents of special needs children. STOMP staff members are spouses of military personnel who thus understand the unique, specialized circumstances and needs of military families. Another government agency, the US Department of Defense, includes the office of the Department of Defense Education Activity (DoDEA) and provides comprehensive guidance to military families with special needs children who are eligible to receive, or are receiving, free appropriate public education (FAPE) as mandated by the IDEA law, whether that education is located in the United States or in other countries.

PROVIDING SPECIAL EDUCATION SERVICES FOR PRESCHOOLERS

If parents observe that their preschooler is not attaining developmental milestones within the expected age ranges or does not seem to be developing in the same way as most other children, they should seek **evaluation** for possible developmental delay or disability. Although 3-to-5-year-olds are likely not in elementary school yet, the elementary school in a family's school district is still the best first contact because the IDEA law specifies that school districts must provide special education services at no family cost to eligible children, including preschoolers. Another excellent source of more information about special education is the National Dissemination Center for Children with Disabilities (NICHCY) of the US Department of Education's Office of Special Education Programs. They partner with nonprofit organizations like the Academy for Educational Development (AED) to produce useful documents for families with special needs children. NICHCY supplies state resource sheets listing main contacts regarding special education services in each US state. Families can obtain these sheets at NICHCY's website or by telephone.

Copyright © Mometrix Media. You have been licensed one copy of this document for personal use only. Any other reproduction or redistribution is strictly prohibited. All rights reserved. This content is provided for test preparation purposes only and does not imply an endorsement by Mometrix of any particular political, scientific, or religious point of view.

INFORMATION SOURCES FOR EVALUATION

Under the IDEA (Individuals with Disabilities Education Act), evaluation information sources include: physicians' reports, the child's medical history, developmental test results, current classroom observations and assessments (when applicable), completed developmental and behavioral checklists, feedback and observations from parents and all other members of the evaluation team, and any other significant records, reports, and observations regarding the child. Under the IDEA, the parents are involved in the evaluation, along with at least one regular education teacher and special education teacher, if the child has these, and any special education service provider working with the child—for children receiving early intervention services from birth through age 2 and transitioning to preschool special education, it may be an early intervention service provider; a school administrator knowledgeable about children with disabilities, special education policies, regular education curriculum, and resources available; a psychologist or educator who can interpret evaluation results and discuss indicated instruction; individuals with special expertise or knowledge regarding the child (recruited by school or parents); when appropriate, the child; and other professionals, for example, physical or occupational therapists, speech therapists, medical specialists, and so on.

INFORMAL ASSESSMENT INSTRUMENTS

Early childhood teachers assess pre-K children's performance in individual, small-group, and whole-class activities throughout the day using informal tools that are teacher-made, school-, program-, or district-furnished, or procured by school systems from commercial educational resources. For classroom observations, teachers might complete a form based on their observations during class story or circle time, organized using three themes per day, each targeting different skills—social-emotional, math, alphabet knowledge, oral language, or emergent writing. They note the names of children demonstrating the specified skill and those who might need follow-up, and provide needed one on one interventions daily. For individual observations, teachers might fill out a chart divided into domains like physical development, oral language development, math, emergent reading, emergent writing, science and health, fine arts, technology and media, social studies, social-emotional development, and approaches to learning, noting one child's strengths and needs in each area per chart. In addition to guided observation records, teachers complete checklists, keep anecdotal and running records, and assemble portfolio assessments of children's work. Tracking children's progress informs responsive instructional planning.

> **Review Video: Assessment Reliability and Validity**
> Visit mometrix.com/academy and enter code: 424680

DIFFERENCES BETWEEN SCREENING AND ASSESSMENT INSTRUMENTS

A variety of screening and assessment instruments exist for early childhood measurement. Some key areas where they differ include which developmental domains are measured by an instrument; for which applications an instrument is meant to be used; to which age ranges an instrument applies; the methods by which a test or tool is administered; the requirements for scoring and interpreting a test, scale, or checklist; whether an instrument is appropriate for use with ethnically diverse populations; and whether a tool is statistically found to have good validity and reliability. Early childhood program administrators should choose instruments that can measure the developmental areas pertinent to their program; support their program's established goals; and include all early childhood ages served in their program. Instruments' administration, scoring, and interpretation methods should be congruent with program personnel's skills. Test/measure administration should involve realistic time durations. Instruments/tools should be appropriate to

Copyright © Mometrix Media. You have been licensed one copy of this document for personal use only. Any other reproduction or redistribution is strictly prohibited. All rights reserved.
This content is provided for test preparation purposes only and does not imply an endorsement by Mometrix of any particular political, scientific, or religious point of view.

use with ethnically diverse and non-English-speaking children and families. Tests should also be proven psychometrically accurate and dependable enough.

TYPICAL APPLICATIONS OF SCREENING AND ASSESSMENT INSTRUMENTS

The ways in which screening and assessment instruments applicable to early childhood education are used include a wide range of variations. For example, early childhood education programs typically need to identify children who might have developmental disorders or delays. Screening instruments are used to identify those children showing signs of possible problems who need assessments, not to diagnose problems. Assessment instruments are used to develop and/or confirm diagnoses of developmental disorders or delays. Assessment tools are also used to help educators and therapists plan curricular and treatment programs. Another important function of assessment instruments is to determine a child's eligibility for a given program. In addition, once children are placed in early childhood education programs, assessment tools can be used to monitor their progress and other changes occurring over time. Moreover, program administrators can use assessment instruments to evaluate children's achievement of the learning outcomes that define their program goals, and, by extension, the teachers' effectiveness in furthering children's achievement of those outcomes.

FORMAL ASSESSMENT INSTRUMENTS

Formal assessment instruments are typically standardized tests, administered to groups. They give norms for age groups/developmental levels for comparison. They are designed to avoid administrator bias and capture children's responses only. Their data can be scaled and be reported in aggregate to school/program administrators and policymakers. The Scholastic Early Childhood Inventory (SECI) is a formal one-on-one instrument to assess children's progress in four domains found to predict kindergarten readiness: phonological awareness, oral language development, alphabet knowledge, and mathematics. Other instruments measuring multiple developmental domains include:

- **The Assessment, Evaluation, and Programming System** (0–6 years) for planning intervention
- **The Bayley Scale for Infant Development** (1–42 months) for assessing developmental delays
- **The Brigance Diagnostic Inventory of Early Development** (0–7 years) for planning instruction
- **The Developmental Profile II** (0–6 years) to assess special needs and support IEP development
- **The Early Coping Inventory** (4–36 months)
- **Early Learning Accomplishment Profile** (0–36 months), both for planning interventions
- **The Infant-Toddler Developmental Assessment** (0–42 months) to screen for developmental delays

SCREENING AND ASSESSMENT INSTRUMENTS MEASURING DEVELOPMENT

The available screening and assessment instruments for early childhood development cover a wide range in scope and areas of focus. Some measures are comprehensive, assessing young children's progress in many developmental domains, including sensory, motor, physical, cognitive, linguistic, emotional, and social. Some other instruments focus exclusively on only one domain, such as language development or emotional-social development. Some instruments even focus within a domain upon only one of its facets, (e.g., upon attachment or temperament within the domain of emotional-social development). In addition, some tools measure risk and resiliency factors influencing developmental delays and disorders. Programs like Head Start that promote general

132

Copyright © Mometrix Media. You have been licensed one copy of this document for personal use only. Any other reproduction or redistribution is strictly prohibited. All rights reserved. This content is provided for test preparation purposes only and does not imply an endorsement by Mometrix of any particular political, scientific, or religious point of view.

early childhood development should select comprehensive assessment instruments. Outreach programs targeting better identification of children having untreated and/or undetected mental health problems should choose instruments assessing social-emotional development. Clinics treating children with regulatory disorders might select an instrument measuring temperament. Prevention programs helping multiple-needs families access supports and services could use a measure for risk and resiliency factors. Multifaceted early childhood programs often benefit most from using several instruments in combination.

AGE RANGES INCLUDED IN VARIOUS SCREENING AND ASSESSMENT INSTRUMENTS

An important consideration for screening and assessment in early childhood is that early childhood development is very dynamic and occurs rapidly. Hence, screening and assessment instruments must be sensitive to such frequent and pronounced developmental changes. Some instruments target specific age ranges like 0–36 months. Others cover wider ranges, such as children aged 2–16 years. The latter may have internal means of application to smaller age ranges; for example, sections respectively for 3–6-month-old babies, 7–12-month-olds, and 12–18-month-olds. Or they indicate different scoring and interpretation criteria by age; for example, some screening tools specify different numbers of test items depending on the child's age to indicate a need for assessment. Choosing screening and assessment instruments covering the entire age range served in an early childhood education program is advantageous—not only because they can be used with all child ages in the program but also because they can be administered and readministered at the beginning and end of programs and/or in between, to compare and monitor changes, which is difficult with separate, age-specific tests.

Special Education Services in Early Childhood

SPECIAL EDUCATION SERVICES FOR PRESCHOOL CHILDREN

Special education for preschoolers is education specifically designed to meet the individual needs of a child aged 3 to 5 years with a disability or developmental delay. The specialized design of this instruction can include adaptations to the content, the teaching methods, and the way instruction is delivered to meet a disabled child's unique needs. Special education for preschoolers includes various settings, such as in the home, classrooms, hospitals, institutions, and others. It also includes a range of related services, such as speech-language pathology services, specialized physical education instruction, early vocational training, and training in travel skills. The school district's special education system provides evaluation and services to eligible preschoolers free of charge. Evaluation's purposes are to determine whether a child has a disability under the IDEA's definitions and determine that child's present educational needs.

POST-EVALUATION AND THE INDIVIDUALIZED EDUCATION PROGRAM

After a preschool child is evaluated, the parents and involved school personnel meet to discuss the evaluation results. Parents are included in the group that decides whether the child is eligible for special education services based on those results. For eligible children, the parents and school personnel will develop an IEP. Every child who will receive special education services must have an IEP. The main purposes of the IEP are (1) to establish reasonable educational goals for the individual child and (2) to indicate what services the school district will provide to the child. The IEP includes a statement of the child's present levels of functioning and performance. It also includes a list of more general instructional goals for the child to achieve through school and parental support along with more specific learning objectives reflecting those goals and specifying exactly what the child will be able to demonstrate, under what circumstances, how much of the time—for example, a percentage of recorded instances—and within what time period (e.g., 1 year).

Copyright © Mometrix Media. You have been licensed one copy of this document for personal use only. Any other reproduction or redistribution is strictly prohibited. All rights reserved. This content is provided for test preparation purposes only and does not imply an endorsement by Mometrix of any particular political, scientific, or religious point of view.

INDIVIDUALIZED EDUCATION PROGRAM GOALS AND OBJECTIVES

In an IEP, the goals are more global, describing a skill for the child to acquire or a task to master. The objectives are more specific articulations of achievements that will demonstrate the child's mastery of the goal. For example, if a goal is for the child to increase his or her functional communicative vocabulary, a related objective might be for the child to acquire x number of new words in x length of time; another related objective could be for the child to use the words acquired in 90% of recorded relevant situations. If the goal is for the child to demonstrate knowledge and discrimination of colors, one objective might be for the child to identify correctly a red, yellow, and blue block 95% of the time when asked to point out each color within a group of blocks. Progress toward or achievement of some objectives may be measured via formal tests; with preschoolers, many others are measured via observational data collection.

PROGRESS MONITORING, UPDATING, AND REVISING IEPS

Once a child has been identified with a disability, has been determined eligible for special education and related services under the IDEA, and has had an IEP developed and implemented, the child's progress must be monitored. Monitoring methods may be related to evaluation methods. For example, if a child identified with problem behaviors was initially evaluated using a behavioral checklist, school personnel can use the same checklist periodically, comparing its results to the baseline levels of frequency and severity originally obtained. If an affective disorder or disturbance was identified and instruments like the Beck Depression Inventory or Anxiety Inventory were used, these can be used again periodically; reduced symptoms would indicate progress. If progress with IEP goals and objectives is less or greater than expected, the IEP team meets and may revise the program. This can include specifying shorter or longer times to achieve some goals and objectives; lowering or raising requirements proving too difficult or easy; resetting successive objective criteria in smaller or larger increments; changing teaching methods, content, or materials used; and so on.

Assessment Methodology

ASSESSMENT METHODS

Effective teaching requires multiple methods of assessment to evaluate student comprehension and instructional effectiveness. Assessments are typically categorized as diagnostic, formative, summative, and benchmark, and are applicable at varying stages of instruction. **Diagnostic** assessments are administered before instruction and indicate students' prior knowledge and areas of misunderstanding to determine the path of instruction. **Formative** assessments occur continuously to measure student engagement, comprehension, and instructional effectiveness. These assessments indicate instructional strategies that require adjustment to meet students' needs in facilitating successful learning, and include such strategies as checking for understanding, observations, total participation activities, and exit tickets. **Summative** assessments are given at the end of a lesson or unit to evaluate student progress in reaching learning targets and identify areas of misconception for reteaching. Such assessments can be given in the form of exams and quizzes, or project-based activities in which students demonstrate their learning through hands-on, personalized methods. Additionally, portfolios serve as valuable summative assessments in allowing students to demonstrate their progress over time and provide insight regarding individual achievement. **Benchmark** assessments occur less frequently and encompass large portions of curriculum. These assessments are intended to evaluate the progress of groups of students in achieving state and district academic standards.

Copyright © Mometrix Media. You have been licensed one copy of this document for personal use only. Any other reproduction or redistribution is strictly prohibited. All rights reserved. This content is provided for test preparation purposes only and does not imply an endorsement by Mometrix of any particular political, scientific, or religious point of view.

Assessment Types

- **Diagnostic:** These assessments can either be formal or informal and are intended to provide teachers with information regarding students' level of understanding prior to beginning a unit of instruction. Examples include pretests, KWL charts, anticipation guides, and brainstorming activities. Digital resources, such as online polls, surveys, and quizzes are also valuable resources for gathering diagnostic feedback.
- **Formative:** These assessments occur throughout instruction to provide the teacher with feedback regarding student understanding. Examples include warm-up and closure activities, checking frequently for understanding, student reflection activities, and providing students with color-coded cards to indicate their level of understanding. Short quizzes and total participation activities, such as four corners, are also valuable formative assessments. Numerous digital resources, including polls, surveys, and review games, are also beneficial in providing teachers with formative feedback to indicate instructional effectiveness.
- **Summative:** Summative assessments are intended to indicate students' level of mastery and progress toward reaching academic learning standards. These assessments may take the form of written or digital exams and include multiple choice, short answer, or long answer questions. Examples also include projects, final essays, presentations, or portfolios to demonstrate student progress over time.
- **Benchmark:** Benchmark assessments measure students' progress in achieving academic standards. These assessments are typically standardized to ensure uniformity, objectivity, and accuracy. Benchmark assessments are typically given as a written multiple choice or short answer exam, or as a digital exam in which students answer questions on the computer.

> **Review Video: Formative and Summative Assessments**
> Visit mometrix.com/academy and enter code: 804991

Determining Appropriate Assessment Strategies

As varying assessment methods provide different information regarding student performance and achievement, the teacher must consider the most applicable and effective assessment strategy in each stage of instruction. This includes determining the **desired outcomes** of assessment, as well as the information the teacher intends to ascertain and how they will apply the results to further instruction. **Age** and **grade level** appropriateness must be considered when selecting which assessment strategies will enable students to successfully demonstrate their learning. Additionally, the teacher must be cognizant of students' individual differences and learning needs to determine which assessment model is most **accommodating** and reflective of their progress. It is also important that the teacher consider the practicality of assessment strategies, as well as methods they will use to implement the assessment for maximized feedback regarding individual and whole-class progress in achieving learning goals.

Assessments That Reflect Real-World Applications

Assessments that reflect **real-world applications** enhance relevancy and students' ability to establish personal connections to learning that deepen understanding. Implementing such assessments provides authenticity and enhances engagement by defining a clear and practical purpose for learning. These assessments often allow for hands-on opportunities for demonstrating learning and can be adjusted to accommodate students' varying learning styles and needs while measuring individual progress. However, assessments that focus on real-world applications can be subjective, thus making it difficult to extract concrete data and quantify student progress to guide future instructional decisions. In addition, teachers may have difficulty analyzing assessment

Copyright © Mometrix Media. You have been licensed one copy of this document for personal use only. Any other reproduction or redistribution is strictly prohibited. All rights reserved. This content is provided for test preparation purposes only and does not imply an endorsement by Mometrix of any particular political, scientific, or religious point of view.

results on a large scale and comparing student performance with other schools and districts, as individual assessments may vary.

DIAGNOSTIC TESTS

Diagnostic tests are integral to planning and delivering effective instruction. These tests are typically administered prior to beginning a unit or lesson and provide valuable feedback for guiding and planning instruction. Diagnostic tests provide **preliminary information** regarding students' level of understanding and prior knowledge. This serves as a baseline for instructional planning that connects and builds upon students' background knowledge and experiences to enhance success in learning. Diagnostic tests allow the teacher to identify and clarify areas of student misconception prior to engaging in instruction to ensure continued comprehension and avoid the need for remediation. They indicate areas of student strength and need, as well as individual instructional aids that may need to be incorporated into lessons to support student achievement. In addition, these tests enable the teacher to determine which instructional strategies, activities, groupings, and materials will be most valuable in maximizing engagement and learning. Diagnostic tests can be **formal** or **informal**, and include such formats as pre-tests, pre-reading activities, surveys, vocabulary inventories, and graphic organizers such as KWL charts to assess student understanding prior to engaging in learning. Diagnostic tests are generally not graded as there is little expectation that all students in a class possess the same baseline of proficiency at the start of a unit.

FORMATIVE ASSESSMENTS

Formative assessments are any assessments that take place in the **middle of a unit of instruction**. The goals of formative assessments are to help teachers understand where a student is in their progress toward **mastering** the current unit's content and to provide the students with **ongoing feedback** throughout the unit. The advantage of relying heavily on formative assessments in instruction is that it allows the teacher to continuously **check for comprehension** and adjust instruction as needed to ensure that the whole class is adequately prepared to proceed at the end of the unit. To understand formative assessments well, teachers need to understand that any interaction that can provide information about the student's comprehension is a type of formative assessment which can be used to inform future instruction.

Formative assessments are often a mixture of formal and informal assessments. **Formal formative assessments** often include classwork, homework, and quizzes. Examples of **informal formative assessments** include simple comprehension checks during instruction, class-wide discussions of the current topic, and exit slips, which are written questions posed by teachers at the end of class, which helps the teacher quickly review which students are struggling with the concepts.

SUMMATIVE ASSESSMENTS

Summative assessment refers to an evaluation at the end of a discrete unit of instruction, such as the end of a course, end of a unit, or end of a semester. Classic examples of summative assessments include end of course assessments, final exams, or even qualifying standardized tests such as the SAT or ACT. Most summative assessments are created to measure student mastery of particular **academic standards**. Whereas formative assessment generally informs current instruction, summative assessments are used to objectively demonstrate that each individual has achieved adequate mastery of the standards in question. If a student has not met the benchmark, they may need extra instruction or may need to repeat the course.

These assessments usually take the form of **tests** or formal portfolios with rubrics and clearly defined goals. Whatever form a summative takes, they are almost always high-stakes, heavily-

Copyright © Mometrix Media. You have been licensed one copy of this document for personal use only. Any other reproduction or redistribution is strictly prohibited. All rights reserved. This content is provided for test preparation purposes only and does not imply an endorsement by Mometrix of any particular political, scientific, or religious point of view.

weighted, and they should always be formally graded. These types of assessments often feature a narrower range of question types, such as multiple choice, short answer, and essay questions to help with systematic grading. Examples of summative assessments include state tests, end-of-unit or chapter tests, end-of-semester exams, and assessments that formally measure student mastery of topics against a established benchmarks.

Project-based assessments are beneficial in evaluating achievement, as they incorporate several elements of instruction and highlight real-world applications of learning. This allows students to demonstrate understanding through a hands-on, individualized approach that reinforces connections to learning and increases retainment. **Portfolios** of student work over time serve as a valuable method for assessing individual progress toward reaching learning targets. Summative assessments provide insight regarding overall instructional effectiveness and are necessary for guiding future instruction in subsequent years but are not usually used to modify current instruction.

> **Review Video: Assessment Reliability and Validity**
> Visit mometrix.com/academy and enter code: 424680

BENCHMARK ASSESSMENTS

Benchmark assessments are intended to quantify, evaluate, and compare individual and groups of students' achievement of school-wide, district, and state **academic standards.** They are typically administered in specific intervals throughout the school year and encompass entire or large units of curriculum to determine student mastery and readiness for academic advancement. Benchmark assessments provide data that enable the teacher to determine students' progress toward reaching academic goals to guide current and continued instruction. This data can be utilized by the school and individual teachers to create learning goals and objectives aligned with academic standards, as well as plan instructional strategies, activities, and assessments to support students in achieving them. In addition, benchmark assessments provide feedback regarding understanding and the potential need for remediation to allow the teacher to instill necessary supports in future instruction that prepare students for success in achieving learning targets.

ALIGNMENT OF ASSESSMENTS WITH INSTRUCTIONAL GOALS AND OBJECTIVES

To effectively monitor student progress, assessments must align with **instructional goals** and **objectives**. This allows the teacher to determine whether students are advancing at an appropriate pace to achieve state and district academic standards. When assessments are aligned with specific learning targets, the teacher ensures that students are learning relevant material to establish a foundation of knowledge necessary for growth and academic achievement. To achieve this, the teacher must determine which instructional goals and objectives their students must achieve and derive instruction, content, and activities from these specifications. Instruction must reflect and reinforce learning targets, and the teacher must select the most effective strategies for addressing students' needs as they work to achieve them. Assessments must be reflective of content instruction to ensure they are aligned with learning goals and objectives, as well as to enable the teacher to evaluate student progress in mastering them. The teacher must clearly communicate learning goals and objectives throughout all stages of instruction to provide students with clarity on expectations. This establishes a clear purpose and focus for learning that enhances relevancy and strengthens connections to support student achievement.

CLEARLY COMMUNICATING ASSESSMENT CRITERIA AND STANDARDS

Students must be clear on the purpose of learning throughout all stages of instruction to enhance understanding and facilitate success. When assessment **criteria** and **standards** are clearly

Copyright © Mometrix Media. You have been licensed one copy of this document for personal use only. Any other reproduction or redistribution is strictly prohibited. All rights reserved. This content is provided for test preparation purposes only and does not imply an endorsement by Mometrix of any particular political, scientific, or religious point of view.

communicated, the purpose of learning is established, and students are able to effectively connect instructional activities to learning goals and criteria for assessment. Communicating assessment criteria and standards provides students with clarity on tasks and learning goals they are expected to accomplish as they prepare themselves for assessment. This allows for more **focused instruction** and engagement in learning, as it enhances relevancy and student motivation. Utilizing appropriate forms of **rubrics** is an effective strategy in specifying assessment criteria and standards, as it informs students about learning goals they are working toward, the quality of work they are expected to achieve, and skills they must master to succeed on the assessment. Rubrics indicate to students exactly how they will be evaluated, thus supporting their understanding and focus as they engage in learning to promote academic success.

RUBRICS FOR COMMUNICATING STANDARDS

The following are varying styles of rubrics that can be used to communicate criteria and standards:

- **Analytic:** Analytic rubrics break down criteria for an assignment into several categories and provide an explanation of the varying levels of performance in each one. This style of rubric is beneficial for detailing the characteristics of quality work, as well as providing students with feedback regarding specific components of their performance. Analytic rubrics are most effective when used for summative assessments, such as long-term projects or essays.
- **Holistic:** Holistic rubrics evaluate the quality of the student's assignment as a whole, rather than scoring individual components. Students' score is determined based upon their performance across multiple performance indicators. This style of rubric is beneficial for providing a comprehensive evaluation but limits the amount of feedback that students receive regarding their performance in specific areas.
- **Single-Point:** Single point rubrics outline criteria for assignments into several categories. Rather than providing a numeric score to each category, however, the teacher provides written feedback regarding the students' strengths and ways in which they can improve their performance. This style of rubric is beneficial in providing student-centered feedback that focuses on their overall progress.
- **Checklist:** Checklists typically outline a set of criteria that is scored using a binary approach based upon completion of each component. This style increases the efficiency of grading assignments and is often easy for students to comprehend but does not provide detailed feedback. This method of grading should generally be reserved for shorter assignments.

COMMUNICATING HIGH ACADEMIC EXPECTATIONS IN ASSESSMENTS

The attitudes and behaviors exhibited by the teacher are highly influential on students' attitudes toward learning. Teachers demonstrate belief in students' abilities to be successful in learning when they communicate **high academic expectations**. This promotes students' **self-concept** and establishes a **growth mindset** to create confident, empowered learners that are motivated to achieve. High expectations for assessments and reaching academic standards communicates to students the quality of work that is expected of them and encourages them to overcome obstacles as they engage in learning. When communicating expectations for student achievement, it is important that the teacher is aware of students' individual learning needs to provide the necessary support that establishes equitable opportunities for success in meeting assessment criteria and standards. Setting high expectations through assessment criteria and standards while supporting students in their learning enhances overall achievement and establishes a foundation for continuous academic success.

Copyright © Mometrix Media. You have been licensed one copy of this document for personal use only. Any other reproduction or redistribution is strictly prohibited. All rights reserved. This content is provided for test preparation purposes only and does not imply an endorsement by Mometrix of any particular political, scientific, or religious point of view.

Effective Communication and Impact on Student Learning

Communicating high academic expectations enhances students' self-concept and increases personal motivation for success in learning. To maximize student achievement, it is important that the teacher set high academic expectations that are **clearly** communicated through **age-appropriate** terms and consistently reinforced. Expectations must be reflected through learning goals and objectives, and **visible** at all times to ensure student awareness. The teacher must be **specific** in communicating what they want students to accomplish and clearly detail necessary steps for achievement while assuming the role of facilitator to guide learning and provide support. Providing constructive **feedback** throughout instruction is integral in reminding students of academic expectations and ensuring they are making adequate progress toward reaching learning goals. When high academic expectations are communicated and reinforced, students are empowered with a sense of confidence and self-responsibility for their own learning that promotes their desire to learn. This ultimately enhances achievement and equips them with the tools necessary for future academic success.

Analyzing and Interpreting Assessment Data

Teachers can utilize multiple techniques to effectively analyze and interpret assessment data. This typically involves creating charts and graphs outlining different data subsets. They can list each learning standard that was assessed, determine how many students overall demonstrated proficiency on the standard, and identify individual students who did not demonstrate proficiency on each standard. This information can be used to differentiate instruction. Additionally, they can track individual student performance and progress on each standard over time.

Teachers can take note of overall patterns and trends in assessment data. For example, they can determine if any subgroups of students did not meet expectations. They can consider whether the data confirms or challenges any existing beliefs, implications this may have on instructional planning and what, if any, conclusions can be drawn from this data.

Analyzing and interpreting assessment data may raise new questions for educators, so they can also determine if additional data collection is needed.

Using Assessment Data to Differentiate Instruction for Individual Learners

By analyzing and interpreting assessment data, teachers can determine if there are any specific learning standards that need to be retaught to their entire classes. This may be necessary if the data shows that all students struggled in these specific areas. Teachers may consider reteaching these standards using different methods if the initial methods were unsuccessful.

Teachers can also form groups of students who did not demonstrate proficiency on the same learning standards. Targeted instruction can be planned for these groups to help them make progress in these areas. Interventions can also be planned for individual students who did not show proficiency in certain areas. If interventions have already been in place and have not led to increased learning outcomes, the interventions may be redesigned. If interventions have been in place and assessment data now shows proficiency, the interventions may be discontinued.

If assessment data shows that certain students have met or exceeded expectations in certain areas, enrichment activities can be planned to challenge these students and meet their learning needs.

Aligning Assessments with Instructional Goals and Objectives

Assessments that are congruent to instructional goals and objectives provide a **clear purpose** for learning that enhances student understanding and motivation. When learning targets are reflected

Copyright © Mometrix Media. You have been licensed one copy of this document for personal use only. Any other reproduction or redistribution is strictly prohibited. All rights reserved.
This content is provided for test preparation purposes only and does not imply an endorsement by Mometrix of any particular political, scientific, or religious point of view.

in assessments, instructional activities and materials become more **relevant**, as they are derived from these specifications. Such clarity in purpose allows for more focus and productivity as students engage in instruction and fosters connections that strengthen overall understanding for maximized success in learning. Aligning assessments with instructional goals and objectives ensures that students are learning material that is relevant to the curriculum and academic standards to ensure **preparedness** as they advance in their academic careers. In addition, it enables the teacher to evaluate and monitor student progress to determine whether they are progressing at an ideal pace for achieving academic standards. With this information, the teacher can effectively modify instruction as necessary to support students' needs in reaching desired learning outcomes.

NORM-REFERENCED TESTS

On **norm-referenced tests**, students' performances are compared to the performances of sample groups of similar students. Norm-referenced tests identify students who score above and below the average. To ensure reliability, the tests must be given in a standardized manner to all students.

Norm-referenced tests usually cover a broad range of skills, such as the entire grade-level curriculum for a subject. They typically contain a few questions per skill. Whereas scores in component areas of the tests may be calculated, usually overall test scores are reported. Scores are often reported using percentile ranks, which indicate what percentage of test takers scored lower than the student being assessed. For example, a student's score in the 75th percentile means the student scored better than 75% of other test takers. Other times, scores may be reported using grade-level equivalency.

One advantage of norm-referenced tests is their objectivity. They also allow educators to compare large groups of students at once. This may be helpful for making decisions regarding class placements and groupings. A disadvantage of norm-referenced tests is that they only indicate how well students perform in comparison to one another. They do not indicate whether or not students have mastered certain skills.

CRITERION-REFERENCED TESTS

Criterion-referenced tests measure how well students perform on certain skills or standards. The goal of these tests is to indicate whether or not students have mastered certain skills and which skills require additional instruction. Scores are typically reported using the percentage of questions answered correctly or students' performance levels. Performance levels are outlined using terms such as below expectations, met expectations, and exceeded expectations.

One advantage of criterion-referenced tests is they provide teachers with useful information to guide instruction. They can identify which specific skills students have mastered and which skills need additional practice. Teachers can use this information to plan whole-class, small-group, and individualized instruction. Analyzing results of criterion-referenced tests over time can also help teachers track student progress on certain skills. A disadvantage of criterion-referenced tests is they do not allow educators to compare students' performances to samples of their peers.

WAYS THAT STANDARDIZED TEST RESULTS ARE REPORTED

- **Raw scores** are sometimes reported and indicate how many questions students answered correctly on a test. By themselves, they do not provide much useful information. They do not indicate how students performed in comparison to other students or to grade-level expectations.

Copyright © Mometrix Media. You have been licensed one copy of this document for personal use only. Any other reproduction or redistribution is strictly prohibited. All rights reserved. This content is provided for test preparation purposes only and does not imply an endorsement by Mometrix of any particular political, scientific, or religious point of view.

- **Grade-level equivalents** are also sometimes reported. A grade-level equivalent score of 3.4 indicates that a student performed as well as an average third grader in the fourth month of school. It can indicate whether a student is performing above or below grade-level expectations, but it does not indicate that the student should be moved to a different grade level.
- **Standard scores** are used to compare students' performances on tests to standardized samples of their peers. Standard deviation refers to the amount that a set of scores differs from the mean score on a test.
- **Percentile ranks** are used on criterion-referenced tests to indicate what percentage of test takers scored lower than the student whose score is being reported.
- **Cutoff scores** refer to predetermined scores students must obtain in order to be considered proficient in certain areas. Scores below the cutoff level indicate improvement is needed and may result in interventions or instructional changes.

FORMAL AND INFORMAL ASSESSMENTS

Assessments are any method a teacher uses to gather information about student comprehension of curriculum, including improvised questions for the class and highly-structured tests. **Formal assessments** are assessments that have **clearly defined standards and methodology**, and which are applied consistently to all students. Formal tests should be objective and the test itself should be scrutinized for validity and reliability since it tends to carry higher weight for the student. Summative assessments, such as end-of-unit tests, lend themselves to being formal tests because it is necessary that a teacher test the comprehension of all students in a consistent and thorough way.

Although formal assessments can provide useful data about student performance and progress, they can be costly and time-consuming to implement. Administering formal assessments often interrupts classroom instruction, and may cause testing anxiety.

Informal assessments are assessments that do not adhere to formal objectives and they do not have to be administered consistently to all students. As a result, they do not have to be scored or recorded as a grade and generally act as a **subjective measure** of class comprehension. Informal assessments can be as simple as asking a whole class to raise their hand if they are ready to proceed to the next step or asking a particular question of an individual student.

Informal assessments do not provide objective data for analysis, but they can be implemented quickly and inexpensively. Informal assessments can also be incorporated into regular classroom instruction and activities, making them more authentic and less stressful for students.

USING VARIOUS ASSESSMENTS

The goal of **assessment** in education is to gather data that, when evaluated, can be used to further student learning and achievement. **Standardized tests** are helpful for placement purposes and to reflect student progress toward goals set by a school district or state. If a textbook is chosen to align with district learning standards, the textbook assessments can provide teachers with convenient, small-scale, regular checks of student knowledge against the target standard.

In order be effective, teachers must know where their students are in the learning process. Teachers use a multitude of **formal and informal assessment methods** to do this. Posing differentiated discussion questions is an example of an informal assessment method that allows teachers to gauge individual student progress rather than their standing in relation to a universal benchmark.

Copyright © Mometrix Media. You have been licensed one copy of this document for personal use only. Any other reproduction or redistribution is strictly prohibited. All rights reserved.
This content is provided for test preparation purposes only and does not imply an endorsement by Mometrix of any particular political, scientific, or religious point of view.

Effective teachers employ a variety of assessments, as different formats assess different skills, promote different learning experiences, and appeal to different learners. A portfolio is an example of an assessment that gauges student progress in multiple skills and through multiple media. Teachers can use authentic or performance-based assessments to stimulate student interest and provide visible connections between language-learning and the real world.

ASSESSMENT RELIABILITY

Assessment reliability refers to how well an assessment is constructed and is made up of a variety of measures. An assessment is generally considered **reliable** if it yields similar results across multiple administrations of the assessment. A test should perform similarly with different test administrators, graders, and test-takers and perform consistently over multiple iterations. Factors that affect reliability include the day-to-day wellbeing of the student (students can sometimes underperform), the physical environment of the test, the way it is administered, and the subjectivity of the scorer (with written-response assessments).

Perhaps the most important threat to assessment reliability is the nature of the **exam questions** themselves. An assessment question is designed to test student knowledge of a certain construct. A question is reliable in this sense if students who understand the content answer the question correctly. Statisticians look for patterns in student marks, both within the single test and over multiple tests, as a way of measuring reliability. Teachers should watch out for circumstances in which a student or students answer correctly a series of questions about a given concept (demonstrating their understanding) but then answer a related question incorrectly. The latter question may be an unreliable indicator of concept knowledge.

MEASURES OF ASSESSMENT RELIABILITY

- **Test-retest reliability** refers to an assessment's consistency of results with the same test-taker over multiple retests. If one student shows inconsistent results over time, the test is not considered to have test-retest reliability.
- **Intertester reliability** refers to an assessment's consistency of results between multiple test-takers at the same level. Students at similar levels of proficiency should show similar results.
- **Interrater reliability** refers to an assessment's consistency of results between different administrators of the test. This plays an especially critical role in tests with interactive or subjective responses, such as Likert-scales, cloze tests, and short answer tests. Different raters of the same test need to have a consistent means of evaluating the test-takers' performance. Clear rubrics can help keep two or more raters consistent in scoring.
- **Intra-rater reliability** refers to an assessment's consistency of results with one rater over time. One test rater should be able to score different students objectively to rate subjective test formats fairly.
- **Parallel-forms reliability** refers to an assessment's consistency between multiple different forms. For instance, end-of-course assessments may have many distinctive test forms, with different questions or question orders. If the different forms of a test do not provide the same results, it is said to be lacking in parallel-forms reliability.
- **Internal consistency reliability** refers to the consistency of results of similar questions on a particular assessment. If there are two or more questions targeted at the same standard and at the same level, they should show the same results across each question.

ASSESSMENT VALIDITY

Assessment validity is a measure of the relevancy that an assessment has to the skill or ability being evaluated, and the degree to which students' performance is representative of their mastery

Copyright © Mometrix Media. You have been licensed one copy of this document for personal use only. Any other reproduction or redistribution is strictly prohibited. All rights reserved. This content is provided for test preparation purposes only and does not imply an endorsement by Mometrix of any particular political, scientific, or religious point of view.

of the topic of assessment. In other words, a teacher should ask how well an assessment's results correlate to what it is looking to assess. Assessments should be evaluated for validity on both the **individual question** level and as a **test overall**. This can be especially helpful in refining tests for future classes. The overall validity of an assessment is determined by several types of validity measures.

An assessment is considered **valid** if it measures what it is intended to measure. One common error that can reduce the validity of a test (or a question on a test) occurs if the instructions are written at a reading level the students can't understand. In this case, it is not valid to take the student's failed answer as a true indication of his or her knowledge of the subject. Factors internal to the student might also affect exam validity: anxiety and a lack of self-esteem often lower assessments results, reducing their validity of a measure of student knowledge.

An assessment has content validity if it includes all the **relevant aspects** of the subject being tested—if it is comprehensive, in other words. An assessment has **predictive validity** if a score on the test is an accurate predictor of future success in the same domain. For example, SAT exams purport to have validity in predicting student success in a college. An assessment has construct validity if it accurately measures student knowledge of the subject being tested.

MEASURES OF ASSESSMENT VALIDITY

- **Face validity** refers to the initial impression of whether an assessment seems to be fit for the task. As this method is subjective to interpretation and unquantifiable, it should not be used singularly as a measurement of validity.
- **Construct validity** asks if an assessment actually assesses what it is intended to assess. Some topics are more straightforward, such as assessing if a student can perform two-digit multiplication. This can be directly tested, which gives the assessment a strong content validity. Other measures, such as a person's overall happiness, must be measured indirectly. If an assessment asserted that a person is generally happy if they smile frequently, it would be fair to question the construct validity of that assessment because smiling is unlikely to be a consistent measure of all peoples' general happiness.
- **Content validity** indicates whether the assessment is comprehensive of all aspects of the content being assessed. If a test leaves out an important topic, then the teacher will not have a full picture as a result of the assessment.
- **Criterion validity** refers to whether the results of an assessment can be used to **predict** a related value, known as **criterion**. An example of this is the hypothesis that IQ tests would predict a person's success later in life, but many critics believe that IQ tests are not valid predictors of success because intelligence is not the only predictor of success in life. IQ tests have shown validity toward predicting academic success, however. The measure of an assessment's criterion validity depends on how closely related the criterion is.
- **Discriminant validity** refers to how well an assessment tests only that which it is intended to test and successfully discriminates one piece of information from another. For instance, a student who is exceptional in mathematics should not be able to put that information into use on a science test and gain an unfair advantage. If they are able to score well due to their mathematics knowledge, the science test did not adequately discriminate science knowledge from mathematics knowledge.
- **Convergent validity** is related to discriminant validity, but takes into account that two measures may be distinct, but can be correlated. For instance, a personality test should distinguish self-esteem from extraversion so that they can be measured independently, but if an assessment has convergent validity, it should show a correlation between related measures.

Copyright © Mometrix Media. You have been licensed one copy of this document for personal use only. Any other reproduction or redistribution is strictly prohibited. All rights reserved.
This content is provided for test preparation purposes only and does not imply an endorsement by Mometrix of any particular political, scientific, or religious point of view.

PRACTICALITY

An assessment is **practical** if it uses an appropriate amount of human and budgetary resources. A practical exam doesn't take very long to design or score, nor does it take students very long to complete in relation to other learning objectives and priorities. Teachers often need to balance a desire to construct comprehensive or content-valid tests with a need for practicality: lengthy exams consume large amounts of instruction time and may return unreliable results if students become tired and lose focus.

ASSESSMENT BIAS

An assessment is considered biased if it disadvantages a certain group of students, such as students of a certain gender, race, cultural background, or socioeconomic class. A **content bias** exists when the subject matter of a question or assessment is familiar to one group and not another—for example, a reading comprehension passage which discusses an event in American history would be biased against students new to the country. An **attitudinal bias** exists when a teacher has a pre-conceived idea about the likely success of an assessment of a particular individual or group. A **method bias** arises when the format of an assessment is unfamiliar to a given group of students. **Language bias** occurs when an assessment utilizes idioms, collocations, or cultural references unfamiliar to a group of students. Finally, **translation bias** may arise when educators attempt to translate content-area assessments into a student's native language—rough or hurried translations often result in a loss of nuance important for accurate assessment.

AUTHENTIC ASSESSMENTS

An authentic assessment is an assessment designed to closely resemble something that a student does, or will do, in the real world. Thus, for example, students will never encounter a multiple-choice test requiring them to choose the right tense of a verb, but they will encounter context in which they have to write a narration of an event that has antecedents and consequents spread out in time—for example, their version of what caused a traffic accident. The latter is an example of a potential **authentic assessment**.

Well-designed authentic assessments require a student to exercise **advanced cognitive skills** (e.g., solving problems, integrating information, performing deductions), integrate **background knowledge**, and confront **ambiguity**. Research has demonstrated that mere language proficiency is not predictive of future language success—learning how to utilize knowledge in a complex context is an essential additional skill.

The terms "authentic" and "performance-based" assessments are often used interchangeably. However, a performance-based assessment doesn't necessarily have to be grounded in a possible authentic experience.

PERFORMANCE-BASED ASSESSMENTS

A performance-based assessment is one in which students demonstrate their learning by performing a **task** rather than by answering questions in a traditional test format. Proponents of **performance-based assessments** argue that they lead students to use **high-level cognitive skills** as they focus on how to put their knowledge to use and plan a sequence of stages in an activity or presentation. They also allow students more opportunities to individualize their presentations or responses based on preferred learning styles. Research suggests that students welcome the chance to put their knowledge to use in real-world scenarios.

Advocates of performance-based assessments suggest that they avoid many of the problems of language or cultural bias present in traditional assessments, and thus they allow more accurate

Copyright © Mometrix Media. You have been licensed one copy of this document for personal use only. Any other reproduction or redistribution is strictly prohibited. All rights reserved. This content is provided for test preparation purposes only and does not imply an endorsement by Mometrix of any particular political, scientific, or religious point of view.

assessment of how well students learned the underlying concepts. In discussions regarding English as a second language, they argue that performance assessments come closer to replicating what should be the true goal of language learning—the effective use of language in real contexts—than do more traditional exams. Critics point out that performance assessments are difficult and time-consuming for teachers to construct and for students to perform. Finally, performative assessments are difficult to grade in the absence of a well-constructed and detailed rubric.

TECHNOLOGY-BASED ASSESSMENTS

Technology-based assessments provide teachers with multiple resources for evaluating student progress to guide instruction. They are applicable in most formal and informal instructional settings and can be utilized as formative and summative assessments. Technology-based assessments simplify and enhance the efficiency of determining comprehension and instructional effectiveness, as they quickly present the teacher with information regarding student progress. This data enables the teacher to make necessary adjustments to facilitate student learning and growth. Implementing this assessment format simplifies the process of aligning them to school and district academic standards. This establishes objectivity and uniformity for comparing results and progress among students, as well as ensures that all students are held to the same academic expectations. While technology-based assessments are beneficial, there are some shortcomings to consider. This format may not be entirely effective for all learning styles in demonstrating understanding, as individualization in technology-based assessment can be limited. These assessments may not illustrate individual students' growth over time, but rather their mastery of an academic standard, thus hindering the ability to evaluate overall achievement. As technology-based evaluation limits hands-on opportunities, the real-world application and relevancy of the assessment may be unapparent to students.

ADVANTAGES AND DISADVANTAGES OF TECHNOLOGY-BASED ASSESSMENTS

Technology-based assessments can have many advantages. They can be given to large numbers of students at once, limited only by the amounts of technological equipment schools possess. Many types of technology-based assessments are instantly scored, and feedback is quickly provided. Students are sometimes able to view their results and feedback at the conclusion of their testing sessions. Data can be quickly compiled and reported in easy-to-understand formats. Technology-based assessments can also often track student progress over time.

Technology-based assessments can have some disadvantages as well. Glitches and system errors can interfere with the assessment process or score reporting. Students must also have the necessary prerequisite technological skills to take the assessments, or the results may not measure the content they are designed to measure. For example, if students take timed computer-based writing tests, they should have proficient typing skills. Otherwise, they may perform poorly on the tests despite strong writing abilities. Other prerequisite skills include knowing how to use a keyboard and mouse and understanding how to locate necessary information on the screen.

PORTFOLIO ASSESSMENTS

A **portfolio** is a collection of student work in multiple forms and media gathered over time. Teachers may assess the portfolio both for evidence of progress over time or in its end state as a demonstration of the achievement of certain proficiency levels.

One advantage of **portfolio assessments** is their breadth—unlike traditional assessments which focus on one or two language skills, portfolios may contain work in multiple forms—writing samples, pictures, and graphs designed for content courses, video and audio clips, student

Copyright © Mometrix Media. You have been licensed one copy of this document for personal use only. Any other reproduction or redistribution is strictly prohibited. All rights reserved. This content is provided for test preparation purposes only and does not imply an endorsement by Mometrix of any particular political, scientific, or religious point of view.

reflections, teacher observations, and student exams. A second advantage is that they allow a student to develop work in authentic contexts, including in other classrooms and at home.

In order for portfolios to function as an objective assessment tool, teachers should negotiate with students in advance of what genres of work will be included and outline a grading rubric that makes clear what will be assessed, such as linguistic proficiency, use of English in academic contexts, and demonstrated use of target cognitive skills.

CURRICULUM-BASED ASSESSMENTS

Curriculum-based assessments, also known as **curriculum-based measurements (CBM)**, are short, frequent assessments designed to measure student progress toward meeting curriculum **benchmarks**.

Teachers implement CBM by designing **probes**, or short assessments that target specific skills. For example, a teacher might design a spelling probe, administered weekly, that requires students to spell 10 unfamiliar but level-appropriate words. Teachers then track the data over time to measure student progress toward defined grade-level goals.

CBM has several clear advantages. If structured well, the probes have high reliability and validity. Furthermore, they provide clear and objective evidence of student progress—a welcome outcome for students and parents who often grapple with less-clear and subjective evidence. Used correctly, CBMs also motivate students and provide them with evidence of their own progress. However, while CBMs are helpful in identifying *areas* of student weaknesses, they do not identify the *causes* of those weaknesses or provide teachers with strategies for improving instruction.

TEXTBOOK ASSESSMENTS

Textbook assessments are the assessments provided at the end of a chapter or unit in an approved textbook. **Textbook assessments** present several advantages for a teacher: they are already made; they are likely to be accurate representations of the chapter or unit materials; and, if the textbook has been prescribed or recommended by the state, it is likely to correspond closely to Common Core or other tested standards.

Textbook assessments can be limiting for students who lag in the comprehension of academic English, or whose preferred learning style is not verbal. While textbooks may come with DVDs or recommended audio links, ESOL teachers will likely need to supplement these assessment materials with some of their own findings. Finally, textbook assessments are unlikely to represent the range of assessment types used in the modern classroom, such as a portfolio or performance-based assessments.

PEER ASSESSMENT

A peer assessment is when students grade one another's work based on a teacher-provided framework. **Peer assessments** are promoted as a means of saving teacher time and building student metacognitive skills. They are typically used as **formative** rather than summative assessments, given concerns about the reliability of student scoring and the tensions that can result if student scores contribute to overall grades. Peer assessments are used most often to grade essay-type written work or presentations. Proponents point out that peer assessments require students to apply metacognition, builds cooperative work and interpersonal skills, and broadens the sense that the student is accountable to peers and not just the teacher. Even advocates of the practice agree that students need detailed rubrics in order to succeed. Critics often argue that low-performing students have little to offer high-performing students in terms of valuable feedback— and this disparity may be more pronounced in ESOL classrooms or special education environments

146

Copyright © Mometrix Media. You have been licensed one copy of this document for personal use only. Any other reproduction or redistribution is strictly prohibited. All rights reserved.
This content is provided for test preparation purposes only and does not imply an endorsement by Mometrix of any particular political, scientific, or religious point of view.

than in mainstream ones. One way to overcome this weakness is for the teacher to lead the evaluation exercise, guiding the students through a point-by-point framework of evaluation.

Chapter Quiz

Ready to see how well you retained what you just read? Scan the QR code to go directly to the chapter quiz interface for this study guide. If you're using a computer, simply visit the bonus page at **mometrix.com/bonus948/ftceprekinprim** and click the Chapter Quizzes link.

Copyright © Mometrix Media. You have been licensed one copy of this document for personal use only. Any other reproduction or redistribution is strictly prohibited. All rights reserved.
This content is provided for test preparation purposes only and does not imply an endorsement by Mometrix of any particular political, scientific, or religious point of view.

Child Guidance and Classroom Behavioral Management

Transform passive reading into active learning! After immersing yourself in this chapter, put your comprehension to the test by taking a quiz. The insights you gained will stay with you longer this way. Scan the QR code to go directly to the chapter quiz interface for this study guide. If you're using a computer, simply visit the bonus page at **mometrix.com/bonus948/ftceprekinprim** and click the Chapter Quizzes link.

Behavior in Early Childhood

PRINCIPLES RELATED TO EARLY CHILDHOOD BEHAVIOR MANAGEMENT

Repetition and consistency are two major elements for managing young children's behavior. Adults must always follow and enforce whichever rules they designate. They must also remember that they will need to repeat their rules over and over to make them effective. Behaviorism has shown it is more powerful to reward good behaviors than punish bad behaviors. Consistently rewarding desired behaviors enables young children to make the association between behavior and reward. Functional behavior analysis can inform adults: knowing the function of a behavior is necessary to changing it. For example, if a toddler throws a tantrum out of frustration, providing support/scaffolding for a difficult task, breaking it down to more manageable increments via task analysis, and giving encouragement would be appropriate strategies. If the tantrum was a bid for attention, adults would only reinforce/strengthen tantrum recurrence by paying attention. Feeling valued and loved within a positive relationship greatly supports young children's compliance with rules. The **"10:1 Rule"** prescribes at least 10 positive comments per 1 negative comment/correction.

AGGRESSION

Preschoolers typically demonstrate some aggressive behavior, which tends to peak around age 4. **Instrumental aggression** is one basic type: younger preschoolers frequently shout, hit, or kick others to get concrete objects they want. Middle preschoolers are more likely to exhibit **hostile aggression**, including getting even for wrongs or injuries they feel others have done to them. Hostile aggression occurs in two subtypes: overt and relational. **Overt aggression** involves physically harming others or threatening to do so, while **relational aggression** involves emotional/social harm, such as rejecting or excluding another from a group of friends or spreading malicious rumors about another. Young boys are more likely to engage in **overt aggression**, while young girls are more likely to engage in relational aggression. These gender preferences in aggressive behaviors tend to remain the same at all ages if aggression exists. While most young children eventually phase out aggression as they learn other ways of resolving social conflicts, some persist in verbally and/or physically aggressive behavior, causing problems.

MINIMIZING AGGRESSIVE BEHAVIOR

While it is normal for preschoolers to exhibit some physical and verbal aggression until they have learned more mature ways of expressing feelings, getting what they want, and settling disputes, there are things adults can do to influence them such that aggressive behavior does not develop into a predominant method of social interaction. Adults set examples for children, and children

148

Copyright © Mometrix Media. You have been licensed one copy of this document for personal use only. Any other reproduction or redistribution is strictly prohibited. All rights reserved.
This content is provided for test preparation purposes only and does not imply an endorsement by Mometrix of any particular political, scientific, or religious point of view.

learn by observing and imitating those examples. Therefore, parents, caregivers, and teachers should not model verbally and/or physically aggressive behaviors such as calling others names, yelling at others, or punishing others' undesirable behaviors using physical force. Not only should adults avoid disciplining children physically, but they should also avoid physically and/or verbally violent interactions with other adults. Social learning theorist Albert Bandura proved that children who viewed violent videos imitated what they observed and engaged in more aggressive behavior, so adults should also prevent young children's exposure to violent TV programming and video games.

MANAGING THE NORMAL BEHAVIOR OF YOUNG CHILDREN

Before reacting to young children's behaviors, adults should make sure children understand the situation. They should state rules simply and clearly, repeat them frequently for a long time for young children to remember and follow them, and state and enforce rules very consistently to avoid confusion. Adults should tell children clearly what they expect of them. They should never assume they need do nothing when children follow rules; they should consistently give rewards for compliance. Adults should also explain to young children why they are or are not receiving rewards by citing the rule they did or did not follow. Adults can arrange the environment to promote success. For example, if a child throws things that break windows, adults can remove such objects and substitute softer/more lightweight items. Organization is also important. Adults should begin with a simple, easy-to-implement plan and adhere to it. They should record children's progress; analyzing the records shows what does and does not work and why, enabling new/revised plans.

> **Review Video: Promoting Appropriate Behavior**
> Visit mometrix.com/academy and enter code: 321015

GENETIC AND ENVIRONMENTAL INFLUENCES ON BEHAVIOR

Research into factors influencing early childhood behavior identifies both genetic variables and environmental ones, like corporal punishment, affecting young children's propensities toward antisocial behavior. Children experiencing more corporal punishment and children who are at greater genetic risk display greater behavior problems. However, boys at higher genetic risk for behavior problems who also experience more corporal punishment exhibit the most antisocial behavior. Therefore, both genetic risk factors and corporal punishment significantly predict preschoolers' antisocial behavior. Additionally, the nature-nurture interaction of genetic risk factors and environmental punishment is statistically significant for young boys but not young girls. Such evidence shows that environmental learning is not wholly responsible for antisocial behavior: genetic variables predispose some young children to antisocial behaviors more than others.

Behavior Management Theory

MANAGING AND MONITORING STUDENT BEHAVIOR

BEHAVIORISM AND CONDITIONING

The theoretical school of **behaviorism** was established by John B. Watson and further developed by Ivan Pavlov and B.F. Skinner. Behaviorism emphasizes the role of environmental and experiential learning in the behavior of animals and humans. Simply put, if a person experiences a desirable result from a particular behavior, that person is more likely to perform the behavior in pursuit of the result. Likewise, undesirable results cause a person to avoid performing an associated behavior. This process of **reinforcing** or rewarding good behaviors and **punishing** unwanted behaviors is known as conditioning. Behaviorists use the terms positive and negative to refer to the mode of conditioning. The term **positive** refers to an added stimulus, such as giving a child a treat as

Copyright © Mometrix Media. You have been licensed one copy of this document for personal use only. Any other reproduction or redistribution is strictly prohibited. All rights reserved.
This content is provided for test preparation purposes only and does not imply an endorsement by Mometrix of any particular political, scientific, or religious point of view.

positive reinforcement or giving added homework as positive punishment. **Negative**, on the other hand refers to removing a stimulus, such as taking recess away as a negative punishment, or taking away extra classwork as negative reinforcement for students performing their homework independently. In the classroom, the teacher has the opportunity to help students learn to meet specific behavioral expectations. The tools of behaviorism may be carefully employed in the classrooms through positive and negative punishments and rewards. Classroom rules and expectations should be made clear as soon as possible and reinforced through verbal praise, prizes, or special privileges. Likewise, negative behaviors should be discouraged through verbal warnings, loss of privileges, and communication with the family or administrators when necessary.

CHOICE THEORY

Choice theory, developed by **William Glasser**, states that behavior is chosen, either consciously or unconsciously, to meet the **five basic needs** of survival, love and belonging, power, freedom, and fun. Rather than implement positive and negative reinforcements to drive behavior, the teacher must aim to teach students self-responsibility for their actions. This includes encouraging students to reflect and consider the reasons for their actions and attempt to rectify any misbehavior. This method relies on the notion that if students understand how their desire to meet certain needs impacts their actions, they are more likely to engage in positive behavior. In the classroom, the teacher focuses on meeting students' **five basic needs** to encourage positive behavior by creating a classroom climate that emphasizes **communication, relationship building**, and **self-reflection**. This includes establishing positive relationships with students, holding class discussions, and teaching conflict resolution skills to create a safe, welcoming learning environment. Instructional activities are tailored to individual needs, and students have a great deal of choice in their own learning with the intention of promoting positive behavior by meeting their needs for power and freedom.

ASSERTIVE DISCIPLINE THEORY

The **Assertive Discipline theory** was developed by **Lee** and **Marlene Canter**. This theory states that the teacher is in charge of **instruction**, **the classroom**, and **students' behavior**. The expectation is that the teacher establishes clear behavioral standards that protect their right to teach and students' right to learn without distraction or disruption. Negative consequences for unwanted behavior are instilled to deter students from deviating from behavioral expectations. This theory argues that if teachers are viewed as firm and consistent, students will have a greater respect for them and ultimately engage in positive behavior. In the classroom, the teacher is in control of **establishing** and **consistently reinforcing** standards for student behavior. This establishes a sense of predictability, as students are clear on what is expected of them as they engage in learning. Students are expected to comply with the teacher's expectations, and a system of **negative consequences** are in place to discourage unwanted behavior. Positive behavior is rewarded to further reinforce desired behavior. The teacher in this classroom believes that creating such an environment enhances students' ability to focus on learning without disruption.

STUDENT-DIRECTED LEARNING THEORY

The **Student-Directed Learning theory**, or the idea of the **Democratic Classroom**, was founded by **Alfie Kohn** and emphasizes the importance of **student choice** and **classroom community** in influencing behavior. This includes having students contribute to the development of behavioral expectations, as this helps students understand their purpose while instilling a sense of ownership and accountability. Instructional activities are tailored to accommodate students' individual interests and natural curiosity while emphasizing cooperation to foster an engaging learning environment that promotes positive behavior. This theory focuses on eliciting students' intrinsic motivation to engage in positive behavior, rather than relying on positive and negative

Copyright © Mometrix Media. You have been licensed one copy of this document for personal use only. Any other reproduction or redistribution is strictly prohibited. All rights reserved.
This content is provided for test preparation purposes only and does not imply an endorsement by Mometrix of any particular political, scientific, or religious point of view.

reinforcements. In the classroom, students primarily direct their own learning based upon their **natural curiosity** while the teacher acts as a **facilitator**. Students contribute to the development of behavioral expectations that are instilled to promote respect and focus on learning. **Active engagement**, **cooperation**, and **collaborative learning** are emphasized over direct instruction. Students may be engaging in differing activities simultaneously as the teacher moves around the classroom to monitor progress and assist as necessary.

SOCIAL LEARNING THEORY AND BEHAVIOR MANAGEMENT

The **Social Learning theory**, developed by **Albert Bandura**, asserts that one's **environment** and the **people** within it heavily influence behavior. As humans are social creatures, they learn a great deal by **observing** and **imitating** one another. This theory is also rooted in the importance of **self-efficacy** in achieving desired behavior, as students must be motivated and confident that they can effectively imitate what they observe. In the classroom, the teacher establishes behavioral expectations and focuses on **modeling** positive behaviors, attitudes, and interactions with the intention of encouraging students to do the same. The teacher recognizes and praises positive behavior from students to elicit the same behavior from others. The teacher also emphasizes a growth mindset in the classroom to promote students' sense of self-efficacy.

BEHAVIOR STANDARDS AND EXPECTATIONS FOR STUDENTS AT DEVELOPMENTAL LEVELS

Behavioral standards that emphasize respect for oneself, others, and property are necessary in creating a safe, positive, and productive learning environment for students of all ages. However, as students at varying developmental levels differ in their capabilities across domains, behavioral expectations must be **realistic**, **applicable**, and reflect an **awareness** of these **differences** while encouraging growth. Young children, for example, are learning to interact with others and function in a group setting. Behavioral expectations must be attuned to this understanding while promoting the development of positive interpersonal skills. Young children also require ample opportunities for active movement and cannot reasonably be expected to sit still for long periods of time. Middle level students are at a unique transitional period in their development and often exhibit characteristics of both young children and adolescents. Behavioral standards for these students must recognize the significant social, emotional, cognitive, and physical changes occurring at this stage by emphasizing self-control, emotional regulation, and positive interactions. As older students prepare for adulthood, they can generally be expected to conduct themselves with a degree of maturity and responsibility in a variety of settings. Appropriate behavioral standards for these students emphasize self-responsibility, respectful interactions, and independently completing necessary tasks.

EFFECTIVE MANAGEMENT OF STUDENT BEHAVIOR
MANAGEMENT PROCEDURES AND SIGNIFICANCE IN POSITIVE, PRODUCTIVE, AND ORGANIZED LEARNING ENVIRONMENT

Promoting **appropriate behavior** and **ethical work habits** while taking specific measures to **manage student behavior** creates a safe, organized, and productive classroom. Such an environment is beneficial for students' motivation, engagement, and ability to focus on learning. This is achieved by communicating and consistently reinforcing **high**, yet **realistic behavioral expectations** for all students. This, when combined with **relationship building** strategies, establishes a positive rapport between the teacher and students that encourages appropriate behavior and ethical work habits. Students are more inclined to adhere to expectations for behavior and work habits when their relationship with the teacher is founded on mutual understanding and respect. In addition, students that feel they are a part of developing academic and behavioral expectations feel a greater sense of **ownership** and responsibility to follow them, and, therefore, it is beneficial to include students in this process. Encouraging students to **self-monitor** their

Copyright © Mometrix Media. You have been licensed one copy of this document for personal use only. Any other reproduction or redistribution is strictly prohibited. All rights reserved.
This content is provided for test preparation purposes only and does not imply an endorsement by Mometrix of any particular political, scientific, or religious point of view.

behavior and utilize conflict resolution strategies furthers this sense of accountability, as it prompts students to positively manage their own actions and work habits. Misbehavior must be addressed appropriately and in a timely manner, and consequences must follow a logical sequence, such as a verbal warning, followed by loss of privileges or communication with family.

> **Review Video: Student Behavior Management Approaches**
> Visit mometrix.com/academy and enter code: 843846
>
> **Review Video: Promoting Appropriate Behavior**
> Visit mometrix.com/academy and enter code: 321015

STRATEGIES

Proactively implementing effective behavior management strategies is beneficial to establishing and maintaining a positive, productive learning environment. The **physical environment** should be arranged in such a way that facilitates ease of movement while limiting the amount of free space that could encourage student disruption. Planning for **smooth transitions** from one activity to the next further discourages behavioral disruptions. Desks should be arranged so that students can easily view the teacher, projector, chalkboard, or other information pertinent to learning. Expectations for behavior, procedures, and routines, including consequences, should be predictable, consistent, succinct, and visible at all times. Allowing students to participate in the development of classroom procedures and routines is valuable in providing students with a sense of personal accountability that increases the likelihood that they will follow them. Students also often respond well to incentives for modeling appropriate behavior, such as a **PBIS reward system**, verbal praise, or a positive phone call home. Nonverbal strategies are valuable in subtly managing student behavior throughout instruction, such as hand gestures, proximity, or eye contact. Misbehavior should be addressed discreetly and privately so as to avoid embarrassing the student or encouraging further disruption.

IMPORTANCE OF CONSISTENCY

Standards for behavior must be enforced consistently in order to establish a well-managed classroom in which students can focus on learning. This includes communicating **clear expectations**, holding all students equally accountable with specific **positive and negative consequences**, and **following through** on implementing them. In doing so, the teacher ensures that students are always aware of the behavior expected from them, and what will happen if they do not adhere to the standards. When students are clear regarding behavioral expectations and assured that they will be enforced, they are more inclined to demonstrate appropriate conduct. This creates a predictable, secure environment that promotes student motivation, engagement, and focused productivity in learning. Consistently enforcing behavior standards gives the teacher a sense of credibility among students, and therefore, students are more likely to respect and adhere to these expectations. In addition, holding all students to the same high behavioral standards contributes to a positive classroom climate in which all students feel they are treated fairly.

Chapter Quiz

Ready to see how well you retained what you just read? Scan the QR code to go directly to the chapter quiz interface for this study guide. If you're using a computer, simply visit the bonus page at **mometrix.com/bonus948/ftceprekinprim** and click the Chapter Quizzes link.

Copyright © Mometrix Media. You have been licensed one copy of this document for personal use only. Any other reproduction or redistribution is strictly prohibited. All rights reserved. This content is provided for test preparation purposes only and does not imply an endorsement by Mometrix of any particular political, scientific, or religious point of view.

Language Arts and Reading

Transform passive reading into active learning! After immersing yourself in this chapter, put your comprehension to the test by taking a quiz. The insights you gained will stay with you longer this way. Scan the QR code to go directly to the chapter quiz interface for this study guide. If you're using a computer, simply visit the bonus page at **mometrix.com/bonus948/ftceprekinprim** and click the Chapter Quizzes link.

Literacy Instruction for Young Children

EMERGENT LITERACY THEORY
EMERGENT LITERACY VERSUS READING READINESS

Historically, early childhood educators viewed "reading readiness" as a time during young children's literacy development when they were ready to start learning to read and write, and taught literacy accordingly. However, in the late 20th and early 20th centuries, research has found that children have innate learning capacities and that skills emerge under the proper conditions. Educational researchers came to view language as developing gradually within a child rather than a child's being ready to read at a certain time. Thus, the term *emergent* came to replace *readiness*, while *literacy* replaced *reading* as referring to all of language's interrelated aspects of listening, speaking, writing, and viewing, as well as reading. Traditional views of literacy were based only on children's reading and writing in ways similar to those of adults. However, more recently, the theory of emergent literacy has evolved through the findings of research into the early preschool reading of young children and the associated characteristics of them and their families.

EMERGENT LITERACY THEORY'S PRINCIPLES ABOUT HOW YOUNG CHILDREN LEARN TO READ AND WRITE

Through extensive research, emergent literacy theorists have found the following:

- Young children develop literacy through being actively involved in reading and rereading their favorite storybooks. When preschoolers "reread" storybooks, they have not memorized them; rather, theorists find this activity to exemplify young children's reconstruction of a book's meaning. Similarly, young children's invented spellings are examples of their efforts to reconstruct what they know of written language; they can inform us about a child's familiarity with specific phonetic components.
- Adults' reading to children, no matter how young, is crucial to literacy development. It helps children gain a "feel" for the character, flow, and patterns of written/printed language, and an overall sense of what reading feels like and entails. It fosters positive attitudes toward reading in children, strongly motivating them to read when they begin school. Being read to also helps children develop print awareness and formulate concepts of books and reading.
- Influenced by Piaget and Vygotsky, emergent literacy theory views reading and writing as developmental processes having successive stages.

PERSPECTIVE REGARDING INSTRUCTIONAL MODELS

The emergent literacy theoretical perspective yields an instructional model for the learning and teaching of reading and writing in young children that is founded on building instruction from the child's knowledge. Emergent literacy theory's assumption is that young children already know a lot

Copyright © Mometrix Media. You have been licensed one copy of this document for personal use only. Any other reproduction or redistribution is strictly prohibited. All rights reserved. This content is provided for test preparation purposes only and does not imply an endorsement by Mometrix of any particular political, scientific, or religious point of view.

about language and literacy by the time they enter school. This theory furthermore regards even 2- and 3-year-olds as having information about how the reading and writing processes function, and as having already formed particular ideas about what written/printed language is. From this perspective, emergent literacy theory then dictates that teaching should build upon what a child already knows and should support the child's further literacy development. Researchers conclude that teachers should furnish open-ended activities allowing children to show what they already know about literacy, to apply that knowledge, and to build upon it. From the emergent literacy perspective, teachers take the role of creating a learning environment with conditions that are conducive to children's learning in ways that are ideally self-motivated, self-generated, and self-regulated.

HOW BABIES AND YOUNG CHILDREN LEARN TO READ AND WRITE

According to the theory of emergent literacy, even infants encounter written language. Two- and three-year-olds commonly can identify logos, labels, and signs in their homes and communities. Also, young children's scribbles show features/appearances of their language's specific writing system even before they can write. For example, Egyptian children's scribbles look more like Egyptian writing; American children's scribbles look more like English writing. Young children learn to read and write concurrently, not sequentially; the two abilities are closely interrelated. Moreover, though with speech, receptive language comprehension seems to develop easier/sooner than expressive language production, this does not apply to reading and writing: first learning activities involving writing are found easier for preschoolers than those involving reading. Research finds that form follows function, not the opposite: young children's literacy learning is mostly through meaningful, functional, purposeful/goal-directed real-life activities. Literacy comprises not isolated, abstract skills learned for their own sake but rather authentic skills applied to accomplish real-life purposes, the way children observe adults using literacy.

DEVELOPMENTALLY INAPPROPRIATE KINDERGARTEN AND PRESCHOOL LITERACY PRACTICES

Research finds some preschools are like play centers but are not optimal for literacy because their curricula exclude natural reading and writing activities. Researchers have also identified a trend in many kindergartens to ensure children's "reading readiness" by providing highly academic programs, influencing preschool curricula to get children "ready" for such kindergartens. Influenced and even pressured by kindergarten programs' academic expectations, parents have also come to expect preschools to prepare their children for kindergarten. However, experts find applying elementary-school programs to kindergartens and preschools developmentally inappropriate. Formal instruction in reading and writing and worksheets are not suitable for younger children. Instead, research finds print-rich preschool environments both developmentally appropriate and more effective. For example, when researchers changed classrooms from having a "book corner" to having a centrally located table with books plus paper, pencils, envelopes, and stamps, children spent 3 to 10 times more time on direct reading and writing activities. Children are found to take naturally to these activities without prior formal reading and writing lessons.

Language and Literacy Development

COMMUNICATION DEVELOPMENT NORMALLY OCCURRING WITHIN A CHILD'S FIRST FIVE YEARS OF LIFE

Language and communication development depend strongly on the language a child develops within the first five years of life. During this time, three developmental periods are observed. At birth, the first period begins. This period is characterized by infant crying and gazing. Babies communicate their sensations and emotions through these behaviors, so they are expressive;

Copyright © Mometrix Media. You have been licensed one copy of this document for personal use only. Any other reproduction or redistribution is strictly prohibited. All rights reserved.
This content is provided for test preparation purposes only and does not imply an endorsement by Mometrix of any particular political, scientific, or religious point of view.

however, they are not yet intentional. They indirectly indicate their needs through expressing how they feel, and when these needs are met, these communicative behaviors are reinforced. These expressions and reinforcement are the foundations for the later development of intentional communication. This becomes possible in the second developmental period, between 6 and 18 months. At this time, infants become able to coordinate their attention visually with other people relative to things and events, enabling purposeful communication with adults. During the third developmental period, from 18 months on, children come to use language as their main way of communicating and learning. Preschoolers can carry on conversations, exercise self-control through language use, and conduct verbal negotiations.

MILESTONES OF NORMAL LANGUAGE DEVELOPMENT BY THE 2 YEARS OLD

By the time most children reach the age of 2 years, they have acquired a vocabulary of about 150 to 300 words. They can name various familiar objects found in their environments. They are able to use at least two prepositions in their speech (e.g., *in*, *on*, and/or *under*). Two-year-olds typically combine the words they know into short sentences. These sentences tend to be mostly noun-verb or verb-noun combinations (e.g., "Daddy work," "Watch this"). They may also include verb-preposition combinations (e.g., "Go out," "Come in"). By the age of 2 years, children use pronouns, such as *I*, *me*, and *you*. They typically can use at least two such pronouns correctly. A normally developing 2-year-old will respond to some commands, directions, or questions, such as "Show me your eyes" or "Where are your ears?"

SALIENT GENERAL ASPECTS OF HUMAN LANGUAGE ABILITIES FROM BEFORE BIRTH TO 5 YEARS OF AGE

Language and communication abilities are integral parts of human life that are central to learning, successful school performance, successful social interactions, and successful living. Human language ability begins before birth: the developing fetus can hear not only internal maternal sounds, but also the mother's voice, others' voices, and other sounds outside the womb. Humans have a natural sensitivity to human sounds and languages from before they are born until they are about 4½ years old. These years are critical for developing language and communication. Babies and young children are predisposed to greater sensitivity to human sounds than other sounds, orienting them toward the language spoken around them. Children absorb their environmental language completely, including vocal tones, syntax, usage, and emphasis. This linguistic absorption occurs very rapidly. Children's first 2½ years particularly involve amazing abilities to learn language, including grammatical expression.

6 MONTHS, 12 MONTHS, AND 18 MONTHS

Individual differences dictate a broad range of language development that is still normal. However, parents observing noticeably delayed language development in their children should consult professionals. Typically, babies respond to hearing their names by 6 months of age, turn their heads and eyes toward the sources of human voices they hear, and respond accordingly to friendly and angry tones of voice. By the age of 12 months, toddlers can usually understand and follow simple directions, especially when these are accompanied by physical and/or vocal cues. They can intentionally use one or more words with the correct meaning. By the age of 18 months, a normally developing child usually has acquired a vocabulary of roughly 5 to 20 words. Eighteen-month-old children use nouns in their speech most of the time. They are very likely to repeat certain words and/or phrases over and over. At this age, children typically are able to follow simple verbal commands without needing as many visual or auditory cues as at 12 months.

Copyright © Mometrix Media. You have been licensed one copy of this document for personal use only. Any other reproduction or redistribution is strictly prohibited. All rights reserved. This content is provided for test preparation purposes only and does not imply an endorsement by Mometrix of any particular political, scientific, or religious point of view.

THREE YEARS

By the time they are 3 years old, most normally developing children have acquired vocabularies of between 900 and 1,000 words. Typically they correctly use the pronouns *I*, *me*, and *you*. They use more verbs more frequently. They apply past tenses to some verbs and plurals to some nouns. 3-year-olds usually can use at least three prepositions; the most common are *in*, *on*, and *under*. The normally developing 3-year-old knows the major body parts and can name them. 3-year-olds typically use 3-word sentences with ease. Normally, parents should find approximately 75 to 100 percent of what a 3-year-old says to be intelligible, while strangers should find between 50 and 75 percent of a 3-year-old's speech intelligible. Children this age comprehend most simple questions about their activities and environments and can answer questions about what they should do when they are thirsty, hungry, sleepy, hot, or cold. They can tell about their experiences in ways that adults can generally follow. By the age of 3 years, children should also be able to tell others their name, age, and sex.

FOUR YEARS

When normally developing children are 4 years old, most know the names of animals familiar to them. They can use at least four prepositions in their speech (e.g., *in*, *on*, *under*, *to*, *from*, etc.). They can name familiar objects in pictures, and they know and can identify one color or more. Usually, they are able to repeat four-syllable words they hear. They verbalize as they engage in their activities, which Vygotsky dubbed "private speech." Private speech helps young children think through what they are doing, solve problems, make decisions, and reinforce the correct sequences in multistep activities. When presented with contrasting items, 4-year-olds can understand comparative concepts like bigger and smaller. At this age, they are able to comply with simple commands without the target stimuli being in their sight (e.g., "Put those clothes in the hamper" [upstairs]). Four-year-old children will also frequently repeat speech sounds, syllables, words, and phrases, similar to 18-month-olds' repetitions but at higher linguistic and developmental levels.

FIVE YEARS

Once most children have reached the age of 5 years, their speech has expanded from the emphasis of younger children on nouns, verbs, and a few prepositions, and is now characterized by many more descriptive words, including adjectives and adverbs. Five-year-olds understand common antonyms, such as big/little, heavy/light, long/short, and hot/cold. They can now repeat longer sentences they hear, up to about 9 words. When given three consecutive, uninterrupted commands, the typical 5-year-old can follow these without forgetting one or two. At age 5, most children have learned simple concepts of time like today, yesterday, and tomorrow; day, morning, afternoon, and night; and before, after, and later. Five-year-olds typically speak in relatively long sentences and normally should be incorporating some compound sentences (with more than one independent clause) and complex sentences (with one or more independent and dependent clauses). Five-year-old children's speech is also grammatically correct most of the time.

PERSONAL NARRATIVES

Personal narratives are the way that young children relate their experiences to others by telling the stories of what happened. The narrative structure incorporates reporting components such as who was involved, where the events took place, and what happened. Understanding and using this structure is crucial to young children for their communication; however, many young children cannot follow or apply this sequence without scaffolding (temporary support as needed) from adults. Adults can ask young children guiding questions to facilitate and advance narratives. They can also provide learning tools that engage children's visual, tactile (touch), and kinesthetic (body position and movement) senses. This reinforces narrative use, increases the depth of scaffolding, and motivates children's participation. Children learn to play the main character, describe the

Copyright © Mometrix Media. You have been licensed one copy of this document for personal use only. Any other reproduction or redistribution is strictly prohibited. All rights reserved. This content is provided for test preparation purposes only and does not imply an endorsement by Mometrix of any particular political, scientific, or religious point of view.

setting, sequence plot actions, and use words and body language to express emotions. Topic-related action sequences or "social stories" are important for preschoolers to comprehend and express to promote daily transitions and self-regulation. Such conversational skills attainment achieves milestones in both linguistic and emotional-social development.

ACHIEVEMENTS OR PROCESSES ENABLED BY ORAL LANGUAGE SKILLS DEVELOPMENT

Crucial oral language development skills enable children to do the following:

- Communicate by listening and responding to others' speech
- Comprehend meanings of numerous words and concepts encountered in their listening and reading
- Acquire information on subjects they are interested in learning about
- Use specific language to express their own thoughts and ideas

Research finds young children's ability to listen to, understand, and use spoken and written language is associated with their later reading, spelling, and writing literacy achievement. Infants typically begin developing oral language skills, which continue developing through life. Babies develop awareness of and attend to adult speech and soon begin communicating their needs via gestures and speech sounds. Toddlers express emotions and ideas and solicit information via language. They start uttering simple sentences, asking questions, and giving opinions regarding their likes and dislikes. Young preschoolers expand their vocabularies from hearing others' speech and from books. They describe past and possible future events and unseen objects, tell fictional or "make-believe" stories, and use complete sentences and more complex language.

BENEFITS OF PLAY-BASED ACTIVITIES

When young children play, they often enact scenarios. Play scenarios tell stories that include who is involved, where they are, what happens, why it happens, and how the "actors" feel about it. Children engage in planning when they decide first what their playing will be about, which children are playing which roles, and who is doing what. This planning and the thought processes involved reflect narrative thinking and structure. Children who experience difficulties with planning play are more likely to avoid participating or to participate only marginally. Since playing actually requires these thought and planning processes, children who do not play spontaneously can be supported in playing by enabling them to talk about potential narratives/stories as foundations for play scenarios. When conflicts emerge during play, conversation is necessary to effect needed change. Narrative development constitutes gradual plot development; play conflicts are akin to fictional/personal narrative problems and result in changed feelings. Adults can help young children discuss problems, identify the changed feeling they cause, and discuss plans/actions for resolution.

CONVERSATION OF ADULTS WITH YOUNG CHILDREN

Adults should converse with young children so the children get practice with hearing and using rich and abstract vocabulary and increasingly complex sentences, using language to express ideas and ask questions for understanding, and using language to answer questions about past, future, and absent things rather than only about "here-and-now" things. To ensure they incorporate these elements in their conversations, adults can consider whose voices are heard most often and who does the most talking in the home, care setting, or classroom; the child, not the adult, should be talking at least half of the time. Adults should be using rich language with complex structures when conversing with young children. Adults should be talking with, not at children; the conversation should be shared equally rather than adults doing all the talking while children listen to them. Adults should also ask young children questions, rather than just telling them things. Additionally,

157

Copyright © Mometrix Media. You have been licensed one copy of this document for personal use only. Any other reproduction or redistribution is strictly prohibited. All rights reserved. This content is provided for test preparation purposes only and does not imply an endorsement by Mometrix of any particular political, scientific, or religious point of view.

adult questions should require that children use language to formulate and communicate abstract ideas.

NATURAL VS. INTENTIONAL

Children enjoy conversing with significant adults, including parents, caregivers, and teachers, and they require practice with doing so. Caregivers tend to talk with young children naturally, sometimes even automatically, throughout the day, which helps children develop significant language skills. However, caregivers can enhance young children's oral language development further through intentional conversations. One element of doing this is establishing an environment that gives the children many things to talk about and many reasons to talk. Another element of intentionally promoting oral language skills development is by engaging in shared conversations. When parents and caregivers share storybook reading with young children, this affords a particularly good springboard for shared conversations. Reading and conversing together are linguistic interactions supplying foundations for children's developing comprehension of numerous word meanings. Researchers find such abundant early word comprehension is a critical basis for later reading comprehension. Asking questions, explaining, requesting what they need, communicating feelings, and learning to listen to others talk are some important ways whereby children build listening, understanding, and speaking skills.

ONE-TO-ONE CONVERSATIONS WITH CHILDREN

When parents, caregivers, or teachers converse one-to-one with individual children, children reap benefits not as available in group conversations. Caregivers should therefore try to have such individual conversations with each child daily. In daycare and preschool settings, some good times for caregivers to do this include when children arrive and leave, during shared reading activities with one or two children, and during center time. Engaging in one-to-one talk allows the adult to repeat what the child says for reinforcement and allows the adult to extend what the child said by adding more information to it, like new vocabulary words, synonyms, meanings, or omitted details. It allows the adult to revise what the child said by restating or recasting it. It allows the child to hear his or her own ideas and thoughts reflected back to them when the adult restates them. Moreover, one-to-one conversation allows adults to contextualize the discussion accordingly with an individual child's understanding. It also allows adults to elicit children's comprehension of abstract concepts.

EXTENDED CONVERSATIONS AND TURN-TAKING

When adults engage young children in extended conversations, including taking many "back-and-forth" turns, these create the richest dialogues for building oral language skills. Adults make connections with and build upon children's declarations and questions. Adults model richer descriptive language by modifying/adding to children's original words with new vocabulary, adjectives, adverbs, and varying sentences with questions and statements. For example, a child shows an adult his or her new drawing, saying, "This is me and Gran in the garden," and the adult can build on this/invite the child to continue by saying, "What is your gran holding?" The child identifies what they planted: "Carrot seeds. Gran said to put them in the dirt so they don't touch." The adult can then encourage the child's use of language to express abstract thoughts: "What could happen if the seeds were touching?" The adult can then extend the conversation through discussion with the child about how plants grow or tending gardens. This introduces new concepts, builds children's linguistic knowledge, and helps them learn to verbalize their ideas.

> **Review Video: What is Sensory Language?**
> Visit mometrix.com/academy and enter code: 177314

Copyright © Mometrix Media. You have been licensed one copy of this document for personal use only. Any other reproduction or redistribution is strictly prohibited. All rights reserved. This content is provided for test preparation purposes only and does not imply an endorsement by Mometrix of any particular political, scientific, or religious point of view.

IN-DEPTH COMPREHENSION OF WORD MEANINGS

To support deeper word-meaning comprehension, teachers can give multiple definitions and examples for the same word and connect new vocabulary with children's existing knowledge. For example, a teacher conducting a preschool classroom science experiment incorporates new scientific concepts with new vocabulary words and conversational practice: Pouring water on a paper towel, the teacher asks children what is happening to the water. A child answers, "It's going into the paper." The teacher asks how. Another child says, "The paper's soaking it up." The teacher confirms this, teaches the word *absorb*, compares the paper to a sponge, and asks how much more water will be absorbed. A child responds probably no more since water is already dripping out. The teacher pours water on a plastic lid, asking if it absorbs. Children respond, "No, it slides off." Confirming, the teacher teaches the word *repel*. This teacher has introduced new science concepts and new vocabulary words, engaged the children in conversation, related new concepts and words to existing knowledge, and added information to deepen comprehension.

ADULTS' NARRATION OF CHILD ACTIVITIES AND ACTIONS

One oral language development technique adults can use is to narrate, or describe what a child is doing as he or she does it. For example, a caregiver can say, "I see you're spreading paste on the back of your paper flower—not too much so it's lumpy, but not too little so it doesn't stick. Now you're pressing the flower onto your poster board. It sticks—good work!" Hence, narration can be incorporated as prelude and segue to verbal positive reinforcement. This promotes oral language development by introducing and illustrating syntaxes. Communicating locations and directionality employs verbs and prepositions. Describing intensity and manner employs adverbs. Labeling objects/actions that are currently present/taking place with new vocabulary words serves immediately to place those words into natural contexts, facilitating more authentic comprehension of word meanings and better memory retention. Caregivers/teachers can narrate children's activities during formal instructional activities and informal situations like outdoor playtime, snack time, and cleanup time, and subsequently converse with them about what they did.

TOPICS THAT YOUNG CHILDREN ENJOY TALKING ABOUT

Personal content is important with young children, who enjoy talking about themselves, such as what their favorite color is or where they got their new shirt; about their activities, like what they are constructing with Legos or shaping with Play-Doh; or about familiar events and things that access their knowledge, like their family activities and experiences with neighbors and friends. Here is an example of how a teacher can make use of children's conversation to reinforce it, expand it, and teach new vocabulary and grammar. The teacher asks a child what he or she is building, and the child answers, "A place for sick animals." The teacher asks, "You mean an animal hospital [or vet clinic]?" and the child confirms. When a child says someone was taken to a hospital "in the siren," the teacher corrects the usage by saying, "They took him to the hospital in the ambulance with the siren was sounding?" This recasts *siren* with the correct word choice, *ambulance*. It incorporates *siren* correctly and extends the statement to a complete sentence.

STORYTELLING

Young children like to communicate about their personal life experiences. When they can do this through narrative structure, it helps them use new words they are learning, organize their thoughts to express them coherently, and engage their imaginative powers. Teachers/caregivers can supply new words they need, model correct syntax for sentences by elaborating on or extending child utterances and asking them questions, and build further upon children's ideas. For example, a teacher asks a child what they did at her sister's birthday party. When the child describes the cake and makes gestures for a word she doesn't know, the teacher supplies "candles," which the child

Copyright © Mometrix Media. You have been licensed one copy of this document for personal use only. Any other reproduction or redistribution is strictly prohibited. All rights reserved. This content is provided for test preparation purposes only and does not imply an endorsement by Mometrix of any particular political, scientific, or religious point of view.

confirms and repeats. When the child then offers, "Mom says be careful with candles," the teacher asks what could happen if you're not careful. The child replies that candles can start a fire. In this way, teachers give young children models of sentence structure, teach vocabulary, and guide children in expressing their thoughts in organized sequences that listeners can follow.

SHARED BOOK READING

When teachers share books with preschoolers, they can ask questions and discuss the content, giving great opportunities for building oral language through conversation. Books with simple text and numerous, engaging illustrations best invite preschoolers to talk about the characters and events in the pictures and the plotlines they hear. Children's listening and speaking skills develop, they learn new information and concepts, their vocabularies increase, and their ability to define words and explain their meanings is enhanced through shared reading. Many children's books include rich varieties of words that may not occur in daily conversation, used in complete-sentence contexts. Teachers should provide preschoolers with fictional and nonfictional books, poetry and storybooks, children's reference books like picture dictionaries/encyclopedias, and "information books" covering single topics like weather, birds, reptiles, butterflies, or transportation whereby children can get answers to questions or learn topical information. Detailed illustrations, engaging content, and rich vocabulary are strong elements motivating children to develop oral language and understand how to form sentences, how to use punctuation, and how language works.

Abstract thought is stimulated by asking young children to think about things not observed and/or current. During/after sharing books, teachers can ask children what else might happen in the story; what they imagine the story's characters could be feeling or thinking—which also engages their imaginations; and ask them the meaning of the story's events using questions necessitating children's use of language to analyze this meaning. Teachers can ask younger children vocabulary words ("What did we call this animal?") and encourage them to use language by asking them to describe story details, like "How do the firemen reach people up high in the building?" Once younger children are familiar with a story, teachers can activate and monitor their retention and recall by saying, "Do you remember what happened to Arthur the day before that?" Teachers can ask older children to predict what they think will happen next in a story, to imagine extensions beyond the story ("What would you do if...?"), and make conclusions regarding why characters feel/behave as they do.

ENHANCING THE EFFECTS OF SHARED READING

According to researchers' findings, the effectiveness of shared reading experiences is related to the ways that adults read with young children. Rather than merely labeling objects or events with vocabulary words, teachers should ask young children to recall the shared reading, which monitors their listening comprehension and retention abilities. They should ask children to predict what will happen next based on what already happened in a book; speculate about what could possibly happen; describe characters, actions, events, and information from the shared reading; and ask their own questions about it. Shared reading with small groups of 1–3 children permits teachers to involve each child in the book by questioning and conversing with them about the pictures and plots. To teach vocabulary, teachers can tell children word meanings; point to illustrations featuring new words; relate new words to words the children already know; give multiple, varied examples of new words; and encourage children to use new words they learn in their conversations.

REPEATING SHARED READING

Young children develop preferences for favorite books. Once they know a story's plot, they enjoy discussing their knowledge. Teachers can use this for extended conversations. They can ask children who the characters are, where the story takes place, and why characters do things and

Copyright © Mometrix Media. You have been licensed one copy of this document for personal use only. Any other reproduction or redistribution is strictly prohibited. All rights reserved. This content is provided for test preparation purposes only and does not imply an endorsement by Mometrix of any particular political, scientific, or religious point of view.

events occur. They can ask specific questions requiring children to answer how much, how many, how far a distance, and how long a time. Teachers can also help children via prompting to relate stories to their own real-life experiences. In a thematic approach, teachers can select several books on the same theme, like rain forests or undersea life. This affords richer extended conversations about the theme. It also allows teachers to "recycle" vocabulary by modeling and encouraging use of thematically related words, which enhances memory and in-depth comprehension of meanings. Teachers can plan activities based on book themes, like painting pictures/murals, sculpting, making collages, or constructing models, which gives children additional motivation to use the new language they learn from shared readings of books.

READING ALOUD

Just before reading a story aloud to young students, the teacher should identify vocabulary words in the story that he or she will need to go over with the children. The teacher can write these words on the board or on strips of paper. Discussing these words before the reading will give the children definitions for new/unfamiliar words and help them understand word meanings within the story's context. Teachers can also give young children some open-ended questions to consider when listening to the story. They will then repeat these questions during and after the reading. Questions should NOT be ones children can answer with yes/no. When discussing vocabulary words, the teacher can also ask the children to relate words to personal life experiences. For example, with the word *fish*, some children may want to talk about going fishing with parents. Teachers can encourage children to tell brief personal stories, which will help them relate the story they are about to hear to their own real-life experience, making the story more meaningful.

Before reading a story aloud, adults should tell young children its title and the author's name. Then they can ask the children what an author does (children should respond "write stories" or something similar). Giving the illustrator's name, the adult also can then ask the children what illustrators do (children should respond "draw pictures" or something similar). Holding up the book, an adult can identify the front, spine, and back and ask the children if we start reading at the front or back (children should respond "at the front"). Adults can show young children the illustration on the front cover of the book and ask them, "From this picture, what do you think is going to happen in this story?" and remind them to answer this question in complete sentences. These exchanges before reading a story aloud activate children's fundamental knowledge regarding print and books, as well as the last example's exercising their imagination and language use.

When a teacher is reading a story aloud to young children, after reading each page aloud, he or she should have the children briefly discuss the picture illustrations on each page and how they relate to what was just read aloud. After reading aloud each plot point, action, event, or page, the teacher should ask the children open-ended (non yes/no) questions about what they just heard. This monitors and supports listening comprehension and memory retention/recall and stimulates expressive language use. When children associate something in the story with their own life experiences, teachers should have them explain the connection. As they read, teachers should stop periodically and ask the children to predict or guess what will happen next before continuing. This promotes abstract thinking and understanding of logical sequences and also exercises the imagination. After reading the story, teachers should ask children whether they liked it and why/why not, prompting them to answer using complete sentences. This helps children to organize their thoughts and opinions and to develop clear, grammatical, complete verbal expression.

ENVIRONMENTAL PRINT

Street signs, traffic signs, store and restaurant names, candy wrappers, food labels, and product logos—all the print we see in everyday life—are environmental print. Just as parents often play

Copyright © Mometrix Media. You have been licensed one copy of this document for personal use only. Any other reproduction or redistribution is strictly prohibited. All rights reserved. This content is provided for test preparation purposes only and does not imply an endorsement by Mometrix of any particular political, scientific, or religious point of view.

alphabetic games with children in the car ("Find something starting with A...with B..." etc.), adults can use environmental print to enhance print awareness and develop reading skills. They can ask children to find letters from their names on colorful cereal boxes. They can select one sign type, such as stop, one-way, or pedestrian crossing, and ask children to count how many they see during a car trip. They can have children practice reading each sign and talk about the phonemes (speech sounds) each letter represents. Adults can take photos of different signs and compile them into a little book for children to "read." By cutting familiar words from food labels, they can teach capitalized and lowercase letters, associate letters with phonemes, have children read the words, and sort words by their initial letters and by categories (signs, foods, etc.).

ALPHABETIC PRINCIPLE

The alphabetic principle is the concept that letters and letter combinations represent speech sounds. Children's eventual reading fluency requires knowing these predictable relationships of letters to sounds, which they can then apply to both familiar and unfamiliar words. Young children's knowing the shapes and names of letters predicts their later reading success: knowing letter names is highly correlated with the ability to view words as letter sequences and to remember written/printed words' forms. Children must first be able to recognize and name letters to understand and apply the alphabetic principle. Young children learn letter names first, via singing the alphabet song and reciting rhymes and alphabetical jump-rope chants ("A my name is Alice, I come from Alabama, and I sell Apples; B my name is Betty..." etc.). They learn letter shapes after names, through playing with lettered blocks, plastic/wood/cardboard letters, and alphabet books. Once they can recognize and name letters, children learn letter sounds after names and shapes and spellings after sounds.

To help young children understand that written or printed letters represent corresponding speech sounds, teachers should teach relationships between letters and sounds separately and in isolation and should teach these directly and explicitly. They should give young children daily opportunities during lessons to practice with letter-sound relationships. These opportunities for practice should include cumulative reviews of sound-letter relationships they have already learned and new letter-sound relationships as well. Adults should begin early in providing frequent opportunities to young children for applying their increasing knowledge and understanding of sound-letter relationships to early experiences with reading. They can do this by providing English words that are spelled phonetically (i.e., spelled the same way that they sound) and have meanings that are already familiar to the young learners.

PRINT AWARENESS

Even before they have learned how to read, young children develop print awareness, which constitutes children's first preparation for literacy. Children with print awareness realize that spoken language is represented by the markings on paper (or computer screens). They understand that the information in printed books adults read comes from the words, not the pictures. Children who have print awareness furthermore realize that print serves different functions within different contexts. They know that restaurant menus give information about the foods available; books tell stories or provide information; some signs show the names of stores, hotels, or restaurants; and other signs give traffic directions or danger warnings. Moreover, print awareness includes knowledge of how print is organized (words are combinations of letters and have spaces in between them). Children with print awareness also know that English print is read from left to right and top to bottom, book pages are numbered, words convey ideas and meaning, and reading's purpose is to understand those ideas and acquire that meaning.

Copyright © Mometrix Media. You have been licensed one copy of this document for personal use only. Any other reproduction or redistribution is strictly prohibited. All rights reserved. This content is provided for test preparation purposes only and does not imply an endorsement by Mometrix of any particular political, scientific, or religious point of view.

One way in which a teacher can get an idea of whether or to what extent a young child has developed print awareness is to provide the child with a storybook. Then the teacher can ask the child the following: "Show me the front of the book. Show me the back of the book. Show me the spine of the book. Where is the book's title? Where in the book are you supposed to start reading it? Show me a letter in the book. Now show me a word. Show me the first word of a sentence. Can you show me the last word of a sentence? Now will you show me the first word on a page? Please show me the last word on a page. Can you show me a punctuation mark? Can you show me a capital letter? Can you find a small letter/lowercase letter?" The teacher should also praise each correct response, supply the correct answers for incorrect responses, and review corrected answers.

Teachers should show young children the organization of books and the purpose of reading. When they read to them, they should use books with large print, which are more accessible for young children to view and begin to learn reading. Storybook text should use words familiar/predictable to young children. While reading together, teachers should point out high-frequency words like *the*, *a*, *is*, *was*, and *you*, as well as specific letters, words, and punctuation marks in a story. Teachers can use index cards to label objects, areas, and centers in the classroom, pairing pictorial labels with word labels, and direct children's attention to them. They can invite preschoolers to play with printed words by making greeting cards, signs, or "writing" shopping lists and personal letters. They should point out print in calendars, posters, and signs. Also, teachers can have children narrate a story using a wordless picture book, write down their narrative on a poster, and reinforce the activity with a reward related to the story (e.g., eating pancakes after narrating the book *Pancakes*).

SELF-CONCEPT

Self-concept development begins during early childhood. Children come to identify characteristics, abilities, values, and attitudes that they feel define them. From 18–36 months, children develop the categorical self. This is a concrete view of oneself, usually related to observably opposite characteristics such as child versus adult, girl versus boy, short versus tall, and good versus bad. A 4-year-old might say, "I'm shorter than Daddy. I have blue eyes. I can help Mommy clean house!" Young children can also describe emotional and attitudinal aspects of self-concept ("I like playing with Joshua. I'm happy today."). Preschoolers do not usually integrate these aspects into a unified self-portrait, however. Also, many preschoolers do not yet realize one person can incorporate opposite qualities; a person is either good or bad to them, rather than having both good and bad qualities. The remembered self develops with long-term memory, including autobiographical memories and things adults have told them, to comprise one's life story. The inner self is the child's private feelings, desires, and thoughts.

PHONICS INSTRUCTION

Because children display individual differences in their speeds of learning sound-to-letter relationships, instruction should consider this; there is no set rate. Generally, a reasonable pace ranges from two to four sound-letter relationships per week. Relationships vary in utility: many words contain the letters *m*, *a*, *t*, *s*, *p*, and *h*, which are high-utility, but *x* in *box*, *gh* in *through*, *ey* in *they*, and *a* in *want* are lower-utility. High-utility sound-letter relationships should be taught first. Teachers should first introduce consonant relationships using *f*, *m*, *n*, *r*, and *s*, which are continuous sounds children can produce in isolation with less distortion than word-initial or word-medial stops like *p*, *b*, *t*, *d*, *k*, and *g*. Teachers should also introduce similar-sounding letters like *b* and *v* or *i* and *e*, and similar-looking letters like *b* and *d* or *p* and *g*, separately to prevent confusion. Single consonants versus clusters/blends should be introduced in separate lessons. Blends should incorporate sound-letter relationships children already know.

Copyright © Mometrix Media. You have been licensed one copy of this document for personal use only. Any other reproduction or redistribution is strictly prohibited. All rights reserved. This content is provided for test preparation purposes only and does not imply an endorsement by Mometrix of any particular political, scientific, or religious point of view.

LANGUAGE EXPERIENCE APPROACH (LEA)

The **LEA** teaches beginning reading by connecting students' personal life experiences with written/printed words. A unique benefit is students using their own language and words, enabling them to interact with texts on multiple levels simultaneously. They thus realize they acquire knowledge and understanding through not just instruction but also their own experiences. The four steps for implementing the LEA with EC groups are as follows:

1. Children and the teacher choose a topic, like an exciting trip, game, or recent TV show, to discuss with teacher guidance
2. Each child takes a turn saying a sentence using his or her own words that advances the discussion/story. The teacher writes the children's words verbatim without corrections, visibly and clearly
3. Every few sentences or several words, the teacher stops and reads the record aloud for children to confirm accuracy
4. The teacher points to each word, they read aloud together, or children repeat after the teacher. The teacher gives children copies of the record for independent review and possible compilation into books of LEA stories

WHOLE LANGUAGE APPROACH

The **whole language approach concentrates** on children's seeking, finding, and constructing meaning in language. As such, young children's early technical correctness is not the priority. Whole language teachers do not ignore children's errors. However, they do not make correction more important than overall engagement, understanding, and appreciation of reading, writing, and literature. Instead, teachers make formative assessments taking into account the errors each child makes. Then they design learning experiences for children that give them opportunities and assistance in acquiring mechanically correct linguistic forms and structures. While this holistic approach finds analytical techniques that break language down into components like phonemes and alphabet letters less useful, children with language processing/reading problems need to learn phonemic awareness, phonics, and other decoding skills to develop reading fluency. The National Reading Panel conducted a study (1997–2000) to resolve controversy over phonics vs. whole language as the best teaching method, finding that any effective reading instruction program must teach phonemic awareness, phonics, reading fluency, vocabulary development, and reading comprehension.

The whole language approach is based on constructivist philosophy and psychology: children construct their own knowledge through their interactions with their environments. In contrast to analytical approaches like phonics and alphabetic learning, constructivism views learning as an individual's unique cognitive experience of acquiring new knowledge, shaped by the individual's existing knowledge and personal perspective. Whole language instruction emphasizes helping children create meaning from their reading and express meaning in their writing. The whole language philosophy emphasizes cultural diversity, integrating literacy instruction across subject domains, reading high-quality literature, and giving children many opportunities for independent reading, small-group guided reading, and being read to aloud by teachers. Whole language believes children learn to read by writing and vice versa. Realistically purposeful reading and writing are encouraged, as is using texts that motivate children to develop a love for literature. Early grammatical/spelling/technical correctness is not stressed, which can be problematic for children with reading/language processing disorders, who need explicit instruction in decoding skills and strategies.

Copyright © Mometrix Media. You have been licensed one copy of this document for personal use only. Any other reproduction or redistribution is strictly prohibited. All rights reserved. This content is provided for test preparation purposes only and does not imply an endorsement by Mometrix of any particular political, scientific, or religious point of view.

ADDRESSING EARLY MECHANICAL ERRORS IN LEARNING READING AND WRITING

The basal reader is America's commonest approach, used in an estimated 75–85 percent of K–8th-grade classrooms. The number of publishers offering basal reading series has decreased to about one-fourth of that in the 20th century, decreasing teacher responsibility for investigating/piloting readers for district approval. Using basal readers is a skills-based/bottom-up approach. Teaching smaller-to-larger reading subskills in systematic, rigid sequence assists students' transition from part to whole. Texts graded by reading level contain narration and exposition organized thematically by unit, including children's literature and diverse other genres. Phonics and other specific instructional strands with practice assignments develop skills, which are assessed with end-of-unit tests. For young children, text decoding is enabled through exact control of vocabulary items and word analysis skills, "big [enlarged] books," and word and picture cards. Twentieth-century and older series sacrificed comprehension and enjoyment for vocabulary control and skill acquisition, but 21st-century series vary methods more (like multiple story versions or book excerpts enabling selection sharing), affording children more motivation to read.

DIRECTED READING ACTIVITY (DRA) AND THE DIRECTED READING-THINKING ACTIVITY (DR-TA)

Using basal readers, the DRA comprises the following:

1. The teacher prepares children for reading by stimulating their motivation and introducing new concepts and/or vocabulary
2. Students read silently, guided by teacher questions and statements
3. The teacher develops student comprehension, and students discuss characters, plots, or concepts to further comprehension
4. After silent reading, students read aloud and read answers to teacher questions, known as "purposeful rereading"
5. Students' follow-up workbook activities/practice review comprehension and vocabulary.

Some selections may include enrichment activities relating them to writing, art, drama, or music. The DR-TA approach is designed to develop critical readers through instruction in group comprehension. It requires children's active engagement in reading by processing information, asking questions, and receiving feedback as they read. The first phase of DR-TA is the teacher's direction of student thought processes throughout reading. The second phase involves developing student skills according to their needs as identified in phase 1 and additional extension or follow-up activities.

DIFFERENCES BETWEEN DRA AND DR-TA APPROACHES

- One main difference is that the DR-TA approach gives teachers all the responsibility and greater flexibility for developing lessons. As such, it contains fewer directions than the DRA approach, which contains specific materials and questions to use, specific guidelines, and is more teacher-manual-oriented and materials-oriented. Therefore, DR-TA can be used for not only basal readers but also planning lessons in other curriculum areas involving reading; the DRA approach applies more directly to basal reader programs.
- DRA manuals use mostly literal, factual questions, requiring only convergent thinking for student responses. However, in DR-TA, questions also demand divergent (creative) thinking of students, stimulating higher-level reading comprehension and interpretation.
- New vocabulary is pretaught in the DRA approach before children read. The DR-TA approach excludes preteaching, realistically requiring student decoding of new vocabulary words during reading.

165

Copyright © Mometrix Media. You have been licensed one copy of this document for personal use only. Any other reproduction or redistribution is strictly prohibited. All rights reserved.
This content is provided for test preparation purposes only and does not imply an endorsement by Mometrix of any particular political, scientific, or religious point of view.

- DRA manuals specify when to teach which skills for reading comprehension. DR-TA approaches do not, requiring more questioning expertise and acceptance of some alternative student responses by teachers.

Teaching English Language Learners

ENGLISH LANGUAGE LEARNERS

CHARACTERISTICS AND NEEDS OF LANGUAGE PROFICIENCY LEVELS

The term **English language learner (ELL)** refers to students acquiring English as a second language, and consists of beginner, intermediate, and advanced levels of English language proficiency. Each proficiency level is determined by specific characteristics and requires differing linguistic supports across listening, speaking, reading, and writing domains. **Beginning** ELLs have little or no ability to understand the English language across domains and rely heavily on linguistic aids such as visual representations, gestures, verbal cues, and environmental print. These students communicate through memorized high-frequency words or phrases and often require individualized instruction. **Intermediate** ELLs have acquired some foundational knowledge on the English language and can communicate with increasing complexity. They are generally able to understand, speak, read, and write in short, simple sentences and follow clear, routine directions. These students are able to seek clarification for misunderstandings but continue to require linguistic supports such as repetition, slowed speech, visual representations, and body language. **Advanced** ELL students are generally able to understand and utilize the English language with minimal error and often do not require extensive linguistic support outside of occasional repetition or clarification. Their proficiency is comparable to that of their native English-speaking peers.

ACQUIRING LISTENING AND SPEAKING SKILLS

The acquisition of **listening** and **speaking** skills are interrelated and often are the first two domains in which English language proficiency is developed. As the ELL hears and observes the teacher modeling proper speech and active listening, they begin acquiring listening skills. Additionally, listening to and observing classmates is integral for the development of listening and speaking skills. By watching and imitating their peers, ELLs build understanding of the nuances of the English language in different settings. When words and phrases heard are linked to a particular action or event, the ELL derives meaning and can utilize the newly acquired vocabulary, thus developing listening and speaking skills simultaneously. The development of listening and speaking skills is enhanced in a **language-rich environment** in which students are provided multiple opportunities to practice and develop their skills in a natural setting. Therefore, the teacher must include opportunities for ELLs to speak, actively listen, and work collaboratively. Incorporating materials such as songs, games, stories, and digital media further immerse the ELL in a language-rich environment and allow them to attach meaning to new vocabulary to build proficiency.

ACQUIRING READING AND WRITING SKILLS

The acquisition of listening and speaking skills in English provides the foundation for developing **reading** and **writing** skills. Reading and writing abilities develop in relation to one another, as when students begin acquiring reading skills, they learn to attach meaning to vocabulary and texts that enable them to express themselves in writing. The development of reading skills begins with understanding simple, high-frequency vocabulary and simple sentence structures as a foundation, building upon this knowledge with increasingly complex vocabulary and sentence structures. Similarly, writing ability increases in complexity from basic labels, lists, and copying and develops into expression though simple sentences on familiar topics, and ultimately, complex writing abilities that employ higher-order thinking on abstract concepts. Reading and writing skill

166

Copyright © Mometrix Media. You have been licensed one copy of this document for personal use only. Any other reproduction or redistribution is strictly prohibited. All rights reserved. This content is provided for test preparation purposes only and does not imply an endorsement by Mometrix of any particular political, scientific, or religious point of view.

development is enhanced through consistent practice in a **print** and **literacy-rich** environment. Students should be provided with multiple opportunities for reading and expressing themselves through writing throughout instruction. Reading materials with varying levels of complexity should be readily available for students, and literacy development must be incorporated into all subject areas to build vocabulary and comprehension.

> **Review Video: Stages of Reading Development**
> Visit mometrix.com/academy and enter code: 121184
>
> **Review Video: The Link Between Grammar Skills and Reading Comprehension**
> Visit mometrix.com/academy and enter code: 411287

PRINT AND LITERACY-RICH LEARNING ENVIRONMENT

A print and literacy-rich learning environment is beneficial for providing an **immersive** experience that promotes the development of students' reading, writing, speaking, and listening skills. Such an environment typically incorporates a variety of learning resources and strategies to encourage literacy. The walls are often decorated with a variety of print materials, such as posters, captions, word walls with high-frequency or thematic vocabulary words, signs, labels, bulletin boards, and anchor charts. Students are provided with authentic printed and digital literacy materials, such as newspapers, magazines, shopping advertisements, video clips, songs, and documentaries to increase relevancy and personal connections. A print and literacy-rich classroom also includes a class library that offers texts of varying genres, formats, and levels of complexity. Learning activities provide multiple opportunities to develop literacy skills in a natural setting, such as opportunities for collaborative learning, self-selected reading, and free-write sessions.

> **Review Video: Print Awareness and Alphabet Knowledge**
> Visit mometrix.com/academy and enter code: 541069

COMPONENTS OF LANGUAGE

All languages are comprised of syntax, semantics, morphology, phonology, and pragmatics.

- **Syntax** refers to the structure and arrangement of words within a sentence, which controls the functions of grammar.
- **Semantics** refers to how language conveys meaning.
- **Morphology** refers to how words are constructed of smaller parts, such as root words, prefixes, and suffixes.
- **Phonology** refers to how words are pronounced.
- **Pragmatics** refers to the practical, social applications of language and its use in the real world, including non-verbal communication.

These components heavily overlap with one another. For instance, morphology is heavily involved in constructing the meaning of a word, which largely falls under the category of semantics and without a logical ordering of the words in a sentence (syntax), the sentence could mean something completely different, or be altogether incoherent. Each of these systems needs to be well-established for communication in English or any other language. Some of these components, such as morphology, can be particularly targeted to support content-based instruction. For instance, a teacher might work on prefixes and root words that commonly occur in science, such as bio-, geo-, tele-, -logy, -scope, and -graphy.

Copyright © Mometrix Media. You have been licensed one copy of this document for personal use only. Any other reproduction or redistribution is strictly prohibited. All rights reserved. This content is provided for test preparation purposes only and does not imply an endorsement by Mometrix of any particular political, scientific, or religious point of view.

ENGLISH LANGUAGE PROFICIENCY FOR LISTENING AND SPEAKING
DESCRIPTORS FOR ENGLISH LANGUAGE PROFICIENCY FOR EACH ABILITY LEVEL

Development of English language proficiency is marked by descriptors for each ability level in listening and speaking. **Beginner** ELLs are highly limited or unable to understand or speak English in any setting. They have difficulty understanding and using simple vocabulary even with the help of linguistic aids and rely on single words for basic communication. Grammatically, they are unable to construct full sentences. **Intermediate** ELLs understand and speak using high-frequency English vocabulary on familiar topics and settings. They speak and understand short sentences and demonstrate a basic understanding of English grammatical patterns for constructing simple sentences but need linguistic aids for unfamiliar vocabulary. Additionally, they make several errors when communicating, but can ask in English for clarification, and are usually understood by those familiar with working with ELLs. **Advanced** ELLs can speak and understand grade-appropriate English with linguistic supports. They understand and participate in longer conversations about familiar and unfamiliar topics, but may rely on linguistic aids, repetition, or clarification. These students still make some errors in communication but are often understood by people unfamiliar with working with ELLs. **Advanced high** ELLs require minimal linguistic support and can understand and speak English at a similar level to native English-speaking peers.

TEACHING STUDENTS AT DIFFERENT PROFICIENCY LEVELS

Teaching students with different proficiency levels for listening and speaking English implies that students will require varying degrees of linguistic support to develop their skills and provide them with an equitable learning environment. Specifically, students with lower proficiency levels in these areas will rely more on linguistic accommodations than students with more developed abilities. Teachers must be knowledgeable of the descriptors for each proficiency level to implement the proper supports and instructional strategies to address individual learning needs for developing listening and speaking skills in English. Instructional strategies should aim to promote the acquisition of skills through building background knowledge and providing context in multiple ways. This includes modeling proper speaking and listening skills, accompanying instruction with verbal cues, slower speech, repetition, gestures, and visual aids to improve student comprehension and build vocabulary. Additionally, incorporating several cooperative learning opportunities provides scaffolding and opportunities to practice and build upon listening and speaking abilities. Content instruction can be supported with the implementation of digital resources that promote the acquisition and development of listening and speaking skills and can be tailored to students' individual abilities.

> **Review Video: ESL/ESOL/Second Language Learning**
> Visit mometrix.com/academy and enter code: 795047

ENGLISH LANGUAGE PROFICIENCY FOR READING AND WRITING
DESCRIPTORS FOR ENGLISH LANGUAGE PROFICIENCY AT EACH ABILITY LEVEL

English language proficiency for ELLs is determined by descriptors for each ability level in reading and writing. **Beginning** ELLs possess little or no ability to read, understand, or write in English. Comprehension is restricted to single, familiar vocabulary words, and writing is limited to lists, labels, and vocabulary accompanied by pictures. These students rely heavily on linguistic supports for understanding, and their writing is unclear to those unfamiliar with working with ELLs. **Intermediate** ELLs can read, understand, and write short sentences and simple language structures on familiar material with the help of linguistic aids. They engage in writing assignments, but their writing contains errors and is unclear to those unfamiliar with working with ELLs. **Advanced** ELLs read, understand, and write using more expansive vocabulary and sentence

Copyright © Mometrix Media. You have been licensed one copy of this document for personal use only. Any other reproduction or redistribution is strictly prohibited. All rights reserved.
This content is provided for test preparation purposes only and does not imply an endorsement by Mometrix of any particular political, scientific, or religious point of view.

structures with the help of linguistic accommodations. They may have difficulty with unfamiliar vocabulary but can read and write at a faster pace with increased accuracy. These students demonstrate more complex writing abilities, and their writing is usually understood by those unfamiliar with working with ELLs. **Advanced high** ELLs can read, understand, and write using grade-appropriate English with minimal linguistic support at a level similar to native English-speaking peers.

TEACHING STUDENTS AT DIFFERENT PROFICIENCY LEVELS

Teaching students with different proficiency levels for reading and writing English means linguistic accommodations in the classroom will need to be scaffolded to address the needs and abilities of individual students and promote the development of skills in these areas. Students with lower proficiency levels in reading and writing will require more linguistic aids than students with more developed abilities. Thus, the teacher must have a deep understanding both of individual student needs and of descriptors for proficiency at each level to effectively support students in their acquisition of reading and writing skills. Instructional strategies should foster the acquisition of these skills through providing several ways to allow students to build background knowledge and context to increase understanding. This includes creating a language-rich classroom environment that emphasizes the development of literacy skills in the form of environmental print, word walls and charts for new vocabulary and high-frequency words, labels, and visual aids. Reading materials on subject content should be available at each reading level. Additionally, the use of graphic organizers and outlines increases comprehension and writing ability through breaking information into smaller portions to provide scaffolding.

CREATING EQUITABLE LEARNING ENVIRONMENT FOR ELLS USING LINGUISTIC SUPPORTS

To create an equitable learning environment, ELL students must be provided with linguistic supports that are applicable across content areas in order to ensure they are provided with an equal opportunity for success in learning. Teachers can implement varying supports appropriate to students' levels of English language proficiency that are beneficial in facilitating both English language and content-specific learning. Such supports include incorporating verbal cues, gestures, and visual representations into instruction to provide context and build background knowledge. The use of environmental print, word walls, and labels are also effective in supporting English language skills while simultaneously providing context for facilitating learning in the content area. Teachers should model speaking and listening skills, and practice slow speech or repetition when necessary to ensure understanding. Scaffolding instruction and activities across content areas through such supports as graphic organizers, outlines, and cooperative learning opportunities serve to assist ELL students in building English language proficiency skills across content areas at a pace appropriate for their ability level. By implementing the proper supports, teachers can effectively foster English language learning in all subject areas while ensuring that students simultaneously learn content-specific material.

INSTRUCTIONAL STRATEGIES FOR ENGLISH LANGUAGE LEARNING IN ALL SUBJECT AREAS

Language acquisition occurs across content areas for ELL students, as each subject is comprised of different vocabulary, grammatical patterns, and methods of expressing ideas. Thus, it is important that teachers provide these students with learning strategies that are applicable in all subject areas in order to effectively support English language acquisition and content-specific learning. Through a metacognitive approach, teachers can facilitate ELL students in thinking about how they learn, reflecting on their strengths and weaknesses, and applying useful learning strategies from one content area to another to develop their English language skills in all subjects. This strategy enhances learning through teaching students how to apply learning strategies from one instructional context to another when developing language skills. By activating students' prior

Copyright © Mometrix Media. You have been licensed one copy of this document for personal use only. Any other reproduction or redistribution is strictly prohibited. All rights reserved. This content is provided for test preparation purposes only and does not imply an endorsement by Mometrix of any particular political, scientific, or religious point of view.

knowledge when introducing new material in a given subject area, teachers promote English language learning through providing context and encouraging students to consider what they may already know about a new concept. Such methods as pre-teaching, anticipatory guides, graphic organizers, and brainstorming allow ELL students to make connections that build their language abilities across content areas.

ADAPTING INSTRUCTION FOR VARYING LEVELS OF ENGLISH LANGUAGE PROFICIENCY

When encountering ELL students with varying English language skills, it is imperative to adapt instruction to accommodate these differences and ensure that all students receive appropriate linguistic support. Instruction must be communicated, sequenced, and scaffolded to support learners with different English proficiency abilities. The teacher must communicate instruction clearly while allowing time for repetition or slowed speech as necessary. In addition, teachers must supplement instruction with linguistic supports such as verbal cues, gestures, and visual representations as needed to provide assistance and context appropriate to individual ability levels. Instruction must also be sequenced logically and clearly communicate the expectations and steps of learning experiences. This is achieved by indicating an explicit beginning, middle, and end to activities through transition words and actions appropriate to students' levels of English proficiency. Teachers must scaffold instruction, activities, and assessments to meet individual students' language learning needs. Supports such as word walls, graphic organizers, charts, labels, and pairing students with others who can provide assistance are effective means of scaffolding learning to accommodate varying ability. By communicating, sequencing, and scaffolding instruction in a way that is tailored to ELL students' individual language needs, teachers effectively foster an equitable environment that promotes success in learning.

Print-Rich Environments for Early Childhood

PRINT-RICH CLASSROOMS

In early childhood classrooms, print-rich environments contain books and texts of different genres and topics, including both audio and digital texts. Walls and shelves have signs and labels to help with classroom procedures and organization. Posters display information related to content students have been studying. Reading, writing, and listening centers are available for students to explore during center time. Puppet theaters and flannel boards are present to encourage oral language and storytelling. There are also many literacy-related materials, such as letter tiles and sight word cards. Word walls are posted.

In **print-rich environments**, students are encouraged to share and display texts they have created. They may add their own stories to the classroom libraries or hang up signs they have made. Materials created during shared and interactive reading and writing experiences may also be displayed.

In classrooms for older students, signs and posters are displayed containing academic vocabulary, content students have been studying, and classroom procedures. Written and digital texts from a range of genres are present. There are also ample resources available for students to use to locate and share information, such as computers, tablets, dictionaries, and thesauri.

PROMOTING LITERACY DEVELOPMENT WITH DRAMATIC PLAY CENTERS

Dramatic play centers are common in early childhood classrooms. These centers allow children to act out realistic situations through play. Examples include pretend restaurants, homes, veterinary clinics, and grocery stores. While engaging in dramatic play, children read, write, listen, and speak for authentic purposes.

Copyright © Mometrix Media. You have been licensed one copy of this document for personal use only. Any other reproduction or redistribution is strictly prohibited. All rights reserved.
This content is provided for test preparation purposes only and does not imply an endorsement by Mometrix of any particular political, scientific, or religious point of view.

As children role-play and interact with other children in dramatic play centers, they develop oral language skills. They engage in conversations and practice using language to accomplish tasks, such as ordering in restaurants. They also listen to peers and follow directions, such as when they are pretending to be restaurant servers.

Children also engage in reading activities in dramatic play centers. Labels and realistic print materials can be included. For example, pretend restaurants may include labeled cabinets and menus. Children can practice writing through dramatic play. For example, children who are pretending to be servers may write down orders on notepads.

BUILDING LITERACY ACTIVITIES INTO DAILY ROUTINES AND ACTIVITIES

Teachers can plan reading, writing, listening, and speaking activities across all subject areas. This can include a mixture of independent literacy activities and shared and interactive reading and writing experiences. Texts focusing on topics that are being studied in all content areas can be accessible in the classroom. Students can also write in all subject areas. For example, they can write the processes used to solve problems in math and create travel brochures in social studies.

Teachers of early childhood and elementary students can plan morning meetings in which daily written messages are read and discussed. Students can share current events and topics of interest with their classmates during these meetings, while other students listen and ask questions.

Early childhood and elementary teachers can also incorporate oral language and listening into daily routines. For example, they may recite specific chants or songs during transitions.

Chapter Quiz

Ready to see how well you retained what you just read? Scan the QR code to go directly to the chapter quiz interface for this study guide. If you're using a computer, simply visit the bonus page at **mometrix.com/bonus948/ftceprekinprim** and click the Chapter Quizzes link.

Copyright © Mometrix Media. You have been licensed one copy of this document for personal use only. Any other reproduction or redistribution is strictly prohibited. All rights reserved.
This content is provided for test preparation purposes only and does not imply an endorsement by Mometrix of any particular political, scientific, or religious point of view.

Mathematics

Transform passive reading into active learning! After immersing yourself in this chapter, put your comprehension to the test by taking a quiz. The insights you gained will stay with you longer this way. Scan the QR code to go directly to the chapter quiz interface for this study guide. If you're using a computer, simply visit the bonus page at **mometrix.com/bonus948/ftceprekinprim** and click the Chapter Quizzes link.

Math Foundations

PREMATHEMATICAL LEARNING EXPERIENCES

Preschool children do not think in the same ways as older children and adults do, as Piaget observed. Their thinking is strongly based upon and connected to their sensory perceptions. This means that in solving problems, they depend mainly on how things look, sound, feel, smell, and taste. Therefore, preschool children should always be given concrete objects that they can touch, explore, and experiment with in any learning experience. They are not yet capable of understanding abstract concepts or manipulating information mentally, so they must have real things to work with to understand **premath** concepts. For example, they will learn to count solid objects like blocks, beads, or pennies before they can count numbers in their heads. They cannot benefit from rote math memorization or "sit still and listen" lessons. Since young children "centrate" on one characteristic, object, person, or event at a time, adults can offer activities encouraging decentration/incorporating multiple aspects (e.g., not only grouping all triangles but grouping all red triangles separately from blue triangles).

PROBLEM SOLVING SKILLS

Being able to solve problems is fundamental to all other components of mathematics. Children learn the concept that a question can have more than one answer and a problem can have more than one solution by participating in problem-solving activities. To solve problems, a child must be able to explore a problem, a situation, or a subject; think through the problem, situation, or subject; and use logical reasoning. These abilities are needed to not only solve routine, everyday problems but also novel or unusual ones. Using problem-solving skills not only helps children think mathematically but also promotes their language development and their social skills when they work together. Children are naturally curious about how to solve everyday problems. Adults can take advantage of this inherent curiosity by discussing everyday challenges, asking children to propose ways to solve them, and asking them to explain how they arrived at their solutions. Adults can also invite children to propose problems and ask questions about them. This helps them learn to analyze different types of problems and realize that many problems have multiple possible solutions.

COMMON STEPS THAT PREPARE CHILDREN TO LEARN MATH

The process of solving problems often involves the following steps:

1. Understanding the problem
2. Coming up with a plan to solve the problem
3. Putting that plan into action, and, finally, observing the outcome
4. Reflecting on whether the solution was effective and whether the answer arrived at makes sense

Copyright © Mometrix Media. You have been licensed one copy of this document for personal use only. Any other reproduction or redistribution is strictly prohibited. All rights reserved. This content is provided for test preparation purposes only and does not imply an endorsement by Mometrix of any particular political, scientific, or religious point of view.

Solving problems not only involves learning this series of steps but also requires children to develop the qualities needed to solve problems. Children who are able to solve problems have a number of characteristics. For example, children who are effective problem solvers are able to focus their attention on the problem and its individual component parts. They can formulate hypotheses about the problem/situation and then test them for veracity. They are willing to take risks within reason. They are persistent if they do not solve a problem right away and do not give up if their first attempt at solving a problem is unsuccessful. They maintain flexibility and experiment with alternate methods. They also demonstrate self-regulation skills.

USING PROBLEM SOLVING SKILLS IN DAILY LIFE

Young children continually explore their environments to unravel mysteries about how things work. For example, preschoolers use math concepts to understand that they have three toys, to comprehend that three fingers equals three toys, or to understand that two cookies plus one more equals three cookies. To do abstract mathematics in the future, young children will need two major skills that are also used to solve problems: being able to visualize a scenario and being able to apply common sense thinking. Thinking and planning to achieve goals within the constraints of the properties of the surrounding environment is a natural behavior for young children. They will persist in their efforts to get an older sibling to stop another activity to play with them, to repair broken toys with tape or chewing gum, to manipulate a puzzle or plastic building blocks to get one uncooperative piece to fit, etc. The great 20th-century mathematician and teacher George Polya stated that problem-solving is "the most characteristically human activity." He pointed out that problem-solving is a skill learned by doing, and that developing this skill requires a great deal of practice.

GAMES/ACTIVITIES THAT ENCOURAGE THE USE OF PROBLEM-SOLVING SKILLS

One method that has been found to enhance children's reasoning skills is using adult-child conversations to play mental mathematics games. For example, once children are able to count beyond five, adults can give them basic oral story problems to solve (e.g., "If you have two plums and I give you two more, how many will you have?"). Using children's favorite foods in story problems, which takes advantage of their ready ability to envision these foods, is a good place to start. Thereafter, adults can add story problems involving pets, toys, cars, shopping, and other familiar objects, animals, or activities. Experts advise adults not to restrict the types of problems presented to a child based solely on the child's grade level. Children can work with any situation if they can form mental imagery. Adults can sometimes insert harder tasks (e.g., problems involving larger numbers, problems involving division with remainders, or problems with negative number answers). Even toddlers can solve problems such as how to divide three cookies between two people. The division may not be fair, but it will likely be efficient. Adults should use the Socratic method, asking guiding questions to allow children to arrive at a solution to a problem themselves, rather than telling them a "right" answer.

BENEFICIAL PRACTICES OF PLAYING MENTAL MATH GAMES

Adults can use children's favorite foods and toys to pose story problems to children that involve addition and subtraction. For example, they can ask them questions like "If I give you [this many] more, how many will you have?" or "If we take away [this many], how many are left?" It is better to ask children questions than to give them answers. It is important to use turn-taking. In this method, the adult poses a story problem to the child, and then the child gets to pose one to the adult. Adults must try to solve the problem, even if the child makes up numbers like "bazillion" or "eleventy." Games should be fun, not strictly factual like math tests. Adults can introduce age-appropriate story topics as children grow older. At the end of early childhood/around school age, children can handle the abstract algebraic concept of variables or unknown numbers (which some experts call "mystery

173

Copyright © Mometrix Media. You have been licensed one copy of this document for personal use only. Any other reproduction or redistribution is strictly prohibited. All rights reserved. This content is provided for test preparation purposes only and does not imply an endorsement by Mometrix of any particular political, scientific, or religious point of view.

numbers") and use this concept in games. Adults can pose riddles where x or n is the unknown number, and children must use an operation (e.g., $x + 4 = 7$) to solve the riddle.

Review Video: Mathematical Operations
Visit mometrix.com/academy and enter code: 208095

REASONING SKILLS

COMMUNICATING WITH CHILDREN TO PROMOTE MATHEMATICAL REASONING SKILLS

Adults should reciprocally talk to and listen to children during communication that is focused on using mathematical skills like problem-solving, reasoning, making connections, etc. To promote young children's understanding, adults can express mathematical concepts using pictures, words, diagrams, and symbols. Encouraging children to talk with their peers and adults helps them clarify their own thoughts and think about what they are doing. Communicating with children about mathematical thinking problems also develops their vocabularies and promotes early literacy and reading skills. Adults should listen to what children want to say and should have conversations with them. Communicating about math can also be accomplished through reading children's books that incorporate numbers and/or repetition or rhyme. In addition to talking, adults can communicate math concepts to children by drawing pictures or diagrams and using concrete objects (e.g., blocks, crayons, pieces of paper, fingers, etc.) to represent numbers and/or solve problems. Children also share their learning of math concepts through words, charts, drawings, tallies, etc. Even toddlers hold up fingers to tell others how old they are.

USING REASONING SKILLS TO UNDERSTAND AND APPLY EARLY MATHEMATICAL AND SCIENTIFIC CONCEPTS

A major component of problem-solving is **reasoning**. Children reason when they think through questions and find usable answers. They use reasoning skills to make sense of mathematical and scientific subject matter. Children use several abilities during the reasoning process. For example, they use logic to classify objects or concepts into groups. They follow logical sequences to arrive at conclusions that make sense. They use their analytical abilities to explain their own thought processes. They apply what they have learned about relationships and patterns to help them find solutions to problems. They also use reasoning to justify their mental processes and problem solutions. To support children's reasoning, adults can ask children questions, give them time to think about their answers, and listen to their answers. This simple tactic helps children learn how to reason. Adults can also ask children why something is as it is—letting them think for themselves rather than looking for a particular answer—and listen to the ideas they produce.

ROLE OF REPRESENTATION SKILLS IN CHILDREN'S LEARNING

Young children develop an understanding of **symbolic representation**—the idea that objects, written letters, words, and other symbols are used to represent other objects or concepts—at an early age. This is evident in their make-believe/pretend play and in their ability to learn written language and connect it to spoken language. As children develop early math skills, representing their ideas and the information they acquire helps them organize, document, and share these ideas and facts with others. Children may count on their fingers; create tallies using checkmarks, tick marks, and/or words; draw pictures or maps; and, as they grow older, make graphs. Teachers must help children apply mathematical process skills as they use learning center materials. For example, when a child enjoys sorting rocks by color, the teacher can state that the child is classifying them, bridging informal math activities with math vocabulary. Asking the child how he or she is categorizing the rocks emphasizes math vocabulary. Asking the child after he or she finishes what other ways the rocks could be classified encourages problem-solving.

Copyright © Mometrix Media. You have been licensed one copy of this document for personal use only. Any other reproduction or redistribution is strictly prohibited. All rights reserved.
This content is provided for test preparation purposes only and does not imply an endorsement by Mometrix of any particular political, scientific, or religious point of view.

MAKING CONNECTIONS AND HELPING CHILDREN TRANSITION FROM INTUITIVE TO FORMAL MATH THINKING

Children informally learn intuitive mathematical thinking through their everyday life experiences. They naturally apply mathematical concepts and reasoning to solve problems they face in their environment. However, one frequent problem among children when they begin formal education is that they can come to see academic mathematics as a collection of procedures and rules, instead of viewing it as a means of finding solutions to everyday, real-life problems. This view will interfere with children's ability to apply the formal mathematics they learn to their lives in a practical and useful way. Teachers can help prevent this outcome by establishing the connection between children's natural intuitive math and formal mathematics. They can do this by teaching math through the use of manipulative materials familiar to children. They can use mathematics vocabulary words when describing children's activities, which enables children to develop an awareness of the natural mathematical operations they use in their daily lives. When a teacher introduces a new mathematical concept to children, he or she can give illustrative examples that draw upon the children's actual life experiences.

RELATIONSHIP OF MATHEMATICS TO EVERYDAY LIFE AND OTHER ACADEMIC SUBJECTS

We use math throughout our lives during everyday activities. There are countless examples and combinations of various mathematical concepts in the real world. Additionally, math concepts inform other academic content areas, including music, art, and the sciences. Therefore, it is important for children not to view math as an isolated set of procedures and skills. Children comprehend math more easily when they can make connections, which involves applying common mathematical rules to multiple, varied functions, processes, and real-life activities. For example, adults can ask children to consider problems they encounter daily and solve them. When a parent asks a child to help put away groceries, the child practices sorting categories of foods and packages, and experiments with comparative package sizes and shapes. Parents need not be concerned with what specific mathematical processes are involved but should simply look for examples of math in everyday life and expose children to these examples on a regular basis. For example, pouring liquid into containers of various sizes and speculating which one will hold the most is an easy, fun activity that incorporates a number of skills and concepts, including estimation, measurement, spatial sense, and conservation of liquid volume.

PATTERNS AND RELATIONSHIPS

Patterns are generally defined as things that recur or are repeated regularly. Patterns can be found in images, sounds, numbers, events, actions, movements, etc. Relationships are generally defined as connections or associations between things that are identified and/or described using logic or reasoning. Being aware of patterns and relationships among aspects of the environment helps us comprehend the fundamental structure of these aspects. This awareness enables us to predict what will occur next in a series of events, even before it actually happens. This gives us more confidence in our environment and in our ability to interact with it. We find patterns and relationships in such areas of life as art, music, and clothing. Math-specific activities like counting numbers and working with geometrical shapes, lines, arcs, and curves also involve patterns and relationships. When children understand patterns and relationships, they can understand repetition, rhythm, categorization, and how to order things from smallest to biggest, from shortest to longest, etc.

Adults can help young children develop their understanding of patterns and relationships in life by looking at pictures and designs with them, encouraging and guiding them to identify patterns within drawings, paintings, and abstract designs such as prints on fabrics and other decorative designs. When children participate in movement activities, including dancing to music, running, skipping, hopping, playing simple musical instruments, etc., adults can help them identify patterns

Copyright © Mometrix Media. You have been licensed one copy of this document for personal use only. Any other reproduction or redistribution is strictly prohibited. All rights reserved.
This content is provided for test preparation purposes only and does not imply an endorsement by Mometrix of any particular political, scientific, or religious point of view.

in their own and others' movements. Adults can encourage young children to participate in hands-on activities, such as stringing wood, plastic beads, or penne and other hollow dry pasta tubes onto pieces of string to make necklaces with simple patterns (e.g., blue-yellow-blue-yellow). As children grow older, adults can encourage them to create more complicated patterns. They can alternate a larger number of colors, and they can vary the numbers of each color in more complex ways (e.g., three blue, two yellow, one red, etc.).

CONTRIBUTION OF NUMBER SENSE AND NUMBER OPERATIONS TO MATH COMPREHENSION

Counting is one of the earliest numeracy skills that young children develop. Even before they have learned the names of all the numbers, young children learn to count to three, then to five, etc. However, **number sense** involves a great deal more than just counting. Number sense includes understanding the various applications of numbers. For instance, we use numbers as tools for conveying and manipulating information, as tools for describing quantities, and as tools for characterizing relationships between or among things. Children who have developed number sense are able to count with accuracy and competence. Given a specific number, they can count upward from that number. They can also count backward. They are able to break down a number and then reassemble it. They are able to recognize relationships between or among different numbers. When children can count, are familiar with numbers, and have good number sense, they can also add and subtract numbers. Being familiar with numbers and being able to count easily helps young children understand all other areas of mathematics.

ACTIVITIES TO HELP DEVELOP NUMBER SENSE AND NUMERACY SKILLS

As children complete their daily activities, it is beneficial for adults to count real things with children and encourage them to count as well. This helps children understand numbers by using their own experiences with objects in the environment and gives them practice counting and using numbers. To help children understand that we use numbers to describe quantities and relationships, adults can ask children to sort objects by size, shape, or color similarity. They can also ask children to sort objects according to their differences (e.g., which object is bigger/smaller). Adults can also discuss with children how numbers are used to find street addresses and apartment numbers and to keep score during games. To help children count upward and downward with efficiency and accuracy, adults can point out that counting allows us to determine how many items are in a group. Adults should point to each object as they count it. They can count on their fingers and encourage young children to do the same. Adults should also help children count without repeating or skipping any numbers.

COUNTING

Counting is considered a math skill milestone for young children. Typical four-year-olds enjoy counting aloud. Experts identify three levels of counting. The first is counting from 1 to 12, which requires memorization. The second level is counting from 13 to 19, which requires not only memorization but also an understanding of the more unusual rules for "teen" numbers. The third level is counting from 20 on. This process is very consistent, and the numbers are ordered according to regular rules. Experts in math education believe that at this level of counting, children are discovering a regular mathematical pattern for the first time, which is base ten (i.e., 20, 30, 40, 50, etc. are 2 tens, 3 tens, 4 tens, 5 tens, etc., and after the base, a number between 1 and 9 is added). Researchers and educators in early childhood mathematics programs recommend encouraging children as young as four years old to learn to count up to 100. They find that doing this helps young children learn about and explore patterns in depth.

Copyright © Mometrix Media. You have been licensed one copy of this document for personal use only. Any other reproduction or redistribution is strictly prohibited. All rights reserved.
This content is provided for test preparation purposes only and does not imply an endorsement by Mometrix of any particular political, scientific, or religious point of view.

PERCEIVING AND IDENTIFYING SHAPES

The three levels of perceiving shapes that children typically move through sequentially are seeing, naming, and analyzing. Very young children recognize simple shapes like circles, squares, and triangles. As their cognitive and language skills develop, they learn the names for these shapes and use these names to identify single shapes. The third level is analyzing each shape to understand its properties. Whereas identifying shapes visually is intuitive and based on association, analyzing their properties is more abstract, since a shape can have a number of different appearances. For example, three-year-olds can differentiate a triangle from other shapes. However, if you show them a very tall and skinny, short and wide, lopsided, or crooked triangle, they will have trouble identifying it as a triangle. At the analysis level, children realize that a triangle has three sides, which are not necessarily equal in length. An activity that young children enjoy is closing their eyes, reaching into a bag of assorted shapes, finding a triangle by touch, and explaining why it is a triangle. This involves both the second and third levels of naming and analysis.

SPATIAL SENSE AND GEOMETRY

Spatial sense is an individual's awareness of one's own body in space and in relation to the objects and other people around the individual. Spatial sense allows young children to navigate environmental spaces without colliding with objects and other people; to see and hear adequately and to be aware of whether others can see and hear them; and to develop and observe a socially and culturally appropriate sense of their own and others' personal space. Geometry is the area of mathematics involving space, sizes, shapes, positions, movements, and directions. Geometry gives descriptions and classifications of our physical environment. By observing commonplace objects and spaces in their physical world, young children can learn about solid objects and substances, shapes, and angles. Adults can help young children learn geometry by identifying various shapes, angles, and three-dimensional figures for them; asking them to name these shapes, angles, and figures when they encounter them in the future; and asking them to describe different shapes, draw them in the air with their fingers, trace drawings of the shapes with their fingers, and then draw the shapes themselves.

ACTIVITIES TO HELP DEVELOP SPATIAL SENSE AND GEOMETRY

Because it involves many physical properties like shape, line, and angle, as well as abstract concepts, young children learn geometry most effectively via hands-on activities. Learning experiences that allow them to touch and manipulate concrete objects, such as boxes, containers, puzzles, blocks, and shape sorters, usually work best. Everyday activities can also help children learn geometry concepts. For example, adults can cut children's sandwiches into various geometrical shapes and let children fit them together and/or rearrange them into new patterns. Children become better able to follow directions and navigate through space when they develop geometric knowledge and spatial sense. Adults can provide activities that promote the development of geometric knowledge and spatial sense. For example, they can let children get into and out of big appliance boxes, climb over furniture, and go into, on top of, out of, under, around, over, and through different objects and structures to allow children to experience the relationship between their bodies and space and solids. As they mature, children can play games in which they search for "hidden" shapes. Such shapes may be irregular, may lack flat bases, or may be turned in various directions.

MEASUREMENT

Measurement is the process of determining how long, wide, and tall something is physically and how much it weighs by using measuring units such as inches, feet, yards, square feet, ounces, and pounds. Measurement is also used to quantify time using units like seconds, minutes, hours, days,

Copyright © Mometrix Media. You have been licensed one copy of this document for personal use only. Any other reproduction or redistribution is strictly prohibited. All rights reserved. This content is provided for test preparation purposes only and does not imply an endorsement by Mometrix of any particular political, scientific, or religious point of view.

weeks, months, years, centuries, and millennia. Measurement is not just a formal means of quantifying size, area, and time. It is also an important method for young children to seek and identify relationships between and among things they encounter outside of school in everyday life. When young children practice measuring things, they are able to understand not only the sizes of objects and beings but also their comparative sizes (i.e., how large or small something is compared to another object used as a reference). Furthermore, they are able to figure out how big or little something is on their own.

While it is obviously important for children to eventually learn standardized measurement units like inches, feet, and yards, adults can facilitate early development of measurement skills by letting children choose their own measurement units. For example, they might use their favorite toy to describe a playmate or sibling as "three teddy bears tall," or they might describe a room as "seven toy cars long." Similarly, when children are too young to know formal time measurements like minutes and hours, adults can support children's ability to quantify time using favorite TV shows. For example, four-year-olds can often relate to the idea of one episode of a show (whether it is 30 minutes or 60 minutes long) as a time measurement. Adults can apply this with statements like, "Daddy will be home in one episode." Numerous everyday activities, including grocery shopping, cooking, sewing, gardening, woodworking, and many others, involve measurement. Adults can ask children to help with these tasks and then discuss measuring with children as they participate.

MEASUREMENT OF TIME

Younger children typically do not have an understanding of the abstract concept of time. However, adults can still help children understand that time elapses and that we count/measure this process. For example, adults can ask younger children simple questions, such as "Who can stand on one foot longer?" This comparison strategy helps children figure out which of two or more actions/activities takes a longer/the longest period of time. Even when children do not yet understand what "five minutes" means, adults should still make such references (e.g., "You can play for five minutes longer, and then we must leave."). Repeating such references will eventually help children understand that time passes. Adults can time various everyday activities/events and tell children how long they took. They can also count the second hand's ticks on a watch/clock (e.g., "one second...two seconds...three seconds..."). This familiarizes children with counting, and with using counting to track the passage of time. Until children are old enough to understand abstractions like today/yesterday/tomorrow, adults can use concrete references like "after lunch" or "before bedtime."

FRACTIONS

Fractions are parts or pieces of a whole. While adults understand this and likely do not remember ever not understanding it, very young children think differently in this regard. As Piaget showed, children in the preoperational stage of cognitive development cannot perform logical or mathematical mental operations. They focus on one property of an object rather than all of its properties, a practice he called centration. Hence, if you cut an apple into pieces, very young children see that there are more pieces than there were before, and they believe that several apple pieces are more than one apple. They cannot yet comprehend the logical sequence of dividing an apple into fractions. To comprehend fractions, children must know what a whole unit consists of, how many pieces the unit is divided into, and whether the pieces are of equal size. Adults can help children understand fractions through informal sharing activities, such as slicing up a pizza or a pan of brownies, and/or equally dividing household/preschool chores and play materials.

Copyright © Mometrix Media. You have been licensed one copy of this document for personal use only. Any other reproduction or redistribution is strictly prohibited. All rights reserved. This content is provided for test preparation purposes only and does not imply an endorsement by Mometrix of any particular political, scientific, or religious point of view.

ESTIMATION

Estimation is making an educated or informed guess about a measurement when no actual measurement is available. Adults often make estimates about the sizes of objects when their exact measurements are unknown, about the amounts of substances that have not actually been measured, and about the numbers of small objects in large collections when the objects have not actually been counted. However, young children are in the process of learning the concepts of sizes and numbers. Children must comprehend concepts of comparison and relativity (e.g., larger, smaller, more, less, etc.) before they will be able to make accurate estimates. When children start to develop the ability to estimate amounts or sizes, this process helps them learn related math vocabulary words, such as *about* or *around*, and *more than* and *less than* [something else]. Through estimating, they also learn how to make appropriate predictions and arrive at realistic answers. It is important for young children to learn how to make estimates, to recognize when it is appropriate to apply the estimation method, and to recognize when their estimates are reasonable.

ACTIVITIES TO HELP DEVELOP ESTIMATION

During everyday activities like shopping or eating, adults can ask children to estimate amounts of foods, numbers of items, or lengths of time. Later, adults can help children compare the actual outcome with their original estimate. This process helps children learn to make realistic/reasonable estimates. Activities promoting estimation skills can be very simple. Adults can ask children, for example, to guess which of their friends is tallest and then test the accuracy of the guess using real measurements. When children grow older, adults can write down estimates and real measurements and can then repeat the exercise described above or present a similar one. With repetition, children will eventually begin making more accurate estimates. The goal is not for children to come up with exact measurements but ones that are close to actual amounts/numbers. Giving children opportunities to practice improves their estimating skills.

PROBABILITIES AND STATISTICS

In general, when people work with statistics, they present them in graphs or charts to organize them, interpret them, and make it easier to see relationships among individual statistics. Graphs are visual alternatives that depict mathematical information and show relationships among individual statistics, especially changes over time. Graphs also allow for the comparison of different groups. Probabilities indicate the likelihood that something will happen. Adults use probabilities to predict things, such as people's risks of developing or dying from various diseases or medical conditions; the chances of accidents; children's risks of experiencing academic difficulties, dropping out, or developing emotional and behavioral disorders; and the chances that a certain area will receive rain or snow. Scientists use probabilities to predict the likelihood of various behaviors or outcomes they are studying. They use statistics to show the numbers and proportions of responses or results obtained in research studies. Calendars are one type of chart. Adults can help children use them to organize daily and weekly activities and to understand how we organize information.

CHARTS AND GRAPHS

According to experts, almost every daily activity can be charted in some way. For example, adults can help children peel the little stickers off of plums, bananas, etc. and stick them to a piece of paper/poster board divided into columns. After a week, they can count each column to determine how many pieces of each kind of fruit they ate. Similarly, adults can show children how to use removable stickers or color forms to document the number of times they performed any daily activity. For example, children could place a color form near the front door every time somebody comes in, goes out, and/or rings the doorbell or knocks. This enables children to count the number of times given events occur by recording them. Some children are better able to understand math

Copyright © Mometrix Media. You have been licensed one copy of this document for personal use only. Any other reproduction or redistribution is strictly prohibited. All rights reserved.
This content is provided for test preparation purposes only and does not imply an endorsement by Mometrix of any particular political, scientific, or religious point of view.

by viewing and making graphs. This is because creating graphs involves representing quantities visually instead of just listing numbers.

RATIONAL NUMBERS AND IRRATIONAL NUMBERS

In mathematics, **rational numbers** are numbers that can be written as ratios or fractions. In other words, a rational number can be expressed as a fraction that has a whole number as the numerator (the number on top) and the denominator (the number on the bottom). Therefore, all whole numbers are automatically rational numbers, because all whole numbers can be written as fractions with a denominator of 1 (e.g., $5 = 5/1$, $68 = 68/1$, $237 = 237/1$, etc.). Even very large, unwieldy fractions (e.g., $9,731,245/42,754,021$) are rational numbers, because they can be written as fractions. **Irrational numbers** can be written as decimal numbers, but not as fractions, because the numbers to the right of the decimal point that are less than 1 continue indefinitely without repeating. For example, the value of pi (π) begins as 3.141592... and continues without end or the square root of 2, $\sqrt{2} = 1.414213$ ..., and so on. There are an infinite number of irrational numbers between 0 and 1. However, irrational numbers are not used as commonly in everyday life as rational numbers.

> **Review Video: <u>Rational and Irrational Numbers</u>**
> Visit mometrix.com/academy and enter code: 280645

CARDINAL, ORDINAL, NOMINAL, AND REAL NUMBERS

- **Cardinal numbers** are numbers that indicate quantity. For example, when we say "seven buttons" or "three kittens," we are using cardinal numbers.
- **Ordinal numbers** are numbers that indicate the order of items within a group or a set. For example, when we say "first," "second," "third," etc., we are using ordinal numbers.
- **Nominal numbers** are numbers that name things. For example, we use area code numbers along with telephone numbers to identify geographical calling areas, and we use zip code numbers to identify geographical mailing areas. Nominal numbers, therefore, identify categories or serve as labels for things. However, they are not related to the actual mathematical values of numbers, and do not indicate numerical quantities or operations.
- **Real numbers** include all rational and irrational numbers. Rational numbers can always be written as fractions that have both numerators and denominators that are whole numbers. Irrational numbers cannot, as they contain non-repeating decimal digits. Real numbers may or may not be cardinal numbers.

INTEGRATING MATH INTO EVERYDAY ACTIVITIES AND USING EARLY CHILDHOOD MATH CURRICULA

Integrating math into the context of everyday activities has been the philosophy of early childhood math education until recently. For example, when teachers have children line up, they ask them who is first, second, third, etc. to practice counting. When children play with blocks, teachers ask them to identify their shapes and whether one block is larger/smaller than another. During snack times, teachers help children learn 1:1 correspondence by having them place one snack on each plate. These activities are quite valuable. However, some educators maintain that they are insufficient when used on their own, because in larger classes, it is not always possible to take advantage of "teachable moments" with every child. Therefore, this educational approach cannot be applied systematically. These educators recommend that in addition to integration strategies, early childhood teachers should use a curriculum. The HighScope curriculum, the Creative Curriculum, and Big Math for Little Kids are just a few examples. Many teachers combine several curricula,

Copyright © Mometrix Media. You have been licensed one copy of this document for personal use only. Any other reproduction or redistribution is strictly prohibited. All rights reserved. This content is provided for test preparation purposes only and does not imply an endorsement by Mometrix of any particular political, scientific, or religious point of view.

selecting parts of different programs. Using a curriculum allows teachers to use a more planned approach to integrate math into all activities.

CLINICAL INTERVIEW
BACKGROUND, METHOD, AND ADVANTAGES

Clinical interviews have long been used by individual and family therapists, as well as by researchers. Piaget used them along with observations and case histories to understand young children's thinking as he formulated his cognitive developmental theory. Interviewers ask structured, semi-structured, and open-ended questions and listen to the responses, often recording them for accuracy. This method gives the interviewer a way to find out what the respondent is thinking and feeling inside, which cannot be determined by observing outward behaviors alone. In educational settings, a teacher might ask a child questions like, "How did you do this?" "What is happening now?" "Can you tell me more about this?" "Why are you doing this?" and "What are you thinking about now?". Flexible questioning helps uncover the child's thought process, which is what is leading him or her to engage in specific behaviors. Just observing the behaviors alone does not allow the child to express his or her knowledge. While fully interviewing each child in a classroom is not practical, teachers can adapt this method by asking clinical interview-type questions as part of their instruction.

USING QUESTIONING

Teachers can gain a lot of information and insight about how children are learning math concepts by observing their behaviors. For children to actually express their knowledge and thinking processes, however, teachers must ask them questions. For example, when a teacher introduces new shapes to young children, he or she can ask them the shapes' names, how they differ from one another, and why they think the shapes differ. Teachers can then use children's various responses to elicit further responses from them. This technique requires children to use language in significant ways during math activities. Therefore, these activities not only teach math skills but also promote literacy development. Asking clinical interview-type questions promotes children's development of math communication skills, one of the essential components of math education. Additionally, being able to put one's knowledge and thoughts into words is a skill that is very important in all areas of education, not just math education. Using clinical interview-type questions helps children learn to use language to explain their thinking, share ideas, and express themselves, promoting and strengthening children's awareness of the functions of mathematical language.

CHARACTERISTICS OF YOUNG CHILDREN'S THINKING AND LEARNING THAT INFORM EARLY CHILDHOOD MATH CURRICULA

Young children think in concrete ways and cannot understand abstract concepts, so effective early childhood math curricula typically use many concrete objects that children can see, feel, and manipulate to help them understand math concepts. Young children also naturally learn through exploring their environments, so good EC math curricula have many exploration and discovery activities that allow and encourage hands-on learning. In everyday life, young children start to observe relationships as they explore their surroundings. They match like objects, sort unlike objects, categorize objects, and arrange objects in simple patterns based on shared or contrasting properties. They start to understand words and phrases like *a little, a lot, more, less*, and *the same* [as...]. Preschoolers use available materials such as sticks, pieces of string, their feet, their hands, and their fingers as tools to measure objects. They also use rulers, measuring cups, and other conventional tools. They use their measurements to develop descriptions, sequences, and arrangements, and to compare various objects.

181

Copyright © Mometrix Media. You have been licensed one copy of this document for personal use only. Any other reproduction or redistribution is strictly prohibited. All rights reserved. This content is provided for test preparation purposes only and does not imply an endorsement by Mometrix of any particular political, scientific, or religious point of view.

ACTIVITIES THAT HELP CHILDREN DEVELOP SPATIAL AWARENESS

When preschool children build structures with blocks and put together pieces of puzzles during play, they are not only having fun but are also developing spatial awareness. The relationships of objects to each other and within space are important concepts for children to learn, and serve as a foundation for the principles of geometry and physics that children will learn later. When they are moving around, preschoolers begin to notice how other people and objects are positioned in space and how their own bodies move through space in relationship to objects and other people. This type of spatial awareness supports children's developing gross motor skills, coordination, and social skills. Young children can and should learn a number of math concepts and skills, such as the ones recommended by preschool math curricula like the HighScope program's "Numbers Plus" preschool mathematics curriculum. These concepts and skills include number symbols and names, counting, shapes, spatial awareness, relationships of parts to the whole, measurement, units, patterns, and analyzing data.

ACTIVITIES AND GAMES THAT MAKE LEARNING FUN

BUTTON BOARD

By gluing buttons of various sizes and colors to a piece of cardboard, teachers can initiate a number of activities that help preschoolers learn math concepts while having fun. Preschoolers are commonly learning shapes and how to draw them. Teachers can give children lengths of string, twine, or yarn or long shoelaces and show them how to wrap them around different buttons to form shapes like rectangles, triangles, and squares. To practice counting and 1:1 correspondence, teachers can ask children to wrap their string around a given number of buttons. Preschoolers need to learn the concept that spoken number words like *five* can equate to a group of five concrete objects (such as buttons), and this activity promotes that learning. The button board is also useful for giving preschool children practice with sorting or classifying objects into groups based on a common characteristic. For example, the teacher can ask children to wrap their pieces of string around all the big buttons, all the little buttons, only the red buttons, only the blue buttons, etc.

BEANBAGS AND HOPSCOTCH

Teachers can encourage preschool children's counting and number development by creating a grid on the floor with the numbers 1 to 10 using masking tape, construction paper, and markers. Teachers could also draw the grid outdoors by drawing on pavement with chalk. The teacher arranges the numbers in ascending order within the grid of 10 squares and asks the children if they can name these numbers. The teacher provides beanbags. Each child gets a chance to throw a beanbag into any one of the numbered squares, which allows them to see how far they can throw and/or practice their aim. Each child names the number inside the square where his or her beanbag lands. The children then play a version of hopscotch by hopping from numbered square to square, collecting their beanbags, and then hopping back. If desired, the teacher can write the number each child's beanbag lands on onto a "scoreboard" graph. Teachers can review learning after the game to assess whether children can count using number words, name selected numbers, and throw accurately with consistency.

REUSING SECTIONED PLASTIC TRAYS

A teacher can wash and reuse the compartmentalized plastic trays from the grocery store that are used for vegetables and fruit to create a preschool counting activity. The teacher supplies beads, pennies, erasers, or other small objects, as well as about a dozen sticky notes, writing a number on each note. For older preschoolers, the teacher can write the numeral and the word (e.g., "7" and "seven"). For younger children, the teacher can write the numeric symbol ("7," for example) plus seven dots or other marks as a clue to that number symbol. The teacher puts one numbered note in

182

Copyright © Mometrix Media. You have been licensed one copy of this document for personal use only. Any other reproduction or redistribution is strictly prohibited. All rights reserved.
This content is provided for test preparation purposes only and does not imply an endorsement by Mometrix of any particular political, scientific, or religious point of view.

each compartment and the supply of small objects in the central dip compartment. Then, he or she guides each child to transfer the correct number of each small object to the correct compartment. The child should count aloud while transferring each small object and should repeat this process until all compartments with a numbered sticky note have the correct number of objects. Children can then repeat the process to practice and perfect their counting, or the teacher can place notes with different numbers in the tray's compartments.

FISHING FOR NUMBERS

Teachers can help preschoolers practice identifying numbers and counting by creating a fun "fishing for numbers" game. Teachers cut 10 fish shapes that are about 6 inches long from pieces of construction paper that are different colors. Teachers then write a single number between 1 and 10 on each "fish." Near each fish "mouth," the teacher punches a hole and inserts a paper clip through it. The teacher makes "fishing rods" by tying strings to dowels and gluing a magnet to each string. After spreading out the fish so the children can easily see the numbers, the teacher assigns each child a number, and they "fish" for it, picking up the fish by bringing the magnet close to the paper clip. The children then "reel in" their catches. This gives children practice correctly identifying number names. The game can be adapted for more advanced math concepts as well. For example, the teacher can cut out fish shapes of various sizes and have children "fish" for larger or smaller fish. The activity can also be adapted to promote literacy development. The teacher can write letters instead of numbers on the fish to give students practice with alphabet recognition, or teacher can write a Dolch word/sight word on each fish to give students practice recognizing and identifying important vocabulary words.

COLLAGES

Fundamental math skills that prepare preschoolers for kindergarten include shape recognition. To introduce children to an activity they will view as fun rather than as work, teachers can show children how to make a collage of a familiar figure. This will also give children the opportunity to experiment with an artistic process. For example, they can create a Santa Claus or an Easter Bunny as a holiday art project. They can make **collages** of other imaginary or real people for various events, seasons, or topics. Teachers cut out paper templates, including circles for heads, triangles for hats, squares for bodies, and narrow rectangular strips for limbs. First, they help children name each shape. They have each child trace the template shapes onto paper and cut them out with child-safe scissors. The teacher then instructs the children to arrange their cutout shapes on a piece of cardboard or construction paper. Once they are in the correct positions, the children glue the shapes in place. Teachers can subsequently teach additional shapes (octagons, ovals, etc.), challenging children to make new, different collages.

GRAB BAG

Young children learn to name numbers in a way that is similar to how they learn to recite alphabet letters. However, learning to associate number symbols with concrete objects in the real world environment is a major advance in their cognitive development. The concept of 1:1 correspondence entails matching number symbols to the quantities they represent, an essential early math skill. Teachers can support the development of this math skill with a simple "grab bag" game youngsters enjoy. The teacher writes a number from 1 to 10 on each of the 10 cards, folding each card in half and putting them into a paper lunch bag. The teacher provides each child with a handful of pennies, play coins, buttons, or little blocks to use as counting tokens. Each child takes a turn closing his or her eyes and pulling a card out of the bag. The child reads the number on the card, counts out the corresponding number of pennies/tokens, and puts them with the card. As children learn, teachers can place additional and/or different numbers (e.g., 11 to 20) in the grab bag. To promote the development of early literacy skills, teachers can also include the name of the number on each card.

Copyright © Mometrix Media. You have been licensed one copy of this document for personal use only. Any other reproduction or redistribution is strictly prohibited. All rights reserved.
This content is provided for test preparation purposes only and does not imply an endorsement by Mometrix of any particular political, scientific, or religious point of view.

PATTERN RESIST ART

A significant mark of progress in early math skills development is the ability to not only identify various shapes but also to draw them. Once young children develop this ability, they typically want to practice it all the time. Teachers can encourage this by helping children make pattern resist paintings. The teacher tapes white paper to children's tables/trays, gives them crayons, and invites them to fill the paper with drawings of different shapes of various sizes and colors. Teachers can introduce young children to new shapes (e.g., ovals, stars, crescent moons, etc.) by drawing them on separate pieces of paper for children to look at and copy. Then, the teacher replaces the crayons with water, watercolor paints, and brushes; shows the children how to dip brushes into paint and water to dilute the colors; and allows them to paint over their crayoned shapes, covering all the white paper with color. The children see the shapes show through the paint, creating the pattern resist. Dipping brushes and diluting various colors also develop children's color recognition skills and their hand-eye coordination.

ICE CUBE NECKLACES

In hot weather, making ice cube necklaces is a fun activity that helps young children cool off while learning to sequence objects. The activity also helps children develop their manual motor skills and learn about liquid and solid states of matter. Regular ice cube trays are fine; those with "fun-shaped" compartments are even better. The teacher cuts plastic drinking straws so that they will fit into each ice cube compartment. The children participate, watching and/or helping pour water into trays and adding various food colorings/fruit juices. The teacher places one straw clipping into each compartment. While putting the trays into the freezer, the teacher tells the children that 32° Fahrenheit/0° Celsius is the temperature at which water freezes. Children practice making scientific observations by noting how long the water takes to freeze. They empty the cubes into a big bowl. The children put on bathing suits or other clothing that can get wet, and the class goes outdoors. The teacher provides strings that are knotted at one end, and calls out a color pattern (e.g., one blue cube, then a yellow cube, etc.). Children follow the teacher's instructions to create color-patterned necklaces they can tie, wear, and watch melt.

RED ROVER

Red Rover is a good game for groups of children who are attending parties or playing outdoors at parks or playgrounds. Two teams take turns calling and roving. The child called runs to the other team and tries to fit into its line. If successful, he or she gets to call another player to bring back to his or her home team. If not, the child joins the opposite team. The game continues until one team has no more members. Teachers can adapt this game to teach shape recognition by cutting out various shapes from construction paper of different colors and pinning a shape to each child's shirt. In large groups, more than one child can have the same shape or color. Instead of children's names, the teacher instructs players to use shapes and colors when calling (e.g., "Red Rover, Red Rover, blue circles come over!"). This supports the development of shape and color recognition skills. Teachers can vary action verbs (e.g., "...hop over/jump over/skip over") to support vocabulary development and comprehensive skills. When children perform such movements, they are also practicing and developing gross motor skills.

COUNTING ON FINGERS

A common practice among preschool children is counting on their fingers. Young children learn concretely before they develop abstract thought, so they must have concrete objects to work with to understand abstract mathematical concepts. They use their fingers to count because fingers are concrete. A simple activity that allows children to continue finger counting while removing additional visual support is "blind finger counting." Using eyesight to count objects we can see is relatively easy. However, when children cannot see objects, they must learn to count mentally

Copyright © Mometrix Media. You have been licensed one copy of this document for personal use only. Any other reproduction or redistribution is strictly prohibited. All rights reserved. This content is provided for test preparation purposes only and does not imply an endorsement by Mometrix of any particular political, scientific, or religious point of view.

instead. This allows them to take another step in their progress from concrete to abstract thinking. To count mentally without visual reinforcement takes practice. Teachers can tape a shoebox lid to the box and cut a small hole in it. Children can fit a hand through the hole, but cannot see inside. Children close their eyes; the teacher drops several small objects into the box; and each child reaches in, counting the objects using only touch. Varying objects and quantities maintains the fun of this activity.

SORTING AND CATEGORIZATION

One of the major learning accomplishments of young children is being able to identify similarities and differences among objects. Developing this ability enables children to sort like objects into groups and to place objects into categories based on their differences. When preschoolers compare and contrast objects, they demonstrate an important early step in the development of critical thinking, analytical, and problem-solving skills. For an easy, entertaining guessing game, adults can select assorted household items familiar to children and put them into a bag/pillowcase. They then give children various clues (e.g., "I stir lemonade with this...," "It's made of wood," "We keep it in the kitchen drawer...," etc.) and ask them to guess which items are in the bag. It is important to give young children one to two minutes to consider each clue before they make a guess. Adults repeat clues when children guess incorrectly. If children guess correctly, they are allowed to look inside the bag. Children greatly enjoy seeing that the object they guessed is actually inside the bag. Adults can gradually make the game more challenging by beginning with very common objects and then eventually progressing to more unusual ones.

BAKING COOKIES

Young children are typically curious about adult activities like baking. They usually want to know more about the process and often ask many questions. They also love to be included and to participate, frequently offering/asking to help. Letting them help builds their self-esteem and self-efficacy (i.e., their confidence in their competence to accomplish a task). Adults can allow children to help while also providing instruction and practice with shape recognition, measurement, sorting, and categorization. The adult prepares a favorite cookie recipe. Some children can help measure ingredients, which helps develop the math skill of measurement. With the dough rolled out, children use cookie cutters of various shapes. Recognizing, naming, and selecting the shapes promote the development of shape recognition skills. Adults "shuffle"/mix the baked cookie shapes and have children separate cookies with like shapes into groups, which promotes sorting skills. Having children identify similar/different shapes, sizes, and colors promotes categorization skills. Arranging cookie shapes into patterns for children to identify promotes pattern recognition skills, which are necessary for the development of math skills and many other skills. Giving each child a cookie to eat afterward is naturally reinforcing.

CREATIVE CRAFTS

Prerequisite abilities that young children need in order to develop early math skills include the ability to identify, copy, expand, and create patterns, as well as the ability to count. Adults can promote the development of these skills by giving children a craft project and introducing them to an interactive game they can play using their crafts. First, the children paint six ping pong balls red on one side to make red-and-white balls. Then, the children paint six ping pong balls blue on one side to make blue-and-white balls. Once the paint dries, the adult puts several balls into an egg carton so that one color is face up. The adult starts making a simple pattern (e.g., two white, then two red, then two blue) and asks each child to continue the pattern. Then, the adult allows each child to create his or her own original color patterns. Once a child masters creating patterns using solid colors, he or she can then use both the white and colored sides of the balls to create more complex patterns. Children can design an infinite number of patterns, which are often quite artistic.

Copyright © Mometrix Media. You have been licensed one copy of this document for personal use only. Any other reproduction or redistribution is strictly prohibited. All rights reserved. This content is provided for test preparation purposes only and does not imply an endorsement by Mometrix of any particular political, scientific, or religious point of view.

SHAPE MATCHING GAMES

In one type of shape matching game, early childhood teachers help children make a game board out of construction paper that is shaped like a tree. Teachers first help the children cut a treetop and leaf shapes from green paper. They discuss children's preferences for tall/short and thick/thin trunks, giving them practice using descriptive vocabulary words, particularly ones related to size. This step builds both general and math concept vocabulary. Children cut trunks from brown paper and glue them on the treetops. While out of the children's sight, the teacher cuts 5 to 10 (or more) pairs of shapes per child/tree from different colors of construction paper. Pairs should not match exactly (e.g., a blue square can be paired with a red square). The teacher glues one of each pair of shapes to each child's tree while the child is not looking. The teacher then gives each child the rest of the shapes and invites children to see how quickly they can match each shape to its "partner" on the tree. The teacher can provide "warmer/cooler" distance clues and should provide reinforcement each time a child correctly matches a pair of shapes. Teachers can make this activity more challenging by using more shapes and/or getting students to match shapes that are different sizes (e.g., children can be asked to match smaller diamonds to larger diamonds).

HOMEMADE BEANBAG GAME

Young children enjoy tossing objects and practicing their aim. Adults can make a beanbag game that helps children learn numbers and identify sets, while also allowing them to construct their own game rules. First, the adult should cover five big, equally-sized coffee (or similar) cans with paper that is adhesive on one side. The adult should then use markers to write a number from 1 to 5 and draw the corresponding number of dots on each can. The next step is to fill 15 tube socks with beans and knot/tie/sew them shut. The following numerals and the corresponding number of dots should be written on each homemade beanbag using markers: the number 1 on five beanbags, the number 2 on four beanbags, the number 3 on three beanbags, the number 4 on two beanbags, and the number 5 on one beanbag. Next, the adult should attach the cans to the floor with tape or Velcro. Then, the adult should mark a line on the floor that children must stand behind, and should direct children ONLY to toss the beanbags into the cans. Children will devise various games/rules. First, they may simply toss the beanbags into the cans; then, some may try to toss beanbags into a can that has the same number as the one marked on the beanbag. Eventually, some may throw three beanbags into the "3" can. They may or may not keep score. Allowing children to determine the details and rules gives them an opportunity to develop their imagination and decision-making skills, and to create their own games while learning number and set identification.

GUESSING GAME

Adults can adapt the format of "20 Questions," "I Spy," and other similar guessing games to focus on numbers and help children learn number concepts. For example, adults could say, "I'm thinking of a number from 1 to 10...." and then give children 10 guesses. Adults give children cues as they guess, such as "higher" and "lower," to help them narrow down the number of possible correct answers. As children improve, adults can increase the number range (e.g., from 0 to 50) or use larger numbers (e.g., from 20 to 40). As children's skills and self-confidence develop, adults can reverse roles, having children think of numbers and give clues while adults guess. Young children enjoy the fun of guessing, getting closer using clues, deducing correct answers, and fooling adults with their own clues. Concurrently, they learn to describe numbers, compare them, and sequence them. Adults can make the game more difficult by limiting the number of guesses allowed and/or setting time limits. They can make it easier by providing a written number line for children to reference. This game requires no materials (or just a basic number line), is a great way to pass time, and entertains children while helping to develop numeracy skills.

Copyright © Mometrix Media. You have been licensed one copy of this document for personal use only. Any other reproduction or redistribution is strictly prohibited. All rights reserved. This content is provided for test preparation purposes only and does not imply an endorsement by Mometrix of any particular political, scientific, or religious point of view.

ARTS AND CRAFTS

According to the US Department of Agriculture, preschoolers need three ½-cup servings of fruit and three ½-cup servings of vegetables daily. However, many young children are picky/resistant. Adults can motivate them to eat produce with a "food rainbow" project. Adults show children a picture of a rainbow and discuss its colors and their sequence (teaching some earth science, optics, and color theory). A fun art project is allowing students to color their own rainbows, which improves fine motor skills. Then, adults can have children cut out pictures from grocery circulars and name each food. The adult can help children find one healthy fruit/vegetable for each color, gluing each food to its corresponding stripe on the rainbow. Adults can then help children pull apart cotton balls and glue them to their rainbow pictures to represent clouds. Children can then post their food rainbows on refrigerators as artwork and as healthy eating reminders. At the bottom, children can draw and color one box (bottom-up) for each food they eat (e.g., blue for blueberries, orange for carrots, red for apples, etc.) to create a bar graph. Children should try to "eat" the entire rainbow every week. This activity gives children the opportunity to produce colorful art, eat better, track and document their diets, and develop graphing skills.

> **Review Video: Data Interpretation of Graphs**
> Visit mometrix.com/academy and enter code: 200439

TREASURE HUNT

A treasure hunt is an ideal outdoor activity for young children and can also be adapted for indoor fun. The treasure can be anything such as a small toy, play money, chocolate "coins," or rocks spray painted gold or silver. The adult should put the treasure in a paper bag marked with a large X. The adult should hide it somewhere where it is not visible but will not be overly difficult for children to find. Then, the adult should make a treasure map, using few words and many pictures, sketching landmark objects in the area (e.g., trees and houses if the activity will be done outdoors, and furniture and walls if the activity will be done indoors). The adult should ensure the map is developmentally appropriate for young children and that they will be able to read it independently. Adults with time and motivation can make the map look authentic by soaking it in tea/coffee, drying it in a 200° F oven, or even charring its edges. Adults should include a dotted line on the map that reinforces the simple directions and indicates the path to the treasure, which is indicated on the map by a large X. Children have fun, use their imaginations, make connections between symbols and images to corresponding real-world physical objects, and begin learning to read maps.

PASTA NECKLACE

Stringing beads/noodles is an activity that helps young children develop hand-eye coordination, which they will need for writing and other everyday activities that require fine motor coordination. Noodles are typically the perfect size for young children's hands. They are inexpensive, usually costing less than comparably-sized beads. Moreover, pasta is non-toxic, an advantage when working with children who put things in their mouths. Hollow, tubular noodles like penne, ziti, and wagon wheels are ideal. Fishing line, craft beading string, and other stiff string is best; soft, limp string/yarn is harder for young children to manipulate. Using multicolored vegetable pasta removes the need to use markers or dye to add color. If using white pasta, children can color the noodles with markers, but adults should keep in mind that the ink can bleed onto skin/clothes even when it is dry. Adults should cut pieces of string that are long enough to allow children to easily slip the necklaces on and off after they are tied. Adults should also use a knot to secure a noodle to one end of the string. By providing more than one noodle shape, adults can invite children to string the noodles to create patterns, which develops pattern recognition and pattern creation abilities. These abilities also inform repetition, rhythm, categorization, and sequencing skills, which are important in math, music, art, literature, and clothing design.

Copyright © Mometrix Media. You have been licensed one copy of this document for personal use only. Any other reproduction or redistribution is strictly prohibited. All rights reserved.
This content is provided for test preparation purposes only and does not imply an endorsement by Mometrix of any particular political, scientific, or religious point of view.

NUMBER DASH

A game for young children that some educators call "Number Dash" (Miller, ed. Charner, 2009) builds foundational math concepts and skills while providing physical activity. It can involve small or large groups (the referenced authors say "the more the merrier"). Help children write large numbers on a paved area with sidewalk chalk. Make sure numbers are spread far enough apart so children will not collide while running. There should be one of each number for each child (e.g., six 1s, 2s, 3s, etc. if there are six children). Use chalk colors that contrast with the pavement color to ensure the numbers will be highly visible. Tell children to run ("dash") to whichever number you call out and stand on it until you call another number. Call out numbers randomly. Encourage children who have located the number to help their classmates/playmates. This game develops gross motor skills, number writing skills, and number recognition skills. It also provides experience with playing organized games, following rules, following directions, and cooperating with and helping others. This game can also be played with letters, colors, and/or shapes.

INTRODUCING STANDARD MEASUREMENT USING A RULER

A teacher is introducing standard measures to her class as part of a unit on measurement, one of the early math skills. She shows the children a ruler, explaining that it is one foot long and that we can use it to measure inches and parts of inches. She demonstrates placing the ruler on paper to measure a given length, explaining that the ruler can also be used as a straight edge for drawing lines. One child asks, "How come you started with zero? Why don't you start with one like when we count?" The teacher responds, "That's a very good question! Zero means none/nothing. When we count, we start with one because we already have at least one of something. When you were born, you were not one year old; your age began at zero. After a year, on your first birthday, you were one year old. We also begin measuring distances at zero/none/nothing. The first unit of measurement is one, not two. The distance from zero to one is equal to one. To get to one inch, for example, we need to start at zero."

LEARNING ABOUT GEOMETRIC SHAPES AND THEIR PROPERTIES

A teacher has been working with students to help them develop their shape identification skills. They can recognize shapes by sight and have also learned the defining properties of different shapes (number of sides, etc.). The teacher shows the class this figure:

She asks how many rectangles they can find in the figure. One student answers, "There is one rectangle," which is incorrect because a square is a rectangle; this figure has four rectangles that are squares. Moreover, the entire figure is itself a rectangle. Another student therefore says, "There are five rectangles." This response is also incorrect. Two adjacent squares also form a rectangle; this means there are three additional rectangles. Three adjacent squares also form a rectangle; this means there are two additional rectangles. Thus, the figure has a total of 10 rectangles. Solving this puzzle requires the use of many skills, including analyzing visual information, synthesizing visual information, recognizing patterns, recognizing shapes, and identifying the properties of shapes.

COLLECTING, ORGANIZING, AND DISPLAYING DATA USING STICKY NOTES AND A TEACHER-MADE CHART

A preschool teacher is teaching her group of ten children about basic data collection, data arrangement, and data display. She shows children yellow, blue, and green sticky notes, and has each child select his or her favorite color. Five children choose yellow notes, three select blue, and

Copyright © Mometrix Media. You have been licensed one copy of this document for personal use only. Any other reproduction or redistribution is strictly prohibited. All rights reserved. This content is provided for test preparation purposes only and does not imply an endorsement by Mometrix of any particular political, scientific, or religious point of view.

two choose green. By choosing one of three colors, each child has participated in data collection. The teacher draws lines to divide a sheet of paper into three columns, and labels each column with one of the colors. She helps the children place their chosen sticky notes in the correct columns. By arranging the colored sticky notes into columns, the teacher and children have organized the data they gathered. Once all notes are in their proper color columns, the completed chart is an example of how collected, organized data can be displayed.

	Yellow sticky note	
	Yellow sticky note	
Blue sticky note	Yellow sticky note	
Blue sticky note	Yellow sticky note	Green sticky note
Blue sticky note	Yellow sticky note	Green sticky note
BLUE	**YELLOW**	**GREEN**

The teacher asks the children which color was chosen the most. Seeing five yellow notes, they answer, "yellow." She asks which color was chosen the least, and they say, "green." She asks them to use numbers to arrange the color choices from most popular to least popular. They arrive at, "five yellow, three blue, and two green." Together, the teacher and the children point to and count 10 children. She tells them 5 equals half of 10, and asks which color half of the children chose. Together, they figure out it was yellow. These are examples of analyzing and interpreting data.

Chapter Quiz

Ready to see how well you retained what you just read? Scan the QR code to go directly to the chapter quiz interface for this study guide. If you're using a computer, simply visit the bonus page at **mometrix.com/bonus948/ftceprekinprim** and click the Chapter Quizzes link.

Copyright © Mometrix Media. You have been licensed one copy of this document for personal use only. Any other reproduction or redistribution is strictly prohibited. All rights reserved. This content is provided for test preparation purposes only and does not imply an endorsement by Mometrix of any particular political, scientific, or religious point of view.

Science

Transform passive reading into active learning! After immersing yourself in this chapter, put your comprehension to the test by taking a quiz. The insights you gained will stay with you longer this way. Scan the QR code to go directly to the chapter quiz interface for this study guide. If you're using a computer, simply visit the bonus page at **mometrix.com/bonus948/ftceprekinprim** and click the Chapter Quizzes link.

Science Foundations

SCIENCE CONCEPTS YOUNG CHILDREN LEARN DURING EVERYDAY ACTIVITIES

Science entails asking questions, conducting investigations, collecting data, and seeking answers to the questions asked by analyzing the data collected. Natural events that can be examined over time and student-centered inquiry through hands-on activities that require the application of problem-solving skills are most appropriate for helping young children learn basic science. In their everyday lives, young children develop concepts of 1:1 correspondence through activities like fitting pegs into matching holes or distributing one item to each child in a class. They also develop counting concepts by counting enough items for each child in the group or counting pennies in a piggy bank. They develop classification concepts when they sort objects into separate piles according to their shapes or some other type of category (e.g., toy cars vs. toy trucks). When children transfer water, sand, rice, or other substances from one container to another, they develop measurement concepts. As they progress, children will apply these early concepts to more abstract scientific ideas during grade school.

SCIENCE CONCEPTS INFANTS AND TODDLERS LEARN IN NORMAL DEVELOPMENTAL PROCESSES

Infants use their senses to explore the environment and are motivated by innate curiosity. As they develop mobility, children gain more freedom, allowing them to make independent discoveries and think for themselves. Children learn size concepts by comparing the sizes of objects/persons in the environment to their own size and by observing that some objects are too large to hold, while others are small enough to hold. They learn about weight when trying to lift various objects. They learn about shape when they see that some objects roll away while others do not. Babies learn temporal sequences when they wake up wet and hungry, cry, and have parents change and feed them. They also learn this concept by playing, getting tired, and going to sleep. As soon as they look and move around, infants learn about space, including large and small spaces. Eventually, they develop spatial sense through experiences like being put in a playpen or crib in the middle of a large room. Toddlers naturally sort objects into groups according to their sizes, shapes, colors, and/or uses. They experiment with transferring water/sand among containers of various sizes. They learn part-to-whole relationships by building block structures and then dismantling them.

NATURALISTIC, INFORMAL, AND STRUCTURED LEARNING EXPERIENCES

Children actively construct their knowledge of the environment through exploring it.

- During **naturalistic learning**, young children's learning experiences are spontaneously initiated by the child during everyday activities and the child controls his or her choices and actions.

Copyright © Mometrix Media. You have been licensed one copy of this document for personal use only. Any other reproduction or redistribution is strictly prohibited. All rights reserved. This content is provided for test preparation purposes only and does not imply an endorsement by Mometrix of any particular political, scientific, or religious point of view.

- **Informal learning experiences** also allow the child to choose his or her actions and activities, but they include adult intervention at some point during the child's engagement in naturalistic pursuits.
- In **structured learning experiences**, the adult chooses the activities and supplies some direction as to how the child should perform the associated actions.

One consideration related to early childhood learning that teachers should keep in mind is that within any class or group of children, there are individual differences in learning styles. Additionally, children from different cultural groups have varying learning styles and approaches. Early childhood teachers can introduce science content in developmentally appropriate ways by keeping these variations in mind.

NATURALISTIC LEARNING EXPERIENCES

Motivated by novelty and curiosity, young children spontaneously initiate naturalistic experiences during their everyday activities. Infants and toddlers in Piaget's sensorimotor stage learn by exploring the environment through their senses, so adults should provide them with many objects and substances they can see, hear, touch, smell, and taste. Through manipulating and observing concrete objects/substances, preschoolers in Piaget's preoperational stage begin learning concepts that will enable them to perform mental operations later on. Adults should observe children's actions and progress and should give positive reinforcement in the form of looks, facial expressions, gestures, and/or words encouraging and praising the child's actions. Young children need adult feedback to learn when they are performing the appropriate actions. For example, a toddler/preschooler selects a tool from the toolbox, saying, "This is big!" and the mother responds, "Yes!" A four-year-old sorting toys of various colors into separate containers is another example of a naturalistic experience. A five-year-old who observes while painting that mixing two colors yields a third color is yet another example.

INFORMAL LEARNING EXPERIENCE

Informal learning experiences involve two main components. First, the child spontaneously initiates naturalistic learning experiences during everyday activities to explore and learn about the environment. Second, the adult takes advantage of opportunities during naturalistic experiences to insert informal learning experiences. Adults do not plan these in advance but take advantage of opportunities that occur naturally. One way this happens is when a child is on the right track to solve a problem but needs some encouragement or a hint from the adult. Another way is when the adult spots a "teachable moment" during the child's naturalistic activity and uses it to reinforce a basic concept. For example, a three-year-old might hold up three fingers, declaring, "I'm six years old." The parent says, "Let's count fingers: one, two, three. You're three years old." Or, a teacher asks a child who has a box of treats if he or she has enough for the whole class, and the child answers, "I don't know." The teacher then responds, "Let's count them together," and helps the child count.

STRUCTURED LEARNING EXPERIENCES

Naturalistic learning experiences are spontaneously initiated and controlled by children. Informal learning experiences involve unplanned interventions by adults during children's naturalistic experiences, which is when adults offer suitable correction, assistance, and support. Structured learning experiences differ in that the adult pre-plans and initiates the activity/lesson and provides the child with some direction. For example, a teacher who observes a four-year-old's need to practice counting can give the child a pile of toys and then ask him or her how many there are. To develop size concepts, a teacher can give a small group of children several toys of different sizes and then ask the children to inspect them and talk about their characteristics. The teacher holds up one toy, instructing children to find one that is bigger or smaller. If a child needs to learn shape

Copyright © Mometrix Media. You have been licensed one copy of this document for personal use only. Any other reproduction or redistribution is strictly prohibited. All rights reserved. This content is provided for test preparation purposes only and does not imply an endorsement by Mometrix of any particular political, scientific, or religious point of view.

concepts, the teacher might introduce a game involving shapes, giving the child instructions on how to play the game. Or, a first-grade teacher, recognizing the importance of the concept of classification to the ability to organize scientific information, might ask students to bring in bones to classify during a unit on skeletons.

KINDERGARTEN ACTIVITY FOR COLLECTING AND ORGANIZING DATA

Preschoolers and kindergarteners continue their earlier practices of exploration to learn new things, and they apply fundamental science concepts to collect and organize data in order to answer questions. To collect data, children must have observation, counting, recording, and organization skills. One activity kindergarteners and teachers enjoy is growing bean sprouts. For example, the teacher can show children two methods: one using glass jars and paper towels saturated with water, the other using cups of dirt. The children add water daily as needed, observe developments, and report to the teacher, who records their observations on a chart. The teacher gives each child a chart that they add information to each day. The children count how many days their beans took to sprout in the glass jars and in the cups of dirt. They then compare their own results for the two methods, and they compare their results to those of their classmates. The children apply concepts of counting, numbers, time, 1:1 correspondence, and comparison of numbers. They also witness the planting and growing process.

SCIENCE PROCESS SKILLS

Science process skills include observation (using the senses to identify properties of objects/situations), classification (grouping objects/situations according to their common properties), measurement (quantifying physical properties), communication (using observations, classifications, and measurements to report experimental results to others), inference (finding patterns and meaning in experiment results), and prediction (using experimental experience to formulate new hypotheses). Inferences and predictions must be differentiated from objective observations. Classification, measurement, and comparison are basic math concepts that, when applied to science problems, are called process skills. The other science process skills named, as well as defining and controlling variables, are equally necessary to solve both science and math problems. For example, using ramps can help young children learn basic physics concepts. Teachers ask children what would happen if two balls were rolled down a ramp at the same time, if two balls were rolled down a ramp of a different height/length, if two ramps of different heights/lengths were used, etc. In this activity, children apply the scientific concepts of observation, communication, inference, and prediction, as well as the concepts of height, length, counting, speed, distance, and comparison.

SCIENTIFIC METHOD

Children are born curious and naturally engage in problem-solving to learn. Problem-solving and inquiry are natural child behaviors. Early childhood teachers can use these behaviors to promote children's scientific inquiry. Scientific inquiry employs the **scientific method**. The first step in the method is to ask a question, which is another natural child behavior. Just as adult scientists formulate research questions, the first step of the scientific method for children is asking questions they want to answer. Next, to address a question, both adults and children must form a hypothesis (an educated guess about what the answer will be). The hypothesis informs and directs the next steps: designing and conducting an experiment to test whether the hypothesis is true or false. With teacher instruction/help, children experiment. For example, they might drop objects of different weights from a height to see when each lands, as Galileo did. Teachers help record outcomes. The

Copyright © Mometrix Media. You have been licensed one copy of this document for personal use only. Any other reproduction or redistribution is strictly prohibited. All rights reserved. This content is provided for test preparation purposes only and does not imply an endorsement by Mometrix of any particular political, scientific, or religious point of view.

next steps are deciding whether the results support or disprove the hypothesis and reporting the results and conclusions to others.

> **Review Video: The Scientific Method**
> Visit mometrix.com/academy and enter code: 191386

PHYSICAL SCIENCE AND MATTER

Physical science is the science of the physical universe surrounding us. Everything in the universe consists of matter (i.e., anything that has mass and takes up space) or energy (i.e., anything that does not have mass or occupy space, but affects matter and space). The three primary states of matter are solid, liquid, and gas. Solids preserve their shape even when they are not in a container. Solids have specific, three-dimensional/crystalline atomic structures and specific melting points. Liquids have no independent shape outside of containers but have specific volumes. Liquid molecules are less cohesive than solid molecules but more cohesive than gas molecules. Liquids have flow, viscosity (flow resistance), and buoyancy. Liquids can undergo diffusion, osmosis, evaporation, condensation, solution, freezing, and heat conduction and convection. Liquids and gases are both fluids, and they share some of the same properties. Gases have no shape, expanding and spreading indefinitely outside of containers. Gases can become liquid and solid through cooling, compression, or both. Liquids and solids can become gaseous through heating. Vapor is the gaseous form of a substance that is solid/liquid at lower temperatures. For example, when water is heated, it becomes steam, a vapor.

> **Review Video: States of Matter**
> Visit mometrix.com/academy and enter code: 742449

LIQUIDS

Of the three states of matter—solid, liquid, and gas—liquids have properties that fall somewhere in between those of solids and gases. The molecules of solids are the most cohesive (i.e., they have the greatest mutual attraction). Gas molecules are the least cohesive, and liquid molecules are in between. Liquids have no definite shape, while solids do. Liquids have a definite volume, whereas gases do not. The cohesion of liquid molecules draws them together, and the molecules below the surface pull surface molecules down, creating surface tension. This property can be observed in containers of water. Liquid molecules are also attracted to other substances' molecules (i.e., adhesion). Surface tension and adhesion combined cause liquids to rise in narrow containers, a property known as capillarity. Liquids are buoyant (i.e., they exert upward force, so objects which have more buoyancy than weight float in liquids, while objects which have more weight than buoyancy sink in liquids). Liquids can be made solid by freezing and can be made gaseous by heating/evaporation. Liquids can diffuse, which means they can mix with other molecules. Liquid diffusion across semi-permeable membranes is known as osmosis.

SOLIDS

Solids maintain their shape when they are not inside of containers, whereas liquids and gases acquire the shapes of containers holding them. Containers also prevent liquids and gases from dispersing. Of the three forms of matter, solids have the most cohesive molecules. Solid molecules are most attracted to each other, and solid molecules are held together most strongly. Solid atoms are organized into defined, three-dimensional, lattice-shaped patterns (i.e., they are crystalline in structure). Solids also have specific temperatures at which they melt. Some substances that seem solid, such as plastic, gel, tar, and glass, are actually not true solids. They are amorphous solids because their atoms do not have a crystalline structure but are amorphous (i.e., the positions of

Copyright © Mometrix Media. You have been licensed one copy of this document for personal use only. Any other reproduction or redistribution is strictly prohibited. All rights reserved.
This content is provided for test preparation purposes only and does not imply an endorsement by Mometrix of any particular political, scientific, or religious point of view.

their atoms have no long-range organization). They also have a range of melting temperatures rather than specific melting points.

GASES

Gases have the least cohesive (i.e., mutually attracted) molecules of the three states of matter, while solids have the most cohesive molecules. Gases do not maintain a defined shape, while solids do. If not contained within a receptacle, gases spread and expand indefinitely. Gases can be elementary or compound. An elementary gas is composed of only one kind of chemical element. At normal temperatures and pressures, 12 elementary gases are known: argon, chlorine, fluorine, helium, hydrogen, krypton, neon, nitrogen, oxygen, ozone, radon, and xenon. Elementary gases can be either monatomic or diatomic, meaning they are either made of single atoms like argon (Ar), or bound pairs of atoms like oxygen (O_2). Compound gases have molecules containing atoms of more than one kind of chemical element. Carbon monoxide (which contains one carbon and one oxygen atom) and ammonia (which contains nitrogen and hydrogen atoms) are common compound gases.

LIGHT

REFLECTION AND SCATTERING

When a beam of light hits a smooth surface like a mirror, it bounces back off that surface. This rebounding is **reflection**. In physics, the law of reflection states that "the angle of incidence equals the angle of reflection." This means that when light is reflected, it always bounces off the surface at the same angle at which it hit that surface. When a beam of light hits a rough rather than a smooth surface, though, it is reflected back at many different angles, not just the angle at which it struck the surface. This reflection at multiple and various angles is scattering. Many objects we commonly use every day have rough surfaces. For example, paper may look smooth to the naked eye but actually has a rough surface. This property can be observed by viewing paper through a microscope. Because light waves striking paper are reflected in every direction by its rough surface, scattering enables us to read words printed on paper from any viewing angle.

ABSORPTION

When light strikes a medium, the light wave's frequency is equal or close to the frequency at which the electrons in the medium's atoms can vibrate. These electrons receive the light's energy, making them vibrate. When a medium's atoms hang on tightly to their electrons, the electrons transmit their vibrations to the nucleus of each atom. This makes the atoms move faster and collide with the medium's other atoms. The energy the atoms got from the vibrations is then released as heat. This process is known as **absorption** of light. Materials that absorb light, such as wood and metal, are opaque. Some materials absorb certain light frequencies but transmit others. For example, glass transmits visible light (and therefore appears transparent to the naked eye), but absorbs ultraviolet frequencies. The sky looks blue because the atmosphere absorbs all colors in the spectrum except blue, which it reflects. Only blue wavelengths/frequencies bounce back to our eyes. This is an example of subtractive color, which we see in paints/dyes and all colored objects/materials. Pigments absorb some frequencies and reflect others.

REFRACTION

When light moves from one transparent medium to another (e.g., between water and air/vice versa), the light's speed changes, bending the light wave. It bends either away from or toward the normal line, an imaginary straight line running at right angles to the medium's surface. We easily observe this bending when looking at a straw in a glass of water. The straw appears to break/bend at the waterline. The angle of refraction is the amount that the light wave bends. It is determined by how much the medium slows down the light's speed, which is the medium's refraction index. For example, diamonds are much denser and harder than water and thus have a higher refraction

Copyright © Mometrix Media. You have been licensed one copy of this document for personal use only. Any other reproduction or redistribution is strictly prohibited. All rights reserved. This content is provided for test preparation purposes only and does not imply an endorsement by Mometrix of any particular political, scientific, or religious point of view.

index. They slow down and trap light more than water does. Consequently, diamonds sparkle more than water. Lenses, such as those in eyeglasses and telescopes, rely on the principle of refraction. Curved lenses disperse or concentrate light waves, refracting light as it both enters and exits, thus changing the light's direction. This is how lenses correct (eyeglasses) and enhance (telescopes) our vision.

MAGNETISM

Magnetism is the property some objects/substances have of attracting other materials. The form of magnetism most familiar to us is certain materials attracting iron. Magnets also attract steel, cobalt, and other materials. Generators supplying power include magnets, as do all electric motors. Loudspeakers and telephones contain magnets. Tape recorders use magnets. The tape they play is magnetized. Magnets are used in compasses to determine the location of north and various corresponding directions. In fact, the planet Earth is itself a giant magnet (which is why compasses point north). Hence, like the Earth, all magnets have two poles: a north/north-seeking pole and a south/south-seeking pole. Opposite poles attract and like poles repel each other. Magnets do not need to touch to attract or repel each other. A magnet's effective area/range is its magnetic field. All materials have some response to magnetic fields. Magnets can turn nearby magnetic materials into magnets, by a process known as magnetic induction. Materials that line up parallel to magnetic force field lines are paramagnetic, while materials that line up perpendicular to magnetic force field lines are diamagnetic.

MODERN THEORY OF MAGNETISM AND WHAT SCIENTISTS DO AND DO NOT KNOW

Scientists have known about the effects of magnetism for hundreds of years. However, they do not know exactly what magnetism is or what causes it. French physicist Pierre Weiss proposed a theory of magnetism in the early 20th century that is widely accepted. This theory posits that every magnetic material has groups of molecules—domains—that function as magnets. Until a material is magnetized, its domains have a random arrangement, so one domain's magnetism is canceled out by another's. When the material comes into a magnetic field—the range/area wherein a magnet is effective—its domains align themselves parallel to the magnetic field's lines of force. As a result, all of their north-seeking/north poles point in the same direction. Removing the magnetic field causes like poles to repel one another as they normally do. In easily magnetized materials, domains revert to random order. In materials that are harder to magnetize, domains lack sufficient force to disassemble, leaving the material magnetized. Later versions of Weiss's theory attribute domain magnetism to spinning electrons.

> **Review Video: Magnets**
> Visit mometrix.com/academy and enter code: 570803

INSULATION, CONDUCTION, AND THE FLOW OF ELECTRICITY

The smallest units of all matter are atoms. The nuclei of atoms are orbited by negatively charged electrons. Some materials have electrons that are strongly bound to their atoms. These include air, glass, wood, cotton, plastic, and ceramic. Since their atoms rarely release electrons, these materials have little or no ability to conduct electricity and are known as electrical insulators. Insulators resist/block conduction. Metals and other conductive materials have free electrons that can detach from the atoms and move around. Without the tight binding of insulators, materials with loose electrons enable electric current to flow easily through them. Such materials are called electrical conductors. The movements of their electrons transmit electrical energy. Electricity requires something to make it flow (i.e., a generator). A generator creates a steady flow of electrons by moving a magnet close to a wire, creating a magnetic field to propel electrons. Electricity also requires a conductor (i.e., a medium through which it can move from one place to another).

Copyright © Mometrix Media. You have been licensed one copy of this document for personal use only. Any other reproduction or redistribution is strictly prohibited. All rights reserved. This content is provided for test preparation purposes only and does not imply an endorsement by Mometrix of any particular political, scientific, or religious point of view.

MOVEMENT OF ELECTRICAL CURRENTS BY A GENERATOR

Magnetism and electricity are related, and they interact with each other. Generators work by using magnets near conductive wires to produce moving streams of electrons. The agent of movement can range from a hand crank, to a steam engine, to the nuclear fission process. However, all agents of movements operate according to the same principle. A simple analogy is that a generator magnetically pushes electrical current the way a pump pushes water. Just as water pumps apply specific amounts of pressure to specific numbers of water molecules, generator magnets apply specific amounts of "pressure" to specific numbers of electrons. The number of moving electrons in an electrical circuit equals the current, or amperage. The unit of measurement for amperage is the ampere, or amp. The amount of force moving the electrons is the voltage. Its unit of measurement is the volt. One amp equals 6.24×10^{18} electrons passing through a wire each second. For example, a generator could produce 1 amp using 6 volts when rotating 1,000 times per minute. Today's power stations rely on generators.

POSITIONS AND MOTIONS OF OBJECTS AND NEWTON'S LAWS OF PHYSICS

Moving physical objects changes their positions. According **to Newton's first law of motion**, an object at rest tends to stay at rest, and an object in motion tends to stay in motion until a force changes the object's state of motion. For example, an object at rest could be a small rock sitting on the ground. If you kick the rock into the air, it moves through the air. The rock will continue to move, but when a force like gravity acts on it, it falls/stops moving. The resulting motion from kicking the rock illustrates Newton's third law of motion: for every action, there is an equal and opposite reaction. The acceleration or change in velocity (a) of an object depends on its mass (m) and the amount of force (F) that is applied to the object. Newton's second law of motion states that $F = ma$ (force equals mass times acceleration). Thus, moving objects maintain their speeds unless acted on by a force, like friction.

HEAT

Heat is transmitted through conduction, radiation, and convection. Heat is transmitted within solids by conduction. When two objects at different temperatures touch each other, the hotter object's molecules are moving faster. They collide with the colder object's molecules, which are moving slower. As a result of the collision, the molecules that are moving more rapidly supply energy to the molecules that are moving more slowly. This speeds up the movement of the (previously) slower-moving molecules, which heats up the colder object. This process of transferring heat through contact is called thermal conductivity. An example of thermal conductivity is the heat sink. Heat sinks are used in many devices. Today, they are commonly used in computers. A heat sink transfers the heat building up in the computer processor, moving it away before it can damage the processor. Computers contain fans, which blow air across their heat sinks and expel the heated air out of the computers.

ACOUSTICAL PRINCIPLES AND THE HUMAN HEARING PROCESS

When any physical object moves back and forth rapidly, this is known as **vibration**. The movements that occur during vibration disturb the surrounding medium, which may be solid, liquid, or gaseous. The most common sound conducting medium in our environment is gaseous: our atmosphere (i.e., the air). An object's vibratory movements represent a form of energy. As this acoustic energy moves through the air, it takes the form of waves, sound waves specifically. The outer ear receives and amplifies the sound and transmits it to the middle ear, where tiny bones vibrate in response to the sound energy and transmit it to the inner ear. The inner ear converts the acoustic energy into electrical energy. The electrical impulses are then carried by nerves to the brain. Structures in the brain associated with hearing receive these electrical signals and interpret

Copyright © Mometrix Media. You have been licensed one copy of this document for personal use only. Any other reproduction or redistribution is strictly prohibited. All rights reserved. This content is provided for test preparation purposes only and does not imply an endorsement by Mometrix of any particular political, scientific, or religious point of view.

them as sounds. The ears' reception of sound waves is auditory sensation, and the brain's interpretation of them is auditory perception.

SOLAR SYSTEM
SOLAR SYSTEM'S LOCATION AND COMPONENTS

The universe is composed of an unknown (possibly infinite) number of galaxies or star systems, such as the Spiral Nebula, the Crab Nebula, and the Milky Way. Our sun, Sol, is one of billions of stars in the Milky Way. The solar system's planets are held in position at varying distances (according to their size and mass) from the Sun by its gravitational force. These planets orbit or revolve around the Sun. From the closest to the Sun to the farthest away, the solar system's planets are Mercury, Venus, Earth, Mars, Jupiter, Saturn, Uranus, and Neptune. Pluto was historically included as the ninth planet but was demoted to a "dwarf planet" by the International Astronomical Union in 2006. Due to angular momentum, planets rotate on their axes, which are imaginary central lines between their north and south poles. One complete Earth rotation equals what we perceive as one 24-hour day. As the Earth turns, different portions face the Sun. These receive daylight, while the portions turned away from the Sun are in darkness. One complete revolution of the Earth around the Sun represents one calendar year.

PLUTO

Since more powerful observatories have enabled greater detection and measurement of celestial objects, the International Astronomical Union has defined three criteria for defining a planet. First, it must orbit the Sun. Pluto meets this criterion. Second, it must have enough gravitational force to shape itself into a sphere. Pluto also meets this criterion. Third, a planet must have "cleared the neighborhood" in its orbit. This expression refers to the fact that as planets form, they become the strongest gravitational bodies within their orbits. Therefore, when close to smaller bodies, planets either consume these smaller bodies or repel them because of their greater gravity, clearing their orbital area or "neighborhood." To do this, a planet's mass must sufficiently exceed the mass of other bodies in its orbit. Pluto does not meet this criterion, having only 0.07 times the mass of other objects within its orbit. Thus, astronomers reclassified Pluto as a "dwarf planet" in 2006 based on its lesser mass and the many other objects in its orbit with comparable masses and sizes.

EARTH

Earth is roughly spherical in shape. Its North and South Poles at the top and bottom are farthest away from and least exposed to the Sun, so they are always coldest. This accounts for the existence of the polar ice caps. The Equator, an imaginary line running around Earth at its middle exactly halfway between the North and South Poles, is at 0° latitude. Sunrises and sunsets at the Equator are the world's fastest. Days and nights are of virtually equal length at the Equator, and there is less seasonal variation than in other parts of the world. The equatorial climate is a tropical rainforest. Locations close to the North Pole, like Norway, are at such high latitudes that their nights are not dark in summertime, hence the expression "Land of the Midnight Sun." They also have very little light in wintertime. As Earth revolves around the Sun over the course of a year, the distance and angle of various locations relative to the Sun change, so different areas receive varying amounts of heat and light. This is what accounts for the changing seasons.

ROCKS FOUND ON THE EARTH'S SURFACE
SEDIMENTARY ROCKS

Earth's rock types are sedimentary, igneous, and metamorphic. These categories are based on the respective processes that form each type of rock. Igneous rocks are formed from volcanoes. Metamorphic rocks are formed when igneous and sedimentary rocks deep inside the Earth's crust

Copyright © Mometrix Media. You have been licensed one copy of this document for personal use only. Any other reproduction or redistribution is strictly prohibited. All rights reserved.
This content is provided for test preparation purposes only and does not imply an endorsement by Mometrix of any particular political, scientific, or religious point of view.

are subjected to intense heat and/or pressure. **Sedimentary rocks** are formed on Earth's surface and characteristically accumulate in layers. Erosion and other natural processes deposit these layers. Some sedimentary rocks are held together by electrical attraction. Others are cemented together by chemicals and minerals that existed during their formation. Still others are not held together at all but are loose and crumbly. There are three subcategories of sedimentary rock. Clastic sedimentary rocks are made of little rock bits—clasts—that are compacted and cemented together. Chemical sedimentary rocks are frequently formed through repeated flooding and subsequent evaporation. The evaporation of water leaves a layer of minerals that were dissolved in the water. Limestone and deposits of salt and gypsum are examples. Organic sedimentary rocks are formed from organic matter, such as the calcium left behind from animal bones and shells.

METAMORPHIC ROCKS

Sedimentary rocks are formed on the Earth's surface by layers of eroded material from mountains that were deposited by water, minerals like lime, salt and gypsum deposited by evaporated floodwater, and organic material like calcium from animal bones and shells. Igneous rocks are formed from liquid volcanic rock—either magma underground or lava on the surface—that cools and hardens. **Metamorphic rocks** are formed from sedimentary and igneous rocks. This happens when sedimentary and/or igneous rocks are deep inside the Earth's crust, where they are subjected to great pressure or heat. The process of metamorphism does not melt these rocks into liquid, which would happen inside a volcano. Rather, the pressure and/or heat change the rocks' molecular structure. Metamorphic rocks are thus more compact and denser than the sedimentary or igneous rocks from which they were formed. They also contain new minerals produced either by the reconfiguration of existing minerals' structures or by chemical reactions with liquids infiltrating the rock. Two examples of metamorphic rocks are marble and gneiss.

IGNEOUS ROCKS

Igneous or volcanic rocks are formed from the magma emitted when a volcano erupts. Magma under the Earth's surface is subject to heat and pressure, keeping it in liquid form. During a volcanic eruption, some magma reaches the surface, emerging as lava. Lava cools rapidly in the outside air, becoming a solid with small crystals. Some magma does not reach Earth's surface, but is trapped underground within pockets in other rocks. Magma cools more slowly underground than lava does on the surface. This slower cooling forms rocks with larger crystals and coarser grains. The chemical composition and individual cooling temperatures of magma produce different kinds of igneous rocks. Lava that cools rapidly on the Earth's surface can become obsidian, a smooth, shiny black glass without crystals. It can also become another type of extrusive rock, such as andesite, basalt, pumice, rhyolite, scoria, or tuff (formed from volcanic ash and cinders). Magma that cools slowly in underground pockets can become granite, which has a coarse texture and large, visible mineral grains. It can also become another type of intrusive rock, such as diorite, gabbro, pegmatite, or peridotite.

EROSION

Erosion is a natural process whereby Earth's landforms are broken down through weathering. Rain and wind wear away solid matter. Over time, rain reduces mountains to hills. Rocks break off from mountains and, in turn, disintegrate into sand. Weathering and the resulting erosion always occur in downhill directions. Rain washes rocks off mountains and down streams. Rains, rivers, and streams wash soils away, and ocean waves break down adjacent cliffs. Rocks, dirt, and sand change their form and location through erosion. They do not simply vanish. These transformations and movements are called mass wasting, which occurs chemically (as when rock is dissolved by chemicals in water) or mechanically (as when rock is broken into pieces). Because materials travel as a result of mass wasting, erosion can both break down some areas and build up others. For

Copyright © Mometrix Media. You have been licensed one copy of this document for personal use only. Any other reproduction or redistribution is strictly prohibited. All rights reserved. This content is provided for test preparation purposes only and does not imply an endorsement by Mometrix of any particular political, scientific, or religious point of view.

example, a river runs through and erodes a mountain, carrying the resulting sediment downstream. This sediment gradually builds up, creating wetlands at the river's mouth. A good example of this process is Louisiana's swamps, which were created by sediment transported by the Mississippi River.

WEATHER, CLIMATE, AND METEOROLOGY

Meteorology is the study of the atmosphere, particularly as it pertains to forecasting the weather and understanding its processes. **Weather** is the condition of the atmosphere at any given moment. Most weather occurs in the troposphere and includes changing events such as clouds, storms, and temperature, as well as more extreme events such as tornadoes, hurricanes, and blizzards. **Climate** refers to the average weather for a particular area over time, typically at least 30 years. Latitude is an indicator of climate. Changes in climate occur over long time periods.

WINDS AND GLOBAL WIND BELTS

Winds are the result of air moving by convection. Masses of warm air rise, and cold air sweeps into their place. The warm air also moves, cools, and sinks. The term "prevailing wind" refers to the wind that usually blows in an area in a single direction. Dominant winds are the winds with the highest speeds. Belts or bands that run latitudinally and blow in a specific direction are associated with convection cells. Hadley cells are formed directly north and south of the equator. The Farrell cells occur at about 30° to 60°. The jet stream runs between the Farrell cells and the polar cells. At the higher and lower latitudes, the direction is easterly. At mid-latitudes, the direction is westerly. From the North Pole to the south, the surface winds are Polar High Easterlies, Subpolar Low Westerlies, Subtropical High or Horse Latitudes, North-East Trade winds, Equatorial Low or Doldrums, South-East Trades, Subtropical High or Horse Latitudes, Subpolar Low Easterlies, and Polar High.

RELATIVE HUMIDITY, ABSOLUTE HUMIDITY, AND DEW POINT TEMPERATURE

Humidity refers to water vapor contained in the air. The amount of moisture contained in air depends upon its temperature. The higher the air temperature, the more moisture it can hold. These higher levels of moisture are associated with higher humidity. **Absolute humidity** refers to the total amount of moisture air is capable of holding at a certain temperature. **Relative humidity** is the ratio of water vapor in the air compared to the amount the air is capable of holding at its current temperature. As temperature decreases, absolute humidity stays the same and relative humidity increases. A hygrometer is a device used to measure humidity. The **dew point** is the temperature at which water vapor condenses into water at a particular humidity.

PRECIPITATION

After clouds reach the dew point, **precipitation** occurs. Precipitation can take the form of a liquid or a solid. It is known by many names, including rain, snow, ice, dew, and frost. **Liquid** forms of precipitation include rain and drizzle. Rain or drizzle that freezes on contact is known as freezing rain or freezing drizzle. **Solid or frozen** forms of precipitation include snow, ice needles or diamond dust, sleet or ice pellets, hail, and graupel or snow pellets. Virga is a form of precipitation that evaporates before reaching the ground. It usually looks like sheets or shafts falling from a cloud. The amount of rainfall is measured with a rain gauge. Intensity can be measured according to how fast precipitation is falling or by how severely it limits visibility. Precipitation plays a major role in the water cycle since it is responsible for depositing much of the Earth's fresh water.

CLOUDS

Clouds form when air cools and warm air is forced to give up some of its water vapor because it can no longer hold it. This vapor condenses and forms tiny droplets of water or ice crystals called

Copyright © Mometrix Media. You have been licensed one copy of this document for personal use only. Any other reproduction or redistribution is strictly prohibited. All rights reserved. This content is provided for test preparation purposes only and does not imply an endorsement by Mometrix of any particular political, scientific, or religious point of view.

clouds. Particles, or aerosols, are needed for water vapor to form water droplets. These are called **condensation nuclei**. Clouds are created by surface heating, mountains and terrain, rising air masses, and weather fronts. Clouds precipitate, returning the water they contain to Earth. Clouds can also create atmospheric optics. They can scatter light, creating colorful phenomena such as rainbows, colorful sunsets, and the green flash phenomenon.

LIVING ORGANISMS

All **living organisms** have fundamental needs that must be met. For example, plants that grow on land need light, air, water, and nutrients in amounts that vary according to the individual plant. Undersea plants may need less/no light. They need gases present in the water but not in the air above the water. Like land plants, they require nutrients. Like plants, animals (including humans) need air, water, and nutrients. They do not depend on light for photosynthesis like most plants, but some animals require more light than others, while others need less than others or none at all. Organisms cannot survive in environments that do not meet their basic needs. However, many organisms have evolved to adapt to various environments. For example, cacti are desert plants that thrive with only tiny amounts of water, and camels are desert animals that can also go for long periods of time with little water. Penguins and polar bears have adapted to very cold climates. Internal cues (e.g., hunger) and external cues (e.g., environmental change) motivate and shape the behaviors of individual organisms.

TYPES OF ANIMAL LIFE CYCLES

Most animals, including mammals, birds, fish, reptiles, and spiders, have simple life cycles. They are born live or hatch from eggs, and then grow to adulthood. Animals with simple life cycles include humans. Amphibians like frogs and newts have an additional stage involving a metamorphosis, or transformation. After birth, they breathe through gills and live underwater during youth (e.g., tadpoles). By adulthood, they breathe through lungs and move to land. Butterflies are examples of animals (insects) that undergo complete metamorphosis, meaning they change their overall form. After hatching from an embryo/egg, the juvenile form, or larva, resembles a worm and completes the majority of feeding required. In the next stage, the pupa does not feed, and is typically camouflaged in what is called an inactive stage. Mosquito pupae are called tumblers. The butterfly pupa is called a chrysalis and is protected by a cocoon. In the final stage, the adult (imago) grows wings (typically) and breeds. Some insects like dragonflies, cockroaches, and grasshoppers undergo an incomplete metamorphosis. There are egg, larva, and adult stages, but no pupa stage.

ECOLOGY

Ecology is defined as the study of interactions between organisms and their environments. **Abiotic factors** are the parts of any ecosystem that are not alive but which affect that ecosystem's living members. Abiotic factors also determine the locations of particular ecosystems that have certain characteristics. Abiotic factors include the sunlight; the atmosphere, including oxygen, hydrogen, and nitrogen; the water; the soil; the temperatures within a system; and the nutrient cycles of chemical elements and compounds that pass among living organisms and their physical environments. **Biotic factors** are the living organisms within any ecosystem, which include not only humans and animals but also plants and microorganisms. The definition of biotic factors also includes the interactions that occur between and among various organisms within an ecosystem. Sunlight determines plant growth and, hence, biome locations. Sunlight, in turn, is affected by water depth. Ocean depths where sunlight penetrates, called photic zones, are where the majority of the photosynthesis on Earth occurs.

> **Review Video: Photosynthesis**
> Visit mometrix.com/academy and enter code: 227035

Copyright © Mometrix Media. You have been licensed one copy of this document for personal use only. Any other reproduction or redistribution is strictly prohibited. All rights reserved. This content is provided for test preparation purposes only and does not imply an endorsement by Mometrix of any particular political, scientific, or religious point of view.

ORGANISM REPRODUCTION

A few examples of the many ways in which organisms reproduce include binary fission, whereby the cells of prokaryotic bacteria reproduce; budding, which is how yeast cells reproduce; and asexual reproduction. The latter occurs in plants when they are grafted, when cuttings are taken from them and then rooted, or when they put out runners. Plants also reproduce sexually, as do humans and most other animals. Animals, including humans, produce gametes (i.e., sperm or eggs) in their gonads through the process of meiosis. Gametes are haploid, containing half the number of chromosomes found in the body's cells. During fertilization, the gametes combine to form a zygote, which is diploid. It has the full number of chromosomes (half from each gamete), which are arranged in a genetically unique combination. Zygotes undergo mitosis, reproducing their gene combination with identical DNA sequences in all new cells, which then migrate and differentiate into organizations of specialized organs and tissues. These specialized organs in biologically mature organisms, alerted by signals such as hormonal cues, undergo meiosis to create new haploid gametes, beginning the cycle again.

PLANT REPRODUCTION

Most plants can reproduce asexually. For example, cuttings can be rooted in water and planted. Some plants put out runners that root new growths. Many plants can be grafted to produce new ones. Plants also reproduce sexually. Plants' sexual life cycles are more complex than animals', since plants alternate between haploid form (i.e., having a single set of chromosomes) and diploid form (i.e., having two sets of chromosomes) during their life cycles. Plants produce haploid cells called gametes (equivalent to sperm and egg in animals) that combine during fertilization, producing zygotes (diploid cells with chromosomes from both gametes). Cells reproduce exact copies through mitosis (asexual reproduction), becoming differentiated/specialized to form organs. Mature diploid plants called sporophytes—the plant form we usually see—produce spores. In sporophytes' specialized organs, cells undergo meiosis. This is part of the process of sexual reproduction, during which cells with half the normal number of chromosomes are produced before fertilization occurs. The spores produced by the sporophyte generation undergo mitosis, growing into a haploid plant of the gametophyte generation that produces gametes. The cycle then repeats.

ECOLOGICAL RELATIONSHIPS

Organisms interact, both with other organisms and their environments. Relationships wherein two differing organisms regularly interact so that one or both of them benefit are known as **ecological relationships**. In **mutualistic** relationships, both organisms benefit. For example, bacteria live in termites' digestive systems. Termites eat wood. However, they cannot digest the cellulose (the main part of plant cell walls) in wood. The bacteria in termites' guts break down the cellulose for them, releasing the wood's nutrients. Reciprocally, the termites as hosts give the bacteria a home and food. In **commensalistic** relationships, one organism benefits and the other one is unaffected. One example is barnacles attaching to whales. Barnacles, which are filter feeders, benefit from the whales' swimming, which creates currents in the water that bring the barnacles food. The whales are not disturbed by the barnacles. In **parasitic** relationships, the parasite benefits, but the host suffers. For example, tapeworms inside animals' digestive tracts get nutrients. The hosts lose the nutrients stolen by the worms and can sustain tissue damage because of the presence of the tapeworms.

Copyright © Mometrix Media. You have been licensed one copy of this document for personal use only. Any other reproduction or redistribution is strictly prohibited. All rights reserved. This content is provided for test preparation purposes only and does not imply an endorsement by Mometrix of any particular political, scientific, or religious point of view.

Chapter Quiz

Ready to see how well you retained what you just read? Scan the QR code to go directly to the chapter quiz interface for this study guide. If you're using a computer, simply visit the bonus page at **mometrix.com/bonus948/ftceprekinprim** and click the Chapter Quizzes link.

Copyright © Mometrix Media. You have been licensed one copy of this document for personal use only. Any other reproduction or redistribution is strictly prohibited. All rights reserved.
This content is provided for test preparation purposes only and does not imply an endorsement by Mometrix of any particular political, scientific, or religious point of view.

FTCE Practice Test #1

SCAN HERE

Want to take this practice test in an online interactive format?
Check out the bonus page, which includes interactive practice questions and
much more: **mometrix.com/bonus948/ftceprekinprim**

Developmental Knowledge

1. The concept of object permanence is best characterized as:

a. "Out of sight, out of mind."
b. "Out of mind, out of sight."
c. "Out of sight, still exists."
d. "Out of sight, out of time."

2. Which of these is more typical of the language development of a two to three year old than of a preschooler?

a. Describing unseen objects
b. Telling "make-believe" stories
c. Speaking in complete sentences
d. Expressing opinions/preferences

3. Which of the following characteristics in children's language development typically occurs latest?

a. Responding to requests ("Give it to Mom") and questions ("More juice?")
b. Wanting to hear the same stories, games, or rhymes repeated many times
c. Answering simple questions about stories they enjoy hearing read or told
d. Being able to point at a few of their body parts when someone asks them

4. Experts recommend including in ECE programs five factors to prevent child abuse and neglect. Two of these are to enhance parental (1) resilience and (2) social connections. Which of the following is NOT one of the other three?

a. Strengthening child development and parenting knowledge
b. Offering concrete help to families when they are needing it
c. Strengthening children's emotional and social competence
d. Strengthening legal punishment for child abuse and neglect

5. According to Piaget's theory, which of these abilities develops earliest in children?

a. Reversibility of actions
b. Conservation of quantity
c. Symbolic representation
d. Object permanence

203

Copyright © Mometrix Media. You have been licensed one copy of this document for personal use only. Any other reproduction or redistribution is strictly prohibited. All rights reserved.
This content is provided for test preparation purposes only and does not imply an endorsement by Mometrix of any particular political, scientific, or religious point of view.

6. How can EC educators engage families in children's education with flexibility for their diverse circumstances, needs, and ways of participating?

    a. They must design preschoolers' IFSPs themselves and always give copies to parents.

    b. They should develop and assign goals to parents for participating in child education.

    c. They are not responsible to furnish transportation or child care for parental visiting.

    d. They can utilize alternative meeting times to accommodate parent work schedules.

7. Which of these is included among things educators can do to involve diverse families in EC education?

    a. If parents cannot attend meetings due to work, educators cannot help it.

    b. It is outside educator responsibility to provide transportation or childcare.

    c. School strategies are in educators' purviews, but not home-use strategies.

    d. Educators can recruit interested family members to help out at preschool.

8. When a child gives reasons for succeeding at something, which of the following reflects an internal locus of control?

    a. "I did well because the teacher helped me."

    b. "I got a good mark because I was just lucky."

    c. "I did well because Danny showed me how."

    d. "I did a good job because I worked so hard."

9. Which of these is true about effective nonverbal communication by teachers?

    a. Unusual or flashy apparel and exaggerated gestures are effective.

    b. Appropriate movements expressing energy and enthusiasm work.

    c. Students will not take teachers who smile while teaching seriously.

    d. Relaxed posture and avoiding eye contact will put students at ease.

10. Which of these most accurately reflects expert recommendations of effective strategies for resolving classroom conflicts?

    a. De-emphasize conflicts by not letting students record them.

    b. Have students record observations, identifying participants.

    c. Discuss student reactions without judging them good or bad.

    d. Have students track conflicts over time and discuss reactions.

11. Which of these is most advisable when designing management plans for common EC behaviors?

    a. Once implemented, a plan should never be altered.

    b. The most effective plans are difficult to implement.

    c. The plan should be complex to cover all possibilities.

    d. Recording progress enables effective management.

12. A teacher observes young children playing in the classroom to inform the kinds of play activities to offer them. To promote development, which students should the teacher offer opportunities for full cooperative play with others?

    a. Students who are playing by themselves

    b. Students playing associatively with peers

    c. Students who are watching others playing

    d. Students playing near but not with others

Copyright © Mometrix Media. You have been licensed one copy of this document for personal use only. Any other reproduction or redistribution is strictly prohibited. All rights reserved.
This content is provided for test preparation purposes only and does not imply an endorsement by Mometrix of any particular political, scientific, or religious point of view.

13. Which form of aggression is most common in younger preschoolers up to around 4 years old?

    a. Overt aggression
    b. Hostile aggression
    c. Relational aggression
    d. Instrumental aggression

14. When preschool teachers provide activities to develop social skills, what is true about some necessary skills that young children should and can learn?

    a. Young children learn to verbalize what they want in cooperative activities.
    b. Preschool children are too egocentric to learn to have empathy for others.
    c. Assigning collaborative projects will not teach preschoolers to cooperate.
    d. Preschool children are not yet cognitively able to learn how to take turns.

15. Which of the following is most effective for teaching pre-math and manipulative skills to preschool children?

    a. Giving them solid objects to manipulate physically
    b. Giving them information for mental manipulation
    c. Giving them math processes to memorize by rote
    d. Giving them lessons to listen to while they sit still

16. Which of the following is the most appropriate pre-math learning activity for preschool-aged children?

    a. Counting numbers in their heads
    b. Counting blocks, beads, or pennies
    c. Counting classmates from memory
    d. Counting toys through a mental list

17. Hands-on, experiential learning activities can further adolescent cognitive and psychosocial development. Which result of these activities is most likely to help preadolescents and younger adolescents resolve the conflict of Industry vs. Inferiority?

    a. Transitioning from concrete to abstract thought
    b. Having experiences of success in school activity
    c. Forming future action plans they find satisfying
    d. Transitioning from intuitive to logical reasoning

18. In an EC aesthetic activity about shape, which sequence of steps is most appropriate?

    a. Helping children arrange shapes to make pictures; discussing shapes in an artwork; reading a story about shapes; having children identify shapes in a story
    b. Having children identify shapes in a story; reading the story about shapes; helping children arrange shapes to make pictures; discussing shapes in an artwork
    c. Reading a story about shapes; having children identify shapes in the story; discussing shapes in an artwork; helping children arrange shapes to make pictures
    d. Discussing shapes in an artwork; helping children arrange shapes to make pictures; having children identify shapes in a story; reading the story about shapes

Copyright © Mometrix Media. You have been licensed one copy of this document for personal use only. Any other reproduction or redistribution is strictly prohibited. All rights reserved.
This content is provided for test preparation purposes only and does not imply an endorsement by Mometrix of any particular political, scientific, or religious point of view.

19. Which of the following can preschool children learn in lessons about the element of color in art?
- a. The names of different colors
- b. Skills of sensory discrimination
- c. Children can learn all of these
- d. Skills for making classifications

20. When preschool teachers engage children in activities such as portraying various emotions through physical postures and movements, which is most accurate about the learning outcomes?
- a. The movements provide negligible exercise.
- b. Children learn ways of expressing emotions.
- c. Children understand feelings but have no fun.
- d. Children have fun but do not think creatively.

21. Using technology, teachers can create multimedia presentations that most afford which benefit?
- a. Accessing different learning styles in individual students
- b. Providing students with objective analysis and feedback
- c. Enabling the viewing of documents but only in the school
- d. Enabling only parents at home to view school documents

22. Which is correct for teachers to consider when teaching ESL/ELL students English?
- a. Spanish-speaking children learn to sound out words in the same ways as in English.
- b. The less English (L2) proficiency students have, the more they rely on cues from L1.
- c. ELL students use the same amount of cognitive energy as native English speakers.
- d. The concept of directionality in reading and writing is the same across all languages.

23. Which of these best reflects research findings about various influences of poverty on children?
- a. Educational, nutritional, medical, and social inequities present certain advantages.
- b. Decreased verbal interactions have no effect on visual and linguistic development.
- c. Acquiring language within culturally specific contexts is a disadvantage to children.
- d. Playing with peers and older children with little adult intervention has advantages.

24. What is recommended for ECE settings regarding emergency first aid and medical treatment?
- a. Written parental consent is unnecessary in real emergencies.
- b. Centers need not file parental doctor or hospital preferences.
- c. Information on family health insurance should be kept on file.
- d. Notifying parents of emergencies is desired but not required.

25. Experts report which of the following about reflective teachers relative to appraisals?
- a. Reflective teachers excel at self-evaluation but resist others' evaluations.
- b. Reflective teachers do not fear evaluations but are unlikely to self-assess.
- c. Reflective teachers want self-improvement informed by other educators.
- d. Reflective teachers are motivated to improve mainly for better appraisals.

Copyright © Mometrix Media. You have been licensed one copy of this document for personal use only. Any other reproduction or redistribution is strictly prohibited. All rights reserved. This content is provided for test preparation purposes only and does not imply an endorsement by Mometrix of any particular political, scientific, or religious point of view.

26. Which teacher practice is an element of logically structuring classes for effective communication and interaction with classes of individually differing students?

a. Presenting problems to students without developing solutions
b. Recounting processes or events out of chronological sequence
c. Showing students how connected ideas relate to main themes
d. Clarifying topics with literal presentations rather than as stories

27. A new fourth-grade teacher in a culturally diverse school is unfamiliar with the backgrounds, experiences, and needs of his students. Which of the following strategies would best help this teacher provide learning experiences that are responsive to all of his students' needs?

a. Self-educating regarding the needs and priorities of the community
b. Working with a mentor teacher to develop effective instructional strategies
c. Integrating students' diversities into the curriculum
d. Recognizing and eliminating personal biases

28. Which of these is correct about one-on-one vs. group conversations between adults and young children?

a. Adults should discuss one on one during whole-group preschool activities.
b. Adults can better reinforce what children say in group discussions.
c. Adults have less chance to extend what children say in one on one context.
d. Adults can better elicit children's abstract idea comprehension one on one.

29. How much usable play space at a minimum do experts recommend for indoor and outdoor early childhood learning environments?

a. At least 35 sq. ft. indoors and 75 sq. ft. outdoors
b. At least 25 sq. ft. indoors and 50 sq. ft. outdoors
c. At least 50 sq. ft. indoors and 100 sq. ft. outside
d. At least 45 sq. ft. indoors and 85 sq. ft. outdoors

30. Which of the following is an example of experiential learning?

a. Watching a video, taking notes
b. Reading a textbook, taking notes
c. Testing a hypothesis, taking notes
d. Listening to a lecture, taking notes

31. In teacher communication strategies, what best describes the effects of some types?

a. Utilizing media will only distract from communicating instructionally.
b. Slide presentations demonstrate reasoning and illustrate processes.
c. Animations and videos are best for the summarization of key points.
d. Boards or overheads give a sense of scale, show dynamic processes.

32. Which of the following most accurately reflects expert recommendations for indoor learning environments to accommodate planned curriculum activities for toddlers and preschoolers?

a. Furniture should be lightweight and easy to move around.
b. Art and cooking activities should be separated from water.
c. Dramatic play, blocks, reading, and music can be combined.
d. Separate areas should be provided for school-age children.

Copyright © Mometrix Media. You have been licensed one copy of this document for personal use only. Any other reproduction or redistribution is strictly prohibited. All rights reserved.
This content is provided for test preparation purposes only and does not imply an endorsement by Mometrix of any particular political, scientific, or religious point of view.

33. For developmentally appropriate instruction of young children, which essential aspects should educators consider?

    a. The child's age is more important than individual child growth patterns.
    b. The child's individual growth patterns supersede any cultural influences.
    c. Cultural influences are more significant than age or growth patterns.
    d. Age, individual growth patterns, and cultural influences are all essential.

34. Among six types of play that she identified, which did Mildred Parten find the most socially mature?

    a. Independent play
    b. Cooperative play
    c. Associative play
    d. Parallel play

35. When teaching elementary school students to analyze and understand information, which of these should teachers do?

    a. Assign students to summarize information, but without rules so they do it their way.
    b. Provide regular formats, which they may refine, to assist students with taking notes.
    c. Teachers should never prepare notes for students; students must do it themselves.
    d. Preparing lessons in outline form affords no benefit to students as they take notes.

36. What is the best way for a teacher to use a slide show presentation related to a lesson plan?

    a. Project it during the lesson to summarize and emphasize main points
    b. Project it instead of lecturing as a visual alternative to verbal delivery
    c. Project it during the lesson to add many details to spoken information
    d. Project it before the lesson to give students a preview of information

37. A group of prekindergarten students is learning about patterns by arranging beads on a string after watching a demonstration from the teacher. Which of the following teacher questions would best promote inquiry and logical reasoning skills as students work?

    a. "What color beads are you using?"
    b. "Why did you choose this bead to go next in your pattern?"
    c. "What kind of pattern are you making with your beads?"
    d. "Which bead comes next in your pattern?"

38. Which kind of informal assessment can provide the most continuity in recording a pre-K child's progress in a given area or domain?

    a. Running records
    b. Anecdotal records
    c. Portfolio assessments
    d. Observational checklists

39. Of the following, which is more typical of a screening instrument than an assessment instrument?

    a. Interpreting scores by weighting various item values
    b. Interpreting scores by reversing point values of items
    c. Interpreting scores by comparisons to national norms
    d. Interpreting scores by comparisons to a cut-off score

Copyright © Mometrix Media. You have been licensed one copy of this document for personal use only. Any other reproduction or redistribution is strictly prohibited. All rights reserved.
This content is provided for test preparation purposes only and does not imply an endorsement by Mometrix of any particular political, scientific, or religious point of view.

40. For teachers to make informal assessments of pre-K classes, which of these would apply?

    a. Teachers assess during small-group rather than whole-class activities.
    b. Teachers only make assessments during activities for the whole class.
    c. Teachers can organize assessments by using around ten themes a day.
    d. Teachers make classroom observations each targeting different skills.

41. What is an accurate statement about selecting screening and assessment instruments according to the age ranges they cover for use in ECE programs?

    a. Tests covering the entire age range served in a program are less useful because they are not age-specific.
    b. Tests covering the entire age range served in a program can be used in mid-program to monitor progress.
    c. Tests that are separate and specific to different ages make it easier to compare before and after programs.
    d. Tests that cover the whole range of ages served in the program are not as accurate for all of the child ages.

42. What is correct regarding predictive validity, sensitivity, specificity, and false-positive and false-negative errors in screening and assessment instruments used with preschool children?

    a. A screening tool identifies a potential mental health disorder which a complete evaluation then diagnoses.
    b. An instrument correctly identifying 6 of 10 children with disorders/delays is said to have a specificity of 60%.
    c. An instrument correctly identifying 8 of 10 children as not having disorders/delays shows sensitivity of 80%.
    d. A screening tool identifying delays or disorders in children where none exists contains false-negative errors.

43. Which of these is generally accepted as indicating possible delayed or atypical intellectual development in a child?

    a. A standardized IQ test score that is ten points lower than the mean
    b. A standardized IQ test score one standard deviation below the mean
    c. A standardized IQ test score two standard deviations below the mean
    d. A standardized IQ test score is never used for indicating this possibility

44. In preparation for the upcoming standardized assessment in English language arts, a third-grade teacher uses formative assessments, short quizzes, and reflection activities to determine students' understanding of the content. Which of the following best describes the intended purpose for implementing these strategies?

    a. Creating an inclusive and engaging learning atmosphere
    b. Identifying areas of whole-class and individual student need
    c. Determining the need for testing accommodations prior to the standardized assessment
    d. Updating students' families on overall progress and development

Copyright © Mometrix Media. You have been licensed one copy of this document for personal use only. Any other reproduction or redistribution is strictly prohibited. All rights reserved.
This content is provided for test preparation purposes only and does not imply an endorsement by Mometrix of any particular political, scientific, or religious point of view.

45. According to Piaget's theory, the term *conservation* means which of these?

    a. The idea that our natural resources are finite and hence, we must conserve them

    b. The idea that amounts/numbers can be retained or conserved in one's memories

    c. The idea that even when we cannot see an object, its existence is still conserved

    d. The idea that amounts/numbers are the same regardless of shape or appearance

46. In Piaget's theory of cognitive development, which stages occur during early childhood, i.e., from birth to the age of eight years?

    a. Sensorimotor, Preoperational, Concrete Operations

    b. Preoperational, Concrete Operations, Formal Operations

    c. Sensorimotor, Preoperational, Formal Operations

    d. None of these stages occur during early childhood.

47. Weikart's High Scope Curriculum helps prepare preschoolers for future understanding of Piaget's concept of conservation through which of its main categories?

    a. Classification

    b. Seriation

    c. Space

    d. Time

48. Of the following, which reflects recommend procedures for ECE facilities if non-custodial or non-authorized adults try to pick up children served at a facility?

    a. ECE administrators should inform unauthorized adults of policies and procedures, including custodial court orders.

    b. If an unauthorized adult refuses to leave, threatens/shows violence, or makes a scene, police should not be called.

    c. After an unauthorized adult leaves, the administrator must notify enrolling adults but need not file written reports.

    d. After an unauthorized adult leaves, the administrator must meet with the custodial adult without filing documents.

49. Which of the following do school districts' professional development committees (PDCs) do to help educators pursue PD?

    a. PDCs work with new teachers and their mentors but never pay workshop tuition.

    b. PDCs ensure PD goals meet district guidelines and document PD for state boards.

    c. PDCs work apart from district administrators by setting only interdisciplinary goals.

    d. PDCs defer to district administrators for setting district professional teacher goals.

50. What is an area commonly addressed by both the FERPA and the IDEA legislation?

    a. Privacy and confidentiality of student education records

    b. The right of students with disabilities to equal education

    c. Privacy and portability of student healthcare information

    d. The FERPA and IDEA legislation share nothing in common

Copyright © Mometrix Media. You have been licensed one copy of this document for personal use only. Any other reproduction or redistribution is strictly prohibited. All rights reserved.
This content is provided for test preparation purposes only and does not imply an endorsement by Mometrix of any particular political, scientific, or religious point of view.

Language Arts and Reading

1. Regarding student problems that teachers may observe which can indicate dyslexia, which is true?

    a. Dyslexic students perform worse on objective tests than their IQ and knowledge.
    b. Students with dyslexia typically have more trouble reading long than short words.
    c. Students who have dyslexia lack fluidity, but fare much better with rote memory.
    d. Dyslexic students have equal trouble understanding words in isolation or context.

2. At the beginning of each month, Mr. Yi has Jade read a page or two from a book she hasn't seen before. He notes the total number of words in the section and the number of times she leaves out or misreads a word. If Jade reads the passage with less than 3% error, Mr. Yi is satisfied that Jade is:

    a. Reading with full comprehension
    b. Probably bored and should try a more difficult book
    c. Reading at her independent reading level
    d. Comfortable with the syntactical meaning

3. Which of these is accurate regarding individual observations a teacher could make for informal assessments of students in pre-K classes?

    a. Teachers would not use a checklist to conduct individual informal assessments.
    b. Teachers might keep running records, but should not utilize anecdotal records.
    c. Teachers cannot assemble portfolio assessments of children's work for these.
    d. Teachers can fill out a chart of various domains with child strengths and needs.

4. Which assessment will determine a student's ability to identify initial, medial, blended, final, segmented, and manipulated "units"?

    a. Phonological awareness assessment
    b. High-frequency word assessment
    c. Reading fluency assessment
    d. Comprehension quick-check

5. A third-grade teacher has noticed that a student is having difficulty recognizing and spelling high-frequency sight words. In addition, when writing, he often skips words and writes letters backwards. Which of the following is the most appropriate response in this situation?

    a. Provide the student with individualized instruction to develop his skills.
    b. Pair the student with another that can provide scaffolding.
    c. Implement response to intervention (RTI) services.
    d. Refer the student for an initial evaluation with the special education department.

6. What statement is accurate regarding normally developing oral language in children?

    a. There is a considerable range of ages within normal individual growth.
    b. There are no individual differences among developmental milestones.
    c. Individual children achieve oral language milestones at specified ages.
    d. Individual children all develop spoken language skills at the same rates.

Copyright © Mometrix Media. You have been licensed one copy of this document for personal use only. Any other reproduction or redistribution is strictly prohibited. All rights reserved.
This content is provided for test preparation purposes only and does not imply an endorsement by Mometrix of any particular political, scientific, or religious point of view.

7. According to linguists, what do invented spellings by young children best signify?

a. Children who invent spellings lack phonemic and phonetic awareness.
b. Children's selections of phonetic spellings are due to adult influences.
c. Inventing spellings for words is evidence of phonetic comprehension.
d. Diverse children choosing the same phonetic spellings is just chance.

8. Which of these correctly shows the normal developmental sequence of children's writing with regard to directional principles?

a. No knowledge; partial knowledge; reverses the direction; correct direction; correct spacing
b. No knowledge; reverses the direction; partial knowledge; correct spacing; correct direction
c. No knowledge; partial knowledge; correct spacing; reverses the direction; correct direction
d. No knowledge; reverses the direction; correct direction; correct spacing; partial knowledge

9. Which of the following statements is accurate according to research regarding students who are revising and rewriting?

a. Students only correct their mechanical errors in revisions.
b. Students often incorporate new ideas when they rewrite.
c. Students retain their original writing goals during revision.
d. Students' planning in prewriting is unaffected in rewriting.

10. A teacher is working with a group of English language learners. She asks them to take two pieces of paper. At the top of the first paper, they are to write *SAME*, and at the top of the other, *DIFFERENT*. Each child will consider what his native country and the United States have in common, and what distinct features each country possesses. The children are using which method in organizing their ideas?

a. Hunt and peck
b. Consider and persuade
c. Evaluate and contrast
d. Compare and contrast

11. With a teacher's guidance, a class brainstorms main ideas, topics, or concepts from a text. Students choose a select number of these ideas and copy them onto separate index cards. The students then individually review the text, recording any supporting evidence on the notecard with the applicable main idea. This activity would be an excellent pre-lesson for teaching which skill set?

a. Working as a group to interpret a text and write an appropriate and realistic sequel, focusing on interpretive comprehension and creative writing
b. Silent reading as a form of comprehension practice
c. Organizing ideas for writing a cohesive and persuasive essay or research paper that asserts supported arguments with valid supporting evidence
d. Literal and figurative comprehension, as well as contributing to group discussions via oral communication skills

Copyright © Mometrix Media. You have been licensed one copy of this document for personal use only. Any other reproduction or redistribution is strictly prohibited. All rights reserved.
This content is provided for test preparation purposes only and does not imply an endorsement by Mometrix of any particular political, scientific, or religious point of view.

12. Which choice most appropriately fills the blanks in this statement? "In writing, _____ is the writer's attitude as evident from the writing, and _____ is the individual way in which the writer expresses themselves through the writing."

a. voice, tone
b. tone, voice
c. style, tone
d. voice, style

13. Which of the following strategies would likely be most effective in teaching prekindergarten students to listen responsively to directions?

a. Implementing listening games with simple multi-step directions
b. Choral reading poems, rhymes, and familiar stories
c. Changing intonation when giving verbal directions
d. Using gestures, body language, and visual cues

14. During a writing activity, a kindergarten teacher prompts students to spell unfamiliar words phonetically. This practice encourages students to use which of the following?

a. Orthographic processing skills
b. Inventive spelling
c. Pre-communicative spelling
d. Decoding skills

15. A third-grade teacher is planning a unit on identifying and writing compound sentences. Which of the following instructional strategies would best support students' understanding of this concept?

a. Creating a word wall with a list of common conjunctions
b. Asking students to identify compound sentences in grade-level reading passages
c. Implementing sentence-dictation exercises
d. Having students practice the concept using sentence-building strips

16. A first-grade teacher is planning to administer a diagnostic pretest before introducing a unit on the structure of simple sentences. Which of the following concepts should this teacher include in the test to ensure students' readiness for instruction?

a. Identifying basic nouns and verbs
b. Segmenting multisyllabic words
c. Recognizing conjunctions
d. Adding inflectional morphemes to words

17. When telling the teacher what he did over the weekend, a kindergarten student says, "I goed to the birthday party and eated some cake." How should the teacher respond in this situation?

a. Rephrasing the student's sentence by repeating it back properly
b. Ignoring the grammatical errors and responding to the student's statement
c. Asking the student follow-up questions to encourage discussion
d. Correcting the student's mistakes and asking them to repeat the sentence

Copyright © Mometrix Media. You have been licensed one copy of this document for personal use only. Any other reproduction or redistribution is strictly prohibited. All rights reserved.
This content is provided for test preparation purposes only and does not imply an endorsement by Mometrix of any particular political, scientific, or religious point of view.

18. Which of these is an example of attributes to seek in good children's literature?
   a. Stable story characters who do not change
   b. Books featuring overtly moralistic themes
   c. Concise summaries of race/gender types
   d. Original yet believable plot constructions

19. What is most accurate regarding the basal reader series used in today's classrooms?
   a. Texts used are by subjects, not reading levels.
   b. Texts used are expository, not narrative work.
   c. Texts used are the children's literature genre.
   d. Texts used are thematically organized by unit.

20. Among four categories of media that teachers instruct students to identify, in which one are books primarily classified?
   a. Media used in one-on-one communication
   b. Media used for entertainment
   c. Media to inform many people
   d. Media for persuading people

21. A kindergarten teacher is planning a lesson on identifying key details and literary elements within a fictional text. The teacher will use a grade-level-appropriate work of children's literature, and will include a read-aloud followed by several corresponding activities. According to Pennsylvania's PreK-4 standards in language arts, the teacher can reasonably expect students to do which of the following by the end of the lesson?
   a. Make inferences based upon literary techniques found in the text.
   b. Cite evidence from the text to support what it says explicitly.
   c. Determine the moral of the story and explain how it is conveyed in the text.
   d. Identify characters, setting, and major events of the story with prompting and support.

22. A third-grade teacher is planning a unit in which students will independently read a work of fictional literature. Which of the following prereading strategies would likely be most effective in enhancing students' overall comprehension of the text?
   a. Administering a diagnostic exam to determine students' level of literacy development
   b. Providing students with a word bank of unfamiliar vocabulary from the text
   c. Scaffolding the text by chunking it into smaller parts
   d. Having students complete an anticipation guide prior to reading the text

23. A third-grade teacher is planning a lesson in which students will independently read an informational text. Prior to beginning the lesson, the teacher will review new vocabulary words and add them to the class word wall. As students read the text, they will fill out a guided summary frame. Afterward, students will discuss their summaries with a table partner. These strategies are likely intended to promote students' skills in which of the following areas?
   a. Irregular sight word recognition
   b. Using text features to locate information
   c. Comprehension of academic language
   d. Understanding the relationship between written and spoken language

Copyright © Mometrix Media. You have been licensed one copy of this document for personal use only. Any other reproduction or redistribution is strictly prohibited. All rights reserved. This content is provided for test preparation purposes only and does not imply an endorsement by Mometrix of any particular political, scientific, or religious point of view.

24. A third-grade teacher is preparing to introduce an informational text to students. As a prereading strategy, the teacher reads a portion of the text aloud to the class and pauses at unfamiliar vocabulary. The teacher then asks students to identify surrounding words that may indicate examples, synonyms, antonyms, or definitions of the new words. This strategy is likely intended to develop which of the following skills?

a. Contextual analysis
b. Structural analysis
c. Phonological processing
d. Decoding and encoding

25. A kindergarten teacher wants to promote students' ability to retell a fictional story in sequential order. Which of the following activities would be most effective in achieving this goal with students of this age group?

a. Providing students with a story map to fill out as they read
b. Having students sort events from the story using picture cards
c. Modeling how to identify transitional words and phrases in the text
d. Having students arrange sentences from the story in the order in which they happened

26. Prior to reading a new story aloud to the class, a kindergarten teacher leads students through a picture walk of the book. This strategy promotes students' overall comprehension by fostering their ability to do which of the following?

a. Make connections between illustrations and text
b. Identify the author and illustrator
c. Use proper book handling skills
d. Make inferences about events in the story

27. A fourth-grade class is reading a short fictional novel over the course of several days. As students read, the teacher prompts them to respond to a series of reflection questions regarding their reactions, thoughts, and opinions about the text using a reading response journal. This strategy is most likely intended to develop students' what?

a. Literal reading comprehension skills
b. Inferential reading comprehension skills
c. Evaluative reading comprehension skills
d. Problem-solving skills

28. Children develop phonological awareness:

a. Only through direct training given by adults
b. Only naturally, through exposure to language
c. Via both natural exposure and direct training
d. Via neither incidental exposure nor instruction

29. A child who omits, substitutes, or distorts certain speech sounds beyond the usual age-range norms is most likely to have:

a. An articulation disorder
b. A type of voice disorder
c. One specific type of aphasia
d. Delayed language development

Copyright © Mometrix Media. You have been licensed one copy of this document for personal use only. Any other reproduction or redistribution is strictly prohibited. All rights reserved.
This content is provided for test preparation purposes only and does not imply an endorsement by Mometrix of any particular political, scientific, or religious point of view.

30. Phonemic awareness is a type of:

a. Phonological awareness. Phonemic awareness is the ability to recognize sounds within words.

b. Phonics. It is a teaching technique whereby readers learn the relationship between letters and sounds.

c. Alphabetization. Unless a reader knows the alphabet, phonemic awareness is useless.

d. Syntactical awareness. Understanding the underlying structure of a sentence is key to understanding meaning.

31. Which of the following most accurately defines information literacy?

a. The set of skills required for reading and comprehending information

b. The set of skills necessary to amass a comprehensive base of knowledge

c. The set of skills required for the finding, retrieval, analysis, and use of information

d. The set of skills necessary for effectively communicating information to others

32. Which of the following is NOT true about the whole language approach to literacy instruction?

a. The whole language approach is effective for children with language processing disorders.

b. The whole language approach is effective for supporting constructivist learning of literacy.

c. The whole language approach is effective for integrating literacy across content domains.

d. The whole language approach is effective for emphasizing cultural diversity in instruction.

33. Coarticulation affects:

a. Blending awareness

b. Phonemic awareness

c. Sequencing

d. Aural awareness

34. A first-grade student is having difficulty blending sounds of multisyllabic words. When asked to read such words aloud, he pronounces each letter sound independently. Which of the following intervention strategies would likely best promote the development of this skill?

a. Scaffolding definitions of new vocabulary words

b. Providing corresponding pictures for vocabulary words to clarify meaning

c. Having the student practice spelling words with letter tiles, reading the words aloud, and clapping out syllables

d. Pointing out examples of rhyming words and alliteration in poems and stories

35. Labeling items throughout the classroom with words and corresponding images is an effective strategy for promoting prekindergarten students' ability to:

a. Understand the purpose of written language

b. Read written text from left to right

c. Describe the connections between pictures and words

d. Identify and name objects

Copyright © Mometrix Media. You have been licensed one copy of this document for personal use only. Any other reproduction or redistribution is strictly prohibited. All rights reserved.
This content is provided for test preparation purposes only and does not imply an endorsement by Mometrix of any particular political, scientific, or religious point of view.

36. When introducing new high-frequency vocabulary, a first-grade teacher uses a mapping activity in which students separate, graph, and tap out the individual phonemes of each new word while reading them aloud. This strategy is likely intended to promote which of the following?

    a. Automaticity
    b. Prosody
    c. Orthographic mapping
    d. Receptive language skills

37. A second-grade teacher is reviewing sight words with students. Included in the vocabulary list are the words "stitch," "witch," and "hitch." Each of these words contains which of the following?

    a. An inflectional morpheme
    b. A consonant trigraph
    c. A vowel digraph
    d. A diphthong

38. A second-grade teacher is having students create vocabulary flip-books to practice adding prefixes and suffixes to root words. As students build each word, the teacher has them read it aloud to a table partner. This activity is likely intended to develop which of the following skills?

    a. Letter-sound correspondence
    b. Morphological awareness
    c. Blending letter sounds
    d. Phonemic awareness

39. Silent reading fluency can best be assessed by:

    a. Having the student retell or summarize the material to determine how much was understood.
    b. Giving a written test that covers plot, theme, character development, sequence of events, rising action, climax, falling action, and outcome. A student must test at a 95% accuracy rate to be considered fluent at silent reading.
    c. Giving a three-minute Test of Silent Contextual Reading Fluency four times a year. The student is presented with text in which spaces between words and all punctuation have been removed. The student must divide one word from another with slash marks, as in the example: The/little/sailboat/bobbed/so/far/in/the/distance/it/looked/like/a/toy. The more words a student accurately separates, the higher her silent reading fluency score.
    d. Silent reading fluency cannot be assessed. It is a private act between the reader and the text and does not invite critique.

40. Which of the following reading comprehension strategies is *most* applicable to differentiating between homonyms without knowing their exact spellings?

    a. Pictures
    b. Phonics
    c. Context
    d. Grammar

Copyright © Mometrix Media. You have been licensed one copy of this document for personal use only. Any other reproduction or redistribution is strictly prohibited. All rights reserved.
This content is provided for test preparation purposes only and does not imply an endorsement by Mometrix of any particular political, scientific, or religious point of view.

41. Which of the following is true regarding children's reading fluency?

a. The lack of reading fluency is always due to word-decoding deficits.
b. Children's motivation to read is unaffected by their reading fluency.
c. Some children need only more reading practice to develop fluency.
d. Fluency has equal impact on school performance at all grade levels.

42. Context clues are useful in:

a. Predicting future action
b. Understanding the meaning of words that are not familiar
c. Understanding character motivation
d. Reflecting on a text's theme

43. Which of the following is correct regarding basal readers for teaching reading?

a. Basal readers involve a top-down approach.
b. Reading sub-skills are taught systematically.
c. Sequencing of teaching sub-skills is flexible.
d. These have become rare in the twenty-first century.

44. Which of the following best explains the importance prior knowledge brings to the act of reading?

a. Prior knowledge is information the student gets through researching a topic prior to reading the text. A student who is well-prepared through such research is better able to decode a text and retain its meaning.
b. Prior knowledge is knowledge the student brings from previous life or learning experiences to the act of reading. It is not possible for a student to fully comprehend new knowledge without first integrating it with prior knowledge.
c. Prior knowledge is predictive. It motivates the student to look for contextual clues in the reading and predict what is likely to happen next.
d. Prior knowledge is not important to any degree to the act of reading, because every text is self-contained and therefore seamless. Prior knowledge is irrelevant in this application.

45. A teacher is working with a group of third graders at the same reading level. Her goal is to improve reading fluency. She asks each child in turn to read a page from a book about mammal young. She asks the children to read with expression. She also reminds them they don't need to stop between each word; they should read as quickly as they comfortably can. She cautions them, however, not to read so quickly that they leave out or misread a word. The teacher knows the components of reading fluency are:

a. Speed, drama, and comprehension
b. Cohesion, rate, and prosody
c. Understanding, rate, and prosody
d. Rate, accuracy, and prosody

46. Which of the following choices represents the smallest unit of language that possesses semantic meaning?

a. Morpheme
b. Grapheme
c. Phoneme
d. Word stem

Copyright © Mometrix Media. You have been licensed one copy of this document for personal use only. Any other reproduction or redistribution is strictly prohibited. All rights reserved. This content is provided for test preparation purposes only and does not imply an endorsement by Mometrix of any particular political, scientific, or religious point of view.

47. A first-grade teacher has noticed that one student struggles to recall stories in the correct sequence. The student often mixes up events from the beginning, middle, and end of the story, and confuses important connecting details. Which of the following strategies would likely best support this student's language skill development in this area?

a. Fostering personal connections between the student's life and events from stories
b. Providing the student aids such as graphic organizers, story maps, and pictures that correspond with events from stories
c. Exposing the student to a variety of texts relevant to her personal interests
d. Reading aloud to the student individually and asking open-ended questions about the story

48. When reading aloud to students, a kindergarten teacher makes sure to speak expressively by pausing at the end of each sentence, changing intonation, and correlating inflection with differences in punctuation within the text. In doing so, the teacher models which of the following?

a. The correct usage of academic language
b. Differences in writing styles of literary and informational texts
c. Interest and enthusiasm for reading
d. The relationship between English grammatical conventions in written and spoken language

49. A kindergarten teacher has noticed that one student is struggling with sight word recognition and decoding skills, and is beginning to fall behind the rest of the class. The teacher is concerned that this may impede the student's development of reading comprehension skills. Which of the following interventions would be most appropriate in this situation?

a. Providing individual instruction with a reading resource teacher
b. Implementing Response to Intervention (RTI) services
c. Contacting the student's parents to address the concerns
d. Developing an Individualized Education Program (IEP) to address the student's learning needs

50. A first-grade teacher is using direct instruction to introduce multiple-meaning words to students. Which of the following additional strategies would reinforce this concept?

a. Having students complete sentence dictation exercises
b. Displaying new vocabulary in the classroom with corresponding images
c. Having students practice segmenting the new words
d. Implementing word-building activities using letter tiles

Mathematics

1. During a unit on geometry, Ms. Nifong instructs her students to sketch two congruent polygons. Which of the following sketches completes this task correctly?

a. Two rectangles with the same perimeter
b. Two polygons with the same shape
c. Two polygons with the same side lengths
d. Two squares with the same area

Copyright © Mometrix Media. You have been licensed one copy of this document for personal use only. Any other reproduction or redistribution is strictly prohibited. All rights reserved.
This content is provided for test preparation purposes only and does not imply an endorsement by Mometrix of any particular political, scientific, or religious point of view.

2. What is the most effective way to facilitate children's comprehension of mathematics?

    a. To preserve mathematics as a discipline separate from other academic subjects and everyday life

    b. To allow children to find their own activities applying math rather than providing activities for them

    c. To help them connect and apply common math rules to many different life activities and processes

    d. To ask/answer questions and explain during formal math lessons, not confusing math with real life

3. Which of the following options represents equivalency between mathematical expressions?

    a. $3 + x + 3x + 3 + x = 5x + 6$

    b. $7x - 2x = 9x$

    c. $2y + 2y + 2y = 6y^3$

    d. $2.5(x + 2) = 2.5x + 2$

4. Which of the following statements is true?

    a. -6 is to the right of -5 on the number line

    b. -7 is to the left of -2 on the number line

    c. 0 is to the left of -1 on the number line

    d. 7 is to the left of -2 on the number line

5. Of the following statements, which is true of how children's mathematical counting skills develop?

    a. Learning to count from one to twelve involves more unusual rules.

    b. Learning to count from thirteen to nineteen requires more memorizing.

    c. Learning to count above twenty involves less consistent rules.

    d. Learning to count from twenty to one hundred, children discover base ten.

6. A prekindergarten teacher wants to begin developing students' understanding of measurement. Which of the following activities would likely best demonstrate this concept?

    a. Providing students with yardsticks and asking them to measure the length of the classroom

    b. Demonstrating how to use various measurement tools

    c. Engaging students in making a simple recipe in which ingredients must be measured

    d. Explaining the difference between the metric and imperial systems

7. What is the distance on a coordinate plane from $(-8, 6)$ to $(4, 3)$?

    a. $\sqrt{139}$

    b. $\sqrt{147}$

    c. $\sqrt{153}$

    d. $\sqrt{161}$

Copyright © Mometrix Media. You have been licensed one copy of this document for personal use only. Any other reproduction or redistribution is strictly prohibited. All rights reserved.
This content is provided for test preparation purposes only and does not imply an endorsement by Mometrix of any particular political, scientific, or religious point of view.

8. Mr. Mancelli teaches fifth-grade math. He is making prize bags for the winners of a math game. If he has eight candy bars and twelve packages of gum, what is the largest number of identical prize bags he can make without having any left-over candy bars or packages of gum?

    a. 2
    b. 4
    c. 6
    d. 8

9. Which of the following is true regarding children's development of number sense?

    a. Children must learn all number names before they learn to count.
    b. Children learn to count before learning all the names of numbers.
    c. Children's number sense is equal to, and a synonym for, counting.
    d. Children's number sense is that numbers only describe quantities.

10. A prekindergarten teacher provides each student with a set of counting chips as they practice learning to count to ten. As students count each number aloud, the teacher instructs them to move a chip from one side of their desk to the other. This strategy is likely intended to help students do which of the following as they develop this pre-numeracy skill?

    a. Name numerals up to ten
    b. Compare numbers between one and ten
    c. Recognize and identify numerals
    d. Keep track of counting

11. If 1 inch on a map represents 60 feet, how many yards apart are two points if the distance between the points on the map is 10 inches?

    a. 1,800
    b. 600
    c. 200
    d. 2

12. As a group of fourth-grade students work independently to practice solving division problems, the teacher walks around and asks questions to check for understanding. Which of the following questions would best promote the development of students' mathematical communication skills?

    a. "What answer did you get for that problem?"
    b. "Can you explain how you got this answer?"
    c. "What step did you take first to solve that problem?"
    d. "What strategy can you use to check your answers?"

Copyright © Mometrix Media. You have been licensed one copy of this document for personal use only. Any other reproduction or redistribution is strictly prohibited. All rights reserved.
This content is provided for test preparation purposes only and does not imply an endorsement by Mometrix of any particular political, scientific, or religious point of view.

13. Which of the following represents the net of a triangular prism?

a.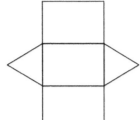

b.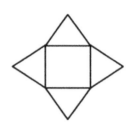

c.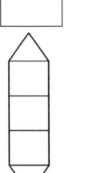

d.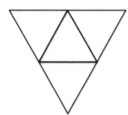

14. A kindergarten teacher wants to begin developing students' ability to think algebraically throughout a unit on adding numbers up to ten. Which of the following strategies would be most effective in achieving this goal?

    a. Providing both verbal and written directions on how to add numbers up to ten
    b. Modeling how to finger count when adding two numbers
    c. Introducing expressions concretely, pictorially, then abstractly
    d. Demonstrating where the concept of addition is applicable in real-world situations

15. A kindergarten student has difficulty arranging numbers in ascending order. Which of the following strategies would likely best support development of this skill?

    a. Leading the class in counting songs, rhymes, and chants
    b. Encouraging rote memorization using flash cards
    c. Having the student practice representing numbers using a number chart and counting chips
    d. Incorporating counting activities into unstructured play time

16. Zach was asked to round each decimal value to the nearest tenth. He incorrectly rounds each value and writes down his answers. If Zach applies the same misconception when rounding the number 14.51, what will his incorrect answer be?

$$8.264 \rightarrow 8$$
$$18.58 \rightarrow 19$$
$$19.79 \rightarrow 20$$
$$0.62 \rightarrow 0$$
$$5.91 \rightarrow 6$$

    a. 10
    b. 14
    c. 14.5
    d. 15

Copyright © Mometrix Media. You have been licensed one copy of this document for personal use only. Any other reproduction or redistribution is strictly prohibited. All rights reserved.
This content is provided for test preparation purposes only and does not imply an endorsement by Mometrix of any particular political, scientific, or religious point of view.

17. Which of the following statements is an example of using ordinal numbers?

 a. "I am four years old and my brother Timmy is two years old."
 b. "I sit at the first table for lunch and my sister sits at the third."
 c. "I play on the junior soccer team. My shirt says number six."
 d. "Two-thirds of my math class are boys and one-third are girls."

18. To which of the following sets of numbers does $\frac{1}{4}$ belong?

 a. The set of real numbers
 b. The set of irrational numbers
 c. The set of integers
 d. The set of whole numbers

19. Identify the cross-section polygon formed by a plane containing the given points on the cube.

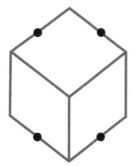

 a. Rectangle
 b. Trapezoid
 c. Pentagon
 d. Hexagon

Copyright © Mometrix Media. You have been licensed one copy of this document for personal use only. Any other reproduction or redistribution is strictly prohibited. All rights reserved.
This content is provided for test preparation purposes only and does not imply an endorsement by Mometrix of any particular political, scientific, or religious point of view.

20. Which of the following pairs of equations represents the lines of symmetry in the figure below?

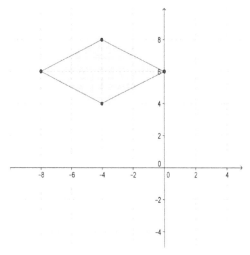

a. $x = -4, y = 6$
b. $x = 4, y = 6$
c. $y = -4, x = 6$
d. $y = 4, x = -6$

21. Which of the following equations may be used to convert $0.\overline{7}$ to a fraction?

a. $9x = 7.\overline{7} - 0.\overline{7}$
b. $99x = 7.\overline{7} - 0.\overline{7}$
c. $9x = 77.\overline{7} - 7.\overline{7}$
d. $90x = 7.\overline{7} - 0.\overline{7}$

22. Which of the following activities is most focused on children's *identifying* patterns?

a. Stringing beads with different colors in a certain order to make a necklace design
b. Counting the number of blue dots before a green dot appears in a printed fabric
c. Arranging alternating pieces of different sizes and gluing them to paper or board
d. Hopping two times on one foot, then the other; then three times each; four; etc.

23. Of the following, which is accurate regarding the relationship of problem-solving skills to math?

a. Children are not interested in solving everyday problems; adults must give incentives.
b. Children learn mathematical thinking; other things promote language and social skills.
c. Children learn through solving problems that there can be multiple possible solutions.
d. Children should not propose problems or ask questions about them; the adults should.

24. Which of the following describes how to find the volume of a regular solid prism?

a. Find the perimeter of the base of the prism and multiply by the height of the prism.
b. Find the area of the base of the prism and multiply by the height of the prism.
c. Find the sum of the areas of the faces and multiply by the length of the prism.
d. Find the sum of the areas of the lateral faces and multiply by the number of faces.

Copyright © Mometrix Media. You have been licensed one copy of this document for personal use only. Any other reproduction or redistribution is strictly prohibited. All rights reserved.
This content is provided for test preparation purposes only and does not imply an endorsement by Mometrix of any particular political, scientific, or religious point of view.

25. A teacher asks children to sort various objects. First the teacher has them put big things in one box and little things in another box. Then the teacher has the children separate hard things from soft things, etc. Which mathematical concept is most supported by this activity?

 a. Patterning
 b. Classifying
 c. Counting
 d. Ordering

26. During an activity, Mrs. Schwartz instructs her students to place coins into three groups, where each group gets progressively lower in total value. Which of the following students correctly completed this activity?

 a. Henry with Group 1: 2 dimes, 2 nickels, and 4 pennies; Group 2: 1 dime, 3 nickels, 2 pennies; Group 3: 2 dimes, 1 nickel, 4 pennies
 b. Graham with Group 1: 1 dime, 5 nickels, and 5 pennies; Group 2: 2 dimes, 2 nickels, 8 pennies; Group 3: 1 dime, 2 nickel, 9 pennies
 c. Landon with Group 1: 3 dimes, 4 nickels, and 9 pennies; Group 2: 2 dimes, 4 nickels, 3 pennies; Group 3: 1 dime, 9 nickels, 2 pennies
 d. Elizabeth with Group 1: 2 dimes, 2 nickels, and 9 pennies; Group 2: 2 dimes, 4 nickels, 1 penny; Group 3: 1 dime, 1 nickel, 7 pennies

27. Ms. Elliott asks her fifth-grade students, "Do you prefer chocolate or vanilla ice cream?" If the probability of her students preferring chocolate ice cream is 0.6, what is the probability of her students preferring vanilla ice cream?

 a. 0.6
 b. 0.4
 c. 0.3
 d. 0.5

28. Which of the following correctly represents the expanded form of 0.593?

 a. $5 \times \frac{1}{10^0} + 9 \times \frac{1}{10^1} + 3 \times \frac{1}{10^2}$
 b. $5 \times \frac{1}{10^2} + 9 \times \frac{1}{10^3} + 3 \times \frac{1}{10^4}$
 c. $5 \times \frac{1}{10^3} + 9 \times \frac{1}{10^2} + 3 \times \frac{1}{10^1}$
 d. $5 \times \frac{1}{10^1} + 9 \times \frac{1}{10^2} + 3 \times \frac{1}{10^3}$

29. A building is 44 feet tall and casts a shadow that is 59.2 ft in length. Which of the following best represents the distance from the top of the building to the end of the shadow?

 a. 39.6 ft
 b. 45.5 ft
 c. 61.9 ft
 d. 73.8 ft

225

Copyright © Mometrix Media. You have been licensed one copy of this document for personal use only. Any other reproduction or redistribution is strictly prohibited. All rights reserved. This content is provided for test preparation purposes only and does not imply an endorsement by Mometrix of any particular political, scientific, or religious point of view.

30. Mr. Orr asks his class to use inductive reasoning as to determine the pattern in this series of numbers. Which number is next in this series?

> 2, 5, 10, 17, ___

    a. 25
    b. 26
    c. 22
    d. 24

31. What is true about facilitating young children's early development of measurement skills?

    a. Adults should discourage children from using their own personal measuring units.
    b. Adults should teach children standardized measurement units in isolated lessons.
    c. Adults should explain measuring to children when demonstrating everyday tasks.
    d. Adults should ask children to participate in everyday tasks and discuss measuring.

32. Regarding young children's early comprehension of fractions, which of these is accurate?

    a. Children must know how many parts a unit is divided into, but not what comprises the unit.
    b. Children must know what makes a whole unit, but not into how many pieces it was divided.
    c. Children must know how many pieces a unit is divided into, but not if they are of equal size.
    d. Children must know what a whole unit is, how many parts there are, and if part sizes match.

33. What things can adults best use to help very young children learn geometric concepts?

    a. Concrete objects
    b. Both of these
    c. Everyday activities
    d. Neither of these

34. Which of the following represents an inversely proportional relationship?

    a. $y = 3x$
    b. $y = \frac{1}{3}x$
    c. $y = \frac{3}{x}$
    d. $y = 3x^2$

35. At the end of the first semester, a second-grade teacher administers a formal exam that consists of all curriculum covered in the first half of the year. Which of the following best explains the purpose of using this assessment approach?

    a. To determine students' level of understanding throughout instruction
    b. To assess students' background knowledge and level of understanding
    c. To provide the teacher with immediate feedback regarding instructional effectiveness
    d. To measure students' progress in relation to achieving district and state academic standards

Copyright © Mometrix Media. You have been licensed one copy of this document for personal use only. Any other reproduction or redistribution is strictly prohibited. All rights reserved. This content is provided for test preparation purposes only and does not imply an endorsement by Mometrix of any particular political, scientific, or religious point of view.

36. Of the following learning objectives involving data analysis for pre-K through Grade 2, which is most likely to have few or no activities that are age-appropriate for pre-K and kindergarten ages?

    a. To pose questions and collect data regarding familiar objects and everyday situations
    b. To sort various objects by their properties and categorize them accordingly in groups
    c. To represent data using line graphs, bar graphs, picture graphs, charts, and timelines
    d. To put objects on table/floor graphs by property and say the group with most/fewest

37. Which of the following activities would best help first-grade students understand the concept of measuring objects?

    a. Measuring the height of the pencil sharpener using a meter stick
    b. Measuring the length of the chalkboard using a tape measure
    c. Measuring the width of their desks using dominoes placed end to end
    d. Measuring the circumference of the trash can using a cloth tape

38. Kevin saves $3 during Month 1. During each subsequent month, he plans to save 4 more dollars than he saved during the previous month. Which of the following equations represents the amount he will save during the nth month?

    a. $a_n = 3n - 1$
    b. $a_n = 3n + 4$
    c. $a_n = 4n + 3$
    d. $a_n = 4n - 1$

39. A prekindergarten teacher places two groups of eight one-unit cubes on a table. In one group, the cubes are arranged neatly into two small rows of four. In the other group, the cubes are spread far apart. When asked which group has more cubes, students chose the pile in which the cubes were spread apart. Which of the following best explains the reason for the students' answer?

    a. The teacher did not ask students to count the unit cubes individually.
    b. Students have not yet learned one-to-one correspondence.
    c. Prekindergarten students have not yet developed an understanding of conservation.
    d. Students did not have the opportunity to physically manipulate the unit cubes.

40. A second-grade teacher wants to promote students' ability to tell time to the nearest five minutes using an analog clock. Which of the following strategies would best support students' development of this skill?

    a. Showing images of analog clocks corresponding to the time of events on the daily class schedule
    b. Using unit cubes to help students learn to skip count by fives and tens
    c. Reviewing addition and subtraction skills to help students determine elapsed time
    d. Introducing digital clocks first to teach the general concept of telling time

Science

1. The distance from the earth to the sun is equal to which of the following?

    a. One astronomical unit
    b. One light-year
    c. One parsec
    d. One arcsecond

Copyright © Mometrix Media. You have been licensed one copy of this document for personal use only. Any other reproduction or redistribution is strictly prohibited. All rights reserved. This content is provided for test preparation purposes only and does not imply an endorsement by Mometrix of any particular political, scientific, or religious point of view.

2. On a topographic map, an area where the contour lines are very close together indicates which of the following?

a. A stream is present.
b. The slope is very gentle.
c. The slope is very steep.
d. The area surrounds a depression.

3. Physical weathering of rocks can be caused by all of the following EXCEPT:

a. The freezing and thawing of water on the surface of rocks
b. Changes in temperature
c. Oxidation
d. Changes in pressure due to the removal of overlying rocks

4. How does the tilt of Earth's axis cause seasons?

a. A hemisphere experiences fall and winter when that half of Earth is tilted away from the sun. It experiences spring and summer when that half of Earth is tilted toward the sun.
b. A hemisphere experiences winter and spring when that half of Earth is tilted away from the sun. It experiences summer and fall when that half of Earth is tilted toward the sun.
c. A hemisphere experiences spring and summer when that half of Earth is tilted away from the sun. It experiences fall and winter when that half of Earth is tilted toward the sun.
d. A hemisphere experiences summer and fall when that half of Earth is tilted away from the sun. It experiences winter and spring when that half of Earth is tilted toward the sun.

5. Limestone is one example of which subtype of sedimentary rock?

a. Clastic
b. Organic
c. Chemical
d. Pegmatite

6. Which of the following processes is NOT part of the formation of sedimentary rock?

a. Layering
b. Cementation
c. Compaction
d. Heat

7. Which of the following soil or rock types has a high porosity and a low permeability?

a. Sand
b. Granite
c. Gravel
d. Clay

8. What phase of the moon follows a full moon?

a. waning gibbous
b. waxing crescent
c. waning crescent
d. waxing gibbous

Copyright © Mometrix Media. You have been licensed one copy of this document for personal use only. Any other reproduction or redistribution is strictly prohibited. All rights reserved.
This content is provided for test preparation purposes only and does not imply an endorsement by Mometrix of any particular political, scientific, or religious point of view.

9. Young children develop many basic science concepts through everyday activities. Of the following, which activity is most related to the development of measurement concepts?

a. Fitting wooden pegs into holes with matching shapes in a toy
b. Pouring sand from one container into a differently sized one
c. Seeing how many coins they have accrued in their piggy bank
d. Separating toys into piles of cars, trucks, animals, people, etc.

10. To teach early physics concepts, an EC teacher gives students an activity of rolling balls down ramps. The teacher asks them questions like what would happen if one ramp were longer or higher; if two different sizes of ramps were used; if they started two balls rolling down a ramp at the same time, etc. Which skills in the scientific process do the children use during this activity?

a. Observation and communication
b. They use every one of these skills.
c. Skills of inference and prediction
d. Measurements and comparisons

11. When young children build structures from blocks and then knock them down or take them apart, which of these science concepts are they learning?

a. Concepts of shape
b. Concepts of weight
c. Part-whole relations
d. Temporal sequences

12. Which of the following foundational science skills is best illustrated by an activity comparing non-standard measures, such as using scales to find the weight ratio when comparing apples and grapes.

a. Observation
b. Inference
c. Communication
d. Classifying

13. Which of the following does NOT display an appropriate or safe use of chemicals?

a. Never taste any chemicals.
b. To test odors, waft the odors towards your nose with a cupped hand.
c. Never return unused chemicals to the stock bottle.
d. When diluting acids, always pour the water into the acid.

14. After a science laboratory exercise, some solutions remain unused and are left over. What should be done with these solutions?

a. Dispose of the solutions according to local disposal procedures.
b. Empty the solutions into the sink and rinse with warm water and soap.
c. Ensure the solutions are secured in closed containers and throw away.
d. Store the solutions in a secured, dry place for later use.

Copyright © Mometrix Media. You have been licensed one copy of this document for personal use only. Any other reproduction or redistribution is strictly prohibited. All rights reserved.
This content is provided for test preparation purposes only and does not imply an endorsement by Mometrix of any particular political, scientific, or religious point of view.

15. Which of the following is a mnemonic strategy used in teaching science?

    a. memorizing the phrase King Phillip Came Over From Greece Saturday to help remember the biological classifications: Kingdom, Phylum, Class, Order, Family, Genus, Species

    b. a guided reading strategy that involves summarizing, generating questions, clarifying, and predicting

    c. think, write, discuss lectures

    d. student-generated experimental procedures to answer a student-generated question

16. Of the following ecological relationships, which ones benefit both organisms involved?

    a. Commensalistic relationships

    b. Mutualistic relationships

    c. Parasitic relationships

    d. None of these does

17. In the human digestive system, which of the following is a part of the large intestine?

    a. The colon

    b. The ileum

    c. The jejunum

    d. The duodenum

18. Which of the human cranial nerves controls sensation in the face?

    a. The facial nerve (VII)

    b. The vagus nerve (X)

    c. The trigeminal nerve (V)

    d. The hypoglossal nerve (XII)

19. Which of the following is the smallest?

    a. tissue

    b. a cell

    c. a muscle

    d. a ligament

20. Which of the following have a simple life cycle, without a metamorphosis?

    a. Frogs

    b. Newts

    c. Grasshoppers

    d. Human beings

21. The following represents a simple food chain. What trophic level contains the greatest amount of energy?

$$tree \rightarrow caterpillar \rightarrow frog \rightarrow snake \rightarrow hawk \rightarrow worm$$

    a. Tree

    b. Caterpillar

    c. Hawk

    d. Worm

Copyright © Mometrix Media. You have been licensed one copy of this document for personal use only. Any other reproduction or redistribution is strictly prohibited. All rights reserved. This content is provided for test preparation purposes only and does not imply an endorsement by Mometrix of any particular political, scientific, or religious point of view.

22. **In an ecosystem, its abiotic factors:**
    a. Are alive.
    b. Are not alive.
    c. Do not affect living organisms.
    d. Include some microorganisms.

23. **In terms of relationships between organisms and between organisms and their environments, the relationship between termites and the bacteria in their digestive systems is classified as:**
    a. Parasitic
    b. Ecological
    c. Mutualistic
    d. Commensalistic

24. **A horse is an example of a(n) _____.**
    a. omnivore
    b. carnivore
    c. decomposer
    d. herbivore

25. **If a population reaches a maximum size and ceases to grow due to a limited availability of resources, which of the following describes the population?**
    a. Unstable
    b. Shrinking exponentially
    c. At carrying capacity
    d. Moving towards extinction

26. **In the scientific process, which skill do children employ most when they see patterns and meaning in the results of experiments they make?**
    a. Measurement
    b. Classification
    c. Inferences
    d. Prediction

27. **Of the following actions, which best represents the science process skill of Inference?**
    a. Formulating new hypotheses based on experimental results
    b. Finding patterns and meaning in the results of experiments
    c. Identifying properties of things/situations using the senses
    d. Reporting experimental results and conclusions to others

28. **When using a light microscope, how is the total magnification determined?**
    a. By multiplying the ocular lens power by the objective being used
    b. By looking at the objective you are using only
    c. By looking at the ocular lens power only
    d. By multiplying the objective you are using by two

29. **All of the following are true regarding wind energy, EXCEPT:**
    a. Wind turbines use space inefficiently, but they have low operational costs.
    b. Wind is not a reliable source of energy in all geographic locations.

Copyright © Mometrix Media. You have been licensed one copy of this document for personal use only. Any other reproduction or redistribution is strictly prohibited. All rights reserved.
This content is provided for test preparation purposes only and does not imply an endorsement by Mometrix of any particular political, scientific, or religious point of view.

c. Wind turbines are expensive to manufacture and install.
d. Wind turbines are a threat to wildlife.

30. Which of the following is currently the greatest benefit of genetically modified crops?

a. Increased profits for farmers
b. Increased nutrition for consumers
c. Increased shelf life of foods
d. Decreased allergens for consumers

31. Once a hypothesis has been verified and accepted, it becomes which of the following?

a. A fact
b. A law
c. A conclusion
d. A theory

32. A student has collected data on the width of tree trunks and average precipitation rates for different locations. The student wants to show the relationship between these two variables. What type of graph should be used?

a. A multi-line graph with the width measurements on the x-axis and precipitation rates on the y-axis.
b. A scatter plot with the width measurements on the y-axis and precipitation rates on the x-axis.
c. A bar graph with the width measurements on the y-axis and precipitation rates on the x-axis.
d. A pie chart with the width of trees shown as a percentage at different precipitation rates.

33. Which of the following is a disadvantage of fossil fuels?

a. Extraction processes are extremely dangerous.
b. There is no way to control pollution from their processing.
c. They are difficult to store safely.
d. Their use contributes to global warming.

34. Among the states of matter, water vapor is classified as:

a. A gas.
b. A solid.
c. A liquid.
d. A plasma.

35. Which of these statements is true regarding magnetism?

a. Only certain electric motors have magnets in them.
b. The planet Earth in itself constitutes a huge magnet.
c. Compasses but not tape recorders contain magnets.
d. Generators contain magnets but telephones do not.

36. Which of the following is NOT true of a chemical reaction?

a. Matter is neither gained nor lost.
b. Heat is absorbed or released.
c. The rate of the reaction increases with temperature.
d. The products have a different number of atoms than the reactants.

Copyright © Mometrix Media. You have been licensed one copy of this document for personal use only. Any other reproduction or redistribution is strictly prohibited. All rights reserved.
This content is provided for test preparation purposes only and does not imply an endorsement by Mometrix of any particular political, scientific, or religious point of view.

37. Which biome is most likely to support the growth of epiphytes?

    a. Deserts
    b. Tropical rain forests
    c. Temperate deciduous forests
    d. Taigas

38. Which of the following represents a chemical change?

    a. Water sublimating
    b. An apple turning brown
    c. Salt dissolving in water
    d. Rock being pulverized

39. What are pure substances that consist of more than one type of atom?

    a. Elements
    b. Compounds
    c. Molecules
    d. Mixtures

40. What is the point of a phase diagram where a substance can exist as a solid, a liquid and a gas?

    a. Isothermal point
    b. Isobaric point
    c. Triple point
    d. Critical point

Copyright © Mometrix Media. You have been licensed one copy of this document for personal use only. Any other reproduction or redistribution is strictly prohibited. All rights reserved.
This content is provided for test preparation purposes only and does not imply an endorsement by Mometrix of any particular political, scientific, or religious point of view.

Answer Key and Explanations

Developmental Knowledge

1. C: Object permanence, which babies develop during Piaget's first, Sensorimotor stage of cognitive development, is the realization that objects still exist even when they are out of sight. (A) is the opposite of this. The other choices are not related to the concept of object permanence.

2. D: The toddler years are typically when children begin to express their opinions, likes and dislikes as well as their feelings and ideas; and to ask questions. The early preschool years are typically when children are able to describe unseen objects (A), tell "make-believe" stories (B), and speak in complete sentences (C).

3. C: Responding to simple requests and questions (A) and recognizing nouns that name familiar objects in their environment are characteristics typical of children aged 7-12 months. Wanting to hear the same stories, games, and/or rhymes repeated many times (B) and being able to point at a few of their body parts when asked (D) are characteristic of the language development of children aged 1-2 years. Children typically enjoy hearing stories read or told to them and can answer simple questions about the stories (C) when they are 4-5 years old, so this is the latest development of the choices given.

4. D: The Center for the Study of Social Policy has recommended an approach to strengthen families that uses five factors for preventing child abuse and neglect. In addition to strengthening parental resilience and social connections, these also include strengthening parents' knowledge about child development and parenting (A); giving concrete assistance to families when they need it (B); and strengthening children's emotional and social competence (C). Increasing legal punishment for child abuse and neglect (D) is NOT included in this approach.

5. D: Object permanence, i.e. the understanding that things still exist when out of sight, develops in babies during Piaget's first, sensorimotor stage of cognitive development. Piaget believed the typical age for this development was around 8-9 months old. Some researchers after Piaget have also found evidence that some babies develop object permanence as young as 3 months old. Reversibility of actions (A) and conservation of quantity (C) develop during the stage of concrete operations, around the ages of 7-11 years. Symbolic representation (D) typically develops in the Early Representational Thought substage near the end of the Sensorimotor stage, around the ages of 18-24 months.

6. D: To be flexible enough to engage families with diverse needs and circumstances in ECE, educators should include parents and other family members in contributing to the development of Individual Family Service Plans (IFSPs) for preschoolers rather than just design these plans themselves (A). Rather than assigning goals for parents to participate in their children's education (B), educators should ask parents and families to develop their own participatory goals that will reflect what they can do and when and how they can do it. To enable parents with diverse situations and needs to attend meetings and school visits, educators can help by arranging transportation and/or child care for parents who do not have these (C). Another way to engage diverse families is to have meetings at different times that consider parents' work schedules (D).

7. D: EC educators can involve diverse families in their children's educations by recruiting family members who express or show interest to help out at the preschool. If parents' work schedules prevent them from attending school meetings, proactive educators can adapt by scheduling the

234

Copyright © Mometrix Media. You have been licensed one copy of this document for personal use only. Any other reproduction or redistribution is strictly prohibited. All rights reserved. This content is provided for test preparation purposes only and does not imply an endorsement by Mometrix of any particular political, scientific, or religious point of view.

meetings at different times (A). Proactive educators can also provide transportation and childcare to facilitate parents' attendance to meetings and visits to the school (B). Educators can also involve diverse parents by sharing individualized strategies they can use at home with their children (B) that will support and extend the strategies used in school.

8. D: When a person attributes his/her success to internal attributes, like hard work or intelligence, psychologist Julian Rotter named this internal locus of control. He described external locus of control as attributing one's success to external factors outside of one's control, like getting help from the teacher (A) or a classmate/friend (C); or luck (B); or other factors, such as other peoples' efforts. Internal and external loci of control apply to people's attribution of causes for failures as well as successes.

9. B: While teachers are advised against wearing distracting apparel or making exaggerated gestures (a), appropriate physical movements expressing energy, enthusiasm, and excitement about content and learning are effective (b). Rather than losing student respect, teachers communicate that they value their own utterances when they smile (c). Teachers should stand up straight and maintain eye contact to project confidence; slouching and looking away do not put students at ease (d).

10. D: Among strategies for effective classroom conflict resolution, experts recommend that teachers have students track conflicts they partake of and/or witness over time; record their observations in journals (a), but keep the identities of participants anonymous (b); and then discuss various student reactions to these conflicts that they have observed, including the advantages and disadvantages of each (c).

11. D: Once adults have implemented a plan to manage a behavior in an EC setting, they must record the child's progress regularly. By analyzing the records they keep, they can determine which parts of the plan are working and which are not; or whether the entire plan is not working. If they find that a plan is ineffective despite adhering to it consistently for a sufficient time, they can figure out why and then replace it with a new plan more suited to the child, the behavior and its function. If only parts of the plan are ineffective, it can be revised to change those parts; hence (A) is incorrect. EC staff should begin with plans that are easy to implement, not difficult (B) and are simple, not complex (C).

12. B: According to Mildred Parten (1932), play indicated social maturity from least to most as unoccupied behavior; independent or solitary play (a); watching others playing (c); playing near but not directly with others (d); playing with others but without structure or rules (b); and playing cooperatively with others, including interest in both the activity and the players as well as structure, rules, and interpersonal interaction. To stimulate growth, the teacher should offer students opportunities to play at the next higher level, i.e., offer those playing associatively (b) opportunities for full cooperative play.

13. D: Instrumental aggression is behavior wherein a child yells, kicks, or hits others to get something they want, usually a toy or other object. It is the most commonly seen form of aggression in early preschoolers through the age of around 4 years, when it often peaks. Hostile aggression (B) is more common in middle preschoolers older than 4 years and involves retaliating against others in return for being wronged or hurt by them. Hostile aggression has two types: overt aggression (A), more common in boys, wherein they physically hurt others and/or threaten to do so; and relational aggression (C), more common in girls, wherein they emotionally and/or socially hurt others through circulating hurtful rumors and/or rejecting them socially.

Copyright © Mometrix Media. You have been licensed one copy of this document for personal use only. Any other reproduction or redistribution is strictly prohibited. All rights reserved.
This content is provided for test preparation purposes only and does not imply an endorsement by Mometrix of any particular political, scientific, or religious point of view.

14. A: When preschool teachers assign cooperative activities, children can learn to verbalize what they want. They can learn empathy (B) through discussion and question-answer groups. They can learn cooperation through small-group collaborative projects their teachers assign (C), as well as how to take turns (D), listen to others, and express what they want verbally.

15. A: Young children must have concrete things they can see, touch, and manipulate. They are not yet cognitively capable of manipulating information mentally (B). They are not yet able to memorize math processes by rote (C), as older elementary-age children can memorize times tables, etc. They are too young to benefit from "sit still and listen" types of lessons (D).

16. B: Preschool-aged children must have solid, concrete objects they can physically manipulate to understand numerical concepts. They are not yet cognitively able to manipulate information mentally, which is required by all of the other choices.

17. B: For preadolescents and younger adolescents to resolve Erikson's psychosocial nuclear conflict of Industry vs. Inferiority (typically described as from age 7-12, but individual differences can make it earlier or later), they must experience success in school. For students to transition from Piaget's cognitive Concrete Operations to Formal Operations stage (a), teachers can start them with logical reasoning involving concrete manipulatives and then gradually progress, scaffolding as needed, to abstract reasoning without concrete objects. Forming action plans for the future that they find satisfying (c) is an activity that helps older adolescents to resolve Erikson's psychosocial conflict of Identity vs. Role Confusion. Students typically need to transition cognitively from intuitive thought to logical reasoning (d), i.e., from Piaget's Preoperational to Concrete Operations stage, during early childhood, not adolescence.

18. C: An EC aesthetic activity focused on shape can begin with the teacher's reading a children's story or book about shapes to preschoolers. Then the teacher can have children identify shapes in the book. After this, the teacher can show the children an artwork and have them identify shapes they see in it. Then the teacher can help the children arrange various solid shapes to create images of people, animals, flowers, houses, cars, etc. Once they have done this, the teacher can supply glue for the children to fix their images to boards or paper. When the glue is dry, children can paint their creations. This sequence is most appropriate by moving from introduction of shapes, to identification of shapes in an easier medium; to identification of shapes in a more challenging, but more real-life medium; to active manipulation of shapes to create recognizable forms. It goes from easier to harder, and from more passive to more active, progressively building knowledge and experience with shape.

19. C: In lessons about color as one element of visual arts, preschool children can learn the names of different colors (A); skills of sensory discrimination (B) in telling different colors apart from each other; and skills of classification (D) by separating different colors and experimenting with mixing colors to see what other colors they produce.

20. B: When preschool teachers prompt children to use different body postures and movements to portray various emotions, the children do get appreciable physical exercise (A); learn ways to express emotions (B) in ways that are concrete so they can understand them and reinforce them through a physical connection; and, while having fun (C) and using creative thinking (D).

21. A: Teachers can access different learning styles whereby individual students learn best by creating presentations that deliver input to multiple modes of sensation and perception. Teachers can provide students with objective analysis and feedback (b) by making video recordings of them

Copyright © Mometrix Media. You have been licensed one copy of this document for personal use only. Any other reproduction or redistribution is strictly prohibited. All rights reserved. This content is provided for test preparation purposes only and does not imply an endorsement by Mometrix of any particular political, scientific, or religious point of view.

during classroom activities. Technology also enables students, teachers, administrators, and other school staff to view documents (c), and enables parents at home to view them as well (d).

22. B: The less proficient in English an ELL student is, the more dependent s/he will be on cues from their first/native language (L1). Spanish-speaking children do NOT learn to sound out words the same ways as English-speaking children (A). In English, students are taught phonics, the 1:1 relationship of each sound to the letter representing it. In Spanish, however, students are taught to sound out words by the syllable, not the letter. ELL students do NOT use the same amount of cognitive energy as native English speakers (C) to develop English-language literacy: they exert TWICE the cognitive effort in attending to new phonemes, structures, meanings, and literacy skills and concepts. Directionality is NOT the same across languages (D): while English and European languages go left-to-right, Hebrew and Arabic letters go right-to-left (but Arabic numbers go left-to-right); and Chinese, Japanese, and Korean traditionally went top-to-bottom, but today may be vertical or horizontal.

23. D: Studies find the fact that poorer children tend to play with peers and older children with little intervention affords them the advantages of self-reliance, a sense of belonging; empathy, cooperation, and self-control. They also gain experience with modeling, observation, and imitation and other teaching styles. Moreover, the rich cultural traditions of many economically disadvantaged families use storytelling, songs, games, and toys which help children acquire language in culturally specific contexts, another advantage (C). Disadvantages of poverty include deficient education, nutrition, social stimulation, and social service support; and increased family stressors and medical illness (A), which lead to delinquency, school dropouts, unemployment, and perpetuated poverty. Also, lack of toys and inadequate verbal interactions are found to limit children's visual discrimination and language development (D).

24. C: ECE settings should keep certain things on file for medical emergencies, including detailed emergency treatment procedures; signed, written parent consent, which is necessary (A); parental preferences in doctors and hospitals (B); and information on the health insurance of children's families (C) as well as parent contact information. Notifying parents of emergencies is legally required (D) by licensing regulations; not notifying parents is subject to legal action.

25. C: Experts report that reflective teachers have no fear of either self-evaluation (a) or evaluation by others (b), but rather want their self-improvement efforts to be informed by feedback from other experienced educators (c) and are motivated to improve mainly to serve their students best rather than to receive better appraisals (d).

26. C: Elements of structuring classes logically to enhance communication with all students include presenting them with problems and then developing solutions (a); recounting processes or events in chronological sequence (b); showing them how interconnected ideas in content are related to its main, overarching themes (c); providing outlines; and presenting topics as stories (d) to help students relate to them through narrative structure instead of viewing them as collections of unrelated or irrelevant information.

27. A: Initial learning experiences among young children typically occur within their family, cultural, and community environments. By self-educating to learn about the community, teachers can gain insight into their students' individual backgrounds, experiences, and needs. This will ultimately allow the teacher to develop more relevant, meaningful, and responsive learning experiences for all students. In addition, by learning more about students as individuals, teachers can begin recognizing areas in which they may have personal biases toward other groups and

Copyright © Mometrix Media. You have been licensed one copy of this document for personal use only. Any other reproduction or redistribution is strictly prohibited. All rights reserved. This content is provided for test preparation purposes only and does not imply an endorsement by Mometrix of any particular political, scientific, or religious point of view.

cultures, and work to eliminate them so as to create an inclusive, welcoming, and supportive learning environment.

28. D: It is easier for adults to find out what young children understand about abstract concepts during one to one conversations than in group conversations. At preschools, adults should engage each child in one on one conversations at times like when children arrive and leave; during center time; and during shared reading activities with 1-2 children rather than during whole-group activities (A). 1:1 conversations enable adults to reinforce what children say by repeating it better in one on one than in group discussions (B). Adults also have *more* chance to extend what children say by adding to it in 1:1 conversations (C); and to restate what children say so they hear their own ideas reflected back to them one on one than in group conversations.

29. A: Early childhood education experts recommend providing at least 35 square feet indoors and 75 square feet outdoors of usable play space for learning environments. (B) would not be enough room for typical young children to engage in usual activities and avoid fighting or competing among age groups. (C) and (D) would be excellent but do not reflect the recommended *minimums*.

30. C: Testing a hypothesis requires conducting research, e.g., doing an experiment, making field observations, or administering a survey and analyzing the results. Watching videos (a), reading textbooks (b), and listening to lectures (d)—even while taking notes—are not experiential learning activities because they do not involve hands-on learning activities in which students participate directly. Rather than passively absorbing information, students learn by doing in experiential activities.

31. D: Chalkboards, dry-erase boards, and overhead projections are useful for showing reasoning visually and teaching dynamically, as well as illustrating processes. Utilizing media need not distract (a); teachers can use media to enhance instructional communication in helping explain, clarify, and illustrate complex ideas. Slide presentations are best for organizing varied content, summarizing ideas, and emphasizing key points (b). Animations and videos are best for imparting a sense of scale and depicting dynamic processes (c).

32. D: School-age children are likely to be working on ongoing projects which toddlers and preschoolers will not; and other activities that are age-appropriate for older children are not for younger ones, so the school-age children should have separate areas provided for their activities. Furniture should NOT be lightweight and easy to move around (A): while this would facilitate rearrangements in other cases, for infants and toddlers to pull up, balance, and cruise, the furniture must be heavy, sturdy, and bolted in place. Art and cooking activities should be near sinks or other water sources (B) to enable easier cleanup. There should be separate areas for dramatic play, block-building, book-reading, and music activities (C).

33. D: Experts in early childhood education identify child age (a), individual child growth patterns (b), and cultural influences (c) as three main, essential aspects for educators to consider in the assessment methods, classrooms, and instructional techniques they use in order to establish developmentally appropriate instructional practices.

34. B: Parten identified, in order of social maturity, (1) Unoccupied; (2) Independent or Solitary play; (3) Onlooker behavior; (4) Parallel play; (5) Associative play; and (6) Cooperative play. She found playing alone, i.e., Independent play (a) less socially mature; then observing others playing (Onlooker behavior); then playing alongside/near others but separately, i.e., Parallel play (d); then interacting with others playing without coordination or organization, i.e., Associative play (c); and

Copyright © Mometrix Media. You have been licensed one copy of this document for personal use only. Any other reproduction or redistribution is strictly prohibited. All rights reserved. This content is provided for test preparation purposes only and does not imply an endorsement by Mometrix of any particular political, scientific, or religious point of view.

the most socially mature as interacting with others in organized, coordinated play including assigned/assumed roles and interest in both activity and playmates, i.e., Cooperative play (b).

35. B: According to research findings, when teachers provide regular formats for note-taking, this gives them guidelines to follow, making note-taking easier, and students can refine these formats as needed. Studies also find that teachers should not only assign students practice in summarizing, but also provide them with rules for summarizing (a). Another research-based recommendation is that teachers may prepare their own notes if needed to help young students learn how to take notes properly (c). Another way teachers can help students take notes is to prepare their lessons in outline form: as students take notes, the notes will naturally follow the same form, making them more organized and easier to review (d).

36. A: Slide show presentations are valuable for providing brief, concise summaries of a lesson's main points, facts, and concepts as the teacher states these while giving additional information. The slides provide redundancy and highlight the most important parts of the lesson. They are meant to accompany, not replace, the teacher's delivery (b). They reduce lesson information to main points rather than adding many details (c), which students can get from the teacher, the textbook, class discussion, etc. They should not be shown only before lessons as previews (d), since students cannot remember everything.

37. B: By modeling how to create a pattern using beads and providing a hands-on learning experience, the teacher implements age-appropriate and meaningful instruction. In asking open-ended questions as students work, the teacher effectively promotes inquiry and challenges students to employ logical reasoning skills to explain their choice in beads. This strategy also supports the development of students' language skills by encouraging them to elaborate upon their thought processes.

38. A: Anecdotal records (B) provide valuable information that may not be captured in forms that teachers fill out for other informal assessments, but they are most often reports of occasional events or observations. Portfolio assessments (C) compile children's work products over periods of time, offering first-hand records of progress and cumulative assessments, but still limit evaluation of progress to separate examples created at separate points in time. Observational checklists (D) completed at regular intervals also show progress and/or change over time, but again only as snapshots of particular moments. Running records (A), however, are the most continuous of the informal assessments named.

39. D: Screening instruments are typically more likely to be simpler to score and interpret, often being possible to complete right after administration for sharing with stakeholders. Screening instruments are often used to indicate whether further assessment is needed. Assessment instruments are typically more thorough and involve more complicated scoring and interpretation that take longer. Results and interpretations can be shared with stakeholders later in scheduled meetings. Some techniques common in standardized assessment instruments include interpreting scores by reversing the point values of some items (B); by comparing a student's scores to tables showing the national norms (C) for students of the same age or grade level; and/or converting raw scores (the actual numbers the administrator gave to student responses) to standardized scores or percentages. In contrast, interpreting scores on screening instruments can be as simple as comparing them to a designated cut-off score (D) for further assessment.

40. D: For informal assessments of pre-K classes, teachers can make classroom observations during story or circle times, each observation targeting different skills like math, alphabet knowledge, social-emotional skills, emergent writing, oral language, etc. They can make these observations

Copyright © Mometrix Media. You have been licensed one copy of this document for personal use only. Any other reproduction or redistribution is strictly prohibited. All rights reserved. This content is provided for test preparation purposes only and does not imply an endorsement by Mometrix of any particular political, scientific, or religious point of view.

during both small-group (A) and whole-class (B) activities. They should organize the assessments using around three themes per day (C).

41. B: It is more advantageous for ECE programs to use tests that cover the entire age range that their programs serve. This is because they not only can assess all ages of children in the program (A) with equal accuracy (D), but also because they are easier to administer and then re-administer later to monitor children's progress in the program than separate, age-specific tests are; they can also be administered during a program for progress monitoring (B); and they are easier to administer at the beginnings and ends of programs for comparison than separate, age-specific tests are (C).

42. A: When a screening tool identifies a potential mental health disorder, and then a complete diagnostic evaluation confirms this prediction by diagnosing an actual mental health disorder, the screening tool has demonstrated good predictive validity. An instrument correctly identifying 6 of 10 children _with_ developmental disorders or delays is said to have a _sensitivity_ of 60%, not specificity (B). An instrument correctly identifying 8 of 10 children _without_ disorders or delays has 80% _specificity_, not sensitivity (C). Identification of delays/disorders where none exist constitutes false-_positive_ errors (D).

43. C: Scoring two or more standard deviations (SDs) below the mean (average) on a standardized IQ test is commonly accepted as indicating that a child may have delayed or atypical intellectual development. Thus one SD (b) is incorrect. On standardized IQ tests used today, one SD = 15 points. Hence 10 points (a) would not be enough to indicate potentially delayed or atypical intellectual development. Since IQ scores are used to indicate possible delayed/atypical intellectual development, (d) is incorrect.

44. B: As students demonstrate understanding in various ways, it is important to implement multiple strategies for determining instructional effectiveness, engagement, and overall understanding. Doing so provides comprehensive feedback regarding individual and whole-class needs, allowing teachers to adjust instructional strategies and activities as necessary to support all students' success in learning.

45. D: Piaget used the term _conservation_ to mean the ability children develop in the stage of Concrete Operations to conserve the concept of the same quantity regardless of changes in appearance, shape, or arrangement. He did not use this term to refer to conserving natural resources (A) or retaining memories of quantities (B). (C) describes what Piaget termed object permanence.

46. A: The Sensorimotor stage is from birth to roughly age 2; the Preoperational stage from roughly ages 2-7 years; and the Concrete Operations stage from roughly ages 7-11 years. Therefore, infants to eight-year-olds are typically in one of these stages. The Formal Operations stage {(B), (C)} is around the age of 11 years and older. Therefore, answers (D) is incorrect.

47. C: The High Scope Curriculum of Weikart et al identifies 58 key experiences, divided into 10 main categories. These include Classification (A), wherein preschoolers sort, match, and describe by shape objects or pictures; Seriation (B), wherein preschoolers arrange things in order by size, number, etc.; Space (C), wherein preschoolers experiment with spaces by filling and emptying variously sized and shaped containers; and Time (D), wherein preschoolers learn concepts of starting, sequencing, and stopping various actions. The activities of the Space category best prepare preschoolers for Piaget's concept of conservation of volume, whereby they will eventually learn

Copyright © Mometrix Media. You have been licensed one copy of this document for personal use only. Any other reproduction or redistribution is strictly prohibited. All rights reserved.
This content is provided for test preparation purposes only and does not imply an endorsement by Mometrix of any particular political, scientific, or religious point of view.

Mometrix

that amounts of solids and liquids stay the same despite being placed into containers of different sizes and shapes.

48. A: If an adult without custody or otherwise unauthorized attempts to pick up a child from an ECE facility, the administrator should inform the adult of the center's policies and procedures, including showing them their copy of the court's custody order (A) if needed. If the adult refuses to leave, threatens or shows violence or makes a scene, the ECE should call the police if necessary (B). If the adult leaves, the ECE administrator must not only notify the parents or other adult(s) who enrolled the child of the incident; s/he must also file a written report of it (C), meet with the custodial adult to review and/or update custody arrangements; document the meeting (D) including signatures and dates, and file the documentation in the child's center record.

49. B: PDCs work with new teachers and their mentors to ensure teachers' PD goals meet school district guidelines, and sometimes they even pay workshop tuition (a). They also provide documentation for state licensure boards of new teachers' efforts to meet state requirements (b) by approving the teachers' PD plans (PDPs). They collaborate with school district administrators in setting both interdisciplinary (c) and subject-specific district-wide professional teacher goals (d).

50. A: FERPA, the Family Educational Rights and Privacy Act (1974), and IDEA, the Individuals with Disabilities Education Act (1975), both give students' parents and eligible students similar rights to privacy, confidentiality, review, inspection, correction requests, formal hearings, contesting, and advance notice and nondisclosure of directory information regarding schools' student educational records. Hence (d) is incorrect. IDEA guarantees the right of students with disabilities to equal education (b), not FERPA. Privacy and portability of student healthcare information (c) is included in HIPAA (Health Information Portability and Accountability Act, 1996).

Language Arts and Reading

1. A: Students with dyslexia tend to perform much worse than their intelligence and knowledge would indicate on objective formats like multiple-choice tests. They are likely to have *equal* amounts of difficulty with reading short function words (e.g., *an, on, in*) as with reading long, multisyllabic words (B). While they do have trouble with fluid thinking, e.g., thinking "on the spot" to produce spoken and/or written verbal responses, they also have equal difficulty with retaining and/or retrieving names, dates, random lists, phone numbers, and other information through rote memorization and recall (C). Students with dyslexia typically have more trouble understanding words in isolation than in context (D), because they rely on the surrounding context to comprehend word meanings.

2. C: When reading independently, students are at the correct level if they read with at least 97% accuracy.

3. D: One way teachers can use individual observations for informal assessments is to fill out a chart divided into domains like physical development, oral language development, math, emergent reading and writing, science, health, fine arts, technology and media, social studies, social-emotional development, and approaches to learning with one child's strengths and needs in each domain per chart. Another way is to complete a checklist (A). Another is to keep running records, and/or use anecdotal records (B) of children's progress. Teachers can also assemble portfolio assessments of children's work (C) as informal assessments of their learning over time.

4. A: The words in this question prompt are most often used to refer to *sounds* made while reading. Initial/onset, medial, and final sounds are decoded in the beginning, middle, and end of words.

241

Copyright © Mometrix Media. You have been licensed one copy of this document for personal use only. Any other reproduction or redistribution is strictly prohibited. All rights reserved.
This content is provided for test preparation purposes only and does not imply an endorsement by Mometrix of any particular political, scientific, or religious point of view.

When a teacher needs to assess an emergent or struggling reader's ability to differentiate between sounds in words, he or she may use a phonological awareness assessment. This tool will provide the teacher with information about the student's current ability to decode or encode words.

5. D: While all children will acquire literacy skills at individual rates, there are general developmental characteristics associated with each age group. Recognizing atypical patterns of development is essential to identifying potential delays or learning disabilities so as to provide early intervention. By third grade, most neurotypical students have developed the ability to recognize and spell high-frequency sight words and write with a degree of accuracy and fluency. In this situation, the student is displaying possible signs of dyslexia, which is a learning disability that can significantly impede literacy skill development, particularly in the domains of reading and writing, if not properly addressed. As such, upon noticing these signs, it is important that the teacher refer this student for an initial evaluation to determine the need for special education services. Doing so will help to ensure he receives the supports and accommodations necessary to promote his literacy skill development.

6. A: Within normal development, individual children do vary (B) as to when they reach developmental milestones in spoken language. Due this variance, normal oral language development is represented in ranges rather than specific ages (C). In addition to developing at different ages within ranges, normally developing children also vary in the rates (D) at which they develop oral language skills.

7. C: Linguists have found through research studies that not only do preschool children invent spellings for words before they have learned their actual spellings, but moreover, preschoolers from diverse backgrounds all choose the same phonetic spellings, at a rate higher than can be attributed to chance (D) or adult influences (B). The researchers have concluded that through these common invented, phonetic spellings, young children demonstrate comprehension—not a lack thereof (A)—of the phonetic characteristics of words, and of how conventional word spellings symbolize these characteristics.

8. A: First, a child typically shows no knowledge of the correct direction in which to write (left-right, top-bottom in English); then partial knowledge, e.g., *either* left-right *or* top-bottom *or* moving from the upper right at the end of one line to the left for the next line; then reversed writing direction; then correct directionality; then correct direction plus correct spacing between words.

9. B: Researchers have found that the writing process both forms a hierarchy and is observably recursive. Moreover, they find that when students continually revise their writing, they are able to consider new ideas and to incorporate these ideas into their work. Therefore, choice B is correct. Students who are rewriting and revising do not merely correct mechanical errors (A); they also add to the content and quality of their writing. Furthermore, research shows that writers (including students) not only revise their actual writing during rewrites, but they also reconsider their original writing goals rather than always retaining them (C), and they revisit their prewriting plans rather than leaving these unaffected (D).

10. D: Asking children to write a list provides them with a visual model that is a side-by-side comparison of the two countries. In creating that visual model, each student first has to organize his or her thoughts mentally, deciding whether each particular item under consideration is shared between both countries or is a difference between them.

11. C: Once the students' notecards have been checked and edited for accuracy, they can easily be used to demonstrate the process of organizing ideas in an essay or research paper. Students can use

Copyright © Mometrix Media. You have been licensed one copy of this document for personal use only. Any other reproduction or redistribution is strictly prohibited. All rights reserved.
This content is provided for test preparation purposes only and does not imply an endorsement by Mometrix of any particular political, scientific, or religious point of view.

their notecards as aids for making their outlines. They simply have to arrange the notecards in an appropriate order and add pertinent information to bridge the ideas together in their writing.

12. B: Tone is the writer's attitude in a given piece of writing, as it is expressed in that writing. Voice can be thought of as the person who the reader "hears"—the particular way an individual writer expresses themselves. Choice B fills in the blanks correctly. Style (C and D) includes both of these and more; it is the effect a writer creates through purposeful use of all the elements of written language, from tone and voice to grammar and structure.

13. A: Implementing activities to promote students' oral language skills is integral to establishing a foundation for literacy development and academic achievement across content areas. Teaching prekindergarten students to listen responsively enhances a variety of skills, including receptive language, communication, and problem-solving. Incorporating listening games that include simple, multi-step directions provides young children with the opportunity to practice this skill in an engaging and developmentally-appropriate setting. When implementing such activities, teachers must ensure directions are clear, concise, and limited to only a few steps, so as not to distract, confuse, or overwhelm students.

14. B: Inventive spelling occurs when students employ their knowledge of letter-sound relationships to spell unfamiliar words. As spelling development occurs in stages, it is important to recognize that many young children will rely on inventive spelling as they begin learning to write. Encouraging this practice has students use their sense of phonemic awareness to sound out new words, ultimately improving their spelling abilities. However, the teacher must correct misspelled words to ensure proper development. Students that continue to use inventive spelling past the normal developmental stage may require additional support and intervention.

15. D: Compound sentences occur when two independent clauses are joined by a conjunction, such as "and" or "but." This concept builds on students' knowledge of simple sentences, which consist of only one independent clause. Teaching the components and formation of compound sentences is important in developing students' ability to write on a more complex level, as well as their understanding of the characteristics and functions of the English language. Introducing compound sentences using kinesthetic materials, such as sentence-building strips, allows students to explore this concept in a hands-on learning setting. This strategy allows students to physically construct sentences using independent clauses and conjunctions, strengthening their understanding.

16. A: Simple sentences are independent clauses that are composed of a single subject and predicate. This sentence structure is typically the first to be introduced in the early childhood classroom once students have acquired a basic command of standard English conventions, which include parts of speech, spelling, grammar, and punctuation. It is important that teachers ensure students possess this foundational understanding prior because the ability to construct simple sentences is essential to writing fluency development. In order to recognize subjects and predicates, students must be able to identify basic nouns and verbs. Administering a diagnostic pretest to assess students' knowledge in this area prior to beginning a unit on simple sentences allows teachers to identify areas of misconception and provide clarification or reteaching as necessary. Students that are adequately prepared with the skills necessary to form simple sentences will be able to express themselves more clearly in writing and ultimately will develop a greater understanding of increasingly complex stylistic techniques.

17. A: Oral language development occurs when young children have multiple opportunities to engage in daily conversations. Doing so allows them to practice using spoken language while building skills as they listen to others. As students will inevitably make errors in grammar, word

Copyright © Mometrix Media. You have been licensed one copy of this document for personal use only. Any other reproduction or redistribution is strictly prohibited. All rights reserved.
This content is provided for test preparation purposes only and does not imply an endorsement by Mometrix of any particular political, scientific, or religious point of view.

choice, and sentence structure, teachers must be diligent to reinforce correct usage while promoting students' confidence in speaking. When such errors occur, it is important that teachers refrain from explicitly correcting students, but rather, rephrase their sentence and repeat it back to model proper language use. This approach allows students to self-correct by listening and imitating the teacher's speech patterns for continuous skill development.

18. D: Good children's books should feature plots that are well-constructed, and are original but not incredible. Narrative books should feature story characters who are believable, which includes their changing (A) and growing as a result of their experiences like real people do, rather than staying the same throughout the story. Adults choosing children's literature should seek books with themes of value to children, but avoid books with overtly moralistic themes (B). Likewise they should avoid books that promote racial, gender, and other stereotypes (C).

19. D: Basal reader series feature texts that are graded by reading levels (A), include both expository and narrative writing (B), and in children's literature and various other writing genres (C) are thematically organized by unit (D).

20. C: When teaching students about various media types, the four categories listed as choices are ways to classify them. One-on-one communication media includes emails, phone calls, and letters but not books. Entertainment media includes movies, TV shows, and video games; novels are included, but not the wider class of books. (Note that there are many more kinds of books than novels.) Informative media includes books, newspapers, websites, and radio news broadcasts. Persuasive media includes advertising, direct mail marketing, telemarketing calls, and infomercials.

21. D: According to Pennsylvania's PreK-4 standards in language arts, kindergarten students can reasonably be expected to demonstrate fundamental reading comprehension, interpretation, and analysis of grade-level-appropriate works of literature. This includes using literary elements within a story to derive meaning, as well as identifying and recalling key details with prompting and support. The teacher can expect that after hearing the story read aloud and engaging in several corresponding activities, students will be able to identify the setting, characters, and major events within the work of literature. While it is important to account for individual differences in developmental levels, teachers can use academic standards as a framework for measuring student progress.

22. D: Prereading strategies enhance overall student engagement and comprehension. Activities such as anticipation guides serve to provide context, establish purpose for reading, and elicit prior knowledge to strengthen understanding, evoke interest, and make the learning experience meaningful and relevant for students. These guides typically ask students to agree or disagree with a series of statements related to the reading, and to make predictions about the text. This encourages students to actively engage with the text as they determine whether their predictions were correct, or whether their original opinions remained the same during and after reading, which promotes comprehension.

23. C: Acquisition and comprehension of academic language is a common challenge among young children. Early language development typically occurs in familiar settings, and reflects children's daily interactions and experiences, whereas academic language is content-specific, often more complex in nature, and therefore harder to understand. However, this skill is necessary for literacy development and success in learning across subject areas. In this situation, the teacher implements before-, during-, and after-reading strategies to promote understanding of the academic language students will encounter in the informational text. The teacher contextualizes new vocabulary by providing definitions and examples before students read the text, creating a framework for

Copyright © Mometrix Media. You have been licensed one copy of this document for personal use only. Any other reproduction or redistribution is strictly prohibited. All rights reserved. This content is provided for test preparation purposes only and does not imply an endorsement by Mometrix of any particular political, scientific, or religious point of view.

increased comprehension. By having students complete guided summary frames as they engage with the text, the teacher encourages close reading that promotes students' ability to summarize, and therefore, demonstrate understanding, of what they have read. Additionally, in instructing students to discuss their summaries with a partner, the teacher encourages students to practice using academic language, thus strengthening their comprehension of its meaning.

24. A: Contextual analysis skills, or the ability to look for clues within a text to decipher the meaning of unfamiliar words, are essential to vocabulary acquisition and reading comprehension. Examples of context clues include synonyms, antonyms, examples, or definitions that are embedded throughout the text and indicate the meaning of the new word. Teaching students to locate and use these clues helps them learn to make educated guesses regarding the meaning of unfamiliar terms, which increases vocabulary and improves reading comprehension skills.

25. B: In language arts, sequencing refers to one's ability to recall and retell events of a text in the order in which they occurred. Teaching this important skill is essential to promoting success across content areas, as it contributes to the development of reading comprehension and writing, as well as the ability to understand and respond appropriately to directions. By kindergarten, students can reasonably be expected to retell the major events of a fictional work of literature in the order in which they occurred using visual aids as support. In this situation, having students sort events from the story using picture cards would most effectively promote their sequencing abilities.

26. A: Familiarizing young children with the illustrations in a story prior to reading the text is highly beneficial in promoting overall comprehension. Doing so helps emergent readers formulate connections between pictures and corresponding text, thus promoting their ability to make predictions, sequence events, recall major details, and grasp the meaning of unfamiliar vocabulary. Activities such as picture walks, in which students are shown and prompted to discuss the illustrations in a story prior to hearing it read aloud, are an effective method for building students' background knowledge and providing context to establish the foundation necessary for greater overall comprehension.

27. C: Reading comprehension refers to one's ability to read and construct meaning from a text. Young children typically develop through three increasingly advanced levels of reading comprehension ability as they build language and literacy skills. Beginning readers first comprehend text on a literal level and can understand the basic meaning of words and sentences. As students progress, they develop inferential reading skills, or the ability to interpret context clues to derive an implied meaning. Evaluative or critical reading comprehension skills occur when readers are able to relate what they have read to their own background knowledge and experiences to form personal thoughts and opinions. Implementing reading response journals into the early childhood classroom is an effective method for developing students' evaluative reading comprehension skills. This versatile resource can be differentiated to align with a variety of purposes and abilities as students are prompted to closely examine various aspects of a given text. In this situation, the teacher asks students to reflect upon their reactions, opinions, and thoughts about the short novel, thus promoting the development of their evaluative reading comprehension skills.

28. C: Children develop phonological awareness through a combination of incidental learning via being naturally exposed to language in their environments, and receiving direct instruction from adults. They do not develop it solely through one or the other, or neither.

29. A: Articulation is the correct pronunciation of speech sounds (phonemes), and articulation disorders are characterized by incorrectly pronouncing one or multiple phonemes beyond the

Copyright © Mometrix Media. You have been licensed one copy of this document for personal use only. Any other reproduction or redistribution is strictly prohibited. All rights reserved. This content is provided for test preparation purposes only and does not imply an endorsement by Mometrix of any particular political, scientific, or religious point of view.

usual age range norms for the speech sound (age norms are older for more difficult sounds). Voice disorders (B) affect voice qualities like nasality, pitch, volume, and tone rather than pronunciation of specific phonemes. Aphasias (C) are cognitive language-processing disorders that affect language comprehension and/or production (e.g., word retrieval, grammatical sentence composition). Delayed language development (D) falls behind normal developmental ranges for understanding and producing language, but not necessarily speech sounds.

30. A: Phonemic awareness is the ability to recognize sounds within words, so it is a type of phonological awareness. Segmenting words and blending sounds are components of phonemic awareness. Phonological awareness includes an understanding of multiple components of spoken language. The ability to hear individual words within a vocalized stream and the ability to identify spoken syllables are types of phonological awareness.

31. C: According to the Association of College and Research Libraries, information literacy is the set of skills that an individual must have for the finding, retrieval, analysis, and use of information. While it is required for reading and understanding information, it is required for more than this, so choice A is incorrect. It does not necessarily or exclusively involve retaining a lot of information or communicating information effectively, so choices B and C are incorrect. Rather, information literacy involves knowing how to find information, how to evaluate information critically, and how to apply information judiciously to meet specific purposes.

32. A: The whole language approach, as its name implies, is holistic in nature and founded on constructivist principles; it supports children in constructing their own knowledge and meaning through interacting with their environments (B). This approach does emphasize the integration of literacy instruction across the various subject content domains (C). It also emphasizes cultural diversity in learners, instruction, and learning (D). However, because it is holistic rather than analytical like phonics, the whole language approach is NOT as effective for children who have language processing disorders and/or reading disorders because they require explicit instruction to learn the decoding skills and strategies that other children learn incidentally as they learn to read and write.

33. B: Coarticulation affects phonemic awareness. Vocalizing words involves arranging a series of continuous, voiced, unvoiced, and stop sounds. As one sound is being uttered, the tongue and lips are already assuming the shape required by the next sound in the word. This process, which is not conscious, can distort individual sounds. One sound can slur into another, clip the end of the previous sound, or flatten or heighten a sound. For children who have difficulty hearing distinct phonemic sounds, individual instruction may be required.

34. C: Blending syllables is an important phonological processing skill that refers to one's ability to connect individual sounds within words. This skill is integral to developing reading comprehension skills, and therefore, it must be addressed when a student is having difficulty. In this situation, having the student practice spelling words using letter tiles, reading the words aloud, and clapping out syllables helps to strengthen awareness of how sounds work together. Such activities provide a multisensory intervention that lets the student visualize, verbalize, and physically manipulate multisyllabic blended words, promoting the development of this skill.

35. D: Learning to name and identify objects is an essential component of speech and language development. This concept should be integrated throughout all areas of the early childhood curriculum. Strategies that promote receptive language skills, such as labeling items in the classroom with words and corresponding images, help young children learn the names of objects

Copyright © Mometrix Media. You have been licensed one copy of this document for personal use only. Any other reproduction or redistribution is strictly prohibited. All rights reserved. This content is provided for test preparation purposes only and does not imply an endorsement by Mometrix of any particular political, scientific, or religious point of view.

around them. This provides consistent exposure to vocabulary in a variety of contexts to reinforce understanding and increase retention.

36. C: Orthographic mapping refers to a process that occurs when the reader uses knowledge of letter-sound correspondence to recognize and recall the spelling, pronunciation, and meaning of written words. This process is necessary to build the word recognition skills and automaticity necessary for developing reading fluency. When introducing new vocabulary, teachers can stimulate orthographic mapping by having students separate the words into individual sounds to demonstrate the phonemic-graphemic relationship. This strategy helps students commit new words to memory, thus promoting vocabulary acquisition and sight word recognition. Further, having students tap out each phoneme as they read it aloud adds a kinesthetic element, thus strengthening connections for greater understanding.

37. B: As young children develop their language and literacy skills, teachers can begin introducing increasingly complex linguistic units into phonics instruction. A trigraph refers to a group of three letters that are pronounced as a single phoneme. Examples include the letter combinations "tch," "ear," "igh," and "eye." Trigraphs can consist exclusively of consonants, vowels, or a combination of both. In the above example, all three words are spelled with the "tch" letter combination to form a single phoneme; thus, all contain a consonant trigraph.

38. B: Students with strong morphological awareness skills are more effectively able to construct, comprehend, and communicate meaning when interacting with language; therefore, they experience greater development across literacy domains. Morphological awareness refers to one's ability to recognize and distinguish the individual morphemes, or units of language, that words are composed of. This knowledge promotes students' phonological and orthographic processing abilities, thus enhancing vocabulary acquisition as well as reading comprehension, writing, speaking, and listening skills. In this situation, the teacher is using a multisensory approach to build students' morphological awareness by having them create vocabulary flip-books to form words out of prefixes, roots, and suffixes. This activity allows students to physically interact with the words and practice using them by reading them aloud to a table partner, thus strengthening their connections and overall understanding of the concept.

39. C: Silent reading fluency can be monitored over time by giving the Test of Silent Contextual Reading Fluency (TSCRF) four times a year. A similar assessment tool is the Test of Silent Word Reading Fluency (TOSWRF), in which words of increasing complexity are given as a single, undifferentiated, and unpunctuated strand. As with the TSCRF, three minutes are given for the student to separate each word from the next.
Itwillcannotschoolbecomeagendaconsistentphilosophysuperfluous is an example of such a strand.

40. C: The most helpful strategy for discerning which of two homonyms (sound-alike words) is correct without knowing the spelling is its surrounding context of the sentence, paragraph, and/or book and subject matter. For example, "Mexico cedes land" and "Mexico seeds land" sound the same, but if the context continues "to the United States," the meaning of "cedes" applies. Pictures (A) help children identify unknown words rather than differentiate homonyms. Phonics (B) help students sound out unfamiliar words, not differentiate meanings. Grammar (D) can help when one homonym is a verb and the other a noun, for example; but "cedes" and "seeds" are the same part of speech with different meanings, so grammar alone does not help as much as context.

41. C: While *some* children's reading lacks fluency due to deficits in their word-decoding abilities, this is not *always* (A) the case: some children simply need more reading practice to develop fluency. Children's motivation to read (B) *is* affected by their reading fluency: when reading is laborious,

Copyright © Mometrix Media. You have been licensed one copy of this document for personal use only. Any other reproduction or redistribution is strictly prohibited. All rights reserved. This content is provided for test preparation purposes only and does not imply an endorsement by Mometrix of any particular political, scientific, or religious point of view.

children do not enjoy it and avoid reading; when reading is easy, children enjoy it and want to read. Fluency has much *greater* impact (D) on the performance of students in higher grades, when the volume of reading required of them in school is exponentially greater.

42. B: Context clues offer insight into the probable meaning of unfamiliar words.

43. B: The basal reader approach is bottom-up in nature, not top-down (A); i.e., sub-skills for reading are taught from smaller to larger parts and parts to whole. Students are aided in transitions from the part to the whole through instruction in a systematic (B) sequence that is followed rigidly, and is not flexible (C). While fewer publishers have issued basal reading series in the twenty-first century than in the twentieth, the basal reader approach to teaching reading is still the most common one in America: approximately 75% to 85% of classrooms in grades K–8 still use basal readers, so they are not at all rare (D). Other than the number of publishers offering them, the main difference is that previous basal reading series before/during the twentieth century emphasized vocabulary control and skill acquisition at the expense of comprehension and pleasure; whereas twenty-first-century basal readers enhance student motivation to read more with multiple versions of stories, book excerpts enabling selection sharing, and other sources of greater variety.

44. B: Prior knowledge, which rises from experience and previous learning, provides a framework by which new knowledge gained from the act of reading can be integrated. Every act of reading enriches a student's store of prior knowledge and increases that student's future ability to comprehend more fully any new knowledge acquired through reading.

45. D: Fluent readers are able to read smoothly and comfortably at a steady pace (rate). The more quickly a child reads, the greater the chance of leaving out a word or substituting one word for another (for example, *sink* instead of *shrink*). Fluent readers are able to maintain accuracy without sacrificing rate. Fluent readers also stress important words in a text, group words into rhythmic phrases, and read with intonation (prosody).

46. A: A phoneme is a unit of language that represents the smallest unit of sound. For instance, the *k* in *kit* or the *ph* in *graph* both represent English phonemes. Graphemes are written phonemes and can be alphabetic letters, numbers, characters, punctuation marks, and so on. Neither phonemes nor graphemes have semantic meaning unless they are used as part of a larger unit of language, such as the morpheme. Morphemes can be roots, prefixes, and suffixes. The word *rechargeable* is comprised of three morphemes: *re*, *charge*, and *able*. Each component of this word has a meaning unto itself, but when combined with the others, each one is used to make a new word with a new meaning.

47. B: Sequencing in language arts is a reading comprehension skill that refers to one's ability to recall and arrange events from a text. If a student struggles with sequencing, the teacher must implement appropriate interventions, as development of this language skill is necessary for success in learning across content areas. For example, sequencing also applies to one's ability to follow a set of directions or steps in the correct order to solve problems; recognize cause and effect; and recall major events from history. In this situation, providing visual aids—such as graphic organizers, story maps, and pictures that correspond with events from stories—supports the student in developing this language skill. The teacher must continuously monitor this student's progress to determine if additional interventions are necessary.

48. D: Recognizing the characteristics and functions of English grammatical conventions is important for reading comprehension development. Further, modeling to students how these patterns apply to spoken language is necessary for fostering reading fluency and expressive

Copyright © Mometrix Media. You have been licensed one copy of this document for personal use only. Any other reproduction or redistribution is strictly prohibited. All rights reserved. This content is provided for test preparation purposes only and does not imply an endorsement by Mometrix of any particular political, scientific, or religious point of view.

language skills. By pausing between sentences, changing intonation, and correlating inflection with variances in punctuation within the text, the teacher effectively models the relationship between English grammatical patterns in written and spoken language.

49. B: Response to Intervention (RTI) is a three-tiered model intended to provide students that struggle in a particular content area with additional support. Each tier consists of increasingly intensive services designed to develop students' skills to a grade-appropriate level. Tier-one RTI services are generally applied to all students to promote universal understanding and achievement. Students that continue to have difficulty are typically referred for tier-two RTI services, in which they receive small-group instruction outside the classroom to develop their skills in the given subject area. Tier-three services are directed toward individual students in need of significant support. In this situation, the student likely has not responded to the tier-one interventions applied to the whole class, and therefore would benefit from receiving tier-two RTI services.

50. B: Developing students' range of vocabulary is essential to building reading comprehension skills. This includes teaching students that some words in English may have multiple meanings. Homonyms are words that are spelled and pronounced the same, but have different meanings, such as "right," "left," "bat," and "well." Providing consistent reminders of the various meanings of such words helps students internalize this difficult concept to promote retention and deepen their understanding of new vocabulary. After introducing homonyms to students through direct instruction, displaying the new vocabulary with corresponding images would give students a visual reference to reinforce the multiple meanings of these words.

Mathematics

1. D: Congruent figures have the same shape and the same size. Two squares have the same shape. If the areas are the same, they also have the same size and are congruent. Choice A is incorrect because two rectangles can have the same perimeter but not the same shape. Choice B is the incorrect because two polygons of the same shape are not necessarily the same size. Choice C is incorrect because two polygons can have the same side lengths but different shapes. Therefore, the correct answer is choice D.

2. C: Parents and other adults can best help children understand math concepts and procedures by helping them realize how these are applied in many different activities, including other academic subjects like the sciences, arts, and music and a variety of everyday life activities. They should NOT isolate math from life and other school subjects (A). They should NOT just let children do whatever they please and hope that they apply math in these activities (B); instead, they can engage them in activities applying math concepts, like sorting when putting away groceries or setting the table. They should not restrict working on math comprehension to formal math lessons (D), but seek and find math concepts and practices in everyday life routines and events. This will help them understand math better, as well as apply it in practical ways.

3. A: $3 + x + 3x + 3 + x = 5x + 6$ correctly shows how the combination of like terms on the left side of the equation results in the expression on the right side of the equation. $7x - 2x = 9x$ incorrectly combines like terms by adding the coefficients rather than subtracting them. $2y + 2y + 2y = 6y^3$ incorrectly adds the exponents of like terms instead of just adding the coefficients of like terms. $2.5(x + 2) = 2.5x + 2$ incorrectly distributes the 2.5 across by parentheses by neglecting to multiply the 2.5 with the last term in the expression.

4. B: The number line orders numbers from least to greatest. When comparing any two numbers, the smaller value will always be to the left of the greater value. Because –7 is less than –2, –7 will

Copyright © Mometrix Media. You have been licensed one copy of this document for personal use only. Any other reproduction or redistribution is strictly prohibited. All rights reserved. This content is provided for test preparation purposes only and does not imply an endorsement by Mometrix of any particular political, scientific, or religious point of view.

always be to the left of –2 on the number line. All of the other options have greater values placed to the left of smaller values. This can never be true on any number line.

5. D: Math education experts believe that when children can count to twenty, thirty, etc., to one hundred, they begin to discover the first consistent mathematical pattern they observe, that of base ten (i.e., twenty = two tens, thirty = three tens, etc., and we add only numbers from one to nine before reaching the next set of tens). Learning to count from one to twelve involves memorization, but NOT more unusual rules (A). Counting from thirteen to nineteen *does* involve less regular rules, in addition to the same amount of memorizing, NOT more (B). However, learning to count above twenty actually involves *more* consistent rules (C), and these facilitate children's recognition of the base ten pattern.

6. C: Introducing the concept of measurement through familiar activities, such as cooking, supports development of young children's' foundational understanding that attributes can be quantified. This strategy allows students to make connections to and expand upon prior knowledge for more effective learning. In this situation, engaging students in making a simple recipe in which ingredients are measured provides a hands-on activity that introduces measurement in a relevant context, supporting their development and learning of this concept.

7. C: The distance may be calculated using the distance formula, $d = \sqrt{(x_2 - x_1)^2 + (y_2 - y_1)^2}$. Substitute the given coordinates into the formula.

$$d = \sqrt{\left(4 - (-8)\right)^2 + (3 - 6)^2}$$
$$d = \sqrt{(12)^2 + (-3)^2}$$
$$d = \sqrt{144 + 9}$$
$$d = \sqrt{153}$$

Therefore, the distance between the two points is $\sqrt{153}$.

8. B: Since Mr. Mancelli has eight candy bars, he can make at most eight identical bags, each containing a single candy bar and a single package of gum; in this case, however, he will have four packages of gum remaining. To determine the greatest number of prize bags he can make so that no candy bars or packages of gum remain, he needs to find the largest number of groups that both 8 and 12 can be split into. In other words, he must find the greatest common divisor (or greatest common factor) of 8 and 12. The factors of 8 are 1, 2, 4, and 8. The factors of 12 are 1, 2, 3, 4, 6, and 12. The greatest common factor between these two numbers is 4. The greatest common divisor of 8 and 12 is 4. He can make four prize bags, each of which contains two candy bars and three packages of gum. Therefore, the correct choice is B.

9. B: Young children learn to count to three before they have learned all of the numbers' names; then they learn to count to five, etc. Thus, they do not know all number names before learning to count (A). Children's number sense does not equate to counting alone (C). It also includes understanding various applications of numbers—not only for describing quantities (D), but also for expressing and manipulating information, and for depicting relationships among things. Children who have developed good number sense can understand these functions as well as count, and they can count forward and backward, dismantle and reassemble numbers, and add and subtract them. These abilities facilitate their developing all other math skills.

10. D: Learning to keep track while counting is an important pre-numeracy skill that supports the ability to understand such concepts as ascending and descending order, cardinality, and one-to-one

Copyright © Mometrix Media. You have been licensed one copy of this document for personal use only. Any other reproduction or redistribution is strictly prohibited. All rights reserved. This content is provided for test preparation purposes only and does not imply an endorsement by Mometrix of any particular political, scientific, or religious point of view.

correspondence. When teaching prekindergarten children to count to ten, providing manipulatives such as counting chips creates an active, hands-on learning experience to support students in developing this skill. This strategy provides a kinesthetic element to learning by allowing students to physically move individual chips as they learn to count to ten, as well as a visual aid to help them keep track of how far they have counted.

11. C: Start by setting up a proportion to solve: $\frac{1\text{ inch}}{60\text{ feet}} = \frac{10\text{ inches}}{x\text{ feet}}$. When the numbers are cross multiplied, you get $x = 600$. Now we need to convert 600 feet to yards. There are 3 feet in 1 yard, so divide 600 by 3 to find the number of yards between the two points: $600 \div 3 = 200$. Therefore, the two points are 200 yards apart.

12. B: Mathematical communication skills are the ability to speak and write effectively using mathematical terms. This includes using mathematical language to discuss one's thoughts, reasoning, and problem-solving strategies. Mathematical communication skills are necessary for developing and building on concept knowledge, as they promote students' understanding of their own thinking, connections between mathematical ideas, and ability to verbalize their processes. In this situation, asking students how they got a particular answer prompts them to consider their own reasoning and explain each step of their problem-solving strategy, promoting mathematical communication skills.

13. A: The net of a triangular prism has three rectangular faces and two triangular faces, and the rectangular faces must all be able to connect to each other directly.

14. C: Promoting students' ability to think algebraically in early elementary school establishes a foundation for thinking abstractly when working with increasingly advanced mathematical concepts. To achieve this, teachers should introduce math experiences gradually as students develop mastery. This method allows young children to progress through increasingly complex levels of algebraic thinking as they learn, while also demonstrating that the same expression can be presented in multiple ways. When introducing a new mathematical concept, teachers should begin by doing so concretely, then pictorially, and ultimately, in abstract terms. For example, in this situation, the teacher could begin by having students work with manipulatives as they solve addition problems, then present the equation using pictures of familiar objects, and eventually, show them only the numerical equation. Doing so helps students learn how to think algebraically when approaching new mathematical concepts.

15. C: Ordering refers to the ability to correctly arrange a series of numbers, either by ones or by periodic intervals, in ascending or descending order. This pre-numeracy skill is necessary for developing understanding of a range of foundational mathematical concepts, so it must be addressed when a student is having difficulty. Having students who struggle in this area practice representing numbers using a chart and counting chips provides a hands-on opportunity to physically manipulate and visualize the difference between numbers. This strategy supports the development of understanding of cardinality, and ultimately, how to correctly order numbers.

16. D: Zach's task was to round each number to the nearest tenth. However, Zach's work shows evidence of rounding each number to the nearest whole number. When 14.51 is rounded to the nearest whole number it becomes 15. If Zach had correctly rounded 14.51 to the nearest tenth, it would have become 14.5.

17. B: Ordinal numbers do not indicate the quantity of things but rather their order in a series or set, i.e., the rank or position of each member—the first and third tables here. Choice (A) is an example of cardinal numbers, which indicate quantity or how many—here, four years and two

Copyright © Mometrix Media. You have been licensed one copy of this document for personal use only. Any other reproduction or redistribution is strictly prohibited. All rights reserved.
This content is provided for test preparation purposes only and does not imply an endorsement by Mometrix of any particular political, scientific, or religious point of view.

years old. Choice (C) is an example of a nominal number, i.e., one that indicates neither rank nor quantity, but rather a number used as a name to identify something—here, the shirt number of a team player (six). Choice (D) is an example of using rational numbers, i.e., divisions/ratios of integers, or more simply, fractions—two-thirds and one-third here.

18. A: The set of integers, $\{-3, -2, -1, 0, 1, 2, 3, \ldots\}$, does not contain fractions. Since $\frac{1}{4}$ is a rational, real number, it cannot be an irrational number.

19. D: The cross-section is a hexagon.

20. A: The vertical line of symmetry is represented by an equation of the form $x = a$. The horizontal line of symmetry is represented by an equation of the form $y = b$. One line of symmetry occurs at $x = -4$. The other line of symmetry occurs at $y = 6$.

21. A: The repeating decimal may be converted to a fraction by writing:

$$\begin{aligned} 10x &= 7.\overline{7} \\ - \quad x &= 0.\overline{7} \end{aligned}$$

which simplifies as $10x - x = 7.\overline{7} - 0.\overline{7}$, or $9x = 7.\overline{7} - 0.\overline{7}$.

22. B: When a child counts how many dots of one color there are in a fabric print before a different color is used, this activity is focused on identifying the pattern(s) in the print. Stringing beads with different colors in a pre-selected order (A), arranging and gluing down pieces of alternating sizes (C), and hopping on each foot for pre-determined different numbers of times (D) are all activities that are focused on *creating,* rather than *identifying,* patterns.

23. C: Children are innately curious about solving everyday problems (A); hence adults can make use of this natural characteristic by asking children to offer solutions. Once a child resolves a problem, the adult should also ask them to explain how they came to their solution. Practicing problem-solving not only teaches children to think mathematically; it also expedites language development and social skills development (B) when they work together with others. Experts advise adults not only to propose problems and ask questions about them to children, but also to have children do these things themselves (D). This gives them practice in how to think through and figure out things for themselves, as well as helping them realize that many problems have multiple and varied possible solutions.

24. B: A regular solid prism is a solid, three-dimensional shape which has length, width, and height. The bases are of the same shape, and the shape of the other faces depend on the shape of the bases. The volume of a regular solid prism can be determined by multiplying the area of the base by the height of the prism.

25. B: By having the children sort objects according to their similarities and differences in properties like size, texture, etc., the teacher is supporting the math concept of classifying, also

Copyright © Mometrix Media. You have been licensed one copy of this document for personal use only. Any other reproduction or redistribution is strictly prohibited. All rights reserved.
This content is provided for test preparation purposes only and does not imply an endorsement by Mometrix of any particular political, scientific, or religious point of view.

known as categorizing or sorting. The children are learning to group things according to common properties, and to separate groups that differ in the properties they share. Patterning (A) would be better supported by an activity in which they arrange objects with alternating properties—e.g., stringing three blue beads, then one yellow, then three blue, etc. Counting (C) would involve things like pointing to each object, identifying it by number "One, two, three…," and stating the total number of objects, rather than sorting them. Ordering (D) would be supported by activities wherein children arrange objects in a sequence from biggest to smallest or vice versa, or longest to shortest, etc., rather than grouping them.

26. B: Graham has placed Group 1 with 40¢, Group 2 with 38¢, and Group 3 with 29¢. Henry has placed Group 1 with 34¢, Group 2 with 27¢, and Group 3 with 29¢. Landon has placed Group 1 with 59¢, Group 2 with 43¢, and Group 3 with 57¢. Elizabeth has placed Group 1 with 39¢, Group 2 with 41¢, and Group 3 with 22¢.

27. B: Since the events are mutually exclusive, the sum of their individual probabilities is 1.0. Subtracting 0.6 from 1.0 yields 0.4. Therefore, the correct choice is B.

28. D: The 5 is in the tenths place, the 9 in the hundredths place, and the 3 in the thousandths place. Thus, 0.593 is equal to the sum of the product of 5 and $\frac{1}{10}$, the product of 9 and $\frac{1}{100}$, and the product of 3 and $\frac{1}{1,000}$.

29. D: The Pythagorean theorem may be used to find the diagonal distance from the top of the building to the base of the shadow. The following equation may be written and solved for c: $44^2 + 59.2^2 = c^2$. Thus, $c \approx 73.8$. The distance is approximately 73.8 ft.

30. B: This series lists the sum of the squares of natural numbers and 1. For example, $1^2 + 1$ is 2, and $2^2 + 1$ is 5. The next number in the series can be determined by $5^2 + 1$, which is 26. Note also that the differences between consecutive numbers in the series are consecutive odd integers starting at 3; for example, $2 + 3$ is 5, $5 + 5$ is 20, and $10 + 7$ is 17, so the next number in the series is $17 + 9$, or 26.

31. D: An effective way to help young children develop early math skills related to measurement is to ask them to help with everyday chores and activities that incorporate measurement—e.g., shopping, cooking, sewing, gardening, etc.—and use these activities to discuss measurement concepts and processes with the children as they participate directly, which is more effective than if they only watch the adult demonstrate (C). Adults should *not* discourage young children from using their own personal units of measurement (A); this is a natural and useful practice, as when a child says his friend is as tall as four teddy bears. Adults can moreover apply this practice to describe measurements in ways young children can understand better than if they tried to teach them standardized units of measurement in isolated lessons (B) with no real-life referents.

32. D: To understand fractions, children must know all of these things: what makes up a particular whole unit; how many pieces that unit is divided into; and whether the pieces are all of the same size or not. Knowing the number of parts but not what makes up the unit (A); knowing what comprises the whole unit, but not how many pieces into which it has been divided (B); or knowing both what makes up the whole unit and how many pieces it has been divided into, but not knowing whether the pieces are equal in size or not (C) will not allow children to comprehend the concept of fractions. For example, a child will not understand the idea of thirds if something is divided into three parts of *unequal* size, because each piece is not equal to one-third of the whole.

Copyright © Mometrix Media. You have been licensed one copy of this document for personal use only. Any other reproduction or redistribution is strictly prohibited. All rights reserved. This content is provided for test preparation purposes only and does not imply an endorsement by Mometrix of any particular political, scientific, or religious point of view.

33. B: It makes it easier for very young children to understand geometric concepts when adults provide them with concrete objects (A) that they can touch and move with their own hands. Very young children will also find it easier and more enjoyable to learn about geometric shapes to incorporate them into their normal everyday activities (C). For example, adults can cut children's sandwiches into various shapes, and then let the children arrange them to fit together and rearrange them to create new and different patterns. Using things that are familiar and pleasant to young children enhances their engagement and comprehension. Adults can also enhance infants' and toddlers' development of spatial sense by letting them play (supervised) in, on, under, around, and through things like large appliance cartons, furniture, etc.

34. C: An inversely proportional relationship is written in the form $y = \frac{k}{x}$, thus the equation $y = \frac{3}{x}$ shows that y is inversely proportional to x.

35. D: Formal benchmark assessments are administered periodically throughout the school year, and are intended to provide feedback regarding students' progress in meeting district and state academic standards in a given content area. The data from these assessments is used for a variety of purposes, including determining student readiness for the next grade level, evaluating instructional effectiveness, identifying potential need for remediation, and guiding teachers in the planning process. In this situation, administering a benchmark assessment at the end of the first semester will give the teacher insight regarding whole-class and individual students' strengths and needs. This will allow the teacher to make any necessary adjustments to instructional strategies, activities, accommodations, and supports to most effectively meet students' learning needs as they progress through the school year.

36. C: Pre-K and Kindergarten students are less likely to be able to display data in line graphs, bar graphs, picture graphs, charts, and timelines than students in grades 1 and 2 are. Younger children can gather common found objects during everyday play and other activities (e.g., acorns, leaves, socks, toys) and then sort them and compare their similarities and differences (A). They can also sort objects (or information) according to one given property, like color, amount, shape, size, etc., and group them accordingly (B). Younger children can additionally place objects onto a table graph or floor graph according to such groupings, and then identify which category or group contains the most or fewest objects (D).

37. A: Since the students are using manipulatives, this is a concrete representation.

38. D: This situation may be modeled by an arithmetic sequence, with a common difference of 4 and an initial value of 3. Substituting the common difference and initial value into the formula, $a_n = a_1 + (n - 1)d$, gives $a_n = 3 + (n - 1)(4)$, which simplifies to $a_n = 4n - 1$.

39. C: When teaching foundational mathematical skills to early childhood students, it is important to recognize the characteristics and abilities of their cognitive developmental levels. Prekindergarten students are in the preoperational stage of cognitive development and have not yet acquired concrete thinking skills. The ability to understand conservation—the idea that altering the appearance of something does not change the quantity—does not develop until the concrete operational stage of development. Therefore, when asked which group of unit cubes contained more, students were unable to recognize that both groups consisted of eight cubes. Rather, they selected the group that visually appeared larger.

40. A: Young children learn effectively when new mathematical concepts are placed in familiar, real-world contexts. This strategy fosters personal connections to learning, as students can see where it is relevant and applicable in their own lives. Showing images of analog clocks helps

Copyright © Mometrix Media. You have been licensed one copy of this document for personal use only. Any other reproduction or redistribution is strictly prohibited. All rights reserved. This content is provided for test preparation purposes only and does not imply an endorsement by Mometrix of any particular political, scientific, or religious point of view.

students internalize how to read them by providing a visual reference of how various times appear. Further, this concept is reinforced by corresponding each image to the time of each event on the class schedule. Doing so connects the idea of telling time with analog clocks to an immediately recognizable situation, making learning meaningful and promoting students' learning and development of this skill.

Science

1. A: The average distance from the earth to the sun is equal to one astronomical unit (AU). An AU is equal to 93 million miles and is far smaller than a light-year or a parsec. A light-year is defined as the distance light can travel in a vacuum in one year, and is equal to roughly 63,241 AU. A parsec is the parallax of one arcsecond and is equal to 2.0626×10^5 astronomical units.

2. C: On a topographic map, an area where the contour lines are very close together indicates that the slope is very steep. Lines very far apart would indicate a more gradual change in elevation. Contour lines help represent the actual shape of the Earth's surface features and geographic landmarks like rivers, lakes, and vegetation. Topographic maps also show man-made features such as roads, dams, and major buildings. They are based on aerial photography, and the quadrangle maps are produced in various scales. The 7.5-minute quadrangle is very common and provides a 1:24,000 scale, where 1 inch represents 2,000 feet.

3. C: Physical weathering of rocks can be caused by changes in temperature and pressure, as well as the freezing and thawing of water on the surfaces of rocks. Oxidation is a chemical process, not a physical one. Therefore, it is considered an example of chemical rather than physical weathering.

4. A: Heat on Earth is generated by the sun. The more direct sunlight an area on Earth receives from the sun, the warmer it will be. The earth is most tilted toward or away from the sun at the solstices between spring and summer or between fall and winter. When the Northern hemisphere is tilted away from the sun, all of the countries in the Northern hemisphere experience fall and winter. At that same time, the Southern hemisphere experiences spring and summer. The same is true when the Southern hemisphere experiences fall and winter; the Northern hemisphere experiences spring and summer.

5. C: Chemical sedimentary rocks are formed from deposits of minerals, as when flooding introduces water, which has minerals dissolved in it, and then the water evaporates, leaving behind layers of precipitated minerals no longer in solution without the water. Limestone is a chemical sedimentary rock, as are gypsum and rock salt. Clastic (A) sedimentary rock forms from clasts or little bits of rock that are compacted and cemented together. Organic (B) sedimentary rock forms from organic material like calcium from the bones and shells of animals. Pegmatite (D) is not a type of sedimentary rock; it is an intrusive igneous rock formed underground from cooling volcanic magma.

6. D: The formation of sedimentary rock does not include heat. Of the three types of rock igneous, sedimentary and metamorphic, heat is essential to two: igneous and metamorphic. Sedimentary rocks are formed by sediments that get deposited and then compacted or cemented together. Sedimentary rocks are classified into detrital, organic or chemical sediments. Answer A, layering, is correct since sediments can be deposited or otherwise formed in layers. Answer B, cementation, is also called lithification. Answer C, compaction, refers to the pressure forming sedimentary rock leading to cementation.

Copyright © Mometrix Media. You have been licensed one copy of this document for personal use only. Any other reproduction or redistribution is strictly prohibited. All rights reserved. This content is provided for test preparation purposes only and does not imply an endorsement by Mometrix of any particular political, scientific, or religious point of view.

7. D: Porosity is a measure of how much water the soil can retain. Permeability is a measure of how easily water can travel through that soil. Clay has a high porosity because it holds a lot of water. Clay has a low permeability. Since it is fine-grained, water flows very slowly through it. Sand and gravel have high porosities and high permeabilities. Granite has a low porosity and a low permeability.

8. A: The next phase after a full moon is a waning gibbous. A waxing crescent (B) is the phase directly following a new moon, and a waning crescent (C) is the phase that comes directly before a new moon. A waxing gibbous (D) is the last phase before a full moon.

9. B: When young children pour sand, water, rice, etc., from one container to another, differently sized (or shaped) container, they are developing basic measurement concepts. Children fitting pegs into matching holes (A) are developing basic 1:1 correspondence concepts. Seeing how many coins they have put into their piggy bank (C) helps children develop basic counting concepts. Separating toys into piles according to type (D), color, shape, size, or any other characteristic helps children develop basic classification/categorization concepts.

10. B: The activity described uses each of these skills. The children use scientific observation to note what happens when they try the different ball-ramp actions the teacher suggests (and think of themselves), and they discuss their findings with and report them to one another and the teacher (A). They use inference when they realize similarities, differences, and patterns among the different actions and what these mean, and they use prediction to answer the teacher's questions about "what would happen if..." before testing them by performing the suggested actions (C). They use measurement to calculate the height and length of the ramps, the speed at which the balls roll down them, the distance they roll, and they count the numbers of balls and ramps. And they use comparison (D) when they find the differences in the effects on speed and distance of varying ramp sizes, ramp numbers, ball numbers, etc.

11. C: When building block structures and then dismantling them, children learn concepts of part-whole relations. They learn concepts of shape (A) when they realize that some objects roll away from them and others do not. They learn concepts of weight (B) when they try to lift different objects and find some are heavier and some lighter. As babies, they quickly learn concepts of temporal sequences (D) when they awaken wet and/or hungry and then their parents change and/or feed them. As toddlers, they also learn temporal concepts through playing, tiring, and sleeping.

12. B: An activity using non-standard measures to compare something like the weight of apples and grapes is helpful in learning inference skills, since students have to try out different combinations to find the balance. Students improve their inference skills by using the outcome of one attempt to inform their next through inference. Observation skills are also exercised in activities like these, as the students have to observe and operate the scales to find their answer, but it is not such a observationally focused activity as studying and describing physical traits of different objects. Communication would be a key feature if this type of activity were used in a group. Classification is not particularly exercised in this type of activity, since the only classifications would be the type of fruit, which is a given in this type of activity.

13. D: When diluting acids, the acid should always be added to the water. This way, if splashing occurs, only water is splashed out of the beaker. Additionally, this procedure ensures that only a small amount of acid is present in a much larger volume of water. This is especially important when diluting sulfuric acid, because large amounts of heat may be released in the hydration process, which could cause a small amount of water to boil rapidly.

Copyright © Mometrix Media. You have been licensed one copy of this document for personal use only. Any other reproduction or redistribution is strictly prohibited. All rights reserved. This content is provided for test preparation purposes only and does not imply an endorsement by Mometrix of any particular political, scientific, or religious point of view.

14. A: Solutions and compounds used in labs may be hazardous according to state and local regulatory agencies and should be treated with appropriate precaution. Emptying the solutions into the sink and rinsing with warm water and soap does not take into account the hazards associated with a specific solution in terms of vapors or interactions with water, soap, and waste piping systems. Ensuring the solutions are secured in closed containers and throwing them away may allow toxic chemicals into landfills and subsequently into freshwater systems. Storing the solutions in a secured, dry place for later use is incorrect, as chemicals should not be reused due to the possibility of contamination.

15. A: A mnemonic is a simpler, sillier, or more memorable series of words or sounds that used to recall a particular set of items. This strategy is often used when item order is especially important, as is the case with biological classifications. Following a guided reading strategy that involves summarizing, generating questions, clarifying, and predicting is a description of the ReQuest reading strategy. Thinking, writing, and discussing lectures are a variety of lecture styles. Following student-generated experimental procedures to answer a student-generated question is an example of an active student inquiry activity.

16. B: In mutualistic ecological relationships, both involved organisms receive a benefit. For example, bacteria living in termites' digestive systems break down the cellulose in the wood that the termites eat, which the termites' digestive systems alone cannot do. In return for this nutritional aid, the bacteria receive a home and nourishment from the termites. In commensalistic relationships (A), one involved organism benefits while the other is unaffected; e.g., barnacles on whales are aided in their filter-feeding by the currents created in the water by the whales' swimming, while the whales are neither harmed nor helped by the barnacles. In parasitic relationships (C), one organism benefits but the other suffers. Common examples include fleas and tapeworms, which derive nourishment from animals, but harm the animals by robbing them of blood (fleas) and nutrition (tapeworms) and causing tissue damage and discomfort. Therefore (D) is incorrect.

17. A: Parts of the large intestine include the cecum, colon, rectum, and anus. The colon itself includes sections called the ascending colon, transverse colon, sigmoid colon, and descending colon. The ileum (B), jejunum (C), and duodenum (D) are all parts of the small intestine rather than the large intestine. The small intestine performs most of the digestive system's digestion and absorption; the large intestine completes the digestion and absorption processes and transports wastes for elimination.

18. C: The trigeminal nerve, which is the fifth (V) cranial nerve, controls facial sensation as well as the corneal reflex of the eye and the chewing function. The facial (seventh/VII) nerve (A) controls facial muscle movements and the front two-thirds of the tongue's taste sensation. The vagus (tenth/X) nerve (B) controls the gag reflex, and soft palate and vocal cord movements. The hypoglossal (twelfth/XII) nerve (D) controls the movements of the tongue.

19. B: Collections of cells form tissues (A), and collections of tissues can form muscles (C), making cells the smallest of the three. A ligament (D) is a type of muscle, meaning that it is also composed of cells, and is therefore larger than a cell.

20. D: Human beings, like other mammals, birds, fish, reptiles, and spiders, have simple life cycles in that they are either born live or hatched from eggs, and then grow to adulthood. Frogs (A), newts (B), and grasshoppers (C) undergo metamorphoses wherein their forms change. Frogs and newts are amphibians; they begin life underwater, breathing through gills, but breathe through lungs by

Copyright © Mometrix Media. You have been licensed one copy of this document for personal use only. Any other reproduction or redistribution is strictly prohibited. All rights reserved. This content is provided for test preparation purposes only and does not imply an endorsement by Mometrix of any particular political, scientific, or religious point of view.

adulthood and move from the water to live on the land. Grasshoppers hatch from eggs into larvae, wormlike juvenile forms that do most of the feeding they need; then they progress to adulthood.

21. A: In the food chain of tree → caterpillar → frog → snake → hawk → worm, the tree is at the trophic level with the greatest amount of energy. Trophic level refers to the position of an organism in a food chain. Energy is lost according to the laws of thermodynamics as one moves up the food chain because it is converted to heat when consumers consume. Primary producers, such as autotrophs, are organisms who are at the base and capture solar energy. Primary consumers are herbivores that feed on the producers. Secondary consumers consume primary consumers and so on. Decomposers get their energy from the consumption of dead plants and animals.

22. B: The abiotic factors of an ecosystem are not alive; hence (A) is incorrect. Abiotic factors include such things as the atmosphere, water, soil, sunlight, temperatures, nutrient cycles, etc. While not living themselves, abiotic factors *do* affect the living organisms (C) in the ecosystem. Living organisms are biotic factors, including humans, other animals, plants, *and* microorganisms; hence abiotic factors do NOT include microorganisms (D).

23. C: The relationship between termites and bacteria in their digestive systems is mutualistic, meaning both organisms benefit. Termites live on wood, but their digestive systems cannot break down cellulose in wood. Bacteria in their digestive tracts do this for them. Termites benefit from the nourishment; bacteria in return benefit from a place to live and nourishment from the termites. In parasitic (A) relationships, one organism benefits but the other is harmed. An example is tapeworms in animal digestive tracts: tapeworms benefit from the food eaten by their hosts, but hosts are deprived of nourishment and suffer tissue damage. Ecological (B) relationships are any regular interactions between different organisms that benefit one or both. In commensalistic (D) relationships, one organism benefits and the other does not but is unharmed. An example is barnacles on whales. Water currents created as whales swim deliver food to barnacles. Whales get no benefit from barnacles, but are unhurt by them.

24. D: Horses eat plants but do not eat meat, so they are herbivores. Omnivores (A) eat plants and meat, while carnivores (B) eat meat but do not eat plants. Decomposers (C) consume only dead plants and animals, as they break down remains as a source of energy.

25. C: A population that reaches maximum size and ceases to grow due to a limited availability of resources is said to be at carrying capacity. The carrying capacity of a species is influenced by many factors such as the amount of land or water available, food supply, and predators. Unstable and moving towards extinction are not correct as carrying capacity does not necessarily mean it is unstable or becoming extinct. Shrinking exponentially is also incorrect as the question says it has stopped growing, not that it is reducing in size.

26. C: When children conduct simple experiments and are able to see patterns and meanings in the results, they are using the scientific process skill of inference. They use the skill of measurement (A) when they quantify the various physical properties of objects, like length, width, height, weight, etc. They use the skill of classification (B) when they group objects, events, conditions, or situations according to the properties they share in common. They use the skill of prediction (D) when they apply their experiences from experimenting to form new hypotheses to test.

27. B: When scientists and students are able to identify patterns and find meaning in the results of their experiments, they are using the process skill of Inference. When they use the results of their experiments to formulate new hypotheses (A), they are using the process skill of Prediction. When they identify the properties of objects or situations using their senses, they are using the process

Copyright © Mometrix Media. You have been licensed one copy of this document for personal use only. Any other reproduction or redistribution is strictly prohibited. All rights reserved. This content is provided for test preparation purposes only and does not imply an endorsement by Mometrix of any particular political, scientific, or religious point of view.

skill of Observation. When they report the results of their experiments and their conclusions based on these results to others (D), they are using the process skill of Communication. These skills are required for solving both math and science problems.

28. A: When using a light microscope, total magnification is determined by multiplying the ocular lens power times the objective being used. The term "ocular lens" refers to the eyepiece, which has one magnification strength, typically 10x. The objective lens also has a magnification strength, often 4x, 10x, 40x, or 100x. Using a 10x eyepiece with the 4x objective lens will give a magnification strength of 40x. Using a 10x eyepiece with the 100x objective lens will give a magnification strength of 1,000x. The shorter lens is the lesser magnification; the longer lens is the greater magnification.

29. A: Pros of wind energy include space efficiency, no pollution, and low operational costs. Cons of wind energy include wind fluctuation, threats to wildlife, and the expense to manufacture and install.

30. A: Currently, the greatest benefit of genetically modified crops is to the farmer, with herbicide-resistant and pest-resistant crops. This increases profits and makes farming a little easier. Currently, foods made from genetically modified crops do not show significant increases in nutrition or shelf life. One of the greatest concerns regarding foods produced from genetically modified crops is the possibility of introducing new allergens into the food supply.

31. D: Once a hypothesis has been verified and accepted, it becomes a theory. A theory is a generally accepted explanation that has been highly developed and tested. A theory can explain data and be expected to predict outcomes of tests. A fact is considered to be an objective and verifiable observation, whereas a scientific theory is a greater body of accepted knowledge, principles, or relationships that might explain a fact. A law is an explanation of events for which the outcome is always the same. A conclusion is more of an opinion and could be based on observation, evidence, fact, laws, or even beliefs.

32. B: Scatter plots are useful for illustrating two sets of numerical data on the two axes and their relationship. In this case, by plotting the width of the tree trunks along the y-axis and the corresponding average precipitation rates along the x-axis, any relationship between the two can be found. Scatter plots are also useful when there are many data points. A multi-line graph is useful for showing sets of data that change over time. A bar graph is a good choice for comparing individual data points. A pie chart is useful for graphically comparing the parts to a whole.

33. D: Benefits to using fossil fuels include that they are cheap and reliable and relatively safe to extract. The technology to control pollution is already developed. The most serious drawback to using fossil fuels is that their pollution contributes greatly to global warming.

34. A: Water vapor is a gas, i.e., the gaseous form of water, which is a liquid (C) at normal temperatures. Vapors are gaseous forms of substances that are liquids or solids (B) at normal temperatures. They form through evaporation and/or heating. Cooling water vapor makes it liquid; freezing liquid water makes it into ice, a solid. Therefore (D) is incorrect.

35. B: The planet Earth is itself a gigantic magnet; its magnetism is the reason that compasses always point north. *All* electric motors, not just some (A), contain magnets. Tape recorders (C) contain magnets, and the tapes they play are magnetized. Loudspeakers and telephones (D), as well as generators, all operate using magnets.

36. D: Chemical equations must be balanced on each side of the reaction. Balancing means the total number of atoms stays the same, but their arrangement within specific reactants and products can

Copyright © Mometrix Media. You have been licensed one copy of this document for personal use only. Any other reproduction or redistribution is strictly prohibited. All rights reserved.
This content is provided for test preparation purposes only and does not imply an endorsement by Mometrix of any particular political, scientific, or religious point of view.

change. The law of conservation of matter states that matter can never be created or destroyed. Heat may be absorbed or released in a reaction; these are classified as endothermic and exothermic reactions, respectively. The rate of the reaction increases with temperature for most reactions.

37. B: Epiphytes are plants that grow in the canopy of trees, and the tropical rain forest has a rich canopy because of its density and extensive moisture.

38. B: An apple turning brown is an example of a chemical change; in this case, oxidation. During a chemical change, one substance is changed into another. Sublimation of water refers to the conversion between the solid and the gaseous phases of matter, with no intermediate liquid stage. This is a phase change, not a chemical reaction. Dissolution of salt in water refers to a physical change since the salt and water can be separated again by evaporating the water. Pulverized rock is an example of a physical change where the form has changed but not the substance itself.

39. B: Elements and compounds are both pure substances. Elements consist of only one type of atom. Compounds consist of more than one type of atom. Molecules may make up either elements or compounds. Mixtures are two or more substances that are physically combined but not chemically united.

40. C: A triple point on a phase diagram indicates a precise temperature and pressure where a substance can simultaneously exist as a solid, liquid, and a gas. Isothermal means constant temperature and would refer to a vertical line rather than a point. Isobaric means constant pressure and would refer to a horizontal line rather than a point. The critical point indicates a particular temperature and pressure beyond which the substance is neither a liquid nor a gas, but a supercritical fluid.

Copyright © Mometrix Media. You have been licensed one copy of this document for personal use only. Any other reproduction or redistribution is strictly prohibited. All rights reserved. This content is provided for test preparation purposes only and does not imply an endorsement by Mometrix of any particular political, scientific, or religious point of view.

FTCE Practice Tests #2 and #3

To take these additional FTCE practice tests, visit our bonus page:
mometrix.com/bonus948/ftceprekinprim

Copyright © Mometrix Media. You have been licensed one copy of this document for personal use only. Any other reproduction or redistribution is strictly prohibited. All rights reserved.
This content is provided for test preparation purposes only and does not imply an endorsement by Mometrix of any particular political, scientific, or religious point of view.

How to Overcome Test Anxiety

Just the thought of taking a test is enough to make most people a little nervous. A test is an important event that can have a long-term impact on your future, so it's important to take it seriously and it's natural to feel anxious about performing well. But just because anxiety is normal, that doesn't mean that it's helpful in test taking, or that you should simply accept it as part of your life. Anxiety can have a variety of effects. These effects can be mild, like making you feel slightly nervous, or severe, like blocking your ability to focus or remember even a simple detail.

If you experience test anxiety—whether severe or mild—it's important to know how to beat it. To discover this, first you need to understand what causes test anxiety.

Causes of Test Anxiety

While we often think of anxiety as an uncontrollable emotional state, it can actually be caused by simple, practical things. One of the most common causes of test anxiety is that a person does not feel adequately prepared for their test. This feeling can be the result of many different issues such as poor study habits or lack of organization, but the most common culprit is time management. Starting to study too late, failing to organize your study time to cover all of the material, or being distracted while you study will mean that you're not well prepared for the test. This may lead to cramming the night before, which will cause you to be physically and mentally exhausted for the test. Poor time management also contributes to feelings of stress, fear, and hopelessness as you realize you are not well prepared but don't know what to do about it.

Other times, test anxiety is not related to your preparation for the test but comes from unresolved fear. This may be a past failure on a test, or poor performance on tests in general. It may come from comparing yourself to others who seem to be performing better or from the stress of living up to expectations. Anxiety may be driven by fears of the future—how failure on this test would affect your educational and career goals. These fears are often completely irrational, but they can still negatively impact your test performance.

Elements of Test Anxiety

As mentioned earlier, test anxiety is considered to be an emotional state, but it has physical and mental components as well. Sometimes you may not even realize that you are suffering from test anxiety until you notice the physical symptoms. These can include trembling hands, rapid heartbeat, sweating, nausea, and tense muscles. Extreme anxiety may lead to fainting or vomiting. Obviously, any of these symptoms can have a negative impact on testing. It is important to recognize them as soon as they begin to occur so that you can address the problem before it damages your performance.

The mental components of test anxiety include trouble focusing and inability to remember learned information. During a test, your mind is on high alert, which can help you recall information and stay focused for an extended period of time. However, anxiety interferes with your mind's natural processes, causing you to blank out, even on the questions you know well. The strain of testing during anxiety makes it difficult to stay focused, especially on a test that may take several hours. Extreme anxiety can take a huge mental toll, making it difficult not only to recall test information but even to understand the test questions or pull your thoughts together.

Copyright © Mometrix Media. You have been licensed one copy of this document for personal use only. Any other reproduction or redistribution is strictly prohibited. All rights reserved.
This content is provided for test preparation purposes only and does not imply an endorsement by Mometrix of any particular political, scientific, or religious point of view.

Effects of Test Anxiety

Test anxiety is like a disease—if left untreated, it will get progressively worse. Anxiety leads to poor performance, and this reinforces the feelings of fear and failure, which in turn lead to poor performances on subsequent tests. It can grow from a mild nervousness to a crippling condition. If allowed to progress, test anxiety can have a big impact on your schooling, and consequently on your future.

Test anxiety can spread to other parts of your life. Anxiety on tests can become anxiety in any stressful situation, and blanking on a test can turn into panicking in a job situation. But fortunately, you don't have to let anxiety rule your testing and determine your grades. There are a number of relatively simple steps you can take to move past anxiety and function normally on a test and in the rest of life.

Physical Steps for Beating Test Anxiety

While test anxiety is a serious problem, the good news is that it can be overcome. It doesn't have to control your ability to think and remember information. While it may take time, you can begin taking steps today to beat anxiety.

Just as your first hint that you may be struggling with anxiety comes from the physical symptoms, the first step to treating it is also physical. Rest is crucial for having a clear, strong mind. If you are tired, it is much easier to give in to anxiety. But if you establish good sleep habits, your body and mind will be ready to perform optimally, without the strain of exhaustion. Additionally, sleeping well helps you to retain information better, so you're more likely to recall the answers when you see the test questions.

Getting good sleep means more than going to bed on time. It's important to allow your brain time to relax. Take study breaks from time to time so it doesn't get overworked, and don't study right before bed. Take time to rest your mind before trying to rest your body, or you may find it difficult to fall asleep.

Along with sleep, other aspects of physical health are important in preparing for a test. Good nutrition is vital for good brain function. Sugary foods and drinks may give a burst of energy but this burst is followed by a crash, both physically and emotionally. Instead, fuel your body with protein and vitamin-rich foods.

Also, drink plenty of water. Dehydration can lead to headaches and exhaustion, especially if your brain is already under stress from the rigors of the test. Particularly if your test is a long one, drink water during the breaks. And if possible, take an energy-boosting snack to eat between sections.

Along with sleep and diet, a third important part of physical health is exercise. Maintaining a steady workout schedule is helpful, but even taking 5-minute study breaks to walk can help get your blood pumping faster and clear your head. Exercise also releases endorphins, which contribute to a positive feeling and can help combat test anxiety.

When you nurture your physical health, you are also contributing to your mental health. If your body is healthy, your mind is much more likely to be healthy as well. So take time to rest, nourish your body with healthy food and water, and get moving as much as possible. Taking these physical steps will make you stronger and more able to take the mental steps necessary to overcome test anxiety.

Copyright © Mometrix Media. You have been licensed one copy of this document for personal use only. Any other reproduction or redistribution is strictly prohibited. All rights reserved. This content is provided for test preparation purposes only and does not imply an endorsement by Mometrix of any particular political, scientific, or religious point of view.

Mental Steps for Beating Test Anxiety

Working on the mental side of test anxiety can be more challenging, but as with the physical side, there are clear steps you can take to overcome it. As mentioned earlier, test anxiety often stems from lack of preparation, so the obvious solution is to prepare for the test. Effective studying may be the most important weapon you have for beating test anxiety, but you can and should employ several other mental tools to combat fear.

First, boost your confidence by reminding yourself of past success—tests or projects that you aced. If you're putting as much effort into preparing for this test as you did for those, there's no reason you should expect to fail here. Work hard to prepare; then trust your preparation.

Second, surround yourself with encouraging people. It can be helpful to find a study group, but be sure that the people you're around will encourage a positive attitude. If you spend time with others who are anxious or cynical, this will only contribute to your own anxiety. Look for others who are motivated to study hard from a desire to succeed, not from a fear of failure.

Third, reward yourself. A test is physically and mentally tiring, even without anxiety, and it can be helpful to have something to look forward to. Plan an activity following the test, regardless of the outcome, such as going to a movie or getting ice cream.

When you are taking the test, if you find yourself beginning to feel anxious, remind yourself that you know the material. Visualize successfully completing the test. Then take a few deep, relaxing breaths and return to it. Work through the questions carefully but with confidence, knowing that you are capable of succeeding.

Developing a healthy mental approach to test taking will also aid in other areas of life. Test anxiety affects more than just the actual test—it can be damaging to your mental health and even contribute to depression. It's important to beat test anxiety before it becomes a problem for more than testing.

Study Strategy

Being prepared for the test is necessary to combat anxiety, but what does being prepared look like? You may study for hours on end and still not feel prepared. What you need is a strategy for test prep. The next few pages outline our recommended steps to help you plan out and conquer the challenge of preparation.

STEP 1: SCOPE OUT THE TEST

Learn everything you can about the format (multiple choice, essay, etc.) and what will be on the test. Gather any study materials, course outlines, or sample exams that may be available. Not only will this help you to prepare, but knowing what to expect can help to alleviate test anxiety.

STEP 2: MAP OUT THE MATERIAL

Look through the textbook or study guide and make note of how many chapters or sections it has. Then divide these over the time you have. For example, if a book has 15 chapters and you have five days to study, you need to cover three chapters each day. Even better, if you have the time, leave an extra day at the end for overall review after you have gone through the material in depth.

If time is limited, you may need to prioritize the material. Look through it and make note of which sections you think you already have a good grasp on, and which need review. While you are studying, skim quickly through the familiar sections and take more time on the challenging parts.

Copyright © Mometrix Media. You have been licensed one copy of this document for personal use only. Any other reproduction or redistribution is strictly prohibited. All rights reserved. This content is provided for test preparation purposes only and does not imply an endorsement by Mometrix of any particular political, scientific, or religious point of view.

Write out your plan so you don't get lost as you go. Having a written plan also helps you feel more in control of the study, so anxiety is less likely to arise from feeling overwhelmed at the amount to cover.

STEP 3: GATHER YOUR TOOLS

Decide what study method works best for you. Do you prefer to highlight in the book as you study and then go back over the highlighted portions? Or do you type out notes of the important information? Or is it helpful to make flashcards that you can carry with you? Assemble the pens, index cards, highlighters, post-it notes, and any other materials you may need so you won't be distracted by getting up to find things while you study.

If you're having a hard time retaining the information or organizing your notes, experiment with different methods. For example, try color-coding by subject with colored pens, highlighters, or post-it notes. If you learn better by hearing, try recording yourself reading your notes so you can listen while in the car, working out, or simply sitting at your desk. Ask a friend to quiz you from your flashcards, or try teaching someone the material to solidify it in your mind.

STEP 4: CREATE YOUR ENVIRONMENT

It's important to avoid distractions while you study. This includes both the obvious distractions like visitors and the subtle distractions like an uncomfortable chair (or a too-comfortable couch that makes you want to fall asleep). Set up the best study environment possible: good lighting and a comfortable work area. If background music helps you focus, you may want to turn it on, but otherwise keep the room quiet. If you are using a computer to take notes, be sure you don't have any other windows open, especially applications like social media, games, or anything else that could distract you. Silence your phone and turn off notifications. Be sure to keep water close by so you stay hydrated while you study (but avoid unhealthy drinks and snacks).

Also, take into account the best time of day to study. Are you freshest first thing in the morning? Try to set aside some time then to work through the material. Is your mind clearer in the afternoon or evening? Schedule your study session then. Another method is to study at the same time of day that you will take the test, so that your brain gets used to working on the material at that time and will be ready to focus at test time.

STEP 5: STUDY!

Once you have done all the study preparation, it's time to settle into the actual studying. Sit down, take a few moments to settle your mind so you can focus, and begin to follow your study plan. Don't give in to distractions or let yourself procrastinate. This is your time to prepare so you'll be ready to fearlessly approach the test. Make the most of the time and stay focused.

Of course, you don't want to burn out. If you study too long you may find that you're not retaining the information very well. Take regular study breaks. For example, taking five minutes out of every hour to walk briskly, breathing deeply and swinging your arms, can help your mind stay fresh.

As you get to the end of each chapter or section, it's a good idea to do a quick review. Remind yourself of what you learned and work on any difficult parts. When you feel that you've mastered the material, move on to the next part. At the end of your study session, briefly skim through your notes again.

But while review is helpful, cramming last minute is NOT. If at all possible, work ahead so that you won't need to fit all your study into the last day. Cramming overloads your brain with more information than it can process and retain, and your tired mind may struggle to recall even

Copyright © Mometrix Media. You have been licensed one copy of this document for personal use only. Any other reproduction or redistribution is strictly prohibited. All rights reserved. This content is provided for test preparation purposes only and does not imply an endorsement by Mometrix of any particular political, scientific, or religious point of view.

previously learned information when it is overwhelmed with last-minute study. Also, the urgent nature of cramming and the stress placed on your brain contribute to anxiety. You'll be more likely to go to the test feeling unprepared and having trouble thinking clearly.

So don't cram, and don't stay up late before the test, even just to review your notes at a leisurely pace. Your brain needs rest more than it needs to go over the information again. In fact, plan to finish your studies by noon or early afternoon the day before the test. Give your brain the rest of the day to relax or focus on other things, and get a good night's sleep. Then you will be fresh for the test and better able to recall what you've studied.

STEP 6: TAKE A PRACTICE TEST

Many courses offer sample tests, either online or in the study materials. This is an excellent resource to check whether you have mastered the material, as well as to prepare for the test format and environment.

Check the test format ahead of time: the number of questions, the type (multiple choice, free response, etc.), and the time limit. Then create a plan for working through them. For example, if you have 30 minutes to take a 60-question test, your limit is 30 seconds per question. Spend less time on the questions you know well so that you can take more time on the difficult ones.

If you have time to take several practice tests, take the first one open book, with no time limit. Work through the questions at your own pace and make sure you fully understand them. Gradually work up to taking a test under test conditions: sit at a desk with all study materials put away and set a timer. Pace yourself to make sure you finish the test with time to spare and go back to check your answers if you have time.

After each test, check your answers. On the questions you missed, be sure you understand why you missed them. Did you misread the question (tests can use tricky wording)? Did you forget the information? Or was it something you hadn't learned? Go back and study any shaky areas that the practice tests reveal.

Taking these tests not only helps with your grade, but also aids in combating test anxiety. If you're already used to the test conditions, you're less likely to worry about it, and working through tests until you're scoring well gives you a confidence boost. Go through the practice tests until you feel comfortable, and then you can go into the test knowing that you're ready for it.

Test Tips

On test day, you should be confident, knowing that you've prepared well and are ready to answer the questions. But aside from preparation, there are several test day strategies you can employ to maximize your performance.

First, as stated before, get a good night's sleep the night before the test (and for several nights before that, if possible). Go into the test with a fresh, alert mind rather than staying up late to study.

Try not to change too much about your normal routine on the day of the test. It's important to eat a nutritious breakfast, but if you normally don't eat breakfast at all, consider eating just a protein bar. If you're a coffee drinker, go ahead and have your normal coffee. Just make sure you time it so that the caffeine doesn't wear off right in the middle of your test. Avoid sugary beverages, and drink enough water to stay hydrated but not so much that you need a restroom break 10 minutes into the

Copyright © Mometrix Media. You have been licensed one copy of this document for personal use only. Any other reproduction or redistribution is strictly prohibited. All rights reserved.
This content is provided for test preparation purposes only and does not imply an endorsement by Mometrix of any particular political, scientific, or religious point of view.

test. If your test isn't first thing in the morning, consider going for a walk or doing a light workout before the test to get your blood flowing.

Allow yourself enough time to get ready, and leave for the test with plenty of time to spare so you won't have the anxiety of scrambling to arrive in time. Another reason to be early is to select a good seat. It's helpful to sit away from doors and windows, which can be distracting. Find a good seat, get out your supplies, and settle your mind before the test begins.

When the test begins, start by going over the instructions carefully, even if you already know what to expect. Make sure you avoid any careless mistakes by following the directions.

Then begin working through the questions, pacing yourself as you've practiced. If you're not sure on an answer, don't spend too much time on it, and don't let it shake your confidence. Either skip it and come back later, or eliminate as many wrong answers as possible and guess among the remaining ones. Don't dwell on these questions as you continue—put them out of your mind and focus on what lies ahead.

Be sure to read all of the answer choices, even if you're sure the first one is the right answer. Sometimes you'll find a better one if you keep reading. But don't second-guess yourself if you do immediately know the answer. Your gut instinct is usually right. Don't let test anxiety rob you of the information you know.

If you have time at the end of the test (and if the test format allows), go back and review your answers. Be cautious about changing any, since your first instinct tends to be correct, but make sure you didn't misread any of the questions or accidentally mark the wrong answer choice. Look over any you skipped and make an educated guess.

At the end, leave the test feeling confident. You've done your best, so don't waste time worrying about your performance or wishing you could change anything. Instead, celebrate the successful completion of this test. And finally, use this test to learn how to deal with anxiety even better next time.

> **Review Video: Test Anxiety**
> Visit mometrix.com/academy and enter code: 100340

Important Qualification

Not all anxiety is created equal. If your test anxiety is causing major issues in your life beyond the classroom or testing center, or if you are experiencing troubling physical symptoms related to your anxiety, it may be a sign of a serious physiological or psychological condition. If this sounds like your situation, we strongly encourage you to seek professional help.

Copyright © Mometrix Media. You have been licensed one copy of this document for personal use only. Any other reproduction or redistribution is strictly prohibited. All rights reserved.
This content is provided for test preparation purposes only and does not imply an endorsement by Mometrix of any particular political, scientific, or religious point of view.

Additional Bonus Material

Due to our efforts to try to keep this book to a manageable length, we've created a link that will give you access to all of your additional bonus material:

mometrix.com/bonus948/ftceprekinprim

Copyright © Mometrix Media. You have been licensed one copy of this document for personal use only. Any other reproduction or redistribution is strictly prohibited. All rights reserved. This content is provided for test preparation purposes only and does not imply an endorsement by Mometrix of any particular political, scientific, or religious point of view.

Printed in the USA
CPSIA information can be obtained
at www.ICGtesting.com
LVHW080821140724
785420LV00014B/939